MESSIAH THE PRINCE

OR

THE INSPIRATION OF THE PROPHECIES OF

DANIEL.

CONTAINING REMARKS ON THE
VIEWS OF DR. PUSEY, MR. DESPREZ, AND DR. WILLIAMS,
CONCERNING THE BOOK OF DANIEL;

A RECTIFIED SYSTEM OF SCRIPTURE DATES,
THROWING LIGHT ON THE PROPHECY OF THE SEVENTY WEEKS;

A

Treatise on the Sabbatical Years and Jubilees;

AND A

COMPENDIUM OF SACRED AND SECULAR CHRONOLOGY,
FROM THE YEAR B.C. 1000 TO THE DEATH OF CHRIST A.D. 33.

BY

J. W. BOSANQUET, F.R.A.S., M.R.A.S.

TREASURER OF THE CHRONOLOGICAL INSTITUTE.

SECOND EDITION.

" Art thou He that should come, or do we look for another ? "—*Matt.* xi. 3.
" I adjure thee by the living God, that thou tell us whether thou be the Christ,
the Son of God. Jesus saith unto him, Thou hast said : nevertheless I say unto you,
Hereafter shall ye see the Son of Man sitting on the right hand of power, and coming
in the clouds of heaven."—*Matt.* xxvi. 63, 64.

LONDON:
LONGMANS, GREEN, READER, AND DYER,
PATERNOSTER ROW.

1869.

101 . e . 208.

Dedicated

TO

OUR BRETHREN OF THE SEED OF ABRAHAM IN THE FLESH,

"THE PEOPLE OF THE SAINTS OF THE MOST HIGH,"

THE INHERITORS OF

"THE KINGDOM" WHICH "SHALL NOT BE LEFT TO OTHER PEOPLE."

"Now to Abraham and his seed were the promises made."

"And if ye be Christ's, then are ye Abraham's seed, and heirs according to the promise."—*Gal.* iii. 16, 29.

PREFACE.

In the first edition of this work one chief object, with a view to the rectification of Scripture chronology, was to establish the historical fact that "Darius the Median," of the book of Daniel (v. 31), was the well-known Persian king Darius, son of Hystaspes; and to show how the history of the last ten years of that king, as given in the books of Daniel, Ezra, Haggai, and Zechariah, that is, from the time when he had attained to the age of 62, even to his 72nd year, when, according to Ctesias, he died, falls in harmoniously with the history of his reign as related by Herodotus.

Many are now willing to admit the reality of the proposed identification, and the light thereby thrown upon sacred history about the time of the return of the Jews from captivity, as also upon the prophecies of Daniel, is sufficiently manifest. But, while making this admission, it is necessary also fully to understand the extent of alteration thus required in the received mode of reckoning of Scripture dates, and also how it is proposed to reconcile the books of Ezra, Haggai, and Zechariah, with the altered position of the book of Daniel. While bearing in mind, therefore, that Daniel's master was the great king of Persia who succeeded Cambyses, the reader will also take into consideration the following facts in corroboration of that truth.

I. That when Daniel (ix. 1) speaks of "the first year of Darius, the son of Ahasuerus, of the seed of the Medes," by repeating the regnal year in connexion with the words preceding, he wishes us to understand that he is not speaking of the first year of his master's reign over the Medo-Persian empire, in B.C. 517,* but of the time "when he was set over the realm of the Chaldeans;" that is, of the time when he was "about threescore and two years old," (v. 31), which the son of Hystaspes was in the year B.C. 492, two years before the battle of Marathon.

II. That when Ezra speaks of the laying of the foundation of the second Temple, in the second year of Darius (Ezra, iv. 24), he likewise speaks of the second year of the reign of Darius over the realm of the Chaldeans (which realm, or satrapy, included the government of Judea), as indicated by the appeal to Darius (v. 17), that search might be made in the treasure-house "which is there at Babylon," and by the fact that Darius is there spoken of as "king of Assyria" (vi. 22); and, moreover, by the leading chronological fact that Ahasuerus, or Xerxes, is about this time referred to by Ezra as holding a government in Persia (iv. 7), which could not have

---

* See p. 371.

been the case much earlier than the time of the battle of Marathon.

III. That when Haggai, also in the second year of Darius (ii. 6, 22, 23), proclaims in the name of the Lord of Hosts,—" Yet once, *it is a little while*, and I will shake the heavens and the earth, and the sea, and the dry land,"—" and I will overthrow the throne of kingdoms,"—" and I will overthrow the chariots and those that ride in them,"—" and I will take thee, O Zerubbabel, and make thee as a signet," though a hidden meaning may, as St. Paul assumes, be contained in these words referring to future times, yet, primarily, the prophet is here clearly foretelling the approach of that tempestuous movement in the political heavens, which, within a little while, even within two years after the words were uttered by the prophet, began to break forth from Persia, when some million and a half of people were stirred up from all quarters of the empire with the object of overwhelming the little state of Greece, and when two great expeditions went forth, to terminate in two great disasters within ten years of each other, the one at Marathon, the other at Salamis, by dry land and by sea.

IV. That when the prophet Zechariah, writing also in the second year of Darius, takes up in vision, as foretold by Isaiah, xiv. 4-7, " the proverb against the king of Babylon," and seeing how " the oppressor had ceased, how the golden city had ceased, and the staff of the wicked and the sceptre of the rulers had been broken," that is, by the final destruction of

Babylon by Darius, exclaims,—" Behold, all the land
(that is, the land of Judea) sitteth still, and is at
rest," (Zech. i. 11)—the prophet cannot be supposed
to be speaking of the early years of Darius, when
indeed revolt at Babylon was twice suppressed, but
the satrapy of Babylonia not put down, but to that
later period in his reign when the city of Babylon
was finally surrendered into the hands of Darius by
Zopyrus, as Herodotus relates, when the power of
oppression ceased by the slaughter of three thousand
of its nobles, when its brazen gates were carried away
and its outer wall destroyed, during the government
of Xerxes, or Ahasuerus, as Ctesias, correcting
Herodotus, relates, and therefore at a time not far
removed from the date of the battle of Marathon.

V. That, when Daniel informs us, after the fall
of Belshazzar, how " it pleased Darius to set over
the kingdom an hundred and twenty princes, which
should be over the whole kingdom" (vi. 1), it cannot
be supposed that he is speaking of any time within
the first twenty-five years of the reign of the son of
Hystaspes, during which we know from Herodotus
that it was the policy of that king to parcel out his
empire into kingdoms, or satrapies, according to its
great national divisions, and when we know from
the inscription at Behistûn that it was actually so
divided into twenty or twenty-two great satrapies ;
but clearly he must be referring to that late period
in the reign of Darius, when, after the suppression
of the rebellion of Aristagoras in Ionia, the burning of Sardis by the Athenians, the replacing of

Æaces on the throne of Samos, and the final subjection of the turbulent satrapy of Babylonia—ever
seeking to establish its independence in the dynasty
of Nabonadius, of whom Belshazzar, or Belsharuser,
was the eldest son,*—it was found necessary by the
king to reverse his previous policy, as Herodotus
relates (vi. 43), and under the advice probably of
his great Jewish minister, to centralize the government in his own hands, by dividing the empire into
many small self-governing municipalities—Daniel
says 120—each accountable to one of the chief presidents set over the whole kingdom. This change
of policy, as exemplified in the satrapy of Ionia,
Herodotus tells us, took place just before the setting
out of the expedition to Marathon.†

From the foregoing illustrations, then, it will
appear that a primary object aimed at in this work
is to remove the date of Belshazzar's feast at Babylon, and the change of dynasty at Babylon from the
Chaldeans to the Persians, which Daniel tells us
took place in the reign of Darius, not in the reign
of Cyrus, from the times of Cyrus I., the father of
Cambyses,—where it never ought to have been
placed,—and where it never could have been placed,
except for the apparent coincidence that Belshazzar was slain at a nocturnal feast, and that Cyrus,
son of Cambyses, entered Babylon during a nocturnal feast—and to place these events at the time
of the final destruction of Babylon by the son of
Hystaspes, in the sixty-second year of his age

* Journ. R. Asiatic Soc. vol. x. part ii. p. 184.   † See p. 208.

(B.C. 492), that is to say, exactly forty-six years later than the common date, B.C. 538.

Now this arrangement occasions a very material alteration in the current scheme of Scripture reckoning, and leads immediately to an apparent difficulty which has not been sufficiently touched upon in the first edition. For if Belshazzar was slain at Babylon in B.C. 492, who is Cyrus, or Coresh, who released the Jews from captivity, and commanded that the temple of Jerusalem should be built, in the first year of his reign over Babylon, as related in the fifth chapter of Ezra, and who is commonly supposed to have reigned after Darius ? Can it be possible that he was Cyrus, father of Cambyses, who reigned from the year B.C. 559 to 530 ? Certainly not. Where, then, in history is there a king to be found, bearing the title Cyrus, to represent the illustrious king spoken of by Isaiah, the Lord's anointed, who should say " to Jerusalem, Thou shalt be built, and to the temple, Thy foundation shall be laid " ? Isa. xliv. 28.

The answer to this question is extremely simple, though much at variance with the current mode of reckoning. In Appendix B to this edition (p. 424) the author trusts that he has succeeded in showing that the Cyrus of Herodotus, the founder of the Persian empire, who began to reign in B.C. 559, could not possibly have been the king who conquered Babylon, as Herodotus affirms, nor he who released the Jews, because he could not have been the offspring of Cambyses and Mandane, which the conqueror of Babylon, as all are agreed was, nor the grandson of Astyages, which Ctesias tells us emphatically he was not; but that he who freed the Jews was the son of king Cambyses and Mandane, and the grandson of Astyages, whose history is related by Xenophon, and whose chief exploits, such as the deposition of Crœsus, and the capture of Babylon, were accomplished before he came to the throne, during the reign of his father Cambyses, and consequently within the well-defined limits of his father's eighteen years' reign, defined by Ctesias as beginning in B.C. 536, and ending in 518.

Now the result of these proposed alterations, and of the bringing down of the close of the Babylonian captivity from B.C. 517 to 492, is to lower the whole range of dates connected with the Jewish monarchy neither more nor less than twenty-five years. Thus, for instance,—

	Common date.	Altered date.	Difference.
The 49th year of Uzziah, king of Judah = 10th year Menahem, king of Israel, will be lowered from . . .	B.C. 762	to B.C. 737	25 years.
The 52nd year of Uzziah=1st Pekah	759	734	,,
The carrying away of the ten tribes by Shalmanezer .	721	696	,,
The threatened attack upon Jerusalem by Sennacherib =14th of Hezekiah . .	714	689	,,
The 1st year of Nebuchadnezzar after the death of Nabopalassar . . .	606	581	,,
The destruction of Jerusalem	588	563	,,

Two remarkable and interesting discoveries, cor-
roborative of the accuracy of this scheme of dates,
have come under the notice of the author since the
publication of his first edition, upon which it is now
necessary to say a few words. First, the discovery
in a contemporary record of the register of a solar
eclipse at Nineveh, in virtue of which the reigns of
Uzziah and Menahem, in connexion with the reign
of Tiglath-pileser, must be lowered exactly twenty-
five years, as stated above. Second, the discovery of
a series of ancient Jewish tombstones at Tschufukale in the Crimea, some of them as old as the
first century, A.D., which reckon the date of the
burials from the year of the captivity of the ten
tribes, and count that year as B.C. 696, twenty-five
years lower than the common date, as above.

As regards the eclipse, the discovery was announced by Sir H. Rawlinson in the " Athenæum "
of the 18th May, 1867; and referring to the Assyrian
Canon or register of annual archons at Nineveh, he
writes, " In the 18th year before the accession of
Tiglath-pileser there is notice to the following effect,
—' In the month Sivan an eclipse of the sun took
place,'—and to mark the great importance of the
event, a line is drawn across the tablet, although no
interruption takes place in the official order of the
Eponymes. Here, then, we have notice of a solar
eclipse which was visible at Nineveh, which occurred
within ninety days of the (vernal) equinox (taking
that as the normal commencement of the year), and
which we may presume to have been total from

the prominence given to the record: and these are conditions which, during a century before and after the commencement of the era of Nabonassar, are alone fulfilled by the eclipse which took place on the 15th June, 763."

Mr. Airy, the Astronomer Royal, has kindly furnished me with the accompanying trace of the shadow of this eclipse, as computed by Mr. Hind from Hansen's and Leverrier's tables, together with the subjoined points of latitude and longitude:—

B.C. 763.	G.M.T.	Long.	Lat.	Long.	Lat.	Long.	Lat.
	h m	° ′	° ′	° ′	° ′	° ′	° ′
June 14	18 54	35 23	37 52	36 3	37 7	36 44	36 20
	19 0	38 29	38 53	39 6	38 4	39 43	37 14
	19 6	41 33	39 46	42 7	38 54	42 39	38 3
	19 12	44 35	40 31	45 4	39 38	45 32	38 46
	19 18	47 34	41 9	47 59	40 14	48 23	39 21
	19 22	50 32	41 40	50 52	40 45	51 12	39 49
		Northern Limit.		Central Line.		Southern Limit.	

The shadow of totality, as drawn upon the map, it will be observed, does not reach the site of Nineveh, but both Mr. Airy and Mr. Hind allow that a very slight and unimportant deviation from the result of the tables would bring the shadow over that city. A further deviation from the tables, however, in the same direction, is required. For it is clear at first sight, as I immediately stated to Sir Henry, that this eclipse,* eighteen years before the accession of Tiglath-pileser, can be no other than that which was either witnessed or foretold by

---

* Hitzig suggested the eclipse of 9th February, B.C. 784, as that foretold by Amos, in connexion with the common reckoning. Dr. Pusey has had the path of this eclipse calculated by the best tables, and finds it scarcely noticeable at Samaria. He himself

the prophet Amos, who wrote two years before
the great earthquake in the reign of Uzziah (Amos,
i. 1; viii. 8, 9.)   The shadow of this eclipse, therefore, must have passed over Samaria, near to which
Amos prophesied (Amos, vii. 11, 12, 13), as well as
over Nineveh : and the assumption of Sir Henry
that the eclipse recorded at Nineveh was total,
which necessarily forms a main element in Mr.
Hind's calculation of the date, is thus proved to be
correct.   For the words of Amos are, in the name
of the Lord, " I will cause the sun to go down at
noon, and will darken the earth in the clear day,"
an effect which can only be produced by a total
obscuration of the sun.   Another leading element
of calculation is also thus obtained by which to
identify the eclipse at Nineveh, viz., that the inclination of the path of its shadow must have been north-
east, in a line to embrace both Samaria and Nineveh.
All these conditions, after a variation of nearly 4°
of latitude in the computed path, are precisely fulfilled
by the solar eclipse of the 15th June, B.C. 763, and by
no other.   We conclude, therefore, with certainty,
that Tiglath-pileser began to reign on the 13th day
of the month Jyar, May, in the archonship of Nabu-
beluzur, as stated in Canon No. 5, whose year of
office, 18 years after the eclipse, coincided with the
years B.C. 745 and 744.   If with Sir Henry Rawlin-

finds none to suit his date for Amos, B.C. 787. He therefore
abandons the idea of Amos having foretold the occurrence of an
actual eclipse, and considers that the words were used meta-
phorically.—PUSEY's " Minor Prophets."

son we place the beginning of the year of office at the vernal equinox, then did Tiglath-pileser begin to reign in May 745. But if, as Dr. Oppert asserts, the year of office began at the autumnal equinox, then did he begin to reign in May 744, which I believe to be the true date. Now, in the Annals of Tiglath-pileser, lately commented upon by Mr. George Smith in the " Zeitschrift,"* it appears that in the year B.C. 734, in the second campaign of this king in Syria, Tiglath-pileser took tribute of Pekah, king of Israel, and of Yahu-khazi, king of Judah, that is, of Pekah and Khuzzi-yahu, or Uzziah. But according to the corrected reckoning, as stated above, the year B.C. 734-3 is concurrent with the 52nd, or last year of Uzziah. In no year, therefore, later than 734-3, could tribute have been taken of Uzziah. And as the 52nd year of Uzziah is concurrent with the 1st year of Pekah (2 Kings, xv. 27), in no year earlier than 734-3 could tribute have been taken of Pekah. The year B.C. 734 was, therefore, the year in which tribute was paid, both according to the Assyrian record and the proposed corrected Biblical reckoning. The coincidence is exact. The invasion of Judea leading to this levying of tribute appears also to be referred to by Isaiah, vi. 1, " in the year that king Uzziah died." Again, the reckoning is confirmed by the fact that, in the year B.C. 738, according to the same Assyrian computation, Tiglath-pileser took tribute of Menahem, king of Samaria, whose last year we have found to be B.C. 737.

* " Zeitschrift für Ägyptische Sprache," Jan. 1869.

I. Thus the solar eclipse of the year B.C. 763 compels us to lower the reign of Uzziah, and, therefore, the reigns of the whole Jewish monarchy, exactly 25 years.

II. The solar eclipse which affected the dial of Ahaz in the reign of Hezekiah,* by altering the position of the shadow on the steps to the extent of " ten steps," an effect which could only be produced by the sun at the winter solstice, and which, therefore, points to the time of the annular eclipse of the 11th January B.C. 689, again coincides with the 14th year of Hezekiah, when lowered to the extent of exactly 25 years.†

---

* See p. 176.

† It has been observed, at p. 183, that the annular eclipse of the sun which affected the shadow on the dial in the palace of Hezekiah, in order to produce the required effect, must have presented at Jerusalem the phase of a large partial eclipse, as represented at p. 184, and we have suggested that a correction of the moon's computed position in the year B.C. 689 might be obtained with accuracy from this assumed observation. We are now in a position to say with certainty that such must have been the actual phase presented by that eclipse. For the same correction of the theory of the moon's secular acceleration, which would bring down the shadow of the eclipse of June B.C. 763, 4°, so as to cover both Samaria and Nineveh, during an eclipse which was at the descending node, would necessarily raise the shadow of the eclipse of B.C. 689, which was at the ascending node, somewhat to the north of the path laid down by Mr. Airy from "Varied Greenwich elements," (see "Journal of the Royal Asiatic Society," vol. xv. Part 2, p. 288), and so produce the phase represented at p. 184. The path of the eclipse of June 763 is probably the most precisely defined path of shadow recorded in history. It cannot be varied northward without uncovering Samaria, nor southward without uncovering Nineveh. The path of the shadow of the

III. The total solar eclipse, known as the eclipse of Thales, which has always been looked upon by chronologists as regulating the time of the fall of Nineveh, and the accession of Nebuchadnezzar to the throne of Babylon, about four years after the eclipse, and which, till within some few years, was generally assumed to be identical with the eclipse of B.C. 610, is now finally recognised by astronomers as the eclipse of May B.C. 585, just 25 years lower than the common date, thus bringing down the first year of Nehuchadnezzar from B.C. 606 to 581, as successor of his father, and to B.C. 582, as leader of his father's armies.

That three such decisive marks of time as three solar eclipses connected with events in Jewish history, in three successive centuries, should thus combine to lower the chain of sacred history at three independent points to the exact extent of twenty-five years, and that, in conformity with the same precise result, deduced from the identification of Daniel's Darius with the son of Hystaspes, is no ordinary proof of the consistency and accuracy of the series of dates above proposed. It is, in fact, proof of the highest order applicable to such subjects, and unanswerable. When, moreover, it shall

eclipse of B.C. 310 (*see* p. 410) must accordingly be thrown north instead of south of Syracuse, in agreement with the fact, that the fleet of Agathocles first supposed that it was sailing towards Italy, then towards Sardinia, Justin. xxii. v. And the path of the eclipse of B.C. 585 (*see* p. 408) must also be thrown further north, yet covering the position where Syennesis of Cilicia, and Labynetus of Babylon, may be supposed to have brought about peace between the Lydians and *Medes after their battle.—Herod.* i. 74.

have been shown, as we propose to show, that another link in the same continuous chain of rectified dates, that is, the date of the captivity of the ten tribes carried away by Shalmanezer from Samaria, B.C. 696, is the date preserved by an old Jewish historian, who wrote 220 years before the Christian era ;* and that this same date, just twenty-five years lower than the common date, B.C. 721, is the starting-point from which the Jews in the Crimea, descendants of the ten tribes, reckoned for many centuries the years of their captivity, as shown by a series of ancient gravestones still extant, some of them as old as the first century, we feel that the reader will be disposed to go along with us while arguing from the above dates in Jewish history as from established data.

Before we proceed to examine the evidence of the Jewish gravestones in the Crimea, it will be interesting, as well as to the point, briefly to consider the position of Biblical chronology under the hands of several able writers who have recently applied themselves to the subject; especially the opinions of those who have the historical evidence derived from Assyrian inscriptions lying open before them, such as Sir Henry Rawlinson, the late Dr. Hincks, Dr. Oppert, and Mr. George Smith, who has recently entered on the field of Assyrian discovery. The disruption and dislocation of the sacred text, proposed by these writers, and their want of confidence in the facts disclosed in the documents they interpret, is very unsatisfactory. For my own part, after care-

* See p 306.

fully examining the materials which they have laid before us, I am satisfied that Niebuhr's predictive words may now be written in the past, and that "in Nineveh, Babylonia, and Persia, centuries long past have come to light again, and that the ancient times do now present themselves clearly and distinctly in all their details :"* moreover, that the details thus disclosed, on close examination, are found to be in strictest harmony with what is recorded of the same events in Holy Scripture.

In the article already alluded to in the " Athen-æum " of the 18th May, 1867, Sir Henry Rawlinson had arrived at the conclusion, " that the numbers of the Hebrew text would have to be altered so as to curtail the interval between Hezekiah and Ahab by about forty years;" and the effect of his adjustment of Assyrian records with Scripture history would have been to expunge from the dynasty of the kings of Judah the reign of Jotham, who reigned for sixteen years after the death of Uzziah, and who immediately preceded Ahaz on the throne. In November and December, 1868, two carefully written articles, full of valuable information, from the pen of Dr. Oppert, appeared in the " Revue Archéologique," suggesting a very different adjustment of the Assyrian Canon to Bible history. His professed object in these articles is to uphold the truth of the sacred record, and the outline of the common marginal reckoning in our Bibles : and finding, as he supposes, that Sir Henry's discovery of the eclipse stands in his way, he proposes to substitute an

* Niebuhr's " Lectures on Anc. Hist." vol. i. p. 63.

annular eclipse visible at Nineveh in June, B.C. 809,
in place of the total solar eclipse of June, 763, as
representing that which is recorded in the fifth
copy of the Assyrian Canon. This idea, however,
can only be supported on the bold and improbable
assumption, that the names of not less than forty-
seven archons have been omitted by the Assyrian
scribes from the continuous list of these annual func-
tionaries. There is, however, no foundation whatever
to be found for this assumption on examination of
the original documents. Having thus extended
the range of the Assyrian Canon over an increased
period of forty-seven years, Dr. Oppert ventures
next to invent a passage of sacred history, which he
thinks may have dropped out of the sacred text,
to fill up a portion of the lengthened period thus
obtained, and by the re-insertion of which he in-
troduces a fictitious king into the list of the
kings of Samaria, viz., a second Menahem, in addition to the king of that name who came to
the throne in the thirty-ninth year of Uzziah,
whose reign cannot be made to fall in with his
reckoning. He then proposes to allow a second
reign to Pekah, king of Samaria, for which there
is no ground whatever in Scripture; and then com-
pletes his manipulation of the sacred text by placing
the invasion of Judea by Sennacherib, not in the
fourteenth year of Hezekiah, as three times stated
in the Jewish annals, but in the twenty-eighth year
of his reign, with the suggestion that this fourteenth
year might signify the fourteenth counted from Hezekiah's recovery from sickness. The late Dr. Hincks

and Professor Rawlinson have both fallen into this arrangement of the reign of Hezekiah.

Again, M. de Saulcy, taking up another portion of sacred chronology, which, as part of a continuous whole, bears indirectly upon Assyrian dates, has lately published an analysis of the books of Ezra and Nehemiah, with the same view of reconciling the history contained in those books with the common view of the history and chronology of the period. Passing over, for want of space, the many valuable observations of M. de Saulcy which show his full appreciation of the difficulties in those books, I will merely point to his bold conclusion (p. 73), where he charges Ezra, or his copyist, with having erroneously inserted the name of Artachshastha for Cambyses in chapter iv. 7, 8. M. de Saulcy does not perceive the invaluable testimony here to be derived from the omission of the name Cambyses by this contemporary sacred writer, in proof of Xenophon's assertion, that Cyrus who conquered Babylon, and therefore he who released the Jews, was not the father, but the " son of Cambyses, king of Persia " who conquered Egypt, a fact which tends to lower the dates of events recorded by Ezra to the same extent as we have found that they must be lowered in the times of the kings of Judah.

The most recent observations upon the contents of the Assyrian inscriptions are to be found in a series of valuable articles from the pen of Mr. George Smith of the British Museum, commencing in the September and October numbers of the " Zeitschrift für Ägyptische Sprache," &c. 1868, in which the history and campaigns of Tiglath-pileser, Sargon, Esarhaddon, and Asshur-bani-pal, are clearly laid open to the general reader.

I have already observed that Mr. Smith has shown from these Assyrian annals that Tiglath-pileser took tribute of Menahem in the reign of Azariah, or Uzziah, king of Judah, in the year B.C. 738, and this date I assume to be absolutely fixed and established. But he immediately throws doubt upon the Assyrian record, by observing that " it is difficult to believe that Menahem was on the throne of Samaria " at so late a date, " and the same difficulty must be felt with reference to the name of Azariah, who only survived Menahem, according to the Book of Kings, for three years." Again he writes, " I think the twenty years of the reign of Pekah in the Book of Kings is an error for ten years, and that Jotham reigned for eleven or twelve years in concert with his father, while Uzziah was a leper."*

Such, then, is the unsatisfactory state of the chronology of the Jewish monarchy in the hands of Assyrian interpreters. Their suggestions are subversive of all faith in the books of Kings and Chronicles as accurate historical records.

Let us now proceed to show how great things these Assyrian scholars have really done by their discoveries towards the rectification of sacred chronology, and how, in fact, they have supplied the means to others of placing the portion of Jewish history now under inquiry in such a position of certainty as not to be disputed. We begin with the reign of Sargon,

* " Zeitschrift," Jan. 1869, pp. 13, 15, 16.

the father of Sennacherib, concerning whom there is scarcely any difference of opinion between them. Sargon's reign is counted with precision from the year B.C. 721–20 to 705–4, by means of a series of tablets, after his sixth year, bearing the date of each regnal year, together with the name of the presiding archon, thus connecting his reign with the Assyrian Canon down to the time of his assassination in the month Ab, in the archonship of Pakkar-bil, B.C. 705–4. Moreover, his thirteenth year as prince of Assyria, B.C. 709, is certified to be his first year as king of Babylon and his sixteenth year in Assyria as his fourth in Babylon, B.C. 706.*

Now, in the "Fastes de Sargon," translated by Dr. Oppert from inscriptions at Khorsabad, the record opens with these words, " Ultu ris sarrutiya adi xv harriya sa," (this is what took place) "from the beginning of my reign to my fifteenth campaign." Sargon then goes on to recount the chief acts of his reign during his several campaigns, without, however, marking the events with the regnal years of their accomplishment, until he comes down to the conquest of Merodach Baladan, son of Yakin, king of Babylon, the Mardocempadus of Ptolemy's Canon, which we know, from the tablets, took place in his thirteenth year, and his taking possession of the throne of Babylon in that year, B.C. 709. This date is in perfect accordance with the date of Ptolemy. He then suddenly adds, " Ultu ris sarrutiya adi sanat iii. ukali kisa ati"—"all was accomplished

* G. Smith, " Zeitschrift," July, 1869.

from the beginning to the third year of my reign." Dr. Oppert seems to refer this passage to the three first years of Sargon, 720, 719, 718; but it is clear that Sargon is counting here not in the years of his campaigns, but in the years of his actual reign, and it is equally clear that this third year of his reign was the year when Babylon was taken, B.C. 709. The first year, therefore, of his reign as supreme or absolute king was B.C. 711.

Let us now return to the reign of Tiglath-pileser, whom we have found taking tribute of Menahem in B.C. 738, and of Pekah in his first year, and of Uzziah in his last, in B.C. 734. These two dates, as we have said, are established points from which to reckon with certainty and precision. Now Pekah we know from the Book of Kings reigned twenty years. If his first year, therefore, was 734, his last year was B.C. 715, after which he was conquered by Tiglath-pileser. (2 Kings, xvi.) Mr. Smith also finds reference in the annals of Tiglath-pileser to the deposition of Pekah (Paqaka), and the setting up of Hoshea (Husie).* So that from the evidence of the inscriptions, in conjunction with the evidence of Scripture, Tiglath-pileser must have been still on the throne in B.C. 715, after which other acts of his reign are recorded. From this date to the year 711, when Sargon began to reign, there are but three years, during which we may assume he continued to live, and thus we arrive at the following succession of kings :—

* "Zeitschrift," Jan. 1869.

Tiglath-pileser reigns 33 years, from B.C. 745–4 to 712.
Sargon, alone, „   7   „   711 „ 704.

And thus also it appears that Sargon, who was elected
prince, or leader, by certain princes at Harrân,* must
have been on the throne in conjunction with Tiglath-
pileser just ten years, from 721 to 712, before his
sole reign began. This we know was a frequent
occurrence in Eastern monarchies, and that it was so
in this particular case we have sufficient corrobora-
tive evidence.

i. When Pekah towards the close of his reign
combined with Rezin to make war upon Ahaz, that
is to say, in his eighteenth year, B.C. 717, we are
told in the second book of Chronicles, xxviii. 16, that
"at that time did king Ahaz send unto the *kings*
of Assyria to help him." Here, then, is evidence of
the fact of a plurality of kings on the throne of
Assyria in that year.

ii. At this time, 717, the prophet Isaiah (viii. 3, 4)
tells us that, taking two witnesses he went unto the
prophetess, and she conceived and bare a son : and
that of this son it was said, " Before the child shall
have knowledge to cry, My father, and my mother,
the riches of Damascus and the spoil of Samaria
shall be taken away," that is to say, that before the
expiration of the year B.C. 715 Samaria shall be
taken and spoiled. Now Sargon tells us, without
naming the date, that in one of his early campaigns
(say in B.C. 716-15), he besieged and took Samaria,
carried off 27,280 captives from the city, and placed

* Oppert, "Revue Archéologique," Dec. 1868, p. 381.

a governor in possession. He then tells us that he imposed upon the city the tribute of the Sar Mahri. Oppert translates the words "the tribute of the antecedent king." The words would seem, however, to be more correctly translated, " of the king prece- dent," that is, the king supreme or paramount. The word מָרֵא, "Mareh," in Chaldee signified lord, and is used by Daniel in the expression "Lord of Kings."[*] "Mahri" in Assyrian is an epithet of Queen Beltis.[†]

The proper meaning of the word "Mahri" is " before," while the proper meaning of the word " Arku," a title attached to the name of Sargon, is "after." So that, to all appearance, in the year B.C. 715 Tiglath-pileser was styled "king prece- dent," while Sargon was styled " king coming after," or appointed successor to the throne. These then were the kings to whom Ahaz sent messengers.

iii. The public acts of the later years of Tiglath- pileser appear to be the same, or closely connected with the early exploits of the reign of Sargon. For instance, Tiglath-pileser, after taking Damascus and putting Rezin to death, lays claim to having slain Pekah and having set up Hoshea in his stead.[‡] All this, therefore, in B.C. 715. While Sargon, who did not become military archon till 719, and passed his first campaign in Elam (say in 718–17), after besieging and taking Samaria, in 715, imposed upon that city, as we have seen, the tribute of the Sar Mahri, Tiglath-pileser, not naming the king deposed.

---

[*] Dan. ii. 47.   [†] Norris's Dictionary, p. 32.
[‡] " Zeitschrift," Jan. 1869, pp. 14, 15, 16.

Again, after the fall of Damascus and Samaria
Isaiah foretells that "the fly in the uttermost part of
the rivers of Egypt, and the bee that is in the land
of Assyria," shall settle down upon the desolate land
of Palestine ; and accordingly Tiglath-pileser tells
us that the Assyrians next descended on the Philis-
tines, drove Hanon, king of Gaza, out of his city,
who fled to Egypt, and that the king of Askelon
died of alarm on hearing of the fate of Rezin.   This,
therefore, we may assume took place in the year 714.
Sargon now takes up the history, and, without mentioning the flight of Hanon to Egypt, relates how
Hanon joined his forces with those of Sebeck (Sabaco
the Ethiopian), tartan or commander-in-chief of the
armies of Egypt, and how they came up together
out of Egypt and offered him battle at Raphia, how
Sebeck fled away defeated, and how he captured
Hanon with his own hands.*   Again Tiglath-pileser
informs us that he marched against Samsi, queen of
the Arabs, carried away camels, and oxen, and other
spoils, and then subdued the tribes of the Sabeans.
While Sargon, about the same year, 714, tells us that
he laid tribute upon Pi-ir-u (Boccoris), king of Egypt,
on Samsi, queen of the Arabs, and on It-Himya the
Sabean, and carried off gold, spices, horses, and
camels.

No one can fail to see that these campaigns of
Tiglath-pileser and Sargon are the same.   The acts
are probably the acts of Sargon, the glory is the
glory of the reign of Tiglath-pileser.   There is no

* "Fastes de Sargon," p. 4.

need, therefore, for cutting short the reign of Tiglath-
pileser by fifteen years and pressing up events, which
must have taken place as late as the year B.C. 715
and 714, as high as the year 784, as proposed by
Assyrian interpreters ; thus disturbing the position
of the reigns of Jotham and of Pekah, and thereby
the dates of the whole Jewish monarchy.

Let us now turn to the evidence to be derived
from the tombstones of the Caraite Jews of the ten
tribes in the Crimea, who appear to have preserved
with exactness the date of the captivity of their forefathers from Samaria in the time of Shalmanezer.
The Caraite Jews, it is well known, are distinguished
from their Jewish brethren of the West by their adherence to the text of Scripture, and their rejection of
Rabbinical traditions. And owing to the jealousy
thus existing between them, and the Talmudical
Jews, and the strangeness of the obsolete chronological eras brought to light in their inscriptions,
doubt has been thrown upon the genuineness of the
sepulchral monuments to which we now draw attention. It is thought improbable that the tradition of
the date of their captivity should have been preserved from so remote a period to the present time
unknown to the Jews of the West. We think, on
the other hand, that the several stages of the tradition may be clearly traced, even from the time of
Shalmanezer down to the first century A.D., in which
century several of the earliest of these monuments
are dated.

What, for instance, is the book of Tobit but an

historical romance preserved in the tribe of Naph-
thali, one of the ten tribes carried away by Shalmanezer, and giving an account of the commencement of the captivity at Nineveh under that king ?
Tobit, we read, was purveyor to King Enemessar, or
Shal-enemessar. Now this book closes with the statement that Tobias, the son of Tobit, died at Ecbatana
at the age of 127 years, "and before he died, he heard
of the destruction of Nineveh which was taken by
Nabuchodonosor and Assuerus, and before his death
he rejoiced over Nineveh." No one, we presume, believes that Tobias lived 127 years. It is the Greek
translator of the book in the second or third century
B.C., to whom we are indebted for this error : while it
is obvious that the year of his death had been counted
from the time when his father's tribe and family
were carried away from Thisbe in Galilee. Tobias
had lived to the 127th year "Ligaluthenu" (after our
captivity), and probably this record had been
engraved on some monumental stone to his memory.
These 127 years could not have been counted from
the year B.C. 721, the common date for the captivity,
because then they would have ended in B.C. 595,
ten years earlier than the eclipse of Thales, when
Nineveh was still standing. But if counted from
B.C. 696, they would have ended in B.C. 570, just
thirteen years after the fall of that city in 583.

That they were counted from that very year we
have reason to believe from the fact, that the dates
of the several captivities under Shalmanezer, Sennacherib, and Nebuchadnezzar, have been accurately

preserved by the Jewish historian, Demetrius, who computed them upwards from the first year of the reign of Ptolemy Philopator, B.C. 222; and Demetrius affirms that the captivity of the ten tribes took place 474 years before the 4th Ptolemy, that is, in B.C. 696. If this, then, was the tradition in B.C. 222, monumental traces of that reckoning were in existence probably amongst the Eastern Jews at that date, and the same record ought in consistency to be found on the sepulchral monuments of the Jews of the ten tribes in the first century A.D. who have always kept themselves distinct from the Jews of the two tribes dispersed from Jerusalem by Titus.

Again, what is the book of Judith but a history preserved in the tribe of Simeon (Ch. ix. 2), one of the ten tribes carried away by Shalmanezer? Her exploits were accomplished in the 18th year of Nabopalassar, father of Nebuchadnezzar, that is, in the year B.C. 608,* just after the establishment of the Scythians at Nineveh, and at the time of their expedition against Ashdod and Ascalon. It is said that she lived to the age of 105, and that "none made Israel afraid in the days of Judith, nor a long time after her death." Now Judith probably did not live to the age of 105 : but if, as is probable, there was inscribed upon her monument that she died in the 105th year "Ligaluthenu," that year, counted from B.C. 696, would be 592, sixteen years after the death of Holofernes ; and it was not till the year 582, or twenty-six years after the death of

* See p. 453.

Holofernes, that Nebuchadnezzar made the kingdom of Judea tributary to Babylon.

We think, then, that there is strong presumptive evidence from these two books that the Jews of the ten tribes had been accustomed from the commencement to reckon, in the years of their exile, from Samaria and Galilee in the days of Shalmanezer.

The following account of the Crimean tombstones is taken from a learned and interesting treatise by Professor Chowlson, which appeared in the "Memoirs of the Imperial Academy of Sciences at St. Petersburg" in 1865.*l

The first reference in modern days to the Jewish burial-grounds at Tschufukale and Mankup, not far from the fortress of Sebastopol, is found in the travels of Pallas in the South of Russia, who visited the Crimea in the year 1793, or 1794. He describes the large two-horned stones in these cemeteries, and speaks of the places as overshadowed by venerable trees, and how, by threatening to cut down these trees, money had frequently been extorted from the Jews by the Khans of the Crimea.† Koppin's Russian work on the Crimea, dated in 1837, gives drawings of these stones, which are copied by Chowlson, and many are said to have sunk deep into the

---

* Chowlson's valuable treatise extends over 134 pages. See also "Adolph Neubauer's Geschichte des Karäerthums." Leipzig, 1866, and "Die Firkowitche Sammlung," "Melanges Asiatiques," vol. v. p. 121, St. Petersburg. Also Dr. Samuel Davidson's observations on these tombstones, printed in the "Jewish Chronicle," Oct. and Nov. 1868.

† "Pallas' Travels," vol. ii. pp. 34, 122.

ground, leaving nothing legible of their inscriptions.

In 1839, Prince Woronzoff, Governor-General of Odessa, and President of the Archæological Society in that place, wrote to Murmzoff, Governor of Sympheropol, requesting information concerning the Caraites of the Crimea. Abraham Firkowitch, a learned Jew of Eupatoria, was then appointed to search in the cities of Caffa, Mankup, Solchat, Tschufukale, and other places where the Caraites dwelt, for manuscripts, epitaphs, and any other antiquities bearing upon the history of these people. He succeeded in collecting fifty-one fragments of the Hebrew Scriptures, and fifty-nine copies of ancient Hebrew epitaphs, eighteen of them from Mankup, the rest from the burial-ground of Tschufukale, or Jews' castle. The oldest of the epitaphs was dated in A.D. 640. The news of these discoveries created much sensation amongst Continental Jews. Some doubted the genuineness of the relics, some the correctness of the copies of the epitaphs. Dr. Stern, of Odessa, was therefore appointed in 1842 to visit the spots pointed out by Firkowitch, and to verify his discoveries. Dr. Stern returned with additional manuscripts, and seven additional epitaphs, the earliest dated in A.D. 598, and certified the correctness of Firkowitch's report. After this, Firkowitch and his son-in-law Gabriel Firkowitch made repeated searches in the Crimea; and in 1853, not less than 700 copies of tombstones, and 150 copies of epigraphs were shown to, and ex-

amined by Professor Chowlson at St. Petersburg, together with a map describing the places where each was found. In 1856 it was suggested that paper impressions should be taken of the inscriptions, and accordingly 100 impressions were taken of 100 epitaphs; and in 1863, Abraham Firkowitch caused the inscriptions upon eight of these tombstones to be sawn off and carried to St. Petersburg, where they now remain deposited in the Asiatic Museum.*

Facsimiles of three of the most ancient of these monuments are here given as illustrations in evidence of the preservation of the date of the captivity B.C. 696. The originals of No. 2, and No. 3, have been carried to St. Petersburg. The original of No. 1, the most ancient of all, remains *in situ*, of which a copy and paper impression only were before Professor Chowlson. The deaths are registered in years of a current era "Ligaluthenu"† (after our Exile).

---

* The value of these relics is at present so little estimated, that they remain hidden in boxes under a library table of the Asiatic department of the Academy of Sciences, where they were lately examined by my friend Mr. J. Harman. It is probable that tombs of still more ancient date might be recovered by deeper excavation in the cemetery.

† Professor Chowlson remarks that a forger of these monuments seeking to support a fictitious date of the exile from Samaria, would not have written simply Ligaluthenu, but Ligaluth Shomron, after the exile from Samaria.

Dr. Geiger of Frankfort writes, "The mention of eras which were unknown at a later date tends to show that no fraud has been committed in these monuments which belong to an age and country uncontrolled by other dates." And again, "The calcu-

The inscriptions have been interpreted by Chowlson, as follows :—

No. 1.

זאת ציון בוקי
בן יצחק כוהן נע
עת ישועת ישר
אל שנת תשב
שנים לגלותנו

"This is the tombstone of Buki, the son of Izchak, the priest ; may his soul be in Eden, at the time of the salvation of Israel. (He died) in the year 702, of the years, or era, of our Exile," that is, in A.D. 6.

No. 2.

ר משח לוי מת
שנת תשבו לגלותנו

"Rabbi Moses Levi died in the year 726, after our Exile," that is, in A.D. 30.

No. 3.

צדוק חלוי בן משה
מת דא ליציח
תשפה לגלותנו

"Zadok the Levite, son of Moses, died 4000 after the Creation, 785 after our Exile," that is, in A.D. 89.

All that we gather from these three venerable inscriptions is, that the Jews of the Crimea at some remote period of their sojourn there were accustomed

lation of the era after the Assyrian exile as presented in these instances is so little intelligible that a forger would not have used it as the basis of his fraud."

2

to register deaths in the years of their Exile :* and
that on one of the stones the year of Exile was
reckoned by them as 4000, less 785 years, = 3215
years after the Creation.

But this figure, 3215 after the Creation, tells us
nothing, unless we know how many years before
the Christian era, or from some other fixed date,
the Crimean Jews placed the time of the Creation.

Now one of the most interesting epigraphs discovered by Abraham Firkowitch, upon a roll at
Mangelis, near Derbend, informs us that in the
reign of the Emperor Julian, in the latter part of
the fourth century, Greek-speaking Jews, whose
ancestors had been placed by Titus in Byzantium,
spread through Trebizond to Metarcha, on the Sea
of Azoff, bringing with them Rabbinical teaching :
and by this means a second reckoning was introduced into the Crimea, called the Metarchian, which
is, in fact, the era now in common use amongst the
Jews throughout the world, and which places the
Creation in the year B.C. 3760–61.

An epitaph on one of the stones which has been
carried to St. Petersburg,† and which had been
inscribed during the period of transition, that is,
before the old Crimean era had been lost and the
Metarchian exclusively used, runs thus :—

"And this is the monument of the tomb of

---

* It may be observed that the date on each of these monuments is given in letters which recall the word Thisbe, the town
in Galilee from whence Tobit was carried by Shalmanezer.

† Chowlson, p. 15.

Esther, the daughter of Solomon, which I have placed above her head : who died in the year [4]536,—may her soul be bound up with the bundle of the living,—after the Creation; that is, [4]385 according to the Metarchians."*

From this monument, then, we learn that the difference between the old Crimean era of Creation and the era of the Metarchians (which latter era is supposed to be the invention of Rabbi Hillel, called Hanasi, in the first half of the fourth century),† was 151 years. And this number of years of difference between the reckonings may be also shown by a comparison of several Caraite epigraphs, and is a point not disputed. So that the original Jewish era of Creation, as preserved amongst the ten tribes, was 3760 + 151 = 3911 before Christ. Now if we deduct the year 3215, which we have found to be concurrent with the year of Exile, from that date, we find that the traditional year of Exile in the Crimea was B.C. 696. Thus,—

> Tombstone, No. 1, dated "702 after our Exile," was set up in A.D. 6.
> Tombstone, No. 2, dated "726 after our Exile," was set up in A.D. 30.
> Tombstone, No. 3, dated "785 after our Exile," was set up in A.D. 89.

It is not surprising that these monuments lead-

---

* "That is, of the Jews of Tamatarcha, or Tmutarakan, now called Taman, in the immediate vicinity of the ancient Phanagoria."—Chowlson.

† Ideler's "Handb. d. Chron." i. pp. 569, 578, 580. Lepsius, "Chron. of the Egyptians," E. Trans. p. 450.

ing to the establishment of the year B.C. 696, as the date of the capture of Samaria, should have been received at first with doubt and suspicion, as bearing testimony to no accepted computation either of Jews or Christians of the present day. But when, on the other hand, we find that this date is in agreement, even to a single year, with a reckoning which we have shown to be founded upon three fixed and indubitable marks of time, and especially with the eclipse of B.C. 763,—the precise path of which will probably form the basis of many a future astronomical computation, and which regulates the chronology of the period now under inquiry, bringing down the latter part of the sixth year of Hezekiah, about which time Samaria was taken, to the year B.C. 696,—the presumption previously adverse to the genuineness of the monuments becomes reversed, and we accept with much safety their testimony as affording additional and valuable confirmation of a reckoning, which we have no hesitation in pronouncing to be the true reckoning of Scripture chronology during the period of the Jewish monarchy.

From these epitaphs we learn that the correct reckoning of time had not been lost amongst the Jews so early as the beginning of the first century A.D., and can understand how it came to pass that Simeon and Anna were found continuously waiting about the temple " for the consolation of Israel" towards the close of Herod's reign, and how Anna was present there just at the time when Jesus, the son of David, was brought into the temple by His mother Mary. For, according to the common reckoning, calculating from B.C. 536, nearly half a century had elapsed since the completion of 490 years from "the going forth of the command to build Jerusalem;" and the coming of the expected Prince would in such case have become almost a matter of despair.

We have dwelt in this preface more particularly on the subject of Scripture chronology, because the great question between Jews and Christians seems now to have narrowed itself almost to a simple question of chronology. Dr. Herman Adler, son of the Chief Rabbi of England, an able and eloquent preacher, has in course of the present year published a series of earnest and interesting sermons, in which he has alluded to this work, "Messiah the Prince;" and he has treated the subject of the Seventy Weeks of Daniel almost entirely from a chronological point of view. Dr. H. Adler endeavours to impress upon his readers that "almost all chronologists" reckon that the destruction of Jerusalem by Nebuchadnezzar took place 588 years before the birth of Jesus of Nazareth. Whereas, he says, Messiah ought to have appeared, according to Christian interpreters, at the expiration of 490 years from that date. Now, as long as Dr. Adler continues to believe that Jerusalem was destroyed in the year B.C. 588, and almost all chronologists shall agree with him, so long, it must be admitted, will Christian interpreters find it difficult to convince even willing believers that Daniel's prophecy was fulfilled in the birth of Jesus

Christ. When, however, a truer reckoning of the
times of Scripture events, in harmony with the many
archæological discoveries of the present day, shall
have become established, and chronologists in general
shall be convinced that the date of the destruction of
Jerusalem was not B.C. 588, but 563—that after the
completion of seventy years of desolation counted
from that date, ending in B.C. 492, Daniel, in the
first year of Darius as king of Babylon, poured
forth his supplication to God that the sanctuary
and city might be restored—and that at the expiration of exactly seventy weeks of years, or 490
years from the date of his supplication, Jesus, the
son of David, was born in the city of David as recorded by the faithful historian St. Luke—then will
this remarkable prophecy appear before our brethren
in all its simplicity, and this reasoning, founded upon
a fictitious mode of reckoning, of necessity fall to
the ground.

Meanwhile we may observe that the prophets
Jeremiah and Daniel, and the writer of the last
chapter of the second book of Chronicles, all understood that God had declared that "seventy years
of desolation," neither more nor less, should be fulfilled on the ruined city, "until the land had enjoyed
her sabbaths : for as long as she lay desolate she
kept sabbath, to fulfil threescore and ten years"
(2 Chron. xxxvi. 21). It is unsatisfactory, therefore, to find Dr. Adler arguing that these three inspired writers were mistaken concerning this precise
prediction, and that instead of seventy years of deso-

lation, not less than 490 were to be accomplished
before the city could be rebuilt. But his readers
will be still more dissatisfied when they find that
these 490 years never were fulfilled in the desolations of the holy city, as foretold, according to
his interpretation. For Dr. Adler himself observes
(p. 111), that the walls of Jerusalem were rebuilt
by Nehemiah in the year B.C. 445, and they certainly were rebuilt within 150 years after the date
he fixes for their destruction; nor would any one
deny that the temple itself had been rebuilt and
the daily worship re-established long before the
restoration of the walls by Nehemiah. But what
is most of all unsatisfactory in Dr. Adler's reasoning is that, after quoting the words of Daniel (ix.
25), "Know, therefore, and understand that from
the going forth of the word *to restore and to build
Jerusalem,* unto the anointed Prince, shall be seven
weeks," &c. (p. 115), he endeavours to persuade
his readers that these seven weeks must not be
reckoned from the time of rebuilding and restoration, but from "the destruction of Jerusalem;"
thus making destruction and restoration, in prophetic language, interchangeable terms.

Again, Dr. Adler quotes the beautiful words of
Isaiah (xi. 1–9) beginning, "There shall come forth
a rod out of the stem of Jesse"—and truly observes
that the prophet predicts that the Messiah will be a
scion of the house of David, and then adds—"Christianity declares its Redeemer to be of Divine origin.
Its professors, therefore, are placed in this dilemma.

If He were Divine, how is it that He is here termed a descendant of Jesse ? If He were not Divine, the foundation of their faith crumbles into dust." But Dr. Adler forgets to remind his readers of the passage in Jeremiah (xxiii. 5), "Behold the days come that I will raise unto David a righteous branch, and a king shall reign and prosper," &c., "and this is His name whereby He shall be called, Jehovah our Righteousness." So that, if Dr. Adler calls in question the Divine nature of Messiah, son of David, he is left in the same dilemma as the Jews of old, who could not answer our Lord's question—"David, therefore, himself calleth Him Lord; and whence is he then his son?" (Mark, xii. 37.)

Once more, Dr. Adler truly observes that in the days of Messiah the scattered tribes of Israel are to be restored to the Holy Land. And this, he says, did not take place in the time of Jesus of Nazareth. Therefore Jesus of Nazareth could not be the Messiah. But he forgets the pathetic words of our Lord weeping over Jerusalem, and saying, " How often would I have gathered thy children together even as a hen gathereth her chickens under her wings, and ye would not, Behold ! your house is left unto you desolate;" and then, alluding to the time of His coming again,—" Ye shall not see me henceforth till ye shall say, Blessed is He that cometh in the name of the Lord " (Matt. xxiii. 37, 39). Do not these words clearly refer to the time of restoration and acceptance of Israel, when He shall come again in glory, "and every eye shall see Him, and they which pierced Him ?" (Rev. i. 7; Zech. xii. 10).

We appeal, then, to the intelligence of our Jewish brethren to reject the erroneous reckoning involved in Dr. Adler's process of reasoning; and we humbly entreat Dr. Adler to search and examine for himself whether there be error, or not, in the proposed reckoning which fulfils the weeks of Daniel in the year of the birth of Jesus Christ. If he shall find no error, then may he be disposed to inquire with the Baptist, " Art thou He that should come, or do we look for another ? " And then would we beseech him to listen with reverence to the conclusive answer which satisfied the inquirer, " The blind receive their sight, the lame walk, the lepers are cleansed, the deaf hear, the dead are raised up, and to the poor the gospel is preached."

But in calling upon our Jewish brethren to confess that Jesus the son of David was " He " indeed, the Anointed Prince "that should come," do we call upon them also to renounce the faith of their ancestors, the chosen of God, or to involve themselves in all the multitudinous and contradictory creeds of Christendom put before them as Christianity? God forbid! Far better that, imbued with steadfast faith in the one great doctrine of the unity of God, they should examine, unfettered by Christian creeds, the sources of Christianity for themselves, and see whether there be anything in the teaching of Jesus opposed to the teaching of Moses and the prophets concerning God and His Messiah. For He said, " Think not that

I am come to destroy the law and the prophets. I am not come to destroy, but to fulfil." (Matt. v. 17). He never taught, like some pious Christians of this day, that those ten great commands, which form the basis of all practical religion in the world, were to become obsolete, and, in course of time, to be no longer binding on his followers. " If thou wilt enter into life," he says, " keep the commandments." (Matt. xix. 17.)

Let Israel continue to hold fast her creed, and confess the everlasting truth,—

" I believe with a perfect faith that the Creator, blessed be His name, is one, that there is no unity like unto Him, and that He only is our God : He was, is, and shall be eternally."

For the Lord Jesus taught no other faith than this, saying, " Hear, oh Israel, the Lord our God is one Lord " (Mark, xii. 29) ; and, praying to God the Father,— His Father and our Father, His God and our God,— exclaimed, " This is life eternal, that they might know Thee the only true God, and Jesus Christ whom Thou hast sent " (John, xvi. 3) ; and again His apostle taught, " There is no God but one" — " There is but one God, the Father, of whom are all things, and we unto Him, and one Lord Jesus Christ, by whom are all things, and we by Him " (1 Cor. viii. 4, 6).

True it is, that the Lord Jesus taught, " I and my Father are one " (John, x. 30) ; that is, truly one in the unity of the same Divine spirit, the same will, and the same Divine purpose, and prayed the

Father that His disciples also might "all be one; as Thou, Father, art in me, and I in Thee, that they all may be one in us" (xvii. 21). For this was the great doctrine of At-one-ment and communion with God taught by Moses, and for the diffusion of the benefits of which, to all mankind, the Lord Himself came down from heaven. This is a doctrine which should not sever, but unite the Jew and Christian. It is the gracious doctrine which hereafter will unite all people and all nations of this world with God,—when "The Lord shall be king over all the earth, and his name one"—when the will of God shall "be done on earth, as it is in heaven"—and when "all the nations which came against Jerusalem shall even go up from year to year to worship the King, the Lord of Hosts, and to keep the feast of tabernacles" (Zech. xiv. 9, 16). For this is the feast which quickly follows that day of all days in the calendar of Moses, the great day of atonement, on which our brethren afflict their souls, and on which hereafter, "in the spirit of grace and of supplication," they will afflict them, and call to remembrance how the guilt of all mankind was laid upon "the Lamb of God, which taketh away the sin of the world" (John, i. 29), and "mourn for him as one mourneth for his only son."

True again it is, that as Moses taught that man was created in the image and similitude of God, so Paul also taught that the Lord Jesus, in the highest sense of perfection, was "the express image of his person,"—"the image of the invisible God,"—

" whom no man hath seen or can see;" and so the
Lord Jesus, in whom " dwelleth all the fulness of
the Godhead bodily," spoke also concerning Himself, in figure, " he that hath seen me hath seen the
Father " (John, xiv. 9). Yet, nevertheless, " though
in the form of God, He aspired not to be equal with
God." And never did either He or His disciples
teach that He and the Father are " one God," or, as
our Romish brethren would say, that " God incarnate
died upon the cross." * For then could not the Son
have cried in mental agony to His Father, " My God,
my God! why hast Thou forsaken me?" Then would
the command have been unmeaning to baptize " in the
name of the Father, and of the Son." Then could not
the Son, "by whom God made the worlds" (Heb. i. 2),
"have through the eternal Spirit offered Himself
without spot to God?" (Heb. ix. 14). Then could not
His disciples, with one consent, have called themselves the servants " of God the Father, and of the
Lord Jesus Christ ;" nor could Paul have preached,
" to us there is one God, the Father," " and one
Lord Jesus Christ." Such was not the Christianity
of Christ's and His disciples. And, therefore, we
submit, with reverence, that we dare not teach our
brethren that the Father and the Son are " one God."

Again, though every pious Jew, with holy David,
would pray to God, " Take not Thy holy spirit
from me,"—"stablish me with Thy free spirit."
Though the Lord Jesus has told us that He " cast
out devils by the Spirit of God," and Paul has

* See p. 28.

taught us that "the Lord is the Spirit," (2 Cor.
iii. 17); though every Christian prays for "the
renewing of the Holy Spirit which God sheds on
us abundantly, through Jesus Christ our Saviour,"
(Titus, iii. 5, 6); though, with St. Augustine, we
may say, that "the Father and the Son, and the
spirit of both, work all things at the same time
equally and harmoniously;" yet, again, we submit
with reverence that we are not at liberty to call
upon our Jewish brethren to go beyond the words
of Christ's apostles, who, while they all confessed
themselves to be the servants "of God the Father,
and of the Lord Jesus Christ," yet never felt constrained to add, servants also of "God the Holy
Ghost proceeding from the Father and the Son."
For this was not the faith delivered to the saints.

Let Israel still hold fast her creed, and confess,—

"I believe with a perfect faith, that to the
Creator, blessed be His name, yea, to Him only, is
it proper to address our prayers, and that it is not
proper to pray to any other."

For the Lord Jesus, when asked by His disciples
to teach them how to pray, replied, say, "Our Father
which art in heaven;" and again, "In that day
shall ye ask me nothing. Verily, verily, I say unto
you, Whatsoever ye shall ask the Father in my
name, He will give it to you" (John, xvi. 23).

Neither Christ, nor His disciples, ever taught
that we should pray to His earthly mother as our
intercessor with Him,—that "it is impossible for
any to be saved who turns away from her, or is dis-

regarded by her,"— and "that God is subject to the command of Mary:"[*] nor, with the last council of the Romish Church at Trent, that "it is good and useful suppliantly to invoke the saints." Above all, He never taught the followers of Moses to blaspheme God's honour, by mutilating His Table of Commandments delivered from Mount Sinai, by striking out the second, to make room for prayers to saints and angels.[†] Our Jewish brethren both in this and in their preceding article of faith are nearer even now to Christianity than the erring Romish Church. Would that the time might quickly come when, with the name of the Father written in their foreheads, they shall sing the song of Moses and the song of the Lamb. When Jew, Mahomedan, and Christian, gathered together in one fold, in fellowship with the great shepherd of our faith, shall be united in one holy bond of faith — the worship of one only God, the Father.

Again, let Israel hold fast her creed,—

"I believe, with a perfect faith, in the personal appearance of the Messiah ; and although He tarry, yet will I wait for Him in expectation of His daily coming."

---

[*] Pusey's "Eirenicon," p. 103.

[†] The following is taken from the "Dottrina Cristiana," the authorised manual of instruction used in Rome :— Q. "How many are the commandments of God?" A. "Ten."—Q. "Say the ten Commandments." A. "1st. I am the Lord thy God, thou shalt not have another God before me. 2nd. Thou shalt not take the name of God in vain. 3. Remember to sanctify the feast-days," &c. &c.—DEAN ALFORD on Rome.

d

We think our Jewish brethren are here again in better preparation for the coming of the Lord than many a Christian. They look for the personal appearance of a heavenly king, "who shall execute judgment and justice in the earth" (Jerem. xxiii. 5). "Rejoice before the Lord, for He cometh, for He cometh to judge the earth : and with righteousness to judge the world, and the people with his truth" (Ps. xcvi. 13). Christians are apt to look for the coming of their Lord, to carry them to heaven, or cast them down to hell. "In His days" (it is written) "Judah shall be saved and Israel dwell safely." "I will sift the house of Israel among all nations." And again: "I will bring again the captivity of Israel, and they shall build the waste cities, and inhabit them" (Amos, ix. 9, 14). But Christians tell us that the day of the Lord's coming is but the day of each man's death; and as for Judah and Israel, these are words extinct, or intended only to represent the Catholic Church, by which all must be taught who seek to go to heaven.

The Lord Jesus said, "Hereafter shall ye see the Son of Man sitting on the right hand of power and coming in the clouds of heaven." And Paul had expectation even in his days that that coming was nigh at hand; for he said, "Yet a little while and He that shall come will come, and will not tarry" (Heb. x. 37); and also looked for "a crown of righteousness which the Lord, the righteous Judge," should give to "all them that love His appearing" (2 Tim. iv. 8). " When He shall

appear," says St. John (1 John, iii. 2), "we shall
be like Him, for we shall see Him as He is." The
Apostles, therefore, like our Jewish brethren, looked
forward to a personal appearance of Messiah upon
earth, and to see Him face to face.

Our brethren are not called upon to make cause
with those unstable, would-be leaders of Israel, who
at a recent Synod,* renounced in these last days the
belief in Israel's restoration — an act which reminds
us of their ancestors, redeemed from Babylon, who,
in want of faith, when the rebuilding of their
Temple was about to be commenced, exclaimed,
" The time is not come, the time that the Lord's
house should be built" (Hag. i. 2). They are not
called upon to seek the personal presence of their
Saviour in the elements of bread and wine, much
less to seek in those elements for the co-redemp-
tress Mary.† But they are called upon to cast off
that partial, nay wilful blindness of which Paul
spoke, and to behold in Jesus the Son of David, of
the root of Jesse, who claimed to Himself the
special title " Son of Man," that " Son of Man " of
whom Daniel wrote, as coming to the Ancient of
days, to whom should be given " dominion, and
glory, and a kingdom, that all people, nations, and
languages "—not in heaven but in earth—" should
serve Him." Christ " said to his disciples, The days
will come when ye shall desire to see one of the
days of the Son of Man, and ye shall not see it.

* The Synod at Leipsic in 1869.
† Pusey's " Eirenicon," p. 163.

And they shall say unto you, See here : or See there : go not after them nor follow them. For as the lightning, that lighteneth out of the one part under heaven, shineth unto the other part under heaven ; so shall also the Son of Man be in his day " (Luke, xvii. 22–24).

Let Israel never swerve from her belief in the personal appearance of the Messiah upon earth. If it is true that this mighty and exalted Being, by whom God made the world, came down from heaven some 1800 years ago, to visit in person His creatures upon earth ; doubtless He will fulfil the promise of His second coming in person to complete the work He then began. Our brethren, we know, will greet Him at His coming with the lofty *name*, " Jehovah our Righteousness." And we ourselves are taught that He hath obtained by inheritance a more excellent *name* than the holy angels, who are commanded to worship Him. Yet let us both remember, that when this blessed, gracious Being dwelt amongst us, though " God of God," and " Light of light," He never ceased to pray to our Father as His God, nor ever claimed identity with the one immortal and invisible Source of all things —" The only true God."

INTRODUCTION TO THE FIRST EDITION.

THE following remarks upon the book of Daniel, written during leisure hours of a busy life, were begun with the intention merely of commenting upon two of the principal prophecies of the book; with the view, first, of pointing out the untenableness of Dr. Pusey's interpretation of the well-known prophecy of the ninth chapter; and secondly, of arguing from the exact and literal fulfilment in Jesus Christ of the words of that chapter, and also from the remarkable historical fulfilment of the words of the second chapter, for the genuineness and inspiration of this most sublime and marvellous book of Holy Scripture. While the work, however, was in progress through the press, the publication of Mr. Desprez's treatise on "Daniel, or the Apocalypse of the Old Testament," accompanied by an Introduction from the hand of Dr. Williams, in which the prophecy of the ninth chapter is ingeniously, and at first sight inextricably, interwoven with certain portions of the eleventh chapter, now commonly supposed to have been written in the time of the Maccabees, rendered it necessary to take into consideration additional matter, and to extend the range of these remarks over a more comprehensive field. The result has been, that some observations which might more properly have formed part of the body of the work, can only be supplied in the form of prefatory matter; for which defect in arrangement the author craves the indulgence of the reader.

The delay thus occasioned has afforded him the advantage of perusing several recent comments on Dr. Pusey's admirable work on "Daniel the Prophet," especially the valuable observations of Mr. J. J. Stewart Perowne, concerning the Chaldee of Daniel, published in the first number of the "Contemporary Review," to which he begs leave to direct the attention of those who are desirous of entering into the linguistic argument. All the arguments which the learning and ingenuity of adverse critics can deduce from the language of the book, with the view of lowering the date of its composition within times subsequent to the reign of Antiochus Epiphanes, have now probably been exhausted; and the result of the discussion of this part of the inquiry has been, we are satisfied, to establish with increased clearness, in the mind of every unprejudiced examiner, the peculiar appropriateness of the prophet's language to the position in which he was placed, viz.—at Babylon; and also its close approximation to the language known to have been used about the time of the Babylonian Captivity, when Daniel professes to have written. On the other hand, the peculiarity of the construction of the book, in successive portions of Hebrew, Chaldee, and Hebrew, and the occasional alternations from the first to the third, and from the third again to the first person, in the composition, seem to favour the idea that all portions of the present text are not the production of the same hand, and lead to the inference, that the dignified and majestic prophecies of Daniel are of an older date than certain dubious passages contained in the book, which seem to betray the hand of a compiler even as late as the time of the Maccabees. Notwithstanding all that has been written concerning the book of Daniel, we submit that it is yet open to more searching examination: and much yet remains to be brought forward towards fixing with precision the date of some of the principal visions, as also towards reestablishing the lofty position, in the scheme of Divine Revelation, which the writings of this prophet are entitled and destined in our opinion yet to hold. It has not yet been determined by the consent of commentators, under what Median or Medo-Persian king Daniel lived and wrote his later prophecies, that is to say, who was the king in secular history that in the book of Daniel bears no other title than Darius, whose dominions extended over a vast portion of the Persian empire, and who unquestionably lived within the

times of authentic Persian history. So long as this preliminary and fundamental question remains undecided, we question the ability of any commentator to do entire justice to the
book of Daniel; and we most certainly deny the competency
of any critic to infer, from the silence of those prophets who
lived after the Captivity concerning Daniel and his writings,
that neither the prophet nor his writings were in existence
in their days; when, for aught that can be shown to the contrary, Daniel may have been living contemporaneously with
those prophets, and, indeed, have been composing some of
his later prophecies at Babylon, at the very time when they
themselves were delivering their divine messages to the people
at Jerusalem. Dr. Pusey has fairly abandoned all hope of
throwing light upon this important historical question, and
together with most modern interpreters, rests satisfied with
the improbable and uncritical suggestion, that the Darius of
Daniel may possibly be identified either with the Astyages of
Herodotus, or the Cyaxares of Xenophon, or with some yet
undiscovered king of Media. On the other hand, we affirm,
without fear of error, and one of the chief objects of the following pages will be to show, that Daniel's master was no
other than the great Persian king, Darius, son of Hystaspes,
one of the best known kings of Persian history; and that one
of the most momentous of Daniel's visions, viz. that of the
ninth chapter, is fixed with precision to the year in which that
king had attained the sixty-second year of his age, that is,
B.C. 492. For it was, as we believe, not till after the final
overthrow of the kingdom of Babylon, in this year, which
had rebelled three times during the reign of Darius,—first
under Naditabirus, a second time under Aracus, both of whom
falsely claimed the title of Nabucodrossor, son of Nabonadius,*
and lastly under Belsharezar, or Belshazzar, the eldest son of
that king†—that "Darius took the kingdom" of Babylon,
razed the walls of the city, and carried away "all its gates."
All which, we may observe, is consistent with monumental

---

* Behistun Inscription.

† Oppert distinguishes the father of Belsharezar from Nabonadius, and places
his reign between B.C. 508 and 488.—*Chron. des Assyr. et des Babylons*, p. 28.

inscriptions, and also with the trustworthy record of Ctesias, who lived many years in Persia; though at variance with what Herodotus has written concerning the capture of Babylon by Darius. So that the chronology of the book of Daniel, if we are correct, so far from remaining the most vague and disputable of all the books of Scripture, will thus become more accurately fixed than that of any other book : while the lives of three of the chief actors in the history, viz. of Daniel, Belshazzar, and Darius, will be brought down within times when Daniel might possibly have been employed, as he tells us that he was employed during the reign of Belshazzar, in transacting "the king's business" in the capital of the Persian empire, that is, at Susa, which could not well have been the case at any time before the conquest of Babylon by the Persians.

The principal objections raised against the genuineness and inspiration of the book of Daniel, are comprised under the following heads :—1st. That it is written partly in Chaldee, or Aramaic, and partly in Hebrew. 2nd. That it is placed in Hebrew Bibles, not amongst the Prophets, but amongst the Hagiographa, or sacred writings. 3rd. That the author's language is interspersed with Greek and Persian words. 4th. That "neither Zechariah nor Haggai, following immediately the return from exile, contain any such allusion to Daniel or his book, as a career so marvellous, and a book so significant, if they had been known, would have rendered natural, if not necessary."* 5th. That the silence of Ezra, Nehemiah, and Jesus, son of Sirach, concerning the book, is tantamount to its exclusion from the Canon. 6th. That the vision of the eleventh chapter comprehends a series of minute historical events, unlike the character of the predictions of any other prophet, and indeed of Daniel himself, ranging over a period of one hundred years, and then suddenly and abruptly terminates in the reign of Antiochus Epiphanes. 7th. That historical and chronological statements throughout the book are irreconcilable with known secular history.

---

* Dr. Williams' Introduction, p. xii.

Now considering that Daniel was resident at Babylon, in the midst of the great stream of commerce flowing to and fro between Greece and Persia, we can see no force whatever in the objection to the authenticity of his writings derived from the occasional use of Greek and Persian words. On the contrary, the use of such words, as argued convincingly by Dr. Pusey and Mr. Perowne, forms one of the most satisfactory proofs of their composition at the time and in the place in which they profess to have been written. While the fact that the book professes to be the production of one of Hebrew descent, living within the metropolis of the Chaldees, sufficiently and satisfactorily accounts for the use of both Chaldee and Hebrew by the same writer. Even Dr. Williams himself seems to be less positive, and places less stress upon the linguistic argument, in his Introduction to Mr. Desprez, than in his original Essay on Bunsen's Biblical Researches.

With regard to the position of the book of Daniel amongst the books of the Hagiographa, though we think that there is every reason to be satisfied that the writings of Daniel must have been known to, and received by, the Jewish church, from very early times after the return from Babylon, and accepting also the tradition of the Talmud as probable, that the authority of Daniel, though absent, was, together with that of Ezra, exercised amongst the members of the "Great Synagogue," in the settlement of the Canon of Scripture after the Return; yet we can perceive no sufficient reason for believing that either Daniel or Ezra, during their lives, had finally closed and determined the contents of the books which bear their names, in the fragmentary form in which they have come down to us, or that they were accepted by the Church from the time of Ezra, as of the same weight and authority as the books of the prophets who immediately preceded Daniel, viz. Jeremiah and Ezekiel. The arguments of Dr. Pusey upon this point appear to us to be far from convincing. The evidence, indeed, seems decidedly to tend the other way. The apocryphal additions, which had been attached to both of these books before the time of their translation into Greek, tend to establish that the limit of the contents of neither of them was then absolutely fixed, while from the book of Ecclesiasticus, we gather distinctly, that by some at least of the Jewish Church, neither Daniel nor Ezra was reckoned amongst those spoken of by the Son of Sirach, as " renowned for their power, giving counsel by their understanding, and declaring prophecies."* We see no reason, therefore, for believing that these books were generally received by the Jews of the first few centuries after the Exile, otherwise than as writings worthy of deep study and contemplation, and placed by them therefore amongst the Hagiographa. And we submit that it is only by the admission of the truth of this position, that the upholders of the authenticity of the book of Daniel can be extricated from the untenable position in which they are placed, as regards the questionable portion of one of the later chapters. The revelations of Daniel were probably looked upon by the Jews for many years after the reception of them at Jerusalem, much in the same light as the Revelations of St. John were looked upon in the early Christian Church, concerning the latter of which, Eusebius, in the fourth century, while enumerating the canonical books of the New Testament, after naming the first epistle of Peter as authentic, adds, " Then is to be placed, if you think good, the Revelation of St. John."†

The prophecies of Daniel, like those of St. John, must for several hundred years after their delivery, have been wholly unintelligible to those who read them ; and as professing to relate to the times of " the latter days " of the Jewish nation, may naturally have remained neglected and unheeded, till the time when to all appearance they were literally coming to pass. It is the exact fulfilment of the words of both these books of revelation, now so plainly perceived after the event, which alone has stamped them with the mark of divine inspiration, never to be effaced.

With regard to the argument drawn from the silence of writers living immediately after the Captivity, concerning Daniel and his writings, it appears to us to be extremely weak and worthless. What reasonable ground, we ask, can there

---

* Ecclus. xliv. 3. † Euseb. " Eccles. Hist." iii. 25.

be for expecting to find amongst the meagre fragments of history which constitute the books of Ezra and Nehemiah, any reference to Daniel, who was at Babylon, when so little is recorded concerning the acts of the leaders who had brought up the Captivity to Jerusalem? And if we are correct in our identification of the Darius of Daniel with the Darius of the books of Haggai and Zechariah, there can be no ground for the assumption that the two prophets writing at Jerusalem, in the second and fourth years of that king's reign, should "necessarily" make reference to the visions of Daniel, who was writing in a distant place in the first and third years of the same king. We accept, however, to the fullest extent, the force of the argument derived from the silence of Jesus, son of Sirach. There were clearly living in his days, as we have already said, those who did not accept the authority of the book of Daniel. And if we will consider for a moment, it could hardly have been otherwise. For how is it conceivable, that the sect of the Sadducees, which we know to have been in existence before the days of the son of Sirach, could have maintained its existence amongst the educated classes of the Jews, believing neither in angel, nor in spirit, nor in the doctrine of the resurrection from the grave, in the face of the book of Daniel—the very text-book of these Pharisaic opinions,—if the book had at that time been generally considered of binding and canonical authority? Dean Milman has eloquently written, " I have no doubt that in one of the noblest books among those called the Apocryphal, we have the work of a Sadducee, or rather, for it is a manifest fusion of several books, a full declaration of the views of the higher Sadducaic anti-traditional party. In the book of Ecclesiasticus there are magnificent descriptions of God's creative power, of His all-comprehending providence, of His chastisement of unrighteousness, of His rewards of godliness ; the most beautiful precepts of moral and social virtue, of worldly wisdom and sagacity, of chastity, temperance, justice, beneficence, but "—" as to angels, in the whole book there is no word recognising any intermediate beings between God and man.'* There is indeed one allusion

* Milman's " History of the Jews," vol. ii. 32.

to the doctrine of the immortality of the soul,* a doctrine then
also entertained by most heathen philosophers, but not one
word on the doctrine of the resurrection, such as it was
afterwards preached by Paul, exemplified by Jesus, scoffed
at by the Athenians, and as it is so plainly taught in
the last chapter of Daniel. Thus then there appears to
be quite sufficient reason for the omission of any allusion
to Daniel in the book of Ecclesiasticus, without being
driven to the conclusion that Daniel's writings were not
known and reverenced by many in the days of the writer of
that book. That they were deeply studied, and held up both
for example and precept, long before the days of the Son of
Sirach, we have the direct testimony of a book derived from
another influential sect, viz. from the Apocryphal book called
the First of Maccabees, the tendency of which is decidedly of a
Pharisaic character. For from thence we learn that Mattathias,
the father of Judas Maccabeus, on his death-bed held up for
example the lives of Ananias, Azarias, Misael, and Daniel;†
and, from the second book bearing that title, that the
doctrine of the resurrection from the dead, taught expli-
citly in the book of Daniel, and which, as we believe, was
a doctrine taught by him with authority in the college of
philosophers at Babylon, had at that time taken such strong
hold upon the minds of the Jewish people, as to have sustained
the courage of seven brethren, together with their mother, in
the presence of Antiochus, when they chose rather to suffer
the penalty of death, than to renounce their religion, trusting,
as they declared, that "the King of the world shall raise us
up, who have died for His laws, unto everlasting life."‡
Except for the words of Dan. xii. 2, the belief of these seven
young men can only be accounted for by inspiration. We agree
then with the objectors, that the book of Daniel was originally
placed where we now find it in the Hebrew scriptures,
amongst the Hagiographa; and moreover that by many it could

---

* Ecclus. xix. 19. Dean Milman appears inadvertently to have spoken of
the doctrine of immortality as not entertained by the Son of Sirach, intending
probably to have spoken of the resurrection of the body.

† 1 Macc. ii. 59, 60.   ‡ 2 Macc. vii. 9.

not have been accepted as of authority even as late as the time of Christ. But we see no sufficient reason to be derived from thence, for entertaining the idea of its having been composed so late as the time of the Maccabees. On the contrary, in our opinion the positive evidence of the books of Maccabees in favour of the reception of the book before the days of Antiochus, far outweighs any negative evidence to be derived from the omission to mention it in the book of Ecclesiasticus.

Such, then, is the mode in which we satisfy our own minds with regard to the first five of the above-enumerated objections. Taken all together, they appear to weigh as nothing against the simple affirmation of the book itself, that it was written from time to time by Daniel, during the reigns of Nebuchadnezzar, Belshazzar, and Darius, the Median king.

We now come to the consideration of the sixth and seventh objections, which are of an historical character. And here we approach the stronghold of the opponents of the authenticity of our book. It is the strong conviction in the minds of acute and well-trained critics that they are substantially right in their historical criticisms, which excludes the possibility of their entering with patience into argument with those who meet them dogmatically with the plenary inspiration of Holy Scripture. While, on the other hand, the inextinguishable feeling that the book cannot have been the mere work of man—that the unity of Scripture is imperfect without the book of Daniel—that to expunge it from the Bible is, as it were, to abstract the very heart from the scheme of Divine revelation to mankind—as strongly disinclines the supporters of the authenticity from listening to any argument which touches the veracity of any portion of the book.

Nevertheless we humbly submit that the truth and exceeding value of the book will become more firmly established by the surrender of some small portion of the present text, which, we shall endeavour to show, is not necessarily to be taken as proceeding from the hand of Daniel. We beg the particular attention of the reader while we offer some few prefatory remarks, pointing out what we conceive to be the

key, not only to the historical difficulties involved in the book
of Daniel, but the key also to many discrepancies of a similar
nature which pervade the history of the Jews from the time
of Solomon to the birth of Christ.

If we turn to the first verse of the tenth chapter of
Daniel, we read, " *In the third year of Cyrus, king of Persia, a
thing was revealed unto Daniel, whose name was called Belteshazzar : and the thing (was) true, but the time appointed (was)
long; and he understood the thing, and had understanding of the
vision.*" It will be observed, that by the reception or rejection of this one single verse, not only the chronology of the
book of Daniel, but the chronology of the whole Jewish
monarchy and upwards, may be very materially altered. For
if, as we are here told, the vision of the tenth and following
chapters was seen in the third year of the reign of Cyrus,
and in the course of the vision Darius the Mede is incidentally
mentioned as having already reigned, it is clear that Darius
the Mede must have reigned before the third of Cyrus. This,
then, is the inference which has been invariably drawn from
the passage.   On the other hand, if that one verse is omitted,
on the assumption that it was not written by Daniel, the
vision then opens with the words : " In those days I Daniel
was mourning three full weeks ;" and " those days " must, of
course, signify the days referred to in the previous chapter,
ix. 1,—that is to say, to the early days of Darius, son of
Ahasuerus ; and the question then remains open for consideration, whether this Darius reigned before or after Cyrus.
Now, except for the evidence of this one particular verse,
there could be no question as to the time when Darius
reigned.   For Daniel himself has informed us that it was at
the expiration of " seventy years," counted from the desolation of Jerusalem (ix. 2), that Darius began to reign at
Babylon ; and the prophet Zechariah informs us (i. 12) that
" seventy years of indignation" had been completed upon
Jerusalem in the second year of Darius, son of Hystaspes.
So that a presumption is thus created that the first verse of
chapter x. is merely the interpolated heading of some pious
interpreter, inserted possibly with the object of raising the

chronology of the reign of Darius at Babylon to the extent of not less than forty-six years—that is to say, of raising the first year of this king as "set over the realm of the Chaldeans," at the age of sixty-two, from B.C. 492, to B.C. 538.

Now, if we examine the passage, we find further reason for concluding that this verse was not written by the hand of Daniel. For, in the first place, it speaks of the prophet in the third person, and informs us of what we already knew, from Daniel himself, that his Chaldean name was Belteshazzar. It reads also at first sight as if it were merely an introductory heading to the vision, much in the same manner as we read the introductory heading to Psalm vii.: "Shiggaion of David, which he sang unto the Lord, concerning the words of Cush the Benjamite," which words we need not necessarily suppose to have been written by David himself. Again, the writer announces that "a thing was revealed unto Daniel," and then adds,—*Veĕmeth haddavar*, "And the thing is true." Now no one could be qualified to make this assertion till after the fulfilment, or the supposed fulfilment, of the vision had taken place; for Daniel expressly informs us that he "understood not"—and that "the words were *closed up and sealed* until the time of the end," xii. 8, 9. The translation of the verse is not correctly given in the English version, and we prefer to follow more nearly that of Rosenmüller,* who has no bias towards the view we are suggesting. The writer goes on to say,—*Vetsaba gadol*, "And it concerns great warfare, or a great army."† *Ubin eth haddavar*, "Therefore, consider the thing." *Ubinah lo bammareh*, "And have understanding *of it* in the vision." These latter words are not at first sight intelligible. What does the writer mean by understanding in the vision the thing revealed? We submit that he here informs us that he is about to offer an explanation in the form of vision of the

---

* "Anno Cyri, Persarum regis, tertio res patefacta est Danieli, qui Belteshazzar nominatus est, eaque vera, et magnorum bellorum. Igitur attende illam, attende, inquam illam per visionem patefactam."

† Καὶ δύναμις μεγάλη.—THEODOTION.

thing revealed, which he has just declared to be true. We
shall return to this. At present we are upon the chronology of the chapter. We have already shown sufficient reason
for suspecting interpolation.   And we think that we have
evidence in Scripture, both as to how, and why, this alteration in the chronology of the book of Daniel has been introduced by the sacred Scribe, and how it came to be received
without objection in his day.

It is a remarkable fact that two different versions of the
history of the Jews under Cyrus and Darius have come down
to us—one contained in the canonical book of Ezra, the other
in the apocryphal book of Esdras ; and, what is still more
remarkable is, that Josephus has adopted the arrangement of
the apocryphal book. The book of Ezra places the register of
those who came up to Jerusalem with Zerubbabel, Mordecai,
and others, in the reign of Cyrus ; the apocryphal book and
Josephus place it in the reign of Darius, son of Hystaspes.
The book of Ezra records an opposition on the part of the
Samaritans to the building of the temple in the reign of
Cyrus, while the apocryphal book and Josephus place the
same act of opposition in the reign of Darius. Here, then, we
meet with very early evidence of wavering and uncertainty
as to whether certain events after the Captivity happened
under one or other of these two reigns.   Whichever of the
two versions may be the true one, it is unquestionable that,
according to the canonical book of Ezra itself, both in the
third year of Cyrus, and again about *the third year of Darius*,
son of Hystaspes (Ezra, v. 3–17), direct hindrance was offered
by the Samaritans to the Jews while building the foundations
of the temple.   Now it is generally assumed by interpreters,
both ancient and modern, that the cause of Daniel's mourning for " three full weeks," when the prince of the kingdom
of Persia withstood him " one-and-twenty days," was connected with some contest carried on at the court of Persia,
concerning the restoration of the temple at Jerusalem, the
result of which was that Daniel " remained there with the
kings of Persia," instead of going up to rebuild the temple as
he wished. The suggestion, therefore, here proposed is, that

the writer of the introductory verse to chap. x., with a view to the application of Daniel's visions which he was about to make to his own times, has thought himself justified in assuming, though erroneously, that the mourning of Daniel took place " in the third year of Cyrus," instead of the third year of Darius, where, except for his interpretation, the words of Daniel place it. The result of this arrangement, as we have said, has been to create the fictitious king, " Darius the Mede," a king quite unknown in secular history, and one who we fearlessly declare never reigned, as distinguished from Darius son of Hystaspes; and thereby also to lengthen the period intervening between the time of the captivity and restoration, to the extent of forty-six years, being about the number of years required by any interpreter who would apply the contents of chap. ix. to the days of the Maccabees. That the mourning of Daniel really took place *" in those days,"* that is, towards the latter part of the reign of the son of Hystaspes, contrary to the view of the sacred Scribe, is confirmed both by the incidental mention by Daniel of the intervention of a *"prince of the kingdom of Persia,"* chap. x. 13, and also by the declaration that he "remained there with the *kings of Persia*," which so well accords with that period of the reign of Darius spoken of by Ezra, chap. v. 6, 7, vi. 14, when Ahasuerus or Artashashtha, the prince associated with Darius, had interposed to obstruct the building of the temple, and who may well be supposed to be the prince that withstood the prophet one-and-twenty days.

If, as we are satisfied, Daniel mourned and prophesied " in those days" which fell soon after Darius was set over the realm of the Chaldeans, and when, accordingly, he was first styled by Ezra king of Assyria (Ezra, vi. 22), and when also Ahasuerus, or Artashashtha, or Xerxes, had recently been placed by him on the throne of Persia—an event, as we shall see, which, according to an Egyptian monument now extant, took place about 12 or 13 years before the death of Darius—then would the words of the prophet,[*] " there shall stand up yet three kings in Persia, and the fourth, that

---

[*] Dan. xi. 2.

is Artaxerxes Mnemon,* shall be richer than they all," have been literally fulfilled befere the coming of the "mighty king" of Grecia. While, on the other hand, if "those days" are placed in the third year of Cyrus, there would have reigned not three only, but at least six great kings in Persia between Cyrus and the last king conquered by Alexander the Great. Assuming then, that Daniel prophesied correctly, it is difficult to conceive how the first verse of chap. x. could have been written by his hand.

These and many other considerations have led the author to the conclusion, that the compiler of the book of Daniel, writing under the conviction that the taking away of the daily sacrifice, spoken of by Daniel, chap. ix. 27, was literally being accomplished before his own eyes in the days of Antiochus, and being thereby constrained to show how "threescore and two weeks" of years, or 434 years, had then in some way been fulfilled, has, by the insertion of this one verse, framed for himself, and for those who come after him, a fictitious mode of Biblical reckoning, by which exactly 434 years are interposed between the falsely assumed first year of Nebuchadnezzar, B.C. 604, and the year B.C. 170, or, as others put it, between B.C. 598 and B.C. 164, the remarkable precision of which interval forms so leading a feature in the arguments of those who would throw doubt upon the authenticity of the book of Daniel.† We see no reason for closing our eyes, as some do, to the remarkable fact thus pointed out. On the contrary, we admire the critical sagacity which has detected the artificial arrangement, and at the same time thank the discoverers for one point at least, which seems to lead to the disentanglement of the historical difficulties in our book.

Again, we have remarked that the compiler has in his introductory heading to chap. x. declared that the thing revealed to Daniel was "true;" and that it concerned

* The vast sum of 50,000 talents is said to have been found by Alexander the Great, laid up by successive kings, at Susa alone." If Babylonian talents, equal to £19,000,000 sterling.—GROTE, vol. iii. p. 201.

† Dr. Williams' Introduction, p. xlii.

" great warfare," or armies; the main feature we know of
the supposed times in which he lived. And he calls upon
his hearers to " consider the matter ;" and to " have understanding *of it* in the vision." We prefer the punctuation which reads *Bemareh* (בְּמַרְאֶה), rather than *Bammareh*
(בַּמַּרְאֶה),—" Have understanding of it in vision," or in a
vision : that is, either by attending to the interpreter's explanation of events given in the form of vision, or by applying the events passing before their own eyes in interpretation
of Daniel's words. We shall hereafter show in detail how
the interpreter has endeavoured to adapt his historical commentary to the text. We will now merely select one
single passage to illustrate the idea — that part of chap. x.
together with the first verse of chap. xi. are merely words
of comment. Let us endeavour to throw ourselves into the
position of one taking up the book of Daniel in the days of
the Maccabees. The writings of the prophet, we have
assumed, had at that time been laid aside and neglected as
incomprehensible for many years ; when suddenly the persecutions of Antiochus, the burning of the holy books, and
the massacre of the people by that king with a view to the
extirpation of the Jewish race, began to force upon the Jews
the conviction that they were living in the very " time of
trouble" spoken of in the last chapter of the book, " the
time of the end," " καιρὸς καταστροφῆς."* To have taught
openly amongst the people this application of Daniel's words
to the events then passing around them, would have led to
the immediate searching for and destruction of the holy
book; to have written of the kings of Syria and Egypt by
name, and to have represented their dynasties as about to
come to an untimely end, would have been looked upon as
treason, and would probably have led to the speedy execution of the writer. The Sadducean party who, as we have
seen, did not accept the writings of Daniel, probably cavilled
at the words of the prophecy itself, when brought to their
attention by the sacred Scribes. It may have been objected

---

* Dan. xii. 9. 1 Mac. ii. 49.

by adverse critics in those days, as it has been objected by some in these days, concerning the vision of chap. x. If the prophet was lying prostrate, as he describes himself, " on his face towards the ground, and in a *deep sleep*," v. 9, how could he have lifted up his eyes and have beheld the vision on the banks of the Hiddekel, and at the same time have witnessed the quaking of his companions, and their fleeing away to hide themselves? We venture to surmise, that in those days certain explanatory portions of chaps. vii. and viii., in answer to Daniel's supplication to know the " truth," may possibly have been referred to commonly as the " Scripture of truth." And we do not think that we are too bold in the suggestion, that " Michael (Who is like God?), one of the chief *sarim*," or princes, may be identified with Mishael who was carried away captive with Daniel, as " of the king's seed, and of the princes," and who, after passing unharmed through the fire, where was seen one " like the Son of God," was afterwards " promoted in the province of Babylon," probably with the secondary title *sar*, a title which was also borne by " the prince of the eunuchs."*

With the danger, then, of publicly offending before his eyes, it seems not unnatural that the interpreter of Daniel should have preferred to adopt the concealed form of vision, while expounding to his countrymen his application of then current events to the words of the prophet, thereby avoiding the necessity of speaking of any king by name; and in the following passage we submit that he appears to commence his explanation by addressing himself to the trifling obscurities in the text. After transcribing Daniel's description of the great vision on the Hiddekel, he goes on in the words of the prophet, chap. x. 7, " And I, Daniel, alone, saw the vision: for the men that were with me saw not the vision; but a great quaking fell upon them, so that they fled to hide themselves. v. 8. Therefore I was left alone, and saw this great vision, and there remained no strength in me: for my comeliness was turned in me into corruption, and I re-

* Dan. i. 10.

tained no strength—*velo atsarti koach.* v. 9. Yet I heard
the voice of his words: and when I heard the voice of his
words, then was I in a deep sleep on my face, with my face
toward the ground. [v. 15. *And when he had spoken such
words unto me, I set my face toward the ground, and I became
dumb.* v. 16. *And behold, one like the similitude of the sons of
men touched my lips : then I opened my mouth and spake, and
said unto him that stood before me, O my Lord, by the vision my
sorrows are turned upon me, and I have retained no strength,—*
velo atsarti koach. v. 17. *For how can the servant of this
my lord talk with this my lord ? for as for me, straightway there
remained no strength in me,* (i. e.) *and there is no breath left
in me.*] v. 10. And behold an *hand* touched me, and set me
upon my knees and upon the palms of my hands : and *he*
said unto me, O Daniel, a man greatly beloved, understand
the words that I speak unto thee, and stand upright: for
unto thee am I now sent. And when *he* had spoken this
word, I stood trembling. Then said *he* unto me, Fear not,
Daniel. [v. 18. *Then there came again and touched me one
like the appearance of a man, and he strengthened me :* v. 19, *and
said, O man greatly beloved, fear not : peace be unto thee : be
strong, yea be strong. And when he had spoken unto me I was
strengthened, and said, Let my lord speak, for thou hast
strengthened me.*] v. 12. For, from the first day that thou
didst set thy heart to understand, and to chasten thyself
before thy God, thy words were heard. [Ch. xi. 1. *Also I,
in the first year of Darius the Mede, even I, stood to confirm
and to strengthen him.*] And I am come for thy words.
v. 13. But the prince of the kingdom of Persia withstood
me one-and-twenty days; but, lo, Michael, one of the chief
princes, came to help me : and I remained there with the
kings of Persia. [v. 20. *Then said he, Knowest thou wherefore I am come unto thee ? And now will I return to fight with
the prince of Persia : and when I am gone forth, lo, the prince
of Grecia shall come . . .* v. 21. *and there is none that
holdeth with me but Michael your prince.*] v. 14. Now I am
come to make thee understand what shall befall thy people
in the latter days . . . Ch. xi. 2. And now will I show

thee the truth. [v. 21. *But I will show thee that which is noted in the scripture of truth.*]

The passage, beginning with v. 15, thus dissected and applied to the text,—the disjointed character of which as it stands in the Bible every reader must have observed,—is in the original one consecutive passage, and has all the appearance of a free paraphrase of the twelve preceding verses of Daniel. It was probably written originally in a marginal column, the disjointed pieces of comment being arranged parallel with the respective portions of text. But the comment being, as we believe, afterwards mistaken for part of the text, the disjointed fragments would appear thus to have become improperly united together. The sacred Scribe seems to borrow his angelic imagery from the words of ch. viii. 15. He softens down the strong expression of " corruption," into " sorrows,"—" deep sleep," into " dumb"ness,—and want of " strength," into want of " breath." The highly poetic expression in the text, "And an *hand* touched me,— and *he* said,"—" O Daniel, a man greatly beloved," he paraphrases by "there touched me one like the appearance of a man," "and he said, O man greatly beloved." He refers the first day of Daniel's chastening himself to the time of his " supplications, with fasting, and sackcloth, and ashes," in the first year of Darius the Mede, ix. 1–3; and as at that time the angel " stood to confirm and strengthen him," that is, Daniel, so he explains, that *now* the angel will "return to fight with the prince of Persia," who had withstood him one-and-twenty days. And then closes with the declaration that he will explain "that which is noted in the scripture of truth," that is to say, what is written in chap. viii., concerning a "king of fierce countenance," who shall in the latter days "take away the daily sacrifice," as he himself had lately witnessed, and who yet should come to an end; and more especially that which is written in chap. vii. concerning the king who shall rise up amongst *ten kings,* who shall make war with the saints, or holy people, and overcome them; a prediction which he considered then to have literally come to pass in the person of Antiochus.

We submit for the consideration of those who are satisfied from history that the " *ten horns*," and the " little horn," of chap. vii. represent kingdoms rising up in the latter days of the *fourth* or Roman empire, whether it is possible to reconcile this unquestionably just interpretation with the fact, that Antiochus Epiphanes is by the writer of chap. xi. represented as a king rising up from amongst neither more nor less than *ten kings*, successors of the *third* or Grecian empire. It is clear that the writer has thus identified Antiochus with, or assimilated him to, the little horn of chap. vii. But, since the Holy Spirit cannot be at variance with itself, the traces of another hand than that of Daniel would seem here to be distinct.

Again, the hand of a commentator of Maccabean days would seem to be betrayed in ch. xi. 14, in the words—" The robbers of thy people shall exalt themselves to establish the vision, and they shall fall." Who are these robbers of the people ? and what is the vision referred to ? St. Jerome and commentators in general apply the words as referring to Onias the high-priest, who, in the reign of Philometor, fled with a body of zealous Jews to Egypt, and endeavoured to set up a temple and altar, in imitation of those at Jerusalem, in the city of Heliopolis, and so " to establish the vision " of Isaiah, xix. 19, or perhaps of Dan. viii. 13 ; but failed in the attempt at that time, though the temple was built by his son Onias at a later date. But Onias and his followers cannot properly be spoken of as robbers. The original words are עַמֶּךָ פָּרִיצֵי בְּנֵי, *beni paritsey ammecca*, sons of the paritsees, or pharitsees, of thy people. Dr. Rule suggests the translation, " sons of the separatists of thy people." Now the Pharisees were separatists. And it might not be improper, perhaps, to translate the words, " sect of the separatists amongst thy people." If this is admissible, the allusion to the Pharisees, under this term of opprobium, would seem to betray the feeling of party spirit which, we know ran high between Pharisees and Sadducees in the days of the Maccabees, also the hand of a writer of that day.

We accept, then, the historical objections raised by critics

against the latter part of the book of Daniel, in as far as
they regard parts of the tenth and the eleventh chapters,
which appear to us to have been written in the days of the
Maccabees.   We also go along with Dr. Williams, where he
observes, that " So little has the book (as now received) the
framework of chronicle, that it presents four kings in succession, Nebuchadnezzar, Belshazzar, Darius, and Cyrus,
whom no discoverable history arranges in that order."   But,
especially, we are ready to express ourselves indebted to the
critics for the boldness with which they have laid bare the
historical character of the passages above referred to, which
have too long been accepted as Holy Scripture; because they
have thereby led to the discovery of the most important link
in the evidence which proves that our book could not have
been written at so late a date as they assume.

When Dr. Williams asks " on behalf of a book, for which
prediction is claimed, that some evidence, or a probability,
however slight, of its existence anterior to the event, should
be shown," we are now enabled to reply :—

1st. That the two books of Maccabees incontestably prove
that certain portions both of the Chaldee and of the Hebrew
parts of Daniel were written and studied before the days of
Antiochus, or the year B.C. 170.

2nd. That the sober, matter-of-fact Josephus, records his
belief that the eighth chapter of Daniel had been shown to
Alexander 160 years before the date of Antiochus.

3rd. That the hand of a commentator attached to the
book itself, about the time of Antiochus, and applying the prophecies of chapters vii. viii. ix. and xii. to events happening
in his own days, clearly establishes the previous existence of,
and reverence shown towards those prophecies at that time :
while the commentator himself attests that the latest vision
in the book was *not* written in his own days, but recorded by
one who was surnamed Belteshazzar, who had lived in the
days of Nebuchadnezzar, king of Babylon, not less than 230
years before the time of Alexander.

Now what is the result of this proposed curtailment of
the chronology of the book of Daniel, and removal from the

text of certain incongruous passages apparently inserted by some sacred scribe? It is, that these sublime, far-reaching revelations, which profess to unfold the gracious purposes of the Almighty as regards the destinies of His holy people, even to the time of the end—but which, when so incumbered, are involved in so much intricacy and obscurity as to defy consistent interpretation, even from the most able hands— have thus become some of the most plain and intelligible of the prophecies of Holy Scripture, and of a distinctness clear as the cloudless heaven whence they came.

The sacred enigma of the Seventy Weeks, the interpretation of which has so long baffled the ability of both believer and sceptic, of both Jew and Christian, remains no longer an enigma to be solved; for the prophetic words of chap. ix. read off as well-known history of the past. And so far from acknowledging the "necessity" claimed by Dr. Williams, "that we should resign cheerfully, like mariners throwing infected goods overboard with their own hands, all those directly Messianic interpretations in which, without the intervention of any earlier person, or without broader suggestions of spiritual principle, Jesus of Nazareth is held to be distinctly, personally, foreseen as Christ," we are enabled to affirm with a distinctness beyond the power of human wit to gainsay, that this same Jesus of Nazareth, the history of whose inimitable career on earth is marvellous beyond the range of fiction to conceive, and the knowledge of whom and of whose divine precepts already tends "to cover the earth as the waters cover the sea," is indeed, and He only, without the intervention of any earlier person, "Messiah the Prince," so clearly foreseen and foretold by Daniel.

Again, the assumed relation of "typo" to "antitype" in chapters xi. and viii. of Antiochus to anti-Christ, a fiction which has afforded the text for many fantastic interpretations of this portion of the book, and by means of which two distinct and separate visions, viz. those of the viith and viiith chapters, are constantly confounded and mixed up together, entirely disappears from the predictions of Daniel, and we find ourselves unmistakably living in those "latter

f

days," when the civilised world is, as it were, occupied by two wide-spread, overwhelming religious powers, of both which it has become well-nigh weary, and whose appointed times are well-nigh spent; both which have prospered for more than twelve centuries of time, and which are portrayed to the life in the visions of this prophet; the one as mighty with the words of his mouth, the other as mighty with the sword of his hand; the one proceeding out of the ten fragments of the fourth, or Roman empire, the other proceeding out of one of the four divisions of the third, or Grecian empire; the one with busy, worldly eyes, seeking to supervise and dictate to the kingdoms of the West, and persecuting "the holy people" till the time of the end; the other, with inexorable fierceness, ruling over the East, which has destroyed "the mighty and the holy people," forsaken the God of his fathers,—the God of the Jews, "keeping the covenant and mercy with them that love him,"—the God of the Christians, known only as "Our Father,"—and has honoured "the God of forces," that is, of irresistible power and might, "in the most strongholds," ruling over many, and dividing the land.

It is through the book of Daniel that we are especially brought to a sense of the nearness of the all-directing hand of the Almighty, "in whom we live, and move, and have our being," moulding like the potter the clay of his creation, and measuring out the times and seasons, not only as affecting His chosen people Israel, but also as regards the kingdoms of the Gentiles, by whom for a time they have been set aside. For while, according to the altered reckoning, we discover, to our amaze, that the destinies of Israel have been laid out in exact and even cycles of time, even from the call of Moses to the time of Christ, so also do we discern how the powers of the heathen world are no less powers ordained of God, and how the vision of the great metallic image, which represents the rise and fall of the four successive empires of the Gentile world, beginning with the date of the vision, B.C. 560, and ending, as we assume, with the close of 1335 years of Mahomedan oppression, comprehends exactly the great predicted period of subjection of the holy people to the Gentiles ; that is, the period of " seven times " spoken of by Moses in Leviticus, ch. xxvi.,—the period of Gentile domination, spoken of by a greater than Moses, Luke, xxi. 24,—the *annus magnus* of 2520 years, at the expiration of which, Jerusalem, we are told, shall cease to be trodden under foot. We learn how, after the fall of the great persecuting Eastern Antichristian power now dominant over the holy city, the holy people, and the holy land, there shall be a time of tribulation such as never was ; and are enabled to comprehend the words of our Lord, how, immediately after that tribulation, " they shall see the Son of Man coming in the clouds of heaven." And lastly, we catch from Daniel the key-note of the days in which we live, when the world from East to West seems hasting towards its final period of regeneration, and learn with certainty, that not until " he shall have accomplished to scatter the power of the holy people" can " all these things be finished." " Oh pray, then, for the peace of Jerusalem ; they shall prosper that love thee."

" I have set watchmen upon the walls of Jerusalem, which shall never hold their peace day nor night. Ye that make mention of the Lord keep not silence, and give him no rest, till he establish, and make Jerusalem a praise upon earth."

DR. PUSEY'S EXPOSITION

OF

DANIEL'S PROPHECY OF THE SEVENTY WEEKS.

ANYTHING proceeding from the pen of so able, earnest, and conscientious a writer as Dr. Pusey, cannot fail at all times to command the most respectful attention : and we feel assured that the "Nine Lectures on Daniel the Prophet," delivered in the Divinity School of the University of Oxford —planned, as he professes, expressly for the purpose of counteracting the tide of scepticism let loose by the publication of "Essays and Reviews,"—will have been sought for and studied by many an earnest inquirer into the truth of Scripture prophecy.

Dr. Pusey has undertaken a task worthy of his position and reputation in the Church, viz. that of rescuing the book of Daniel from the grasp of modern critics, who, with much triumph and defiance, have consigned it to the domain of fiction or forgery: pronouncing it to be a work written in the time of the Maccabees, and innocently intended by the writer to encourage the Jews in their great struggle against Antiochus Epiphanes. In vain have the works of Jahn, Hengstenberg, Auberlen, Barnes in America, and a host of

B

English writers, taken up the defence of this most remarkable book of Scripture. The wonderful predictions contained in it, professing to unfold the destinies of Daniel's people, from the time of their captivity at Babylon, when he wrote, even to the far distant times of their dispersion amongst the nations, and future restoration into favour with God —predictions which, as a matter of history, have sustained the constancy and energies of that people, not only through their deadly struggle with the powers of heathenism in the days of Antiochus, but also through that still more trying period of desolation and oppression with which they have been afflicted, even to the present day—these sublime and majestic visions, we say, are deliberately classed in the minds of modern expositors together with the vague poetical prophecies of Virgil or the Sibylline books, and condemned by some of the most acute and learned critics of the age as premeditated works of fiction. "The ungenuineness of Daniel," writes Auberlen, "has become an axiom in modern theology, so that it is thought quite superfluous to adduce any proof of that assertion ; and the most recent commentator says, in a very short and explicit manner, no sensible man can entertain a doubt on the subject."[*]

Dr. Williams, the Essayist, speaking of the prophecy of the Seventy Weeks, asserts that "two results are clear beyond fair doubt, that the period of 'weeks' ended in the reign of Antiochus Epi-

* Preface to Auberlen on the Prophecies of Daniel, &c.

phanes, and that those portions of the book supposed to be specially predictive are a history of
past occurrences up to that reign."* "The original place of the book amongst the later Hagiographa of the Jewish Canon, and the absence of
any mention of it by the Son of Sirach, strikingly
confirm this view of its origin: and if some obscurity rests upon details, the general conclusion,
that the book contains no predictions, except by
analogy and type, can hardly be gainsaid."†

If this indeed be so, how painful and degraded
is the position of those whose faith in Christianity
is grounded upon the exact fulfilment of Daniel's
prediction of Christ: who have been accustomed to
value this book as the chief connecting link between the histories of the Old and New Testament;
and to look upon it as occupying a distinct and defined position, otherwise left blank and dreary, in
the continuous scheme of Providence laid open in
Scripture, from the day of the selection of the sons
of Abraham as God's "holy people," even to the
yet future time "when he shall have accomplished
to scatter the power of the holy people, and all
these things shall be finished." If the records contained in the book of Daniel are records of real
events, and the predictions were written at the
time when Daniel professes to have lived, then does
it follow of necessity, that inspiration, prophecy,
and miracle,—the three impossibilities of modern
philosophy, in connection with the past history of

* "Essays and Reviews," p. 69.　　† P. 76.

the world, inasmuch as they are assumed to be subversive of the fixed and undeviating laws of the
Creator, have been signally exemplified in the events
recorded in this book. If, on the contrary, this
single book of Scripture can be shown to be fiction,
the foundation of Christianity is undermined : the
undying expectations of Judaism, based upon the
words of successive prophets, fade into empty air as
childish dreams : we doubt whether the whole volume
of sacred history may not be the work of designing
priests ; and the only wise course to be pursued
would seem to be, to place ourselves at the feet of
those profound philosophers who have laid bare the
great deception, and who profess to teach the will
and ways of the Creator from the surrounding works
of His creation. " The writer of this book," observes Dr. Pusey, " were he not Daniel, must have
lied on a most frightful scale, ascribing to God prophecies which were never uttered, and miracles which
are assumed never to have been wrought. In a word,
the whole book would be one lie in the name of
God." *

Can any intelligent and sensitive mind consent
to remain in doubt on such a question ? Tell me,
cries the despairing, yet unlearned inquirer, conscious of his inability to examine for himself, is it
true that some of the ablest and best instructed
men of modern days have believed, and undertake
to prove, that this book of Daniel was written,
not, as it professes to have been, in the time of

* "Introductory Lecture," p. 1.

the captivity of the Jews at Babylon, but some
three hundred years later, in the time of the Maccabees? Dr. Williams and his associates have much
to answer for, when they put forth the hasty, yet
authoritative reply, that certain forms of language
made use of in the book of Daniel "remove all
philological and critical doubt as to the age of the
book," as having been written long after the times
of the captivity.*

Dr. Pusey, as Regius Professor of Hebrew in
the University of Oxford, undertakes to show that
this assertion is utterly false, and without foundation; and it requires no great depth of knowledge
of Hebrew and Chaldee to follow him through his
analysis, and to feel assured that he has established
satisfactorily this one decisive fact, that the language
of Daniel is the same, or nearly the same, as the language of the book of Ezra, and that, so far as any
test can be applied, it is not the language of the
times of the Maccabees. He boldly affirms, that
"no opponent has ever ventured to look steadily
at the facts, of the correspondence of the language
of Daniel and Ezra, and their difference from the
language of the earliest Targums."† And again,
"the question which any opponent has to solve

---

* "Not only Macedonian words such as *symphonia* and
psanterion, but the texture of the Chaldaic, with such late forms
as לְכוֹן, דְּ, and אֲלֵן the pronominal ם, and ה, having passed
into ן, and not only minute descriptions of Antiochus's reign, but
the stoppage of such description at the precise date, B.C. 169,
remove all philological and critical doubt as to the age of the
book."—*Essays and Reviews*, p. 76.   † P. 56.

is this, whence this marked agreement between the Aramaic of Daniel and Ezra, and this marked difference of the Aramaic of both from that of the Targums of Onkelos and Jonathan? Men are dishonest to themselves and to others when they try to escape from this broad question under cover of the dust of other counter-questions."* Dr. Pusey has spared no pains to satisfy himself that the language of Daniel coincides with his age and circumstances. "I have examined," he says, "expressly for this object, every notable word and idiom used in the Hebrew of Daniel, and have set down under four heads,—

" 1. What is peculiar to Daniel.

" 2. What he has in common with the middle period of language, *i.e.* words or idioms not occurring in the Pentateuch, but received in books free from the influence of Aramaic.

" 3. What Daniel has in common with the later writers, *i.e.* words or idioms, which in our remaining Hebrew, do not occur before the times bordering on the captivity, such as Jeremiah.

" 4 What like other writers of the same date he has revived out of the Hebrew of the Pentateuch."

" There is," he says, " for the most part little characteristic in any of this language,"—" what *is* characteristic falls in with the time of Daniel."†

He then proceeds to analyze the Aramaic portions of Daniel, especially the pronominal forms *hon* and *con*, *den* and *illeen*, which are said so dis-

* P. 42.   † P. 36.

tinctly to mark the late date of the language; and sums up his observations thus: "These endings, which are to be so characteristic as to establish the later date of the Aramaic of Daniel, are endings belonging to all Aramaic. The other forms are exceptional archaisms apparently in the language both of Daniel and Ezra." . . . "Criticism, which should have made endings which are an integral part of the language, which occur not in one dialect of it only but in three, not in one case but in several, characteristic of a later date of a book in which they occur, could not have been imagined in any well-known language. It would have carried on its face its own refutation. In fine, then, the Hebrew of Daniel is exactly that which you would expect in a writer of his age, and under his circumstances. It has not one single idiom unsuited to that time. The few Aryan or Syriac words remarkably belong to it. The Chaldee marks itself out as such as could not have been written at the time when, if it had not been a Divine or prophetic book, it must have been written."*

The Rev. J. M'Gill, to whom Dr. Pusey refers, sums up a condensed essay on the Chaldee of Daniel and Ezra with these words: "Thus we have seen that the biblical Chaldce is distinguished by many peculiarities which mark an early stage of the development of the language. Some of the peculiarities are also found in Syriac: others have altogether disappeared from the Aramean, or are

* P. 55.

found in the later language only as exceptional
cases which rarely occur.   And we have certainly
seen that Daniel does not approach nearer than Ezra
to the language of the Targums.   On the contrary,
there are one or two phenomena which show that
the book of Daniel was written a considerable time
before that of Ezra."*

Again, Dr. Pusey has dispersed the mists in
which some have endeavoured to envelope the book
of Daniel from the occurrence here and there of
Aryan and assumed Macedonian expressions.   He
has shown that the supposed Macedonian Greek is
not Macedonian ; and has truly remarked, that
nothing can be more agreeable to the circumstances and position of Daniel than the occasional
use of words of Aryan extraction, and of two or
three Greek words for musical instruments, living
as he did at Babylon, in the midst of the great
stream of commerce to and fro, from East to West,
where foreign productions of every description must
have been daily exposed in the markets, and where
foreign names for these productions must have been
on the lips of hundreds of persons passing backwards and forwards through that great commercial
city.   As regards the suggested proof of the late-
ness of the composition of the book, from the omission of all reference to Daniel by Jesus, son of
Sirach, any such inference is entirely neutralized by
the fact, that the author of the book of Ezra stands
precisely in the same position as Daniel in this re-

* Journ. Sac. Lit., Jan. 1861, p. 373.

spect; for the name of Ezra is also omitted from the list of Jewish worthies in the book of Ecclesiasticus, yet no one doubts that the book of Ezra was written before the days of the Son of Sirach. We have already observed that the author of Ecclesiasticus, being a Sadducee, could hardly have been expected to make reference to such a book as Daniel.*

Dr. Pusey has grappled fearlessly and success-fully with the philological arguments of his oppo-nents; and, as far as regards the Chaldee portions, or one-half at least of the book, we think that no future student of Daniel, after perusing Dr. Pusey's work, will be disposed to allow that the composition could have been so late as the time of the Macca-bees, or anywhere but near the times of the captivity. On the contrary, when he considers the fact of the combination of the two languages — Hebrew and Chaldee — in the books of Daniel and Ezra, and in these two books of Scripture only, with the excep-tion of a single verse of Chaldee in Jeremiah, a fact which distinguishes these writings from all other books of the Canon, he will be disposed to look upon the book of Daniel as stamped with the pe-culiar mark which could only appropriately belong to a composition written at a time, when Hebrews, accustomed to the use of their native tongue, were dwelling captive in the land of the Chaldees.†

* Introduction, p. xiii.

† Auberlen, we think, has rightly explained the cause of the difference of Daniel's language in different parts of his book. The Chaldee portions relate chiefly to the history of the kingdoms of the heathen world, and may probably have been intended for the ears

Dr. Pusey, in conscious triumph, closes this portion of his work with the words, "Rationalism may rebel, as it has rebelled, but it dare not now, with any moderate show of honesty, abuse philology to cover its rebellion." *

Assuming, then, that the question of the language of Daniel, as a substantive proof of unauthenticity, has been set at rest, and that his prophecies, therefore, unless forged by some ingenious impostor, were written somewhere near the time when Ezra wrote his book, we will now proceed to examine some of the other arguments which have been raised to prove that the book was a forgery of the time of the Maccabees.

It is not our purpose, even were we qualified, to follow Dr. Pusey through the whole course of his able arguments in refutation of his opponents, and in support of the genuineness of the book of Daniel. We are content to rest the issue of the genuineness and inspiration of that book on two main features of internal evidence—on the fulfilment or non-fulfilment of the two most remarkable predictions contained in it, viz., of the symbolical prophecy of the great image in the second chapter, with its supplementary expansions in the seventh and twelfth chapters; and of the well-known prophecy of the " Seventy Weeks."

---

of Chaldeans as well as Jews. The Hebrew portions chiefly relate to events immediately affecting the Jews, and are specially written in the sacred language for them.— *Auberlen on Daniel*, p. 31.

   * P. 57.

If it can be shown that these two plain historical predictions—the one comprehending a series of events extending over not less than twenty-four centuries of time, the other over a long period of four hundred and ninety years—have been literally and exactly fulfilled, in a manner not to be mistaken, then will the inspiration of the writer of these predictions, and the genuineness of the writings, so tested, have been made manifest beyond contradiction. And if, again, the great outline of the world's history, to the end of time, as prophetically laid down in this book of Daniel, shall be shown to have been accomplished hitherto in minute accordance with his predictions, then will the objections of those who cavil at the minuteness of fulfilment of other less extended prophecies, be looked upon by impartial inquirers as both idle and out of place.

A deeper and more reverential study of the book of Daniel will, we humbly submit, lead the mind into wide and interesting fields of contemplation, both as regards the past and future intercourse of God with His chosen people, not open at once to view on the first superficial reading of the book. This is a proposition which we hope to be able to establish in the course of the following observations. Meanwhile, we confess that the study of this book of Scripture, beyond all others, has ever afforded to our understanding the most convincing and sustaining evidence, under all temptations to doubt, that the hand of God is ever near and about His creatures, and that the events of this world are continuously and immediately under the guidance of His directing power.

There stands the great image still before our eyes, as it stood some 2400 years ago ; in the same vivid outline and exceeding brightness, as it appeared to the mental vision of King Nebuchadnezzar in his dream ; with its head of gold; its breast and arms of silver; its belly and thighs of brass; its legs of iron; and its feet, part of iron, and part of miry clay. And there also stands affixed to this symbolic figure a superscription, written at the time, showing that its distinct, five-fold division was intended to represent, first, four great empires then about to rise in succession on the theatre of the world; and then, the division into ten fragmentary kingdoms of the last and most powerful of these empires; the head of the image, as declared by the superscription, touching the times of the Babylonian empire, and its feet reaching down to " the days when the God of Heaven shall set up a kingdom never to be destroyed." No honest interpreter of this superscription can deny the distinctness of the interpretation, nor that it was the intention of the writer of it to carry the mind of the reader over periods reaching far into futurity, even to the end of this world. Did ever impostor, foretelling the future, we may ask, venture to subject his predictions to so lengthened an ordeal of actual events, or ever so clearly define the meaning of his own predictions?

But, again, the times of the ten fragmentary kingdoms proceeding out of the last empire are, in the seventh chapter, more minutely unfolded, and described as extending over a definite yet lengthened period of time, marked by the domination

of a most peculiar and anomalous power, which,
it is said, shall prevail till "*the saints of the
Most High* shall take the kingdom, and possess
it for ever and ever." For out of these ten
kingdoms, we are told, shall come up a power,
"diverse from the first," an arrogant and domineering power, symbolically described as "a horn that
had eyes, and a mouth that spake very great
things," into whose hands the *saints of the Most
High* shall be given, "until a time, times, and the
dividing of time," that is, as we consider it should
be interpreted, for a definite period of 1260 years.*
And after the destruction of this remarkable
power, it is again declared that "the greatness of
the kingdom under the whole heaven shall be given
to *the people of the saints* (עַם קַדִּישֵׁי) *of the Most
High*." Lastly, lest any doubt should exist as to
the meaning of the expression "Saints of the Most
High," mention is made again, in the twelfth chapter,
of the very same period, of "time, times, and a half,"
followed immediately by the words, "And when He
shall have accomplished to scatter the power of the
holy people (עַם קֹדֶשׁ), all these things shall be finished."† We have, then, but to satisfy ourselves as
to who are the "holy people," or "saints of the
Most High," here spoken of, and the whole vision,
as interpreted in the superscription from the days of
the Babylonian king to the present time, will be
vividly represented before our eyes.

Now there can be no question as to the people

---

* Dan. vii. 25.   † xii. 7.

who are described throughout Scripture as the "holy people" of God. Of whom, except of the sons of Abraham, has it been said, " Thou art a holy people (עַם קָדוֹשׁ) unto the Lord God, the Lord thy God hath chosen thee to be a special people unto Himself, above all people that are on the face of the earth?" Of whom had it been foretold, except of the sons of Abraham, " the Lord shall scatter you among the nations, and ye shall be left few among the heathen ?" Of what other people in the world has it been said, " If any of them be driven out unto the utmost parts of heaven, from thence will the Lord thy God gather thee, and from thence will He fetch thee?" And, again, what other people in the world, existing as a nation when these words were uttered, now lies scattered, though yet distinct, throughout every kingdom of the earth, except the sons of Abraham ? Of the sons of Abraham, therefore, in their exile and dispersion, does the prophecy of Daniel speak, when he foretells the oppression of the " saints " for a period of 1260 years, trodden down by that peculiar and tyrannous power which proceeds out of the embers of the Roman empire, and which is elsewhere unmistakably described as seated on the seven hills, and drunk with " the blood of the saints, and" also " with the blood of the martyrs of Jesus."

In this opinion we have the support of Auberlen, who writes, " By the people of 'the saints of the Most High,' to whom dominion is given, Daniel evidently could only understand the people of Israel, as distinguished from the heathen nations and king-

doms, which were to rule till then.   In this point
Roos, Prieswerk, Hofman, agree with Hitzig, Ber-
tholdt, and others.   The prophet's words refer to
the re-establishment of the kingdom of Israel, concerning which the disciples asked our Saviour
immediately before His ascension."*

We are aware that many would interpret the
giving up of the kingdom and dominion to " the saints
of the Most High," as representing the future triumphant reign of the Gentile Church of Christ, that is to
say, of that ecclesiastical hierarchy and its branches
which now stands prominent among the religions of
the world as the representative of Christendom,
seated on, and clinging to, its throne on the seven
hills of the Eternal City.   And, unquestionably, the followers of Christ are throughout the New Testament
looked upon and designated as " saints," that is, true
worshippers of Christ, as distinguished then from the
world of unbelievers.   But when, it may be asked,
except in this primitive state of innocence and purity,
has the Christian Church ever been cast down and
persecuted, meek and trodden under foot ?   When,
alas ! except in its early innocence, has it ever been
otherwise than haughty, worldly, persecuting, cruel,
steeped in human blood ?   God forbid that the kingdoms of this world should ever again be subject to
the triumphant and uncontrolled supremacy of a
domineering ecclesiastical Power such as this.   God
forbid, also, that they should be witness to the domination even of God's ancient holy people while yet

* Auberlen on Daniel, p. 216.

remaining in their unbelief of Christ. When Daniel
speaks of the future glory of the children of Israel
as "saints" in the kingdom of the Son of Man, and
of the accomplishment, or termination, of the dispersion of the "holy people," he clearly refers to
those then far-distant times when the chosen people
of God shall again recognise their God, and God
shall again "take pleasure in His people;" to those
very times, indeed, which are so distinctly and pa-
thetically described by Zechariah, the contemporary
of Daniel, when he exclaims, in the name of God,
"I will pour upon the house of David, and upon
the inhabitants of Jerusalem, the spirit of grace and
supplication, and they shall look upon me whom
they have pierced," &c.—" I will hear them: I will
say, It is My people: and they shall say, The Lord
is my God,"—" and His feet shall stand in that day
on the Mount of Olives,"—"and the Lord my God
shall come, and all the saints (כָּל־קְדֹשִׁים) with thee."[*]
Daniel and Zechariah both refer to the times spoken
of also by that zealous and learned Hebrew of the
Hebrews,[†] brought up at the feet of Gamaliel, Paul
of Tarsus, where he says, " There shall come out
of Zion the Deliverer, and turn away ungodliness
from Jacob;"[‡] when the branches of the olive-tree,
" wild by nature," viz., the Christian branches sprung
from the Jewish Church, shall no longer boast
against the " natural" branches, for a time cut off,
viz., unbelieving Israel; but when the root shall

* Zechariah, xii. 10; xiii. 9; xiv. 5.
† Phil. iii. 5.　　‡ Rom. xi. 26.

be re-established as nourishing the branches, and
both shall be united and grow together in one goodly
olive-tree,—that blessed day of union into one fold,
under one shepherd, when the receiving again of the
children of Israel into favour shall be, as Paul
assures us, to both Jew and Gentile, " as life from
the dead:" when " they shall sing the song of Moses,
the servant of God, and the song of the Lamb,
saying, Great and marvellous are Thy works, Lord
God Almighty ; just and true are Thy ways, Thou
King of *saints*."*

Such was the interpretation set by Daniel upon the
words, "saints of the Most High." Such has ever been
the interpretation of Jewish commentators, looking
for the restoration of Israel in the kingdom of the
Messiah ; and such should be the interpretation
of every Christian who believes that the " Son of
Man," "the anointed Prince," " the righteous Branch
unto David," came into the world, though rejected of
His own, to be " a light to lighten the Gentiles," and
" *Hereafter,*"—as He himself declared to Caiaphas,
when He said, " Ye shall see the Son of Man sitting
on the right hand of power and coming in the clouds
of heaven "†—" *to be the glory of His people Israel.*"‡

Thus, then, it appears that there has been lying
open before us, for more than two thousand years, a
page of the sacred volume professing to contain a distinct revelation from the Most High of the history of
His elect people, the seed of Abraham, even down to
the time when they shall again possess the kingdom.
When the Son of Man shall be king over all the earth,

* Rev. xv. 3. † Matt. xxvii. 64. ‡ Luke, ii. 32.

C

judging the earth in righteousness with all who worship Him in spirit and in truth, both Jew and Gentile,
as His " saints:" For the Gentiles, by faith in Christ,
the seed of Abraham, are also "Abraham's seed,
and heirs according to the promise."[*]　"The dream
is certain, and the interpretation thereof sure."

And, therefore, side by side this sacred volume,
the page of secular history has been slowly, yet continuously, recording the same great outline of events,
in perfect agreement with Daniel's interpretation of
the vision.　The records of history are but the records of the acts of God.

Every well-instructed youth can tell us how,
immediately after the fall of the Babylonian empire,
rose the empire of the Medes and Persians, which,
first by the hand of Cyrus, and afterwards more
completely by the hand of Darius, destroyed that
empire, levelling the mighty walls of Babylon to
the ground, and carrying off the far-famed gates
of brass;[†] when the last of their local kings, Belshazzar, as Daniel informs us, was slain, and the
kingdom passed into the hands of the Persians
(*U-pharsin*); how the Persians in their turn were
overthrown by the Greeks under Alexander of
Macedon; and how the Greek empire in the East,
on the death of that prince, was divided into four
parts amongst his successors; and how at length
that empire also was overthrown by the greatest
and most powerful of all empires, the empire of
Rome.　He could also tell us, how the Roman
empire in its latter days, with one foot planted in

[*] Gal. iii. 29.　　　[†] Herod. iii. 159.

the East, the other in the West, upon the seven hills, preserved its dominion even till the middle of the sixth century; and how, in the course of that century, an overwhelming torrent of barbarians from the North swept over Italy, and caused the empire of the West to cease: how these barbarians were, as it were, swallowed up and absorbed amongst the conquered Romans, "prostrating themselves, half savage and half heathen as they were, at the feet of the high-priest of Rome:"* and how this great and terrible empire had then become split into many kingdoms, truly represented by the ten toes of the image, composed partly of the iron strength of the old Empire, and partly of the fragile materials of the Gothic invaders. Again he would remember, how, when Rome itself had sunk to the very lowest point of abasement, and seemed well-nigh doomed to destruction by these barbarian hordes, about the beginning of the seventh century,† it began again to lift up its head, and rising as it were from its ashes, assumed a form of power " diverse " from any which had yet presented itself to the world; spiritual, yet also temporal; possessed of no material power, yet exercising an influence in the world to be compared even with that of the ancient empire ; " a little horn," yet " with a mouth speaking very great things," even down to the present day.

The germ of this remarkable power was planted by the genius and virtues of Pope Gregory the Great, whose wisdom and Christian spirit, had they always

---

* D'Aubigné's *Reformation* (English Translation), book i. chap. i.   † Gibbon, viii. 158 171.

prevailed with his successors, might have established, as some would now persuade us to believe that Papism is yet capable of establishing, a spiritual kingdom on the seven hills, as a model of sanctity, a beacon light, spreading through the world its pure and holy rays, and making ready the way for the coming of the kingdom of the Son of man. With worldly power, however, came worldly passions, and thirst of worldly sway. The Papal hierarchy quickly forfeited the high position to which it had attained, and assumed that character for superstition, cruelty, intrigue, and falsehood, which it has maintained till this day. Claiming in its chief to represent the meek and peaceful spirit of Christ upon earth, its hands are dipped in blood. Putting forth dogmas of the most inconceivable nature to be received under penalty of non-salvation. Establishing a system of "lying wonders," to deceive the multitude into devout submission. Usurping the more than godly power of canonizing sinners into saints. At one time causing by its scandals and corruptions, the revolt of the Reformation in Germany; at another, the furious outburst of infidelity in France; debasing the minds and energies of those nations which have submitted to the influence of its clergy; till at length, even in the birth-place of its power, it is felt that it would be a blessing to mankind if so intriguing, worldly, and superstitious a power were removed from its high estate, as a chief impediment in the way of the progress of truth and civilisation, and of the final gathering of all religions throughout the world into one fold. Speaking of the barbarian

hordes which invaded Italy, D'Aubigné writes, " It
was the sturdy shoulders of these children of the
idolatrous north that succeeded in placing on the
supreme throne of Christendom a pastor on the
banks of the Tiber.　At the beginning of the seventh
century, these events were accomplishing in the
West precisely at the period when the power of
Mahomet arose in the East."　And both these remarkable powers have maintained their political and
spiritual existence for upwards of 1200 years.　Their
decline and fall, within their own exactly appointed
times, already manifestly taking place before our eyes,
will form the proper subject of exposition when treating upon the viith and viiith chapters of Daniel.

Such is the striking and plain fulfilment in history
of the vision of the great image to the present time.
We wait "the accomplishment of the scattering of the
power of the holy people," and the exaltation of " the
saints of the Most High," to complete the consummation.　And who that surveys the state of the surrounding nations of the world can fail to recognise
amongst them " the holy people," still bowed down
by oppression, yet already shaking off with no gentle
hand the grasp of the oppressor,—still scattered
over the face of the earth, and yet preserved distinct
by the Almighty, as " a special people unto Himself
above all people that are on the face of the earth,"
as if for the very purpose here foretold; patiently
waiting and watching, in accordance with the
twelfth article of their faith, till " the kingdom, as
it was originally, shall return to the people of Israel,
and they shall inhabit their own land, build their

temple and offer sacrifices, as they did in their primitive station; the priests shall attend their service,
and the Levites glorify God in their hymns,"[*]
"For God hath not cast away His people which He
foreknew."[†] The covenant with Abraham was to
give unto him, and to his seed after him, "all the
land of Canaan for an everlasting possession."[‡]
Moses spoke of this people from the beginning as a
nation of priests, and how a fiery law was given
at Mount Sinai unto his "saints."[§] Isaiah, speaking of the future exaltation of Israel, cries, "Say
ye to the daughter of Zion, Behold thy salvation
cometh;" "and they shall call them the holy peo-
ple, (עַם־הַקֹּדֶשׁ), the redeemed of the Lord."[||] While
Daniel foretells how "the little horn" from amongst
the ten kingdoms of the broken Roman empire,
shall in the course of his domination "make war
with the saints,"[¶] (עִם־קַדִּישִׁין), a persecution which
commenced in the seventh century,[**] was fulfilled to
the letter in the times of the Crusades and of the Inquisition, and which has been carried on at Rome even
till the present day: no allusion being made by Daniel,
here or elsewhere, which is most remarkable, to the
existence of the great Roman Gentile Church, except
under this form of oppression. "The chief point,"
writes Auberlen, "which it is necessary to recognise
distinctly, and to express simply, is, that the com-

---

* Jewish Catechism.   † Rom. xi. 2.   ‡ Gen. xvii. 6.
§ Deut. xxxiii. 2. || Isa. lxii. 12.   ¶ Dan. vii. 21, 22.
** See Da Costa's "*Israel and the Gentiles,*" pp. 217–19, con-
cerning the cruel decrees of the Councils of Toledo against the
Jews in the early part of the 7th century.

mencement of the kingdom spoken of in the 2nd and 7th chapters of Daniel is nothing else but the second coming of our Lord Jesus Christ," "the re-establishment of the kingdom of Israel."*

We are then content, as we have said, to rest the genuineness and inspiration of the book of Daniel on the fulfilment or non-fulfilment of this great prophecy. Had it been written even in the present day, after the events, in simulation of prophecy, we can scarcely conceive anything more pointed than the description contained in it, of what has actually come to pass.

Nevertheless, we regret to find ourselves not entirely at unison with Dr. Pusey in this interpretation. Most are agreed as far as the division of the Roman empire into many kingdoms. But the peculiar power which should rise up amongst them, and which is said to have dominion for " a time, times, and dividing of time," that is, for a period which we con-- sider to have now just expired, and which we interpret to be the Papal power, Dr. Pusey looks for as one yet to come into existence.† The future destinies and glory of God's elect, but cast-off people, which we cannot but feel form the chief subject of Daniel's predictions, do not seem to come even within the range of

* Auberlen, p. 216.

† Dr. Pusey here seems to be at variance with the Pope himself, who, in his Allocution in October, 1866, writes:—" By a singular disposition of Divine Providence, it was ordered that when the Roman Empire was overthrown and divided into many kingdoms, the Roman Pontiff, in the midst of this diversity of kingdoms, and in the present state of human society, should possess a civil princedom." This little civil princedom answers precisely to Daniel's expression " little horn."

his contemplation; while in his tenderness towards
Rome, so far from looking upon the Papal power as
the oppressor of the " holy people," he seems to hint
at the present persecution of the See of Rome itself
as the fulfilment of the prophecy.* The difference
between us is a broad one, and has formed with some
minds an important spring of action. So much so,
that we have seen such men as Dr. Newman, in-
fluenced by the same admiration of the Church of
Rome, and deep contempt for the scarcely more
erring Jewish Church, actually driven from communion with the Church of England, as he tells us,†
by the idea of a Protestant bishop,—a bishop of the
circumcision, one who boasted of his Jewish descent
—being placed at Jerusalem. This was " the blow
which finally shattered the faith in the Anglican
Church," of this most frail of religious barques, as if
the tendency of the movement were not in accordance
with the revealed purposes of God, and not indeed
a first step at least, though a remote one, towards
the restoration of His holy people to their own land,
in communion with the Church of Christ. But we
do not wish to dwell upon the unfulfilled portion of
this prophecy. We have stated our convictions.
The time is yet future, and events will decide the
question, whether Papal Rome is looked upon in
prophecy as the persecutor or the persecuted, the
erring or the perfect Church. We will merely add,
that what was foreknown to Divine prescience in
the days of Daniel, is now known to us by the experience of past history; and it is inconceivable to

* P. 77.   † Newman's Apologia, p. 248.

the student of history, that prophetic foresight should have overlooked in these visions two of the most prominent events of history which have acted in retardation of the establishment of the kingdom of God, and the restoration of his "saints," the chief object and burthen of Daniel's visions, viz., Papal, and Mahomedan domination, both which would appear to have been overlooked, if Dr. Pusey's mode of interpretation is the true one. We have before us clearly represented in the book of Daniel:—

1st. The prostrate, cast-off people of God, stiff-necked, yet earnest, waiting for the restoration of the kingdom to Israel, and for "the kingdom of God." The seed of Abraham in the flesh.

2nd. The ever-swelling multitude of devout Gentile worshippers of the Son of Man, represented by the stone "*cut out without hands*," silently, yet unceasingly, lifting up the prayer, "Thy kingdom come." The seed of Abraham by adoption.

And there also, we feel assured, from the known events of history, must be represented,—

3rd. The great apostasy of the East, which has now literally trodden under foot, with one short interval of relief, the holy land, and holy city Jerusalem, for more than twelve hundred years; to the exclusion from thence of God's "holy people." The little horn of the eighth chapter.

4th. The great harlot church of the West, seated on the seven hills, casting out its flood of idolatry, falsehood, and superstition, to the deep abhorrence of God's "holy people," and forming an impassable barrier to their union with the visible

Church of Christ. The little horn of the seventh chapter.

Here are portrayed the "two witnesses" of the Apocalypse prophesying in sackcloth. Here are "the beast" and "the false prophet," domineering till "the Ancient of days did sit," and till the appearance of "the Son of Man coming with the clouds of heaven." And here are the redeemed on Mount Zion, who shall sing the song of Moses, the servant of God, and the song of the Lamb.

Surely the "Times of the Gentiles," which, we are told, shall not close till Jerusalem shall cease to be trodden under foot,*—the commencement of which times may perhaps be placed at that marked epoch in the history of the Jewish Church, when ten out of twelve parts of the holy people were cast off as unworthy of the lofty title of the people of God, —have now nearly run their course. Philosophy and literature, which from that time began to diffuse their light throughout the world, have already accomplished all that they can, and were intended to accomplish for the advancement of human intellect, and more than could have been accomplished singly by the then Jewish Church; for though "the world by wisdom knew not God," yet religion without wisdom, clergy without laity, endowed Church without secular superintendence, except under a theocracy, tend but to degeneracy and superstition. The Gentile Church would seem, at length, to have lost its savour. The world has grown weary of disputation upon dogma, tradition, ritual, and gar-

* Luke, xxi. 24.

ments, to the stifling of the breath of holiness. Intellect and philosophy have now outrun piety and reverence, and religion sighs and prays for the arrival of that dispensation, which the holy Daniel has put into our hearts to long for and expect, as now soon about to dawn in the horizon; when the tabernacle of David, which is fallen down, shall be rebuilt,* and the house of Judah shall once again be made holy and exalted amongst the kingdoms of the world.

Let Israel but once accept the everlasting truth, that the Spirit of the Almighty Creator, pervading all things, may, without derogation from His unity take up his abode within the souls of holy men, and that once at least, in furtherance of His beneficent purposes towards mankind, He has thus manifested Himself in human form, in the person of "The Most Holy,"† who took to Himself the title "Son of Man," and the day will not be far 'distant, when the courts of the Temple of Jerusalem shall echo again to the praise of the Almighty :—

> "O sing unto the Lord a new song:
> Let the congregation of the saints praise him.
> Let Israel rejoice in him that made him:
> And the children of Zion be joyful in their King."

Then shall the grandeur and simplicity of the creed of Israel, which recognises but one eternal and indivisible Spirit, and which suffers no worship of created beings, a creed adapted to the understanding, and reaching to the heart of every enlightened being upon earth, stand forth in contrast with

---

* Acts, xv. 16.   † Dan. ix. 24.

that degraded faith, fitted only to an age of ignorance and darkness, which dims the majesty of the
Almighty in clouds of incense to Virgin, saints,
images, and angels; which dares to speak to us
of the "mother of God," and to dogmatize on the
mode of her conception; and which professes to
create, localize, and sacrifice God by the hands of
its benighted priests.* Then shall the dry bones
of the house of Israel, whose hope was lost, come
again together, bone to his bone, and rise, as it
were, again from their graves;† then shall Ephraim
and Judah be united together as one people. The
Sanctuary shall be re-established, "the place of my
throne and the place of the soles of my feet," on a
scale of magnificence and dimensions suited to the
sanctuary of the whole earth. A river of living
waters shall flow abundantly towards the East, not
from the seven hills of Rome, but from the sanctuary
of Jerusalem; the holy hill of Zion. "There shall
be a very great multitude of fish:" "and every-
thing shall live whither the river cometh."‡

But modern critics profess to have made the discovery, that this pretended vision is a forgery written after the facts, and merely founded upon the
events of Jewish history up to the time of Antiochus Epiphanes. Now we are not amongst those
who would deny the exercise of human judgment

---

* Dr. Manning, in his late Pastoral, speaks of "the Dogmatic
Bull of the Immaculate Conception:" of "the Divine worship of
the holy Mass:" and of "God incarnate dying on the cross."
This doctrine of the death of the Almighty and Eternal God is
truly appalling.

† Ezek. xxxvii. 1–17.   ‡ Ezek. xlvii. 1–9.

in the investigation of the contents of Holy Scripture: on the contrary, we rejoice to see the free and searching examination now applied to them. But how have the critics performed the task which they have undertaken? Dr. Pusey has well exposed the shifts and shuffles to which they have been reduced, in their endeavour to reduce the times of the four distinct empires of Daniel within the compass of three; and those who will consult his work will find that there is no absurdity or contradiction which they have not entertained in order to effect this hopeless purpose. The most approved method seems to be, by placing Daniel captive amongst the Assyrians at Nineveh, instead of amongst the Babylonians, and thus making Assyria the first of the four empires; and this in the face of circumstantial history, be it written when and by whom it may, connecting him first with the Babylonian Empire, and then with the Persian, under both which we are told that Daniel held high office near the throne. " Ewald is right," said Bunsen, " that Daniel was led captive in the first Assyrian invasion, and lived and prophesied in Nineveh, not in Babylon." But how can Ewald be right, in the face of the words of the writer of the book of Daniel to the contrary? What does Ewald, or Baron Bunsen, know concerning Daniel, more than what is written in the book of Daniel itself? It is true, that we find the names of " Noah, Daniel, and Job," * twice coupled together

* " Though Noah, Daniel, and Job were in it, as I live, saith the Lord God, they shall deliver neither sons nor daughters; they shall but deliver their own souls." Ezek. xiv. 20.

as examples of holiness in the book of Ezekiel, which
book precedes in date that of Daniel ; and no unprejudiced mind can fail to admit the difficulty involved
in these passages, of believing that one so young as
Daniel must then have been, and one who was then
associated with the magicians, and astrologers of
Babylon, should have been ranked, while yet alive,
with the most revered saints of antiquity in Jewish
history. This is the only semblance of an argument
for placing Daniel in the earlier time of the Assyrian
Empire. But, on the other hand, is it conceivable
that a saint unheard of, according to these critics,
except through the two passages in question, should
have thus been placed on a level with Noah and Job?
And again, if it is reasonable, in explanation of the
difficulty, to accept with Ewald the hypothesis of an
unknown Daniel, together with an unknown history
of him entirely at variance with all tradition concerning him, would it not be equally reasonable, we
may ask, to adopt the more simple solution, of the possibility of an error in transcription, and surmise that
in this particular chapter of Ezekiel, where the name
Daniel is now read, the name perhaps of David *

---

* In Greek, the transition from Δαυιδ, N.T. to Δανιηλ would
not be difficult. Dr. Pusey has incidentally remarked, (p. 47) that
" a fuller orthography, implying a more prolonged pronunciation
(Daveed for David), has long been recognised as belonging to the
later Hebrew of the O.T." The equivalent Hebrew letters for
Daveid, or Daveed, would have been דואיד, or דוייאד, which latter
formation is not far removed from דניאל. Such, however, is not
the formation adopted in our present copies of Ezekiel, in writing the name of David. The pronunciation Daood, in Persian
and Arabic, on the other hand, indicates a contraction of דָּוִיד into דָּוִד

may have been originally written. For the name of
David, it may be observed, is truly most applicable to
the passages. · The name of Daniel would seem to
be quite inapplicable. Daniel probably had neither
sons nor daughters to deliver, for the tradition is that
he was a eunuch in the palace.* How then could
it be said of him that he should "deliver neither
sons or daughters?" Whereas, when Jerusalem
was threatened † in the days of Hezekiah, as now
in the days of Ezekiel, it is said to have been saved
"for David's sake;" and so the sons and daughters
of Noah were saved for their father's sake: while
Job offered sacrifice continually for his sons and
daughters, and so till the time of his last trial, we
may presume, they had been saved for his sake.‡
Again, it may be observed, that in the orthography of
proper names in Scripture compounded of אֵל, el, God,
such as Daniel, there are not unfrequent instances in
Hebrew and Syriac of a tendency towards contraction by dropping the א, as for instance in Josh. xix. 4,
בְּתוּל, Bethul, is written for בְּתוּאֵל, Bethuel, 1 Chron. iv.
30; חָמוּל, Hamul, Gen. xlvi. 12, for חָמוּאֵל, Hamuel,
1 Chron. iv. 26; and in Syriac, Abnil for Abniel, a
Syrian god :§ so that it might not be impossible for one
transcribing a cursive manuscript of Ezekiel to have
misread דּוִיד, David, for the contracted form דָּנִיל,
Danil, if so written in the manuscript. But if "David," not "Daniel," may possibly have been here
originally written, where is the ground for Bunsen's

---

* Jos. Ant. x. x. i. † 2 Kings, xix. 34; viii. 19. ‡ Job, i. 5.
§ Assemanni. Biblioth: Orient: Tom. i. 26.

authoritative decision, that Ewald is right in supposing Daniel to have prophesied at Nineveh? This
is a fair sample of the criticism, by which the time
of the composition of the book of Daniel is called in
question! It is satisfactory to find, that it is only by
accepting such bold assertions as these, that the reach
of this great prophecy beyond the times of Antiochus can effectually be set aside. Some with the
view of making four empires out of three, would
make Nebuchadnezzar, individually, to represent the
first of the four empires, and his successors the second.
Some, reckless of history, would divide the empire
of the Medes and Persians, such as it existed after
the fall of Babylon, into two distinct empires; and
some again would make two kingdoms of Alexander
and his successors. All have undertaken to com-
press four distinct empires, so described by Daniel,
within three, as distinctly recorded in history; each
contradicts the other in his arrangement; and if all
these inconsistent views are equally applicable to
the words of the prophecy in the opinion of the
writers, it is clear, without entering into further
detail, that the application must be of such an extremely loose character, as to afford no such proof
as we have a right to demand, that these prophecies
are mere repetition of history to the times of the
Maccabees. We have neither space nor inclination
to follow this unsatisfactory attempt at exposition into
all its details. Dr. Pusey has conscientiously done
so, after reading all the various explanations; and
our own conviction, after a careful perusal of his
work, is that, as far as regards the prophecy of the

great symbolic image, the attempts of critics to show that the writer of the book of Daniel, in the second and seventh chapters, was describing events of history with a view to the time of Antiochus, is not only a most signal failure as an act of criticism, but that it has been simply undertaken to meet the exigencies of the foregone conclusion, that Daniel could not be a prophet.

Nevertheless, we are not disposed to quarrel with those who would endeavour to determine which are, and which are not, the genuine writings of Daniel, in the compilation bearing his name which has come down to us. And when we meet with earnest and religious-minded men, such as the late Dr. Arnold, men of esteemed character, and of approved judgment in questions of criticism in general, who have thought it their duty to take exception to a certain portion of the book, of no very great extent, as incapable of bearing any reasonable spiritual construction, and have expressed their opinions that the style and character of the composition of the part objected to is totally unlike the 'character of real prophecy, so grandly exemplified in this particular book of Scripture, we cannot think it reasonable that such opinions should be impatiently set aside as worthless by the mere dictum of authority, but rather that they should be carefully weighed and examined, with the view of turning them, if possible, to profitable account.

Let it be remembered that there is much reason for believing that the book of Daniel, written not

in Judea, but at Babylon, by one not trained to
the prophetic office like his predecessors, but engaged in the secular affairs of two great heathen
kingdoms, was not received into the canon of Scripture, as settled at Jerusalem, till long after the
death of the writer: and that at the time when it
was there received, as testified by the earliest Greek
translation, it had become encumbered with several
questionable additions, rejected indeed by the compiler of the Hebrew canon, and since pronounced
by Protestant expositors to be apocryphal writings
to which the name of Daniel had been improperly
attached; but pronounced to be genuine portions
of the book by the authoritative and infallible decision of the Church of Rome. From the Septuagint translation, or rather paraphrase, of Daniel, we
collect, that at the time of that version the hymn
supposed to have been sung by the three children
in the fiery furnace had become incorporated with
the third chapter of some copies of the Chaldee
book, as then known at Jerusalem, or Alexandria;
and from a comparison of the last words of the sixth
chapter of the Septuagint version with the first
words of the story of Bel and the Dragon,* it may
be inferred, that that legend also, though not so
placed by the translator, had once been appended

---

* Καὶ ὁ βασιλεὺς Δαρεῖος προσετέθη πρὸς τὸ γένος αὐτοῦ, καὶ Δανιὴλ
κατεστάθη ἐπὶ τῆς βασιλείας Δαρείου, καὶ Κύρος ὁ Πέρσης παρέλαβε τὴν
βασιλείαν αὐτοῦ. Sept. Dan. vi. 28.

Καὶ ὁ βασιλεὺς Ἀστυάγης προσετέθη πρὸς τὰς πατέρας αὐτοῦ, καὶ
παρέλαβε Κύρος ὁ Πέρσης τὴν βασιλείαν αὐτοῦ καὶ ἦν Δανιὴλ συμβιωτὴς
τοῦ βασιλέως, &c. Bel and the Dragon, i. 1. Walton's "Polyglot."

to the sixth chapter of the Chaldee.   Traces of this
junction we conceive to be still remaining in the
last words of the sixth chapter as generally read :
" So this Daniel prospered in the reign of Darius ;"
—"And in the reign of Cyrus." Where the last
words would seem to have been left, as in the last
verse of the second book of Chronicles, to show
where the legend once joined, but which, as now
read, in their fragmentary state, lead to the false
assumption that Darius was the predecessor of
Cyrus in Babylon.   We have no hesitation in affirming, on chronological grounds alone, that there is
something dubious in the arrangement of the tenth
and eleventh chapters, dated in the reign of Cyrus,
and which now follow the ninth chapter, dated in
the reign of Darius.   And we are confirmed in this
opinion by the fact, that where the Hebrew text of
xi. 1, now writes " Darius," both the Septuagint and
Theodotion have written " Cyrus."

We shall enter hereafter into the question of the
genuineness or otherwise of this portion of the book
of Daniel, when touching on the work of Mr. Desprez.   For the present we will merely observe that
the eleventh chapter clearly relates to the times of
Antiochus Epiphanes, and differs from the ordinary
style of Daniel, inasmuch as it treats of individual
kings, instead of kingdoms, of minute events, rather
than of great periods of history.   Yet, nevertheless,
if not genuine prophecy, then is the remarkable
persecution of the holy people in the days of that
king nowhere prophesied of in Scripture, which, at

first sight, it is hard to conceive. Leaving this subject, however, as a matter for separate examination,
we now hasten to the consideration of the main subject of our observations, viz., Dr. Pusey's exposition
of the prophecy of the "Seventy Weeks."

Many will be disposed to decide upon the success
cess or failure of his work as a whole by the manner
in which he has executed this, the most difficult part
of his undertaking. All are aware how this plainly-
worded and apparently simple prophecy has been
the subject of difference and controversy, even
amongst those who firmly believe in its fulfilment,
for a period of nearly 1700 years; and how some
of the most profound intellects which ever existed
—scholars, theologians, philologists, mathematicians,
and historians — have tested their powers in the
endeavour to interpret it, yet hitherto confessedly
without success. From the time when Josephus
maintained that the Emperor Vespasian was the
" anointed prince" foretold by Daniel, even to the
present day, one continuous series of discordant
interpretations have succeeded each other. Africanus, Clemens of Alexandria, Eusebius, among the
Fathers; the author of the " Seder Olam," Rabbi
Isaac, and David Gantz, amongst Jewish writers;
Scaliger, Petavius, Sir I. Newton, Marsham, Blayney,
Lloyd, Ussher, Marshall, Lancaster, Prideaux, Jack-
son, Faber, Lyall, Parker, Greswell, Galloway, Lord
Arthur Hervey, Hengstenberg, Auberlen, Hofman,
and Ewald, are some few of the interpreters whose
works have come under the notice of the writer,

in evidence of the labour and ability which has been
bestowed on its · solution.   Some of these writers
have proposed to adopt the reading of the Septuagint translation—"Seven and Seventy"—in preference to the "Seventy" of the Hebrew; some
count in lunar years, most in solar years; some commence the period with the decree of Cyrus, some
with the decree of Darius of the book of Ezra, supposing that king to be Darius Nothus; some count
from the seventh year of Artaxerxes Longimanus,
others from the twentieth year of the same king,
and some from the twentieth year of Xerxes; some
terminate the "weeks" with the birth of Christ,
and most with his baptism or ministry ; some look
upon the periods of "seven weeks," "threescore
and two weeks," and "one week," as forming together a continuous period of "seventy weeks,"
while some would separate from the rest the "seven
weeks," and others the "one week," as periods yet
to be fulfilled in future time ; some few maintain
that the whole period of weeks should be commensurate with those actual sabbatical weeks which were
commanded to be observed, and which we know
were observed in Judea after the captivity ; and,
amongst them, Dr. Pusey seems to feel the force
of this restricting principle; and, lastly, not a few
modern critics have arrived at the great discovery,
that all this labour has been in vain, because this
supposed prophecy is, in fact, merely a fiction of
the days of Antiochus Epiphanes, and the period
of weeks spoken of in it was fulfilled in the reign

of that prince, some 170 years before the birth of Christ. Every fresh interpreter only adds to the force of our conviction, that some radical error lies at the foundation of all Christian interpretations, and that until this source of error shall have been discovered, the Seventy Weeks of Daniel will continue to remain unexplained, and unexplainable, to the comprehension of any unprejudiced inquirer.

From the multitude of varying expositions thus offered to him, Dr. Pusey seems to have selected that of Prideaux, which he follows in all main particulars. We can only regret that we are unable to agree with one so earnest, and so well entitled to attention, either in his selection or mode of treating the subject. Let us first point out one or two preliminary objections which have occurred to us in our progress through this part of the work.

One of the fundamental positions taken up by Dr. Pusey, and one without which his explanation must fall to the ground, is, that Daniel was carried captive from Jerusalem in the third year of Jehoia-kim,* king of Judah, counted from the death of King Josiah, and *before* Nebuchadnezzar had ascended the throne of Babylon ; from which it is inferred that Daniel may thus have been educated in the learning of the Chaldeans for three full years, as we are told he was, and yet have interpreted the king's dream at the close of the *second* year of his reign. This position has been objected to on the ground, that Daniel would thus be brought to Babylon during the

* Dan. i. 1.

first year of Nebuchadnezzar, which was commensurate with the fourth year of Jehoiakim;* and that the second year of the reign of that prince could not have fallen three full years after the arrival of Daniel at Babylon.

Dr. Pusey appeals to the history of Berosus, to show that Daniel may have been one amongst those Jewish captives which Berosus tells us had been taken by Nebuchadnezzar before his father's death, and whom he ordered to be conducted to Babylon by the ordinary route, while he himself hastened over the desert to take the throne. Can anything, however, be more clear than the words of Berosus,† as quoted by Dr. Pusey,‡ to show that those captives, together with Daniel, if he was amongst them, arrived at Babylon *not before*, but after the accession of the king to the throne? So that, if Daniel was brought to Babylon, as we infer, " to stand in the king's palace," to be there nourished and educated for three full years in " the learning and the tongue of the Chaldeans,"§ it is quite clear that those three years could not have been completed till the fourth year of the king's reign. And if so, it is simply impossible that Daniel, as Dr. Pusey supposes, could have interpreted the king's dream in the second year of his reign. The idea proceeds on the supposition, that Daniel interpreted the dream in the last of his three years of probation; that he had commenced his education before his arrival at Babylon; and that a siege of Jerusalem had taken place, not spoken of in the histories contained in the books of Kings or Chro-

---

* Jer. xxv. 1.
† See Josephus cont. Apion. i. 19.   ‡ P. 60.   § Dan. i. 4.

nicles, and before the fall of Pharaoh Necho, at Carchemish,* its then supreme lord. But if Daniel was
thus carried away captive in the third year of Jehoiakim, and from this year, as assumed, the period of seventy years' captivity of the nation at Babylon is to be
counted, how comes it to pass, that the author of the
last chapter of Jeremiah, who enumerates the several
occasions when captives were carried off in the reign
of Nebuchadnezzar, makes no mention of this the
most important captivity of all? The writer knew of
no carrying away of captives from Jerusalem before
the seventh year of Nebuchadnezzar, that is to say,
in the very year in which Jehoiakim fell into the
hands of the Babylonian king and ceased to reign.†

In agreement with Jeremiah, the writer of the
second book of Chronicles, who wrote after the
seventy years of captivity were ended, and when the
precise limits of the captivity therefore were understood, makes no reference, either to this supposed
important siege, or to this commencement of the
captivity. He simply tells us that Jehoiakim reigned
eleven years, and that "against him came up Nebuchadnezzar, king of Babylon, and bound him with
fetters to carry him to Babylon. Nebuchadnezzar
also carried of the vessels of the house of the Lord,
and put them in his temple at Babylon,"‡ evidently
alluding to the same carrying away of part of the
vessels, which is spoken of in the beginning of the
book of Daniel, as having occurred in the third
year of Jehoiakim. So that the third year of this

* Jer. xlvi. 2.   † Jer. lii. 28, 29, 30.
‡ 2 Chron. xxxvi. 6, 7.

king, spoken of by Daniel, would appear to have
been the same as the eleventh, or last year of Jehoiakim, mentioned in Chronicles.

Again, this view is confirmed by the writer of
the second book of Kings,* who is particular in describing the sieges of Jerusalem, and informs us that
Jehoiakim became servant of Nebuchadnezzar for
three years, that is, for the years 5-6, 6-7, and 7-8,
of the Jewish king's reign, after which he rebelled
and became independent. He then reigned in independence for *three years*, that is, during the years
8-9, 9-10, and 10-11, of his entire reign, when in
that eleventh year, called the *third* year of Jehoiakim by Daniel, being the seventh year of Nebuchadnezzar according to Jeremiah, he was bound in
fetters to be carried to Babylon; and his successor,
Jechoniah, who reigned only three months, was in
the following year, or eighth of Nebuchadnezzar,†
carried to Babylon, and his father slain after the
first siege of the city in that king's reign, known to
the writer of the book of Kings.

Again, Ezekiel knows of no other commencement
of the captivity at Babylon than that which began
in the eighth year of Nebuchadnezzar.

Josephus reckons that Daniel was carried away
even as late as the time of Zedekiah. The " Seder
Olam Rabba," with no chronological bias, has the
words, " Daniel is to be understood as speaking of
the third year after the rebellion of Jehoiakim;"
and as regards the year of the interpretation of the

* 2 Kings, xxiv. 1-11.   † Ibid. xxiv. 12.

dream,—" Scripture reckons the years from the destruction of the temple."*

Hippolytus also considered that Daniel was carried captive, not in the third year of Jehoiakim, son of Josiah, but at the time when "Jehoiakim, *son of Eliakim*," that is, Jehoiakin, or Jechoniah, was taken prisoner to Babylon. So also did Clement of Alexandria, Cedrenus, and many others. The strong inducement which has led Prideaux, and those who follow him, to adopt the opposite interpretation, is, the absolute necessity for adopting it, in order to obtain the semblance of a beginning for the seventy years' "*desolations* of Jerusalem," which number of years we know preceded the delivery of the seventy weeks' prophecy.† These desolations, however, are clearly marked in the second book of Chronicles,‡ as beginning with the *burning of Jerusalem*, not with the third year of Jehoiakim, when Jerusalem, so far from being desolate, had not yet even been besieged by the king of Babylon. The idea that Daniel was made captive in the third year from the accession of Jehoiakim, is simply an invention of late Christian days; and when disproved, the first principle upon which most modern interpretations of Daniel's weeks are founded, falls to the ground.

With reference to the " second year of Nebuchadnezzar," and "third year of Jehoiakim," as spoken of by Daniel, we think we can discover the principle upon

* A translation of the " Seder Olam" will be found in Vol. ii., Part ii., of the " Transactions of the Chronological Institute," Longmans.　　† Dan. ix. 2.　　‡ 2 Chron. xxxvi. 19–21.

which Daniel reckoned the reigns of the successive
princes of whom he writes.   We know from the first
words of his ninth chapter that his mind had been
dwelling intently upon the prophecies of Jeremiah ;
and Jeremiah, we know, had foretold the coming of
that "righteous branch* unto David," under whom
"Judah should be saved and Israel dwell in safety:"
and also spoke of a time when there should enter the
gates of Jerusalem "kings and princes sitting on the
throne of David, riding in chariots and on horses, they
and their princes," &c., &c.† It had also already been
revealed to Daniel how four successive empires, beginning with the Babylonians and the Persians, should
have rule over the holy people, after which "the God
of heaven should set up a kingdom never to be destroyed." "The kingdom," therefore, which occupied
the thoughts of Daniel was the kingdom of David,
or the kingdom of Messiah, the future seat of which
kingdom should be Jerusalem.   Counting, therefore,
like Ezekiel, from the time of his own captivity, he
first seems to mention the third of Jehoiakim, that is,
his third year of independence at Jerusalem, as
marking the date of his captivity, and then to have
begun by reckoning the eleven years of the vassalage of Zedekiah till the destruction of the holy city ;
then the second year of Nebuchadnezzar, not from
the time of his accession to the throne of Babylon,
but from the time of his finally taking the government of Judea into his hands : then, again, the years
of Cyrus, not from his accession to the throne of

* Jer. xxxiii. 5, 6.   † Jer. xvii. 25.

Persia or Media, but from the time when Babylon was subdued, and Judea thereby came under his dominion ; and, lastly, when he says "Darius took the kingdom," he counts not from the time of the accession of Darius to the throne of Persia, but from the time of the fall of Belshazzar, when he "took the kingdom being about threescore and two years old," and when Judea and Jerusalem came more immediately under the control of the Persian king.

Again, Dr. Pusey abandons all hope of discovering who was the reigning prince when the prophecy of the seventy weeks was delivered to Daniel. Daniel tells us plainly enough that his master's title was Darius : that Darius reigned over kingdoms subject to the laws of the Medes and Persians, and therefore after the Medes had fallen under the power of the Persians : and that his dominions comprehended "all people, nations, and languages that dwell in all the earth."* His kingdom, therefore, would appear to have been coextensive even with that of Cyrus, to whom "the Lord God of heaven had given all the kingdoms of the earth." Dr. Pusey, however, assumes that this king reigned before the first year of "Cyrus, king of Babylon :" that he was a subordinate prince set up by that king over Babylon, and that his title was anything but Darius. "It is a question," he observes,† " of secular, not of Biblical history, whether Cyrus placed on the throne the Cyaxares II. of Xenophon, or Astyages, or neither, but a Median

---

* Dan. vi. 25.   † P. 124.

descendant of the celebrated sovereign Acashwerosh,
Cyaxares :" and thus he shrinks from the consideration of one of the main questions necessary for deter-
mining whether the prophecy has, or has not, been
fulfilled within the time foretold.   If, also, the Darius
of Daniel was no other than Cyaxares, son of Astyages, and, at the same time, the title Ahasuerus, as
he suggests, is equivalent to the title Cyaxares, why,
it may be asked, has Daniel designated the King
"Darius son of Ahasuerus," and not rather Ahasuerus,
son of Ahasuerus? and how does it come to pass
that, in this case, the title Ahasuerus is applied both
to Cyaxares and Astyages?   If, as an alternative,
Daniel's Darius was no other than Astyages, then
must Astyages, the grandfather of Cyrus, have been
sixty-two years of age at the time of the taking of
Babylon, just eight years before the death of his grandson, according to Dr. Pusey's reckoning, in B.C. 530,
as some say, at the age of seventy, and certainly at
not less than fifty years of age?   In the one case both
grandfather and grandson would have been of the
same age at the taking of Babylon: in the other, of
the respective ages of sixty-two and forty-two.   Dr.
Pusey is not altogether responsible for these extra-
vagant suggestions, which seem to form the staple
of most modern interpretations.   His alternative " or
neither," shows his distrust and distaste for such
illustration: nevertheless, he wishes us to believe
that this great monarch, who after the conquest of
Babylon by the Persians claimed to be sovereign
over " all people, nations, and languages that dwell

in all the earth," was merely a viceroy over the
province of Babylon, whose name was not worthy of
record in secular history: thus leaving ample room
for the doubts of the sceptic, whether the writer
of the book of Daniel was truly acquainted with
the history of the time in which he professes to
have lived.   We trust that no such latitude of
doubt need be left to the sincere inquirer, however
sceptical his turn of mind may be.   Daniel knew
his own master's title, and that title we have no
right to doubt was Darius.

Having thus decided that the king in whose reign
the prophecy was delivered is, according to our
present knowledge, past discovery, and that the
" desolations of Jerusalem " had commenced nineteen
years before Jerusalem had been made desolate,
Dr. Pusey proceeds to analyze the great period
of Seventy Weeks, which he declares to be divided
into three parts, which follow each other in succession, in the order of seven weeks, sixty and two
weeks, and one week.*   He then observes, that
the whole period of seventy weeks, or 490 years,
must   necessarily   terminate   with   the   anointing
of a "holy of holies," or an ALL-HOLY, that is,
our Lord Jesus Christ; in which last conclusion
all Christian readers will agree with him.   " Seventy
seven-times," he writes, " are determined upon
thy people and upon thy holy city, to close the
transgression, to seal up sins, and to make reconciliation for iniquity;" "to bring in everlasting

* P. 170.

righteousness, and to seal up vision and prophecy, and *to anoint a Holy of holies.* These were to be the gifts of God *at the close of that seventieth week.*"* "Once in the future, *at the end of the seventy weeks,* there should be an atoning for all iniquity." Then, again, he most truly points out† that "the symbolical meaning of the anointing is fixed by the next words of the prophecy—*unto Messiah the Prince.* The word is repeated. The last of the six blessings was *to anoint an All-Holy—limshoach kodesch kodashim.* He resumes at once, unto one Anointed, a Prince — ad *Mashiach* nagid. No one wishing to be understood, would unite so closely words relating to the same period of time, *the end of the seventy weeks,*‡ had they not related to the same object—'to anoint an All-Holy :' 'unto one Anointed.'" How clearly and forcibly has Dr. Pusey here set forth the true mode of interpreting the words of the prophecy in the abstract! Who will venture to gainsay his position ? Could any words of his, however, have led us more logically to the conclusion, that the order of the successive periods cannot be, as above stated, $7 + 62 + 1 = 70$:

$$
\begin{array}{rcl}
\text{But } 1 \text{ week} &=& 7 \text{ years} \\
7 \quad \text{,,} &=& 49 \quad \text{,,} \\
62 \quad \text{,,} &=& 434 \quad \text{,,} \\
\hline
70 \quad \text{,,} &=& 490 \text{ years.}
\end{array}
$$

For if, in the words of Daniel, "unto Messiah the Prince," or unto one Anointed a Prince, "shall be

* P. 177.   † P. 180.   ‡ These last italics are our own.

seven weeks and threescore and two weeks," that
is, sixty-nine weeks; and if "the *end* of the seventy
weeks," in the words of Dr. Pusey, is the time determined "to anoint an All-Holy," which is the same
event, clearly no place remains for the period of " one
week," except as preceding the seven and sixty-two.
No interpretation of the prophecy we submit can be
the true one which does not coincide with this leading
principle of interpretation, so clearly, though not in-
tentionally, laid down, viz. that the seventy, and the
sixty-nine, both terminate at the same point. Again,
if " seven weeks and threescore and two weeks," are
thus shown to have closed at the same point of time
as the " seventy," the inference is equally clear and
undeniable, that all that is spoken of as about to
happen, "*after threescore and two weeks*,"—viz., the
cutting off of Messiah: the coming of a prince to
"destroy the city and the sanctuary:" " the confirming
the covenant with many for one week," and " the
causing of the sacrifice and oblation to cease," must
necessarily be excluded from the series of events comprehended within the Seventy Weeks. Having thus
discovered the clue to the interpretation, and, as it
were, with the key in hand ready to unlock the mystery, Dr. Pusey deliberately casts it away, and sur-
rendering himself into the hands of Prideaux, proceeds
to explain the words of the prophecy on a principle
the reverse of that which he has himself laid down.
Disappointment and perplexity alone can be the
result. Let us trace the series of difficulties into
which the scheme of Prideaux leads him.

The wording of the prophecy is remarkably distinct, particular, and minute.　We read not only of the definite periods of " seventy," of " threescore and two," of " seven," and of " one week," but the prophet even marks with a very prominent event the minute division, one half of a week.　" In the midst of the week," or in half a week, " he shall cause the sacrifice and the oblation to cease."　Each of these separate divisions of time we must assume was intended to be fulfilled with exactness.

Nevertheless, when Dr. Pusey comes to interpret, we find that the anointing of an All-Holy, which, according to his own interpretation, ought to have taken place at the end of seventy, is actually placed by him at the baptism of Jesus Christ, when He was anointed with the Holy Ghost to preach the Gospel, at the end of precisely sixty-nine weeks,[*] and he is, therefore, constrained to suggest, that the Holy Spirit, maybe, " did not declare, so that it should be certainly known beforehand, the precise year when the Messiah should come, and should be cut off; "[†] and that " the event, which was to change and regenerate millions upon millions, was fixed beforehand, within some surplus upon 490 years."[‡]　Fully agreeing with Dr. Pusey, that a veil of obscurity was intended to hang over this deeply spiritual prophecy, for a period, reaching far indeed beyond the time of its accomplishment, and seeing also how effectually

[*] P. 170.　　　[†] P. 164.　　　[‡] P. 165.

E

this veil continues to be upheld even to the present day, we are yet unable to admit that any vagueness of intention can possibly be concealed under such manifest precision and minuteness of expression; nor can we believe that Dr. Pusey himself would have yielded to this suggestion, except under the extreme urgency of the position in which he is placed by his own arrangement.

Again, Dr. Pusey writes — " The date when those 490 years began is described in words which leave no large or uncertain margin, *from the going forth of a commandment to restore and rebuild Jerusalem unto Messiah the Prince.*"* Why does he omit the words which immediately follow, — " *shall be seven weeks, and threescore and two weeks,*" that is, exactly 483, *not* 490 years? The confusion thus introduced is extreme. For having already shown that the periods of sixty-nine weeks, and of seventy weeks, must necessarily have ended together with the same event, viz., the " anointing of an All-Holy," and the coming of " one Anointed," at the *end* of the seventieth week, he is here endeavouring to show how the same periods of sixty-nine, and seventy weeks, must also have begun at the same point, viz., " the going forth of the commandment to restore and rebuild Jerusalem," and how the anointing of Messiah, the All-Holy, took place not at the end of the seventieth, but of the sixty-ninth week : two different propositions which cannot coincide.

* P. 165.

The fact is, that Dr. Pusey, being unable to show
how the successive " periods of 49, 434, and 3½ years
twice repeated," in all 490 years, ended with the
anointing of an All-Holy, which is what he sets out
to prove, proposes to combine this arrangement, correct in principle, as pointing out the final event which
should mark the 490th year, though not so fulfilled,
with another arrangement, said indeed to have been
fulfilled, though wholly incorrect in principle, which
places the anointing at the end of 49, and 434 years,
and the termination of the whole period at the end
of a further term of 3½ years, once only fulfilled,
"not twice repeated," in all 486½ years : thus
making the redundancy of years in one scheme
supply the deficiency of years in the other : and in
the fulness of his conviction that the prophecy must
in some way have been fulfilled, he allows himself to
describe and hold up this combination of inconsist-
encies for admiration, as " completeness of symme-
try" and " complicated harmony." *   If it were lawful
to interpret the words " anointed " and " anointing "
in two different senses in the same prophecy, that is
to say, by ending the sixty-nine weeks with the
anointing of Messiah to the priesthood, as Dr. Pusey
proposes, and by ending the seventy weeks by
anointing Messiah to the burial, as proposed by Dr.
Prideaux, a certain sort of complicated harmony
might indeed thus be produced, by the combination
of two different modes of interpretation.   But any such

* P. 188.

complication is distinctly forbidden by the precise
words of the prophecy, "unto Messiah the Prince,"
not "unto Messiah the Priest;" from which it is clear
that "to anoint" has reference, neither to the priesthood or ministry, nor to the burial or sacrifice of
Messiah, but distinctly, and undeniably, to His *birth*
as "Prince" of the house of David, and to His
anointing to the kingdom, and that only.

Thus far regarding Dr. Pusey's exposition of the
main period of 490 years. Can anything, we ask, be
more confused and indistinct? We now proceed to
consider how the minor periods of seven, sixty-two,
and one week, are treated by him.

Dr. Pusey places the commencement of the
7 + 62, or sixty-nine weeks, that is, of the period of
483 years, "unto Messiah," in the year B.C. 458–7,
or 457–6, about the seventh year of the reign of
Artaxerxes Longimanus, when Ezra is said to have
received his commission to re-establish at Jerusalem
the laws and institutions of the Jews; and ends this
period with the baptism of our Lord in A.D. 26, and
the whole period of seventy weeks in A. D. 33. This
arrangement, however, is clearly inadmissible, because
it places the baptism of Christ in the thirteenth year
of Tiberius, and thereby sets at nought the exact record of St. Luke, who fixes the baptism in the fifteenth
year, and thus puts an end to this interpretation.
Neither the beginning nor the ending of this period
of 483 years can be satisfactorily accounted for by
this arrangement. For if our Lord was baptized in
the fifteenth year of Tiberius, A.D. 28, which few

would now be disposed to deny, then was the seventh
year of Artaxerxes too early for the beginning.   If
the seventh of Artaxerxes was the beginning, then
was the ending, A.D. 28, out of time.   So that neither the period of 490 years, nor that of 483, is
capable of any secure or satisfactory solution, nor
do the two periods terminate, as they ought, and
as Dr. Pusey has determined, at the same point of
time.

Again, Dr. Pusey places the crucifixion in A.D.
29, and thus is in difficulty concerning the surplus
of three years and a half after the death of Christ,
which, according to his view, yet remain to complete
the seventieth week in A.D. 33 : while the fact of the
existence of this surplus distinctly nullifies his leading principle, that the " seventy weeks," and also the
sixty-nine weeks, terminate with the anointing of
an All-Holy, that is to say, either with the birth,
ministry, or death of Christ.

Dr. Pusey well observes,* " Every word in this
condensed prophecy has its place and meaning, and
the division (7 + 62) would be unmeaning, unless
something were assigned to this first portion.   The
text does assign it.   It says, ' The street shall be
built again, and the wall,' and that " in troublous
times."   Nevertheless, he is so entirely at a loss to
show how the street and the wall of Jerusalem were
built at the termination of this first portion of " seven
weeks," or 49 years,—a most significant period in Jew-

* P. 172.

ish reckoning, and one which to the ear of every Jew
would naturally recall the remembrance of the period
of Jubilee, within which we know that the whole
series of institutions in the Jewish Church, now about
to be restored, were appointed to run their course,—
that he is induced to say, " De minimis non curat
lex." " When the whole distance is spanned over, it
matters not whether we can make out some lesser
details."* Few, we think, will be disposed to rest
content with such a mode of dealing with this most
significant period. He does, indeed, endeavour
vaguely to account for it, by inferring that Ezra
and Nehemiah may have consumed upwards of forty-
five years in restoring the Jewish polity, supposed to
be figuratively referred to in the prophecy by the
expression, building of the " street " and the " wall."
But the only argument brought forward in support
even of this opinion, and for thus lengthening the
duration of Nehemiah's administration, is, what
would appear to be a perversion of the words of Nehemiah. For he assumes that in Nehem. xiii. 28,
Joiada, the son of Eliashib, not Eliashib himself, is
there spoken of as high-priest,† a point which we
believe to be untenable, and without which his
reckoning falls to the ground. The prophecy,
as usual, is distinct enough, and plainly points to

---

* P. 171.

† " And one of the sons of Joiada, the son of Eliashib, the
high-priest, was son-in-law to Sanballat." If the title high-
priest does not here apply to Eliashib, it must apply to the son of
Joiada, not to Joiada himself.

the building of "the wall" of Jerusalem as
marking the completion of the period.   Dr. Pusey's
interpretation again rests upon forced and uncertain
grounds.

Another fatal objection to Dr. Pusey's exposition,
in our opinion, as also to most modern interpretations, with one great exception, that of Sir Isaac
Newton, is, that the period of "seven weeks" cannot
be made to tally with so many Sabbatical weeks, ending with a Jubilee, as reckoned at Jerusalem after
the return from captivity.   It is undoubtedly true
that Ezra restored the computation and observance
of the Sabbatical years, and that the forty-ninth
year, counted from his supposed arrival at Jerusalem
in autumn, B.C. 458, would end in autumn 408, at
the end of a Sabbatical year.   But no one can point
out any event which took place in that year to mark
a year of Jubilee ; while, on the other hand, we
know that the marking of the boundaries of the
walls of walled cities was one of the express duties
to be performed in the year of Jubilee;* as was also
the revision of the genealogies, as stated by Michaelis
and Ewald,† both which duties were undertaken by
Nehemiah at the time of the dedication of the wall
of Jerusalem.   Dr. Prideaux openly declares his inability to produce correspondence between the weeks

---

* *Seder Olam Rabba*, ch. xxx.   Dwelling-houses within the
walls, and beyond the walls, were differently treated in the year
of Jubilee.   (Levit. xxv. 29, 30.)   Therefore the boundaries had
to be ascertained at the end of every forty-nine years.

† Smith's *Dict.*, note on word "Jubilee."

of Daniel and the Sabbatical years and Jubilees of
the Jews, and therefore pronounces the latter to be
"useless, because they help not to the explaining
anything either in the Holy Scriptures or the histories of the times" of which he treats.* He places
the death of Christ, and the causing of the sacrifice
and oblation to cease, at the conclusion of the last
week, instead of "in the midst of the (last) week."
Dr. Pusey, by arbitrarily placing the death of Christ
in A.D. 29, one year only after the true date of his
baptism, according to St. Luke, proposes to obviate
this difficulty, but thereby falls into one equally inadmissible, viz., of completing the events in sixty-
nine weeks and a half, instead of seventy weeks, and
of contradicting his principal authority. We submit
that no interpretation can be the true one which
does not conform to most, if not to all, of the following plain propositions :—

Daniel, ix. 1, 2.

In the first year of Darius, son of Ahasuerus, of the seed of
the Medes, what time he was made King over the realm of the
Chaldeans, in the first year of his reign, I, Daniel, understood
by books the number of the years whereof the word of the Lord
came to Jeremiah the prophet, that he would accomplish seventy
years in the desolations of Jerusalem.†

1. That the prophecy was delivered in the reign
of a king known to Daniel only by the title Darius.

2. That this Darius, called "son of Ahasuerus,"

* Prideaux's Connec. : Pref. p. xvi.

† "Would let pass seventy years over the ruins of Jerusalem."
—Dr. Benisch.

or Cyaxares, "of the seed of the Medes," may have
been son, or grandson, by birth, adoption, inheritance, ancestral descent in male or female line, son-
in-law,* or simply successor† to the throne of this
Median king.

3. That this Darius reigned over 120 provinces,
comprising "all people, nations, and languages,
which dwell in all the earth:" and was, therefore,
no subordinate king set over a limited portion of the
empire of some greater king. (Dan. vi. 1, 25.)

4. That the dominions of Darius were subject to
"the laws of the Medes and Persians;" and that he
"took the kingdom" of the Chaldeans, which included
that of David, when Babylon passed from the hands of
Belshazzar to the Persians (U-Pharsin). Dan. v. 25-31.

5. That the prophecy was delivered when Jerusalem had been *desolate* for nearly seventy years;
and therefore not earlier than the reign of Darius,
son of Hystaspes, who even on the supposition that
Jerusalem was destroyed as early as B.C. 588, was on
the throne in the seventieth year after the destruction and desolation of that city, and who, therefore,
unless two mighty kings bearing the same title reigned
at the same time, was the Darius known to Daniel.

6. That Darius was "about threescore and two
years old" when the prophecy was delivered; and
since Darius, son of Hystaspes, died at the age of
seventy-two,‡ it was delivered about ten years before

---

* 1 Sam. xxiv. 16.   † 1 Chron. iii. 16.

‡ Ctesiæ Frag.: Muller, p. 49.

his death, and not earlier therefore, according to any reckoning, than B.C. 495.

7. That the second year of Darius, son of Hystaspes, counted from "the time that he was made king over the realm of the Chaldeans," was a year of rest, and freedom from oppression throughout the land of Judea. (Zech. i. 11; Levit. xxv. 5; Isa. xiv. 7.*)

8. That it was not till this "second year," when Darius was about sixty-three years old, that the "*indignation*" against Jerusalem ceased (Zech. i. 1–12), and the words of reconciliation were uttered, "I am returned to Jerusalem with mercies: my house shall be built in it, saith the Lord of hosts, and a line shall be stretched forth on Jerusalem." (Zech. i. 16.)

9. That it was not, therefore, till after *seventy* years of "*desolation*," and *seventy* years of "*indignation*" against Jerusalem, had ceased, that the reckoning of seventy weeks of mercy on that city could have begun.

Verse 24.

Seventy weeks are determined upon thy people and thy holy city, to finish the transgression, and to make an end of sins, and to make reconciliation for iniquity, and to bring in everlasting righteousness, and to anoint a holy of holies.

10. That these "seventy weeks" are weeks of years, or seventy "Sabbaths of years," each ending

---

* "And it shall come to pass in the day that the Lord shall give thee rest from thy sorrow and thy fear, and the hard bondage wherein thou wast made to serve, that thou shalt take up this proverb against the king of Babylon, and say, How hath the oppressor ceased! the golden city ceased." . . . "The whole earth is at rest, and is quiet."

with a shemittah, or year of release, such as were
commanded to be observed by the Levitical law.
(Lev. xxv. 1–8 ; Deut. xv. 1.)

11. That the end of these seventy weeks is
marked by the anointing of "a holy of holies;"
that is, literally, of the most holy portion of the
sanctuary of the Jewish temple; but here applied
figuratively to the "Holy of Holies" of the Spiritual
Church of God, that is, to the most holy portion
of that spiritual temple "of which Jesus Christ is
the chief corner-stone," "in whom we also are
builded together as a habitation of God through the
Spirit" (Eph. ii. 20–22), to the Redeemer, the holy
one of Israel," (Isaiah, xlviii. 17.)

Verse 25.

Know, therefore, and understand, that from the going forth of
the commandment to restore and to build Jerusalem, unto Messiah,
the Prince, shall be seven weeks, and threescore and two weeks :
the street shall be built again, and the wall, even in troublous
times.

12. That this period of "seven weeks" represents a period of "seven Sabbaths of years," or
"forty and nine years," ending with a year of
Jubilee. (Lev. xxv. 8–9.) And also ending with
the dedication of the wall of Jerusalem.

13. That these "seven weeks, and threescore
and two weeks," end with the coming of "one
Anointed, a Prince:" and that this anointed Prince
is he who is before spoken of as the "Holy of
Holies" of Christ's spiritual temple.

14. That "to anoint," therefore, has reference

neither to the time of the burial, nor of the ministry
of the Anointed one, but expressly to the time of his
birth as Prince, and of his consecration to the kingdom of his father David.

15. That, if the "seventy weeks," and "the seven
and threescore and two weeks," both end together
in the birth of the Anointed, the remaining one week
must necessarily precede the "seven, and threescore
and two," thus, $1 + 7 + 62 = 70$.

16. That if the "threescore and two weeks" end
with the "seventy," all that is spoken of as occurring "after threescore and two weeks," must necessarily be excluded from what is comprised within
the seventy.

17. That the "commandment to restore and to
build Jerusalem" has reference to "the commandment of Cyrus," of whom it was foretold that he
should "say to Jerusalem, Thou shalt be built, and
to the temple, Thy foundation shall be laid," (Isaiah,
xliv. 28), which commandment was recovered and
reissued, and first put in execution, in the fourth,
fifth, or sixth year of Darius, when Arta-Xerxes
had been associated on the throne with Darius
(Ezra, vi. 14; Herodotus, vii. 1-4).

18. That Jesus of Nazareth, "of the house and
lineage of David," was born about thirty years
before the fifteenth year of Tiberius, and therefore
towards the end of the year B.C. 3, or beginning
of the year B.C. 2.

Verse 26.

And after threescore and two weeks Messiah (the Prince)

shall be cut off, and (the kingdom shall be) not to him :* and the people of the prince that shall come shall destroy the city and the sanctuary, and the end thereof shall be with a flood, and unto the end of the war desolations are determined.

19. That these words refer to the death of Messiah the Prince, the invasion of Judea by Vespasian and Titus, the destruction of the city and temple of Jerusalem, and the continuation of the war till the whole land should become desolate. (Mark, xiii. 14.)

Verse 27.

And he shall confirm the covenant with many for one week, and in the midst of the week he shall cause the sacrifice and the oblation to cease, and for the overspreading of abominations he shall make it desolate, even until the consummation, and that determined shall be poured upon the desolate.

20. That the "covenant" here confirmed "with many" is the two-fold covenant made with Abraham:—1st. That in his seed, that is, in Messiah, "shall all the nations of the earth be blessed." 2nd. That to Abraham and his seed after him shall be given all the land of Canaan as "an everlasting possession." (Gen. xxii. 18; xvii. 7, 8.) The "covenant and mercy," for the fulfilment of which Daniel prayed. (Dan. ix. 4; Luke, i. 72, 73.)

21. That, "for one week," has reference, figuratively, to the Sabbatical week, A.D. 27–34, or seven years of covenant, from the preaching of the kingdom of the Messiah by John to the Jews, until the calling of the Gentiles in Cornelius: literally, to the Sabbatical week, A.D. 65–72, or seven years of

* "And there is none to help him."—Dr. Benisch.

covenant, during which the Jews partially regained possession of the promised land of Canaan, and resisted the power of the Romans.

22. That the "causing of the sacrifice and oblation to cease," "in the midst of the week," has reference, figuratively, to the death of Messiah, in A.D. 32: literally, to the ceasing of the morning and evening sacrifice and oblation, on the seventeenth of Panemus, or Tamuz, A.D. 70. (Jos. Bell. Jud. l. vi. c. 2.)

23. That, "until the consummation," has reference to the time "when he shall have accomplished to scatter the power of the holy people," and to the time when Jerusalem shall cease to be trodden down by the Gentiles. (Dan. xii. 7; Luke, xxi. 24–27).

Now, if the foregoing propositions have been fairly deduced from the words of Daniel and elsewhere, then is it clear, that there is scarcely one single principle of interpretation which has not either been violated, or overlooked, in Dr. Pusey's exposition. 1. The Darius of Daniel is identified by him either with Cyaxares, or Astyages, or with some yet unheard-of king. 2. The prophecy is supposed to have been delivered at the end of *fifty*, not of seventy years of "*desolation*," at Jerusalem. This period of desolation is spoken of as a period of "captivity,"* not of "*desolation;*" and the years of captivity are counted from a point eight years earlier than any captivity spoken of by Jeremiah or Eze-

---

* P. 162.

kiel. 3. Darius is supposed to be a mere viceroy
under Cyrus, not a king. 4. Dr. Pusey's Darius
cannot appropriate the words of Isa. xiv. 3–7, concerning the fall of Babylon, because the prophet
Zechariah has applied them to the times of Darius,
son of Hystaspes, i. 11. 5. The age of Darius, one
of the special marks of time recorded by Daniel for
our guidance, is not in any way brought to bear on
the prophecy. 6. Darius is assumed to have been a
Mede, and not a Persian. 7. The events of the
prophecy are comprehended within sixty-nine weeks
and a half, instead of seventy. 8. The three periods
comprised within the seventy weeks are placed in the
order of $7 + 62 + 1 = 70$: instead of $1 + 7 + 62 = 70$.
9. The events spoken of as occurring *after* this
last period of sixty-two weeks, are supposed to
have taken place *before* the expiration of that
period. 10. The baptism of Christ is placed two
years earlier than it is fixed by St. Luke. 11.
"Seventy weeks" counted backwards from the fifteenth of Tiberius are not Sabbatical weeks. 12. The
"seven weeks" cannot be made to coincide with a
period of Jubilee, nor to end with the completion
of the wall of Jerusalem. 13. "Unto Messiah the
Prince" is made to signify unto Messiah the Priest.
14. "The commandment to restore and to build
Jerusalem" is not fulfilled by the restoration of the
literal "street" and "wall," nor referable to the
decree of Cyrus, who commanded the restoration of
the literal holy city; but to a decree of Artaxerxes,
which is said to have been fulfilled in a figurative

building of the street and wall, that is, in the restoration of the Jewish polity in Judea.

Thus are the distinctness and precision of Daniel's words departed from almost at every step, in this, the most recent of Christian interpretations : and such is the approved mode of interpretation entertained by one of the most esteemed and eminent of Christian writers of the present day, concerning a prophecy upon which the momentous doctrine of the Messiahship of Jesus of Nazareth is chiefly founded. The Jew has had too much ground for observing, " that those who will examine the books of the Nazarenes will find, that there is nothing clearly known amongst them concerning either the beginning or the ending of the weeks,— one placing them here, another there : and that there is no agreement between them as to the date of the crucifixion of Jesus of Nazareth."*

But if it is incumbent upon Christians to make plain before the world the manner in which they consider that this remarkable prophecy has been fulfilled in the person of Jesus of Nazareth, whom they worship as the Messiah here foretold,—in which it must be admitted that they have not yet been successful, except in the eyes of willing believers,—how much more is it imperative upon " God's holy people," to whom this divine oracle was originally delivered, whose faith and hope is centred in the doctrine of a Messiah, to tell us plainly in

* *Munimen Fidei* of Rab. Isaac, p. 342.

what rational way, and by whom, they conceive
that the coming and cutting off of "One Anointed
a Prince," at the expiration of 490 years after the
delivery of this heavenly message to Daniel, can
have been accomplished, if not in the person of
Him who was born, as we shall see, at the very
time appointed, of the seed of Abraham, of the
house and lineage of David, concerning whom, at
His birth, it was declared, "The Lord God shall
give unto Him the throne of His father David,"* of
whom, during His ministry, the officers of the chief
priests and Pharisees testified, "Never man spake
like this man,"† and who, at the close of a pure and
spotless life, condemned to die, when solemnly ad-
jured by the high-priest to declare whether He were
"the Christ the Son of God," replied "*Thou hast
said.* Nevertheless, I say unto you, Hereafter shall
ye see the Son of Man sitting at the right hand of
Power, and coming in the clouds of heaven."   If
they cannot explain when, and by whom, this prophecy has been accomplished, then we would inquire what is the present state of Israel's belief as
regards these words of Daniel.   To whom do they
apply?   The time of his appearance is long past.
Let us examine a few of the interpretations which
have been put forth by the Jews themselves in contrast with those of Christian expositors, with the
view either of explaining or of avoiding the force of
the prediction.

In the "Seder Olam Rabba," one of their oldest

* Luke, i. 32.   † John, vii. 45–46.

comments, we read :—" The seven weeks are those
which they passed in exile until they went up," that
is, to Jerusalem. " The sixty-two weeks are those
in which they remained in the land of Israel after
their return. But, one week, is that in which they
were partly in the land, and partly out of the land.''

Again, we read : —" Rabbi Jose teaches us that
the seventy weeks are to be reckoned from the
destruction of the first temple to that of the latter
one by the Romans. That is to say, seventy years
during which it remained broken down and destroyed, and 420 during which it stood when rebuilt. But what do you mean by seventy weeks,
when seventy years of the destruction had already
been accomplished? It may be truly said that that
decree had been ordained seventy years before."*

The explanation of David Gantz is to the same
effect. For, after referring to the passage in Isaiah,
where Cyrus is spoken of as Messiah, or Anointed :
" Thus saith the Lord to his Messiah Cyrus," &c.
he adds ; "In the first year of Cyrus the Lord
stirred up his spirit to build the house of his sanctuary ; and Zerubbabel and the captivity went up
to Jerusalem. But when the building ceased to
go on, Daniel, amazed and perplexed, says, ' I,
Daniel, knew by books the number of the years
whereof the word of the Lord came to Jeremiah
the prophet, that he would accomplish seventy
years in the desolations of Jerusalem.' The angel
replies to him, ' Seventy sevens are cut out upon

* " Seder Olam Rabba," chap. xxviii.

thy people,' &c., from which we learn, that the seventy years were to be computed from the captivity of Zedekiah, and the destruction of the temple, not from the captivity of Daniel." *

Rabbi Isaac, son of Abraham, in an able treatise against Christianity, dwells much and forcibly upon the future state of calm and peacefulness, which, according to Isaiah and other prophets, shall mark the time of the kingdom of Messiah—when "the wolf shall lie down with the lamb," and when " the earth shall be full of the knowledge of the Lord as the waters cover the sea ;"† and contrasting this state of peace and happiness with the strifes and contentions which have existed, now for 1800 years, since the coming of Jesus of Nazareth, who declared that He came " not to send peace, but a sword,"‡— strongly urges that Jesus therefore cannot be the Messiah. He accordingly thus explains away the weeks of Daniel,—" Seventy weeks are 490 years, and this is the number of years which elapsed between the destruction of the first temple and the destruction of the second. Thus seventy years were fulfilled by the people in captivity at Babylon, and during 420 years the second temple was standing." §

Again, " The first period of seven weeks, or 49 years, was fulfilled from the desolation of the first temple to the beginning of the building of the second, which took place in the first year of Cyrus, king of Persia. For Cyrus was called anointed prince, where Esaias, chap. xlv., writes, ' Thus saith

* David Gantz, "Zemach David," p. 52.   † Isa. ii. 4; xi. 9.
‡ Matt. x. 34.   § Rabbi Isaac's " Munimen Fidei," ch. xlii. p. 333.

the Lord to his anointed Cyrus,'—'He shall build the city,'" &c.*

David Levi, in his letters to Dr. Priestly, p. 68, makes Cyrus the Messiah, unto whom he considers that there should be reckoned "seven weeks." The Masoretic punctuation also, of Dan. ix. 25, places the principal stop after the words "seven weeks," with a view no doubt to the same interpretation.

Such has been the mode of interpretation propounded by learned and devout Jews of days gone by. These interpretations are one and the same, more or less fully expressed. Our Jewish brethren, it appears, have been willing, at least in former days, to accept Cyrus, king of Persia, the heathen prince, as that "Anointed One," whose coming and cutting off holds so conspicuous a place in the sublime prophecies of Daniel. They have persuaded themselves to believe, that the seventy weeks of mercy on the holy city were fulfilled between the destruction of the first and second temple; and would have us to agree with them, that the second temple, built by the hands of Zerubbabel, in the days of Darius, stood for exactly 420 years, till its final destruction by Titus. Even the learned Maimonides has fallen into these untenable opinions.†

It would be waste of time to enter on a refutation of opinions, which must now be looked upon merely as remnants of a dark age of literature, and which are probably regarded by Jews themselves as obsolete. No enlightened Jew of

---

* Rabbi Isaac's "Munimen Fidei," chap xliii. p. 338.
† Maimonides "de Shemitha et Jubileo," cap. x.

the present day, we presume, will uphold such
plainly erroneous reckoning.   He is too well instructed in history to deny that 490 years, counted
from the destruction of Jerusalem by the Babylonians, must have ended many more than a hundred
years before the destruction of the holy city by the
Romans, and too well exercised in judgment to
maintain, that the period marked out by Daniel as
to elapse "From the going forth of the commandment to *restore* and to *build* Jerusalem, unto Messiah the Prince," can have begun with the going
forth of the commandment of Nebuchadnezzar to
burn and to *destroy* that city, or have ended with
the decree of Cyrus to restore and to build the city,
with which apparently it should have commenced.

Thus, then, both Jew and Christian, though de-
voutly earnest in their belief in the Divine revelations of Holy Scripture, and firm in their conviction
that this special prophecy of the " seventy weeks "
has been, and must have been, in some way fulfilled before their eyes in days long past, are yet
unable, either of them, to satisfy the other of the
time or mode of its accomplishment.   While every
impartial inquirer, looking on upon the controversy,
is compelled to admit, that both Jew and Christian,
are equally at fault in their mode of reckoning of
ancient time, that both have departed much from
the strict words of the prophecy in their proposed
interpretations, and that, if such are the only explanations which can be offered, the prophecy apparently has never been fulfilled.

How remarkable and interesting is the attitude
of these two steadfast, earnest "witnesses" of God,
now that the days of ignorance are past, standing
forward in the light of day and testifying in truth
and sincerity of heart concerning this their common
article of faith—their belief in a Messiah.   There
lies the humble and devoted Christian, prostrate in
love and adoration at the feet of his crucified Lord,
filled with the conviction that in Him, and Him
alone, is to be found that promised offspring of the
woman, that "rod out of the stem of Jesse," on
whom the Spirit of the Lord should rest,* that seed
of Abraham, by and through whom all the nations
of the earth are, and shall be, blessed.   And there
erect beside him stands unmoved the firm and steadfast Jew, refusing to recognise in Him thus dying
on the cross, one single feature of that glorious
Messiah promised to him and his forefathers; acknowledging no trace of fulfilment through Jesus
of Nazareth of that covenant with Abraham, that
his seed should possess the land of Canaan as an
everlasting possession, or of that covenant with
David, "There shall not fail thee a man in my
sight to sit on the throne of Israel:"† no similitude, during 1800 long, weary years of insult and
oppression, of those days of peace and rest which
surely mark the time of the kingdom of Messiah :
no sign or symptom of the mode in which the words
of the holy Simeon shall be accomplished, that this

---

* Isaiah, xi. 1.   † 1 Kings, viii. 25.

Jesus of Nazareth, who has indeed, according to
the promise, been a Light to lighten the Gentiles,
shall yet also be the glory of God's people Israel.
Again, we change the scene, and behold the Priests
and Pharisees of Christ's Gentile church, arrayed
in robes, absorbed in rites, each in his little synagogue putting on the air of God's high-priest, pointing with scorn to the temple, which is cast down,
to Jerusalem, which is trodden under foot, to sacrifices which have ceased, to the ceremonial law
which is extinct, and loudly proclaiming that the
sons of Abraham, though once the loved and chosen
of God, are now cast off for ever for their unbelief; and that, should they ever hereafter acquire
footing in the land of promise, it will probably be
only as "preparing the way of Anti-Christ"* on
earth. While the Jew, on the other hand, bowed
down with grief and shame, smites on his breast
saying, "God be merciful to me a sinner;" and
weeping amid the stones of Zion, points to the
Word of God, which cannot lie, and says, that
temple shall be restored on a scale exceeding what
has ever yet been seen;† to the word of Jesus

* Pusey's "Daniel," p. 189.
† Ezek. xl.; Tobit, xiv. 5. "For I surely believe those
things which Jonas the prophet spake, That Jerusalem shall be
desolate, and the house of God in it shall be burned, and shall be
desolate in it for a time; and that again God will have mercy on
them and bring them again into the land, where they shall build
a temple, but not like to the first, until the time of that age be
fulfilled; and afterward they shall return from all places of their
captivity, and build up Jerusalem gloriously, and the house of
God shall be built in it for ever."

Himself, "Jerusalem shall be trodden down of the Gentiles," (but only) "until the times of the Gentiles be fulfilled;" to the holy prophet, who, when the land shall be divided again for inheritance, speaks of the burnt-offerings, and meat-offerings, and peace-offerings, which the Prince shall give to make reconciliation for the house of Israel ;* to the going up, from year to year, of every one that is left of all the nations which came against Jerusalem, "to worship the King, the Lord of Hosts, and to keep the feast of tabernacles ;"† and still once more to the emphatic words of Jeremiah—"If my covenant be not with day and night, and if I have not appointed the ordinances of heaven and earth, then will I cast away the seed of Jacob, and David my servant, so that I will not take any of his seed to be rulers of the seed of Abraham, Isaac, and Jacob."‡ Again, he looks around at Christianity as exemplified in Christendom, and points to the doctrines and practices of that chief and prominent body of professing Christians, who in the eyes of their protesting brethren are chargeable with superstition and idolatry, and believing in his heart that their teaching and practice are deeply displeasing in the sight of God, and conscious of his mission, declares with boldness that "the heathenish elements in Christianty are destined to be eliminated through Judaism, to be cast off, and buried in the sea of oblivion for ever."§

* Ezek. xlv. 17.   † Zech. xiv. 16.   ‡ Jer. xxxiii. 25, 26.
§ "Question at issue between Judaism and Christianity," by Dr. Benisch, p. 5.

The Christian appeals with pride and triumph to the superior purity and excellence of the precepts of Jesus, his Messiah, as compared with those of Moses. The Jew, hard pressed, admits their excellence and purity, but only as refinements upon what had been already delivered to Moses and the prophets, and in reply dwells with keenness upon the impracticable nature of these precepts, pronouncing that any society attempting literally to act up to them in spirit and in truth could not long be self-maintained. This modern weapon of Judaism against Christianity is too curious and remarkable to be passed over without observation. We produce it in the words of the learned and estimable Jew before quoted. Speaking of a perfect Christian he writes :—

"As a faithful disciple of Jesus he would, were he born to riches, give them all to the poor, reduce himself to beggary, deprive himself of all the influence and advantages which wealth bestows, would promote pauperism, and assist in bringing on mankind all those evils which social economy so clearly proves to be the consequence of mendicancy. Were he a magistrate or judge on the bench, he would, instead of pronouncing sentence on the culprit, declare, 'let him that is guiltless cast the first stone,' and permit the offender to escape, with a paternal admonition to sin no more. Were he a prime minister, he would tamely submit to an insult from a foreign power rather than vindicate the honour of his country by severe measures, since a perfect Christian is not allowed to resent harsh terms, and is only to employ gentle words. Were he a general, he would throw away the sword before the battle, as the effusion of blood does not become a soldier of the Prince of Peace. Were he a wayfarer, he would have to present his inner garment to the robbers just stripping him of the outer one. Were he assailed, he would have humbly to ask the ruffian for an additional blow on the cheek spared the infliction. Is it necessary to dilate upon the state of a society consisting of such perfect Christians ? The Italian proverb, that he that makes himself a lamb will be devoured by the wolf, would soon be exemplified."*

Now it cannot be said with justice to our Jewish brethren, that truth lies only on one side of this picture. We are compelled to believe with them that the glorious Messiah of the prophets has not yet appeared in glory, and that the promised peace and happiness of his kingdom have not yet been established upon earth. And yet, consistently with this admission, we believe, and ask our Jewish brother to believe, that " this same Jesus which was taken up from us into heaven, shall so come in like manner as He was seen to go into heaven," and that " like a Son of Man " He shall be seen hereafter " coming in the clouds of heaven," with power and great glory to establish that kingdom for which our brother so long and patiently has waited. We believe that the Jew has too truly pointed out the Pagan element which lurks in the religion of Christendom, though not in Christianity, and that Christianity has yet to be relieved from these lingering corruptions through Judaism in the West, as it was relieved from similar corruptions by Mahommedanism in the East. We agree with him that the transcendent purity of Christ's precepts are incompatible with the present government of the kingdoms of this world, and also that they are, and

* " Christianity and Judaism," p. 14.

can be, practised only by the few. But we also
remember the words of Christ, " My kingdom now
is not of this world;" my precepts now are not
acceptable to "the children of the kingdom," who
are cast out.* The code of laws which issued
from Mount Sinai, and which by means of Christianity has been effectually spread over and enforced
in all quarters of the world, is yet but too well
adapted to the corrupt and degraded state of man ;
yet, nevertheless, no argument in reason can be
drawn from thence, that the purity and refinement of
the religion of Jesus is not that of the kingdom of
Messiah. Far be it from the "holy people," chosen
from amongst the nations of the world to be a
nation of pure and holy priests, to say to Him that
calls them, Thy precepts are too pure and holy.
What is the nature of the kingdom for which our
brethren seek ? Is it not a kingdom of peace and
perfect love ? Are we not told that in that kingdom the swords are ploughshares, spears are prun-
ing-hooks ; that "they shall neither hurt nor destroy
in all my holy mountain?" Are not, then, the precepts
of Jesus the very essence and constitution of such
a kingdom as this ? Shall they not prevail when
"the kingdom under the whole heaven shall be
given to the saints of the Most High"? Now the
Lord Jesus declared expressly that He was sent
unto "the lost sheep of the house of Israel," to
preach "the gospel of the kingdom of God," saying,

* Matt. viii. 12.

"The kingdom of heaven is at hand." Will Israel, then, be content to resign the holy office to which she has been called, and for which apparently she is still preserved, when now the onward progress of mankind has again commenced its rapid course, and seems to call for progress also in approach toward God? Yea, rather, let her wake to a sense of her own proud position, let her deck herself in the garments of the loved and chosen bride, and, casting herself down in the spirit of grace and supplication, confess, that the kingdom of the Messiah whom she seeks is indeed a kingdom of "love, joy, peace, long-suffering, gentleness, goodness, faith, meekness, temperance;"* that such a kingdom could have been announced and preached only by Messiah Himself, and that, though such precepts are yet far removed above the practice of the millions of this earth, they are still within the reach and practice of the select and holy few to whom the kingdom shall be given; when the Son of Man, if there be truth in His words, shall again "drink of the fruit of the vine" with His disciples, ruling over the twelve tribes of Israel, when many "shall sit down with Abraham, and Isaac, and Jacob, in the kingdom of heaven," and when, through the medium of "the children of the kingdom" and the example of his "holy ones," the whole race of mankind shall gradually be brought into union with their Maker, and become "the sons of God." Once, then, we submit to our brethren, has Messiah

* Gal. v. 22.

come in humility to His own, to be rejected ; once again, we trust, He shall come to reign *with them* in glory. " Rejoice greatly, O daughter of Zion ; shout, O daughter of Jerusalem ; behold, thy King cometh unto thee : He is just, and having salvation; lowly, and riding upon an ass, and upon a colt, the foal of an ass."*

Let Israel hearken to the deep pathetic words of Him who, seated thus upon the ass, and coming towards Jerusalem amid the acclamations of the multitude, " when he beheld the city, wept over it, saying, If thou hadst known, even thou, at least in this thy day, the things which belong unto thy peace! but now they are hid from thine eyes. For the days shall come upon thee, that thine enemies shall cast a trench about thee, and compass thee round, and keep thee in on every side, and shall lay thee even with the ground, and thy children within thee; and they shall not leave in thee one stone upon another; because thou knewest not the time of thy

---

* Zech. ix. 9. We read in the Talmud concerning this passage (Talm. Bab. Sanhedrin, fol. 98, col. 1), " R. Joshua, the son of Levi, objects that it is written in one place, ' Behold, one like a son of man came with the clouds of heaven ;' but in another place it is written, 'lowly and riding upon an ass.' The solution is, if they be righteous, He shall come with the clouds of heaven. If they be not righteous, He shall come lowly and upon an ass." Saadiah Gaon, interpreting the words of Daniel, " One like a Son of Man," &c., says, " This is the Messiah our righteousness. But is it not written of the Messiah, 'Lowly, and riding upon an ass?' Yes, but this shows that He will come in humility, and not in pride upon horses.'—Quoted in Dr. M'Caul's translation of David Kimchi's " Commentary on Zechariah," p. 93.

visitation."*   Let her also hearken to His words of promise, " Verily I say unto you, ye shall not see me, until the time come, when ye shall say, Blessed is he that cometh in the name of the Lord."†

And when the Son of Man shall thus appear again in glory with his saints, and when "his feet shall stand in that day on the Mount of Olives,"‡ we would ask those who look malignantly upon any future attempt of the "holy people" to regain possession of their land, as leading to and preparing the way for Anti-Christ, of whom does the prophet speak at the time of this second coming—of Jews, or of Gentiles—when he says in the name of the Lord, " I will pour upon *the inhabitants of Jerusalem* the spirit of grace and supplication, and they shall look upon me whom they have pierced?"   Of whom is that "third part" composed, of Jews, or of Gentiles, of which it is said, " They shall call upon my name, and I will hear them; I will say, It is my people; and they shall say, The Lord is my God?"§   If not of Gentiles, but of Jews, why this jealous feeling concerning their restoration to their own land?   Does it not savour of the spirit of Anti-Christ himself, to entertain so bitter enmity against those chosen ones of whom it is thus declared that they shall become again the people of the Lord, and that indeed in Jerusalem itself?||

We now pass on to another earnest class of

---

* Luke, xix. 41–44.   † Luke, xiii. 35.
‡ Zech. xiv. 4.   § Zech. xii. 10; xiii. 9.
|| Zech. xii. 6.

interpreters of the book of Daniel — those who would allow of no special providence of the Creator over the affairs of this world; who consider that all things in nature are regulated by fixed and undeviating laws, from which they cannot swerve; and that miracle, inspiration, and prophecy are, therefore, out of place, if not wholly inconsistent with a divine system of organisation. The plainness and precision of the prophecy of the " seventy weeks " is naturally a source of trouble to these philosophers. The words of prophecy may in some cases be ingeniously explained away and declared to be no prophecy at all : it may be alleged in others that opportunity has been open to the prophet of retouching his own words, and of adapting them more pointedly to events after they have come to pass : and, again, it may be contended that certain historical parts of Scripture have been so disarranged and misplaced as to bear the appearance of prophecy, which does not really belong to them. No such allegations, however, are applicable to this one central and most momentous prophecy of all contained in Scripture. No one ventures to deny that the writer of the words of this prophecy, whether he be Daniel or not, existed more than a century and a half before the birth of Christ; no one calls in question, to any material effect, the integrity of the text; and no one can fail to admit the plainness, precision, and freedom from ambiguity of all its expressions.

If, then, the words of Daniel can be shown to have reference to, and to have been fulfilled, with

unmistakable exactness, in connexion with the person of that Being who for 1800 years past has been
looked upon by millions as the "Anointed One"
there spoken of, so signal an instance of inspiration
and of prophecy will have been exhibited, as to set
aside the philosophy of these writers, as inconsistent
with fact, and to remove for ever this stumbling-
block of their philosophy away from the path of
the inquiring believer.   Great efforts, therefore, are
made by these critics, and we believe in perfect sincerity, to explain how the writer of this prophecy
must have framed it rather with reference to past
history than to future events, and how, in fact, he
must have lived even in the time of the events
which he professes to foretell.   The efforts of these
writers, as we have seen, are fruitless, in this respect,
as regards the prophecy of the great image.   But as
regards the prophecy of the " seventy weeks," the result arrived at is looked upon by them as one of the
most signal triumphs of modern criticism ; and it is
now declared to be " clear beyond fair doubt that
the period of ' weeks ' ended with Antiochus Epiphanes."*   In a recent publication,† Dr. Williams
claims a candid hearing for a writer who has undertaken to place this view of the subject in a clear and
intelligible light.   We rejoice to see that the writer
thus put forward, Mr. Desprez, is not only a scholar,
but one who has given much thought to the subject

---

* "Essays and Reviews," p. 69.
† Introduction to Philip S. Desprez' work on Daniel, p. xlii.

and that he has expressed himself clearly, temperately, and apparently with sincerity, in all that he has advanced.

Dr. Pusey has with much labour and fidelity examined the various expositions of the German section of these interpreters, and any one anxious to enter fully into their arguments will do well to consult his work.   We propose to lay before the reader the results arrived at, rather than the reasonings of this class of critics.   Their interpretations in fact resolve themselves, as we shall presently show, into three very distinct prophetic enigmas, or cabalistic formulæ, by which seven times seventy, or 490 years, may by some mysterious process be comprehended within, either 429, or 441, or 424 years.

Mr. Desprez's work, however, which treats the subject in a popular manner for English readers, requires somewhat more examination.   He has had the benefit of the ideas of those who have gone before him in this line of interpretation, and has embodied clearly and distinctly what appears to be most tenable in all that they have advanced.   The words of Daniel we have seen present to us several very distinct ideas :—

1st. A command to restore and to build Jerusalem, from which certain weeks of years are to be computed.

2nd. The appearance of one anointed a prince.

3rd. The cutting off or death of this prince.

4th. The destruction of the city and sanctuary of Jerusalem.

G

5th. The ceasing of the sacrifice and oblation in the temple.

6th. The overspreading of abominations causing it to be made desolate.

7th. The anointing of "a holy of holies" at the end of certain weeks.

8th. The fulfilment of these various events at certain epochs in a then well-understood cycle of Sabbatical years.

Now the book of Maccabees records a remarkable persecution of the Jews in the days of Antiochus Epiphanes, whose reign lasted from B.C. 175 to 164, during which the daily sacrifice and the oblation in the temple of Jerusalem was caused to cease, the altar was profaned for exactly three years, and "the abomination of desolation" was set up.* It informs us how Judas Maccabeus, an anointed prince, was slain in battle in the year B.C. 161; and how "Jerusalem lay void as a wilderness"— "the sanctuary also was trodden down, and aliens kept the stronghold : the heathen had their habitation in that place, and joy was taken from Jacob:" † and how again, at the end of three years, the sanctuary was cleansed from pollution, and the "holy of holies" re-anointed, or consecrated.

Here then are a series of remarkable events in Jewish history which strike Mr. Desprez, as they cannot fail to strike the mind of every candid reader acquainted with their history, as peculiarly applicable to the words of Dan. ix. 26, 27. So appli-

* 1 Macc. iii. 45.   † 1 Macc. i. 54.

cable, indeed, as to have induced some of the most
eminent biblical critics of the present day to look
upon them as the actual counterpart of Daniel's
words. It is observed also by these critics that the
eleventh or last chapter but one of the book, manifestly consists of a minute detail of historical
events, written in prophetic style, from the days of
Alexander down to the days of the Maccabees,
and that the writer, after giving an account of the
ceasing of the daily sacrifice at Jerusalem, the setting up in those days of " the abomination which
maketh desolate," and the destruction of the king
who had inflicted these evils on the Jews, there suddenly drops all detail, and goes off into events which,
after an interval of two thousand years, have certainly not even yet come to pass.

It is urged, with much critical justice, that this
eleventh chapter is unlike the style of prophecy
either in this or in any other book of Scripture, and
that, from the extreme minuteness of the detail, the
writer can only be supposed to have lived after, or
about, the time of Judas Maccabeus, when the events
occurred of which he speaks. But if these remarks
are just, they would seem at first sight to be decisive
of the character of the book. For, if the writer
of this chapter was the writer of the whole book, then
was the whole book merely an uninspired production
of the days of the Maccabees. This, then, is the inference of Mr. Desprez and of the whole of this class
of critics. The hero of Daniel's poem is declared
to be King Antiochus Epiphanes, and the events

of his reign are said to be found to run like a thread through the whole of this supposed prophetic book of Scripture.*

Nothing can be more plain and definite than this theory of interpretation, and it brings the question of the prophetic character, or otherwise, of the book of Daniel at once to issue. It involves, however, the necessity on the part of those who maintain it, to explain, at least with some degree of plausibility, how the several visions and narratives contained in the book can, in the mind of the writer, have been associated with the times and history of Antiochus and the Maccabees. Mr. Desprez seems to feel perfectly satisfied and at ease as regards this point. The chief substance, indeed, of his work is an attempt to point out modes of application and resemblance between the several chapters of Daniel and the times of Antiochus, which certainly would not have occurred to the mind of an ordinary reader, and his view of the subject is thus illustrated. Speaking of the dream of Nebuchadnezzar, chap. ii., he observes: "It is thought that the dream of Nebuchadnezzar is only one phase of analogous visions, moulded into its present shape with a view of enabling the writer to append an historico-prophetic interpretation, accommodated to the circumstances of the Maccabean period."† With regard to the scene on the plain of Dura, chap. iii., he says: "The coincidence between the scenes we have depicted, and the circumstances of the holy people,

* Desprez, p. 162.   † P. 38.

(in the days of Antiochus) is too obvious to need comment. A second Nebuchadnezzar had arisen in the person of Antiochus, whose religious intolerance declared itself in the attempt to coerce all those with whom he came in contact, to worship the gods of his own adoration. The dedication of the golden image on the plain of Dura, corresponds to the dedication of the temple of Jupiter Olympius,* and the compulsory worship of the three children to similar religious coercion in the village of Modin.† The destruction of the men who execute the king's command reappears in the slaughter by Mattathias of the king's commissioners; and the escape of Shadrach, Meshach, and Abednego, from the fiery furnace, in that of Mattathias and his sons in the mountains. The faithfulness of the martyrs in the age of Daniel is reproduced in the steadfastness of those of the days of Antiochus; and the reward of those who were ' promoted in the province of Babylon, exceeded by the promise of a better resurrection.'"‡ The madness of Nebuchadnezzar, chap. iv., is assimilated to the mad acts of Epiphanes, which had caused him to be called Epimanes, or madman: and is supposed to be brought forward by the writer with the view of drawing a parallel between the circumstances of the Babylonian and Syrian monarchs.§ Again, the scene in the banqueting-hall of Belshazzar, chap. v., leading to the interpretation of the handwriting on the wall, is viewed by Mr.

* 2 Macc. vi. 2.   † 1 Macc. ii. 15.
‡ P. 45.   § P. 54.

Desprez solely with reference to the impiety towards
the God of heaven then exhibited by the Babylonian king, who is thus forced into comparison with
Antiochus; and Mr. Desprez feels himself justified
in observing, that " from the comparison instituted
between these leaders of impiety, it will be seen that
their respective circumstances present a singular
conformity with each other ; the type fitting so
closely to its antitype, as to leave room for the
impression that the writer drew an imaginary Belshazzar in Antiochus."* The scene, of Daniel condemned by Darius to be devoured by lions, chap. vi.,
is touched upon with reference to the one single
point of contact between Darius and Antiochus, viz.—
the assumption to himself by each of the honours of
divinity. And the "little horn," of chap. vii., which
rises up amongst the *ten* kingdoms of the fourth
empire; and the " little horn," which stands up in
the latter days on the platform of the *four* kingdoms of the third empire, chap. viii., are both identified with Antiochus, notwithstanding the dissimi-
larity of the portraits—the one being portrayed as
mighty with his mouth, the other mighty with his
sword. " The portion of the book," adds Mr.
Desprez, " which may be called the biography of
Daniel, ends with this deliverance (of Daniel from
the lions), the remaining part being chiefly occupied
with an historico-prophetic narration of the events,
extending to the times of Antiochus Epiphanes.
And it is only when viewed in the light in which

* P. 67.

we have attempted to present the subject, that the former part of the book can be regarded in unity with the latter. Apart from the consideration that the history is illustrative of the prophetical portion, no sufficient reason can be given for the intermixture of personal biography and prophetic vision in a work purporting to be written by the same individual. But when it is perceived that the scenes on the plain of Dura and at Babylon prefigure those else-where enacted; that the idolatrous deifications of the monarchs of Babylon and Media reflect impieties of a subsequent age; that the deliverances of the ser-vants of God, who trusted in Him in old time, fore-shadow the triumphs of those saints who should in later days possess the kingdom; the unity is restored; the plan of the writer is seen to be consistent; and the prophetic vision resolves itself into one grand whole of absorbing interest, having for its object the suffering and rescue of the holy people."*

We have thus endeavoured to give a fair sketch and outline of Mr. Desprez's critical exegesis of the book of Daniel; which may also be taken as repre-senting the views in general of the sceptical class of critics. And we ask of every candid and unpre-judiced reader, can anything be more forced or fanci-ful than the whole series of comparisons, assump-tions, and reasonings here set forth? How much more natural is the view of those who treat each separate chapter in the light in which it is plainly and obviously presented to us by the writer. We

* P. 79.

absolutely deny that any one of these seven chapters,
excepting the last, bears any appearance of having
been written with an eye to events in the reign of
Antiochus. The prophecy of the great image, as
we have seen, reaches down to the time when "the
God of heaven shall set up a kingdom never to be
destroyed," a kingdom which "shall be given to
the people of the saints of the Most High, whose
kingdom is an everlasting kingdom," and reaches
therefore far beyond the wretched times of persecution under Antiochus, when the kingdom of the
holy people, so far from being set up, was nearly
destroyed. The deliverance of the "three children" from the furnace, has no more resemblance
to anything which occurred in the reign of that
king, than to any instance of Jewish deliverance
from persecution which might be picked from the
times of the Crusades, or of the Inquisition. The
scene in the palace of Belshazzar and his death obviously mark, and are intended to mark, the exact
time of transition of the empire of the East, from the
hands of the Babylonians to those of the Medes and
Persians, even down to the minute particular of the
age of the Persian king at the time of his overthrow
of Babylon;* the description is written with the view
of marking the fulfilment of the prediction concerning the rise of the second or Medo-Persian empire,
the completion of the predicted seventy years of
servitude at Babylon, and of fixing the exact date of
the commencement of the predicted Seventy Weeks.†

* Dan. v. 31.   † Zech. ii. 7.

It bears no similitude whatever (except in common acts of impiety) to the events of the reign of Antiochus, during whose reign no great dynastic change affecting the destinies of the holy people took place. The scene of Daniel in the lions' den, according to the chronological reckoning which we adopt, marks the time of the struggle between the dying corruptions of the popular worship of Persia in the days of Darius Hystaspes, and the then revival of ancient monotheism in that empire — a struggle leading to the establishment of Daniel in one of the highest positions of the state,—to the proclamation of Darius, " that in every dominion of my kingdom men tremble and fear before the God of Daniel," *—and to the all-important decree of Darius, which naturally resulted from this proclamation, upon which the temple of Jerusalem was builded and finished in the sixth year of that same king's reign, as then for the first time styled king of Assyria,† when provision was also made of bullocks, rams, and lambs, " that they may offer sacrifices of sweet savours unto the God of heaven, and pray for the life of the king and his sons."‡ We have already expressed our conviction that the prophecy of the " little horn," of chap. vii. which leads down to the time when " one like a son of man shall come with the clouds of heaven and come to the Ancient of Days," has reference to events yet fulfilling on the holy people chiefly in the West: and that the prophecy of the " little horn" of chapter viii., which leads down to the times of " the

* Dan. vi. 26.   † Ezra, vi. 22.   ‡ Ezra, vi. 9, 10, 14.

last end of the indignation" has reference to events yet fulfilling and to be fulfilled on the holy people in the East, and that they can have no possible connexion therefore with the past days of the Syro-Grecian king. We feel satisfied that no unprejudiced reader of Daniel will be able to bring himself to see what Mr. Desprez has persuaded himself that he sees in these historical parallels; and we question whether he has not in these forced similitudes made himself amenable to the terms of reproof contained in the following words of his own quotation: " To suppose that we can serve God's cause by shutting our eyes to the light; much more to suppose that we can serve it by asserting that we see what we do not see, *because we wish to see it*, is simply intellectual atheism." * Lest, however, we ourselves should also be found subject to the words of this pointed admonition, let us be careful, while differing from Mr. Desprez's mode of interpretation, neither to close our eyes to facts, nor to be found slurring over, or keeping out of sight, any one observation which may appear to be adverse to our conviction of the inspired character of the book.

How is it, it is asked, that the book of Daniel is so profuse and detailed in its description of the times of the Greek empire in Syria, and of those times only, and that the composition of the book, while dwelling on those times, is found to be in the most prosaic style of human annals?† How is it that

* P. 4.

† The historical detail of chap. xi. descends even down to

this minute description of events stops suddenly short in Maccabean days? And how is it that the whole remainder of the prophetic portion of the book is so magnificently grand in outline, while foreshadowing the rise and fall of mighty empires and kingdoms, not of petty kings, and so altogether at variance with the prosaic style of this one chapter?

We see no reason to be unthankful to modern critics for having drawn attention to these remarkable phenomena in the book of Daniel. They have opened a subject for inquiry which demands and is entitled to searching and dispassionate investigation, and one which we trust in due time will receive its proper explanation. Meanwhile, however, we cannot agree with them that the hasty solution which they have given is either the true one, or one that necessarily flows even from the facts which they have pointed out. It yet remains a question, even for their own consideration, whether the author of chapter xi. was the author of the whole book.

If critics in these days are struck with the resemblance of events during the Maccabean struggle such minutiæ as these: "The king's daughter of the south shall come to the king of the north to make an agreement: but she shall not retain the power of the arm; neither shall he stand, nor his arm: but she shall be given up, and they that brought her, and he that begat her, and he that strengthened her in these times." (Ch. xi. 6.) And again, "Both these kings' hearts shall be to do mischief, and they shall speak lies at one table," &c. &c. (Chap. xi. 27.) Contrast these expressions with the sublime imagery of the prophetic text, x. 5, 6, and xii. 7.

to the events foretold by Daniel, chapter ix. 26, 27,
how much more powerfully must the minds of those
who lived in the days of that struggle, and when
these remarkable events were coming to pass, have
been led towards the same application: when nothing
of a similar nature had yet occurred in their history,
since their return from captivity, which could in
any way be supposed to be applicable to Daniel's
words, and yet when all around them seemed then to
be fulfilling almost exactly as he had foretold.   We
know how prone we are in these our own days,—
and many similar instances in history might be
pointed out,—to press the words of prophecy and
even to pervert the words of prophecy, into conformity with the events of our own times, and those
apparently coming to pass: to concentrate all that
is spoken of as future, if possible, within our present
age.   We cannot, therefore, doubt that pious Jews,
intensely moved by the apparent correspondence
between the troubles and calamities depicted by
Daniel and the calamities which were inflicted upon
them daily in the reign of Antiochus, were in the
habit of pointing out to each other how the prophecy
was to all appearance then being accomplished in
the events.   Turning their minds intently upon the
mysterious yet encouraging words of Daniel, till then
but little heeded, and comparing them with Jewish
history, they saw clearly,—

1st. How a decree of Cyrus, king of Persia, for
the rebuilding of the temple, by which Jerusalem
had become a second time the "holy city," had been

promulgated in agreement with the words of that book.

2nd. How this heathen Prince Cyrus had been specially designated by the Lord Himself as "His Messiah," or His anointed, that is, as one selected for this particular purpose of restoring the "holy city." How Zerubbabel, who was associated with the high-priest Jeshua, had been spoken of as one of the two "sons of oil," or anointed ones, "that stand by the Lord of the whole earth;"* that is, as one probably selected to fulfil events predicted at the end of Daniel's "seven weeks :" and how again their own Judas Maccabeus, now fighting in honour of that temple, might also properly be looked upon as the Messiah, or anointed one, foretold, by whom the supremacy of Israel might yet have to be established.

3rd. They saw how this anointed prince had nevertheless, been cut off in battle, while striving to deliver the "holy people," in B.C. 161.

4th. They saw how "the city and the sanctuary" had been laid desolate and trodden down for three full years, or for nearly "half a week."

5th. How the daily "sacrifice and oblation" in the temple had ceased during the term of desecration, and the abomination of desolation had been set up.

6th. And how the sanctuary had again been cleansed, and "the holy of holies" anointed by the valiant Judas, their anointed prince, towards the close of a Sabbatical week, in B.C. 165.

* Zech. iv. 14.

Who could fail in Maccabean days, notwithstanding many obvious difficulties in the application,
to couple vaguely these events with Daniel's words?
We have sufficient evidence before us of the fact,
that they were then so applied.   And yet, nevertheless, we confidently dispute their applicability as
urged by critics then and in the present day.

Dr. Pusey has already drawn attention to the
fact, that the Septuagint translator of Daniel, who,
it may be assumed, lived some time after the days
of the Maccabees, and whose Greek version was for
a long time the received version of the Church, has
endeavoured so to paraphrase or pervert the words
of Daniel, ix. 24, 25, as to apply them to the days of
Antiochus.   Dr. Pusey writes :—" In the prophecy
of the seventy weeks the translator repeatedly falsi-
fies the time, in order to make it fit in with that of
Epiphanes.   For the dates of the original he twice
substitutes 'seven, and seventy, and sixty-two,'*

---

* This reading is adopted as the true one by Dr. Blaney, Archbishop Magee, Mr. Galloway, and others.   They reckon seven-
and-seventy weeks as equal to 539 years, and interpret the period
as reaching from the supposed first of Cyrus, B.C. 538, to the birth
of Christ. This interpretation, in its details, is very confused. We
would suggest that the translator may perhaps have considered
the words " Seventy weeks are determined upon thy people and
upon the city of Sion" (ix. 24) as accomplished on the termination of the seventy sabbaths kept during the desolation of Jerusalem, which seventy sabbaths added to 420 years, during which
the first temple had stood, would make up 490 years. But that
the seven-and-seventy and sixty-two, or 973 years (v. 25), were
to be reckoned from the establishment of the city of Sion, in the
days of David or Solomon, and supposed to have ended with the

making 139. This, according to the Era of the Seleucidæ, which the Jews used, comprised the second year of the reign of Epiphanes" (B.C. 174 = E.S. 139), "soon after whose accession Onias was deposed, to which act this writer probably alluded in his unfaithful paraphrase, 'chrism shall be removed.'"* This translator also paraphrases the coming of "the ships of Chittim" (xi. 30), as the interference of the Romans in favour of the Jews, which we read took place in the reign of Antiochus. "And the Romans shall come and expel him, and rebuke him angrily."

Josephus also, we know, professedly, though erroneously in our opinion, interpreted what is related concerning the little horn of the vision of the ram and the goat of chapter viii. as applicable to Antiochus Epiphanes. For after correctly identifying the he-goat with Alexander, the first king of Greece, who conquered the Persians, and the four kingdoms which followed him, as the kingdoms of his successors, he goes on to say how Daniel foretold that "from among them there should arise a certain king who should overcome our nation and their laws, and should take away their political government, and should spoil the temple, and forbid the sacrifices to be offered for three years time : and indeed it so came to pass that our nation suffered

---

extinction of the Asmoneans, on the accession of Herod. This would fix the date of the translation to about 30 years before the birth of Christ.

* Pusey on Daniel, p. 379.

these things under Antiochus Epiphanes according to Daniel's vision." *

Again, the sober and accurate writer of the first book of Maccabees, who wrote some fifty or sixty years after the death of Antiochus, clearly had in his mind the application of chapters viii. and ix. of Daniel, to that king, when he began his history by describing how Alexander smote " Darius, the king of the Persians and Medes," (that is, how the he-goat " smote the ram and brake his *two* horns;") how his servants after his death put crowns upon their heads, and their sons after them, and how " there came out of them a *wicked root*, Antiochus Epiphanes, son of Antiochus the king," who " entered proudly into the sanctuary," who wrote letters to " forbid burnt-offerings and sacrifice, and drink-offerings in the temple," and " set up the abomination of desolation upon the altar, and builded idol altars throughout the cities of Judah on every side."†

Another striking evidence of the tendency of the Jews in the days of Antiochus, to apply the prophecies of Daniel to their own times, is found in the third Sibylline book, in which the " ten horns" of the

* Ant. x. xi. 7. It may be observed, that Josephus, while thus incorrectly pointing out the supposed fulfilment of ch. viii., in the acts of Antiochus, makes no allusion to ch. xi., which so clearly refers to that king.

† 1 Macc. i. 9, 10, 45, 54. If the writers of the two books of Maccabees had received ch. xi. as prophecy, they could hardly fail to have made some reference to it as having been accurately fulfilled by Antiochus.

fourth kingdom of Dan. ch. vii. are clearly referred
to as representing some supposed tenfold division of
the empire of Alexander, and the "little horn" of that
vision represented by a "horn" (κέρας), which rises
up from amongst the ten (ἐκ δέκα δὴ κεράτων). The
writer thus using the very expressions of the prophet.
"The third Sibylline book," writes Dr. Pusey, "is
now generally held to be the work of a Jew in the
time of Antiochus Epiphanes. It threatens unhesi-
tatingly that all the evils which had been done by
the Romans in Asia should be requited with usury
upon them"—"The writer three times fixes his date
by annexing the prophecies of the conversion of the
heathen to the date of the seventh king who should
rule over Egypt"—"The date then of the writer
cannot be later than about B.C. 170." *   This Sibylline book affords strong evidence, therefore, as Dr.
Pusey observes, of this portion of the book of Daniel,
viz., chap. vii. having been in existence before that
date.   And the inference to be drawn from the fact
of these repeated applications of the prophecies of
Daniel to the times of Antiochus, is, that the reign
of that king must be looked upon as one of those
deeply disturbed and excited periods in the history
of God's people which were for ever recurring at
intervals even to the time of Hadrian, in which men's
hearts are troubled, and found "failing them for
fear, and for looking after those things which are
coming on the earth," and when the tendency is to
appropriate prophecy if possible, whether truly

* Pusey's "Daniel," pp. 160, 364.

H

applicable or not, to the events which so powerfully
agitate their minds.

A feverish impression then pervaded the nation,
that their lot had fallen in the time of " the latter
days ;" that the " time of trouble, such as never
was since there was a nation, even to that same
time," foretold by Daniel, had at length come upon
them ; that the day of resurrection was at hand—
the day when the holy "people shall be delivered,
every one that shall be found written in the book."
The imagination of the multitude began to people
the atmosphere around them with supernatural
beings, their old men dreamed dreams, and their
young men saw visions. " Then it happened that
through all the city, for the space almost of forty
days, there were seen horsemen running in the air
in cloth of gold, and armed with lances like a band
of soldiers, and troops of horsemen in array, en-
countering and running one against another with
shaking of shields, &c. &c."*   The contest between
Pharisees and Sadducees ran high in those days.
The freethinking Sadducees, who say "there is no
resurrection, neither angel, nor spirit," and who
were carried away by the influence of the intellectual
but unbelieving Greeks, with whom they associated,
no doubt rejected all such spiritual dreams ; but
the Pharisees, who were then the ruling party, and
looked up to with reverence by the multitude,
dwelt much upon the doctrine and promise of the

* 2 Macc. v. 2, 3.

resurrection, adding at the same time doubtful traditions and superstitions to their belief especially as regarded the superintending agency of angels and spirits over the affairs of this world. The book of Daniel was especially a stronghold of Pharisaic opinions. The strange doctrine of the distribution of the kingdoms of the earth, " according to the number of the angels of God,"* and of the appointment by God of special guardian angels to watch over the affairs of each separate kingdom, supposed to be contained in this book, seems to have emanated from the Pharisees of these times; while a morbid inclination had grown up amongst the people of seeking after signs, and of listening with ready ears to the dreams and revelations of pretended prophets. Judas Maccabeus, who piously waited in expectation of the coming of a prophet,† on one occasion encouraged his followers by the recital of a dream, in which the prophet Jeremiah appeared to present him with a golden sword.‡ While John Hyrcanus, the high priest, who was a Pharisee, is especially mentioned as claiming to himself the gift of prophecy. We may judge of the superstitious and secular character of his pretended revelations, from two instances mentioned by Josephus, one in which being alone in the temple, offering incense, a voice proclaimed to him that his sons who were fighting with Antiochus

---

* Deut. xxxii. 8, Septuagint translation.
† 1 Macc. iv. 46.　　　　　　‡ 2 Macc. xv. 12–16.

Cyzicenus had conquered their enemy ;* another in which " he foresaw and foretold that his two eldest sons would not continue masters of the government " after his death.† Judas also, of the sect of the Essenes, living in those days, is said to have exhibited his powers of prophecy in many instances of a similar secular character.

Such, then, being the excited and superstitious temper of the times under the reign of the Maccabees, it is not unreasonable to assume that there were many more such instances besides those to which we have referred, of attempted application of the words of Daniel vii. viii. and ix. to those troublous days, and that even words of pretended prophecy may not have been too readily rejected by those who were then re-collecting copies of the sacred books, many of which had been burnt, and destroyed by order of Antiochus, and nearly lost during the war.‡

With the deepest feelings of veneration, therefore, for the contents of this most wondrous holy book, and humbly trusting in the guidance of the Spirit which dictated it, we venture to submit, that the portion of Daniel which has given so much offence to seriously minded critics, and which bears about it the appearance of so comparatively low and human a style of composition, is, in fact, merely one of these many forced attempts at application of pro-

---

* Jos. Ant. xiii. 3.   † Bell. Jud. i. 2, 8
‡ 2 Macc. ii. 14.

phecy to the days of the Maccabees.   We agree
with Arnold that "there can be no spiritual meaning made out of the kings of the north and south,"*
and the passages, therefore, containing those histories carry no internal evidence of being words
of prophecy.   On the contrary, they bear internal
marks of being neither more nor less than pure
history; and though written indeed in the form of
prophecy, as was the style and manner of the day,
with a view probably to increased dignity, yet in
their original form, as we shall endeavour to show,
they were not intended by the writer to be considered words of prophecy at all.   We believe them
to represent merely a sober instance of illustrative
paraphrase, written by the hand of some zealous
Pharisee † of Jerusalem, soon after the days of Antiochus, and that they were inserted marginally,
with the intention of concentrating on Antiochus
and his days prophecies which were never really
intended to apply to him, but which by means of
this appended comment are clearly made so to bear :
and that they were inserted with the idea of illustrating, first the prophecy of ch. vii. as regards the
ten horns, out of which "a little horn," falsely
assumed to be Antiochus Epiphanes, should arise,
and of connecting that chapter with ch. viii. which
refers to another "little horn" to arise, "when the

---

* Life of Arnold, vol. ii. p. 195.
† The contest of angels in ch. x. is clearly Pharisaic.

transgressors are come to the full," falsely interpreted to be Antiochus the Great ; secondly, of
applying the words of chap. ix. as regards the setting
up of the abomination of desolation at Jerusalem,
and the ceasing of the daily sacrifice, to the reign of
Epiphanes; and, lastly, of coupling these three
chapters with chap. xii. and the times of the resurrection, which were then probably supposed to be
close at hand.*

It would be difficult, as we have said, to believe
there were not many such comments in existence
in the days of the Maccabees: and less difficult,
we think, to believe that this condensed history
of the Greeks in Syria down to that time, written
thus in prophetic style, and displaying much historical accuracy on the part of the writer, may have
been inserted marginally, that is to say, in the alternate columns of the roll of the book of some pious
and esteemed authority of those days, even of John
Hyrcanus himself, and so, in deference to that authority in after time, and also to the unquestioned
value of the comment, or even in later days with
the view of shutting out more true interpretation of
chap. ix., may have been suffered by the Jewish
Scribes to stand annexed to the text of the authorised copies of the book itself.   In this view we
may also call to remembrance the extreme license
taken by pious Jews about that time, in assuming
the prophetic style in their compositions, and even

* 2 Macc. vii. 6, 9, 11, 14, 23, 29, 36.

the names of holy men who had gone before them, as instanced in the prophecies of the Second Book of Esdras, and in the book of Enoch, and especially in the well-known apocryphal additions to this very book of Daniel. The principal interpolation lies between chap. x. 14, and chap. xi. ver. 35, exclusive of a genuine passage, xi. 2, 3, 4, and professes to be an explanation of "that which is noted in the Scripture of Truth," that is to say, noted in "the book" of Holy Scripture then lying before the interpreter, a comment founded upon which must not be mistaken for prophecy. We think that the marks of paraphrase may clearly be discovered both at the beginning, middle, and end of the passage: and it may also be observed that when this passage is read parenthetically as comment, the sublime and lofty character of Daniel's composition, which seems to be disturbed by its insertion, is preserved throughout the vision without break.

It had not been our intention to have touched again upon this portion of the book of Daniel, as not lying strictly within our province, and we would gladly have avoided doing so. The whole of Mr. Desprez's arrangement, however, concerning the seventy weeks, seems interwoven with this one doubtful chapter : and while reading it again with a view to his observations, the words of Dr. Arnold and others have come back upon us so forcibly, and have seemed to suggest the means of so efficient an explanation of his difficulties, that we cannot refrain from offering the above suggestion for consideration, even at the risk of offending some whose judgment we respect.   Dr. Arnold writes, "I have long thought that (the greater?) part of Daniel is most certainly a very late work of the times of the Maccabees, and the pretended prophecy about the kings of Greece and Persia, and the north and south, mere history. In fact, you can trace distinctly the date when it was written, because the events up to that date are given with historical minuteness, totally unlike the character of real prophecy."*   Dean Milman also writes : "The prophecies down to Antiochus read so singularly like a transcript of the history, and are in this respect so altogether unlike any other in either testament, that they might almost be used, so plain are they, and distinct, and unvisionary, as historical documents.   On the other hand there is something so vast, Oriental, imaginative, in the manner in which the earlier events are related, that, in full confidence that the main facts are historically true, I use them as mainly historical."†   Now let any one compare the words of Daniel, ix. 27 : "He shall confirm the covenant with many,"—"He shall cause the sacrifice and oblation to cease,"—"and for the overspreading of abominations he shall make it desolate,"—"until the consummation,"—"and that

* Life of Arnold, vol. ii. p. 95.
† History of the Jews, vol. i. p. 413.

determined shall be poured out ; "—with ch. xi.
30–36, according to the present arrangement of that
chapter. " He," Antiochus, " shall have indignation
against the covenant,"—" shall take away the daily
sacrifice," — " shall place the abomination which
maketh desolate,"—" shall prosper till the indignation be accomplished," — " for that determined
shall be done ; "—and say whether it is possible
to conceive that this repetition of the same phrases
in the same order is the result of mere coincidence,
or whether these latter words are not put together
with reference in some way to the former. But
if so, since the latter words unquestionably refer to
the times of Antiochus, and all believers in prophecy are satisfied that the former apply with equal
certainty to the times of Titus, the conclusion is
pressed upon us that the latter words are probably
mere words of application, and form therefore no
part of the original prophecy of Daniel. Again,
the connexion between the following passages is, if
possible, still more striking. Compare ch. xi. 36,
" The king shall do according to his will ; " 41,
" He shall enter also into the glorious land; " 45,
" He shall come to his end, and none shall help
him; " with the words of ch. xi. 16, 19, " He that
cometh against him," Antiochus the Great, " shall
do according to his own will ; " " He shall stand in
the glorious land ; " " He shall stumble and fall, and
not be found." Arnold and the German critics we
think, have done service to the cause of truth in

boldly speaking out, and thus forcing on inquiry. Let no one, however, suppose that our suggestion tends in any way to countenance the idea, that the prophecies of Daniel, in general, could possibly have been composed in the time of the Maccabees. On the contrary, when a portion of this one questionable chapter is separated from the text, as representing mere comment on preceding chapters, the theory which would apply the tenor of the whole book to Antiochus necessarily falls to the ground, since the main argument, if not the only plausible argument, in support of such application is founded on this one single chapter. The hero of the supposed prophetic poem, on removal of a portion of chapter xi., entirely disappears: each chapter of the book which has been forced into connexion with his history then remains to be explained in the spirit of its own plain contents: while the fact of an appended comment if it can be established affords an indisputable argument that the text itself was *not* then composed, and that much veneration was attached to the text at the time the comment was made.

But if this be the true view of the question, and we do not fear that it can be entirely set aside, then would it appear that the persecutions of Antiochus have been nowhere made the subject of prophecy throughout the book of Daniel, and that, so far from it being " clear beyond all doubt," as Dr. Williams assures us, " that the period of weeks ended in the reign of Antiochus," the only foundation for that ill-supported idea would seem to be traced to the delusions of those troubled days. And yet we have before remarked, that it would seem hard to be believed that the prophet should thus have overlooked in vision those days of persecution. The answer seems to be, that it is a fact that chap. ix. certainly does pass over, and does take no notice of the troubles in that reign, but leads us on to times which have not even yet come to pass; that chap. vii. which unfolds the latter times of the Roman empire, leads on the time of the second coming of the son of man; that chap. viii. speaks of the times of "the last end of the indignation;" and that the events predicted in the genuine fragments of chap. x. and xi., together with ch. xii., professedly apply to "the latter days," and not, therefore, to the comparatively early days of Antiochus.

Another inference to be drawn from our suggestion is, that if the greater part of chap. xi. consists of comment on other parts of this and earlier chapters of the book of Daniel, the writer of that comment was probably the compiler and editor of the book, as it now stands, and that the time of its admission therefore, not into the Canon of Prophets, but into the section of Ketubim or Hagiographa, was not earlier than the days of the Maccabees, as first pointed out by sceptical critics. The several genuine writings of Daniel, though already well known at Jerusalem, may now have been selected

from amongst the other spurious writings attributed
to the prophet, and put together in consecutive form
as one book, the text collated and fixed, and some
slight additions in the way of comment, such as
chap. i. 21, "And Daniel continued unto the first
year of Cyrus," and vi. 28, " So this Daniel prospered in the reign of Darius—and in the reign of
Cyrus," and possibly some few other passages besides those already pointed out, may have been then
appended by the compiler.

Thus the authorised copies of the book of Daniel
in the subsequent days of Hillel and Shammai, like
our authorised copies of the Bible in present days,
with their appended comments, may have been
arranged, as we have suggested, in alternate columns, in connexion with this supposed valuable
historical interpretation, and yet in a manner not
then misunderstood by the learned Rabbis of those
ante-Christian days, who had the key to the arrangement in their minds ; and in the same manner
may the authorised manuscripts have continued for
ages to have been transcribed, and so faithfully
have been transmitted to posterity.   And yet, nevertheless, they may at length have been misunderstood
by Rabbis of a later and a darker age, and so both
text and comment have become merged together in
one continuous text.   As regards the LXX. translator, who was probably some Greek proselyte better
versed in his own language than in the traditions
of the Scribes, nothing can be more natural than

To face p. 111.

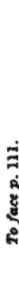

ROLL OF THE BOOK OF DANIEL.

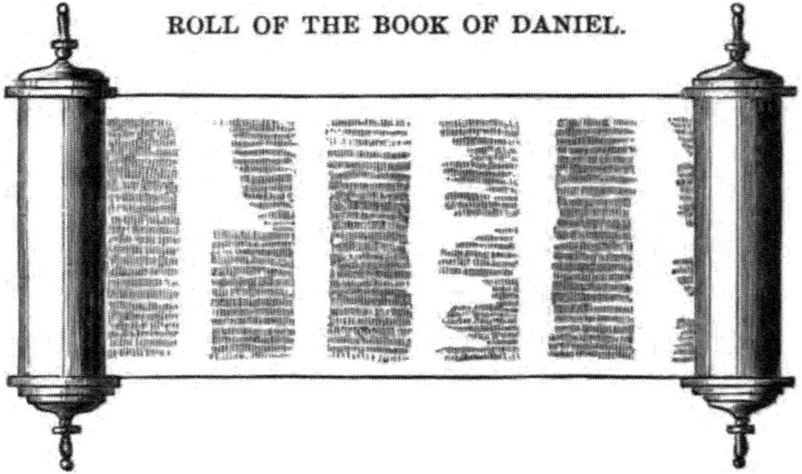

Consecutive Passages of Text and Comment in the Book of Daniel.

Text.	Comment.	Text	Comment.	Text.	Comment.
ChXI.v.36 to ChXII.v.13.	ChXI.v.5 to ChXI.v.35	ChXI.v.2 to ChXI.v.4	ChX.v.15. to ChXI.v1.	ChX.v.2 to ChX.v.14	ChX.v.1

that he should have copied both text and comment consecutively, and that those, therefore, who in early Christian days were only acquainted with the Scriptures in the Greek version, should through that version have accepted without question the whole as the words of Daniel. Nor, in such a case, would any later translator, such as Theodotion, or Jerome, or the learned infidel writer Porphyry, be more open to the charge of carelessness, than our own eminent critics of the present day, for not having detected and expunged this innocent and unintended interpolation, considering that, on reference to Hebrew manuscripts, both Greek and Hebrew apparently agree.

DANIEL'S PROPHECY OF THE LATTER DAYS.

N.B. The reader is requested to read consecutively, pp. 112, 114, 116, 118, 120, 122, 124, 126, *and then the Paraphrase.*

CHAPTER X.

2 In those days * I Daniel was mourning three ful weeks.†

3 I ate no pleasant bread, neither came flesh nor wine iu my mouth, neither did I anoint myself at all, till three whole weeks † were fulfilled.

4 And in the four and twentieth day of the first month as I was by the side of the great river, which is Hiddekel;

5 Then I lifted up mine eyes, and looked, and behold ; certain man clothed in linen, whose loins were girded witl fine gold of Uphas :

6 His body also was like the beryl, and his face as th appearance of lightning, and his eyes as lamps of fire, anu his arms and his feet like in colour to polished brass, and th voice of his words like the voice of a multitude.

7 And I Daniel alone saw the vision: for the men tha were with me saw not the vision; but a great quaking fel upon them, so that they fled to hide themselves.

---

* " In those days,"—that is, in the reign of Darius son of Hystaspes, th king spoken of in chap. ix. 1; in the first, or possibly the third year of his reig over the Chaldeans, in the year B.C. 493 or 490, not, as explained in the mar ginal comment, " in the third year of Cyrus king of Persia."

† " Weeks of days," in the original; to distinguish them from the weeks c years of chap. ix.

PARAPHRASTIC COMMENT,

AND ADAPTATION OF THE PROPHECY OF THE LATTER DAYS TO THE TIMES OF ANTIOCHUS EPIPHANES.

MARGINAL COMMENT.

Text, Ch. x. 2. " In those days."

Introductory Comment. Ch. x. 1. *In the third year of Cyrus* king of Persia a thing was revealed unto Daniel, whose name was called Belteshazzar; and the thing is true; and it concerns great warfare;† therefore consider the thing, and have understanding of it in vision,*

---

* The interpreter here considers that the words, ' In those days,' that is to say, the days when Daniel ' was mourning three full weeks of days,' and when ' the prince of the kingdom of Persia withstood him one and twenty days,' x. 13, must have reference to the days spoken of by Ezra, ch. iv. 5, which may be placed with much probability in the third year of Cyrus. Following the same interpretation therefore, the LXX. and Theodotion, both read Cyrus, instead of Darius, in chap. xi. 1, with a view to consistency between chap. x. 1. and xi. 1. But the interpreter has truly written "Darius," not Cyrus, in xi. 1, as referring the words, " From the first day thou didst set thy heart to understand," x. 12, to the time spoken of in Dan. ix. 23, that is, in the first year of Darius. By inserting Darius, instead of Cyrus, in each passage of Daniel, chronological order throughout the genuine text of the book may be restored. The chapters in Chaldee would then fall consecutively in the reigns of Nebuchadnezzar, Belshazzar, and Darius son of Hystaspes. No vision would have been seen in the reign of Cyrus.‡ And in the Hebrew, the reigns of Belshazzar and Darius would fall into the same order as in the Chaldee.

† Job, vii. 1, margin. Δύναμις μιγάλη. Theodotion.

I

Ch. x. 8. Therefore I was left alone, and saw this great vision, and there remained no strength in me; for my comeliness was turned in me into corruption, and I retained no strength.

9 Yet heard I the voice of his words: and when I heard the voice of his words, then was I in a deep sleep on my face, and my face toward the ground.

10 And behold an hand touched me, which set me upon my knees and upon the palms of my hands:

11 And he said unto me, O Daniel, a man greatly beloved, understand the words that I speak unto thee, and stand upright: for unto thee am I now sent. And when he had spoken this word unto me, I stood trembling.

12 Then he said unto me, Fear not, Daniel:

Text, Ch. x. 9. "And when I heard the voice of his words, then was I in a deep sleep on my face, and my face to the ground."

Comment, Ch. x. 15. *And when he had spoken such words unto me, I set my face toward the ground, and I became dumb.**

16. *And behold, one like the similitude of the sons of men*† *touched my lips: then I opened my mouth, and spake and said :*

Text, x. 8. "My comeliness was turned in me into corruption, and I retained no strength."

Comment, 16. *O my Lord, by the vision my sorrows are turned upon me, and I have retained no strength.*‡

17 *For how can the servant of this my lord talk with this my lord ? for as for me straightway there remained no strength in me, neither is there breath left in me.*

Text, x. 10. "And behold an hand touched me."

Comment, 18. *Then there came and touched me one like the appearance of a man, and he strengthened me.*

Text, x. 11. "And he said unto me, O Daniel, a man greatly beloved."

Comment, 19. *And said, O man greatly beloved.*

Text, x. 12. "Fear not, Daniel."

*Comment,*19. *Fear not; peace be unto thee; be strong, yea, be strong.*

Text, x. 11. "And when he had spoken this word unto me, I stood trembling."

Comment. 19. *And when he had spoken unto me, I roused myself, and said, Let my Lord speak, for thou hast strengthened me.*

---

* "And I became dumb,"—"neither is there breath left in me," v. 17. The interpreter seems to prefer the idea of speechlessness to sleep, as more agreeable to a waking vision.

† The similitude of the hand of a man. LXX.

‡ "I retained no strength." Verses 16, 17, 18, and 19, all comment on the renewal of the prophet's strength.

Ch. x. 12.   For from the first day that thou didst set thine heart to understand, and to chasten thyself before thy God, thy words were heard, and I am come for thy words.

13 (For the prince of the kingdom of Persia withstood me one and twenty days; but lo, Michael, one of the chief princes, came to help me [Daniel]: and I remained there with the kings of Persia.)

14 Now I am come to make thee understand what shall befall thy people in the latter days: for yet the vision is for many days.

CHAP. xi. 2.   And now I will show thee the truth. Behold, there shall stand up yet three kings in Persia;* and the fourth shall be far richer than they all:† and by his strength through his riches he shall stir up all against the realm of Grecia.

3 And a mighty king shall stand up, that shall rule with great dominion, and do according to his will.

4 And when he shall stand up, his kingdom shall be broken, and shall be divided toward the four winds of heaven; and not to his posterity, nor according to his dominion which he ruled: for his kingdom shall be plucked up, even for others beside those.

[*The Prophecy continued p.* 122.]

* This vision was seen in the first, or third year of Darius, when he was about sixty-two or sixty-four years of age (B.C. 492 or 490), and the book of Ezra certifies that Arta-Chshastha, or Xerxes, had then already been raised to the throne in conjunction with Darius (Ezra, iv. 7; vi. 14.) The four kings, therefore, who reigned in Persia, after this vision, were Artaxerxes Longimanus, Darius Nothus, Artaxerxes Mnemon, and Ochus. Eight years after the death of Ochus, the last king, viz., Darius Codomanus, was dethroned by the "mighty king," Alexander. "The prince of the kingdom of Persia," here spoken of is, therefore, Xerxes; "the kings of Persia," Darius and Xerxes united; "Michael, one of the chief princes," is he whose name was originally written Mishael, "of the king's seed," Dan. i. 3, 6, but probably changed to Michael after his deliverance from the fire, and promotion in the province of Babylon, iii. 30.

† Ochus.

Text, Ch. x. 12.   "And I am come for thy words."

Comment, Ch. x. 20.   *Then said he, Knowest thou wherefore I come unto thee ?*

Text, Ch. x. 13.   "The prince of the kingdom of Persia withstood me one and twenty days."

Comment, Ch. x. 20.   *And now will I return to fight* * *with the prince of Persia: and when I am gone forth, lo, the prince of Grecia shall come."*

Text, Ch. x. 14.   "Now I am come to make thee understand what shall befall thy people in the latter days."——
Ch. xi. 2. "And now I will show you the truth."

Comment, Ch. x. 21.   *But I will show thee that which is noted in* SCRIPTURE AS TRUTH : †

Text, Ch. x. 13.   "Lo, Michael, one of the chief princes,‡ came to help me, &c."

Comment, Ch. x. 21.   *And there is none that holdeth with me in these things, but Michael your prince.*

Text, Ch. x. 12.   "From the first day that thou didst set thy heart to understand."

Comment, Ch. xi. 1.   *Also I in the first year of Darius § the Mede,‖ even I, stood to confirm and strengthen him* (i.e. Daniel).¶

* "Fight with the prince of Persia." The doctrine that angels fight for the kingdoms committed to their charge, is here first introduced into the Bible. The interpreter applies the text to the days of Codomanus, and the invasion of Alexander. It really applies to the days of the son of Hystaspes.

† That is to say, what is written in chap. vii. 16 and 19, in answer to the words, "I asked him the truth," "Then I would know the truth." Also in chap. viii. where in viii. 26 it is declared that "the vision of the evening and the morning which was told is true." In other words, "I will show thee what is noted," in chap. vii., chap. viii., chap. ix., and chap. xii.

‡ Michael (who is like unto God ?), the same as Mishael (who is that which God is ?), one of the Jewish princes. The interpreter makes him to be an angel.

§ Compare Daniel, ix. 1, 23. As now in the third year of Cyrus, so "also I in the first year of Darius," stood to strengthen Daniel.

‖ "Darius the Mede," truly, Darius son of Hystaspes, the Persian. The Medes and Persians still spoken of as Medes. See 2 Esdras, i. 3. The interpreter, however, supposed this king to have reigned before Cyrus, as a Median king.

¶ The word "him" is not expressed in the LXX., Theodotion, or the Vulgate. In the Syriac we read "he stood to confirm me." From one of Kennicott's MSS. it seems doubtful whether the reading was "him" or "me" in the Hebrew. See Rosenmüller.

The angel having thus announced in chap. x. 14, that he is to come to speak of events which shall befall the people of Daniel in "*the latter days*," and that the vision shall yet be "*for many days*," begins by enlarging, in chap. xi. 2, 3, 4, upon the vision of chap. viii. 20, 21, 22, concerning the kingdoms of Persia and Grecia. He shows how the kingdom of the mighty king of Grecia should be broken into four parts, and not descend to his posterity, and how again these four kingdoms should be plucked up "even for others beside those," that is, first for the Romans, and then for the Saracens, and thus leads back the mind of the reader to the words of chap. viii. 23, where he suddenly breaks off into a vision of far-distant days, viz., the vision of the "king of fierce countenance," who shall appear at "the *last end of the indignation*," viii. 19, and who shall stand up *in the latter time* of those kingdoms, which were to be formed on the platform of Alexander's empire in the East, in "the latter days." And in conformity with this preamble, he goes on therefore to speak of the last days, when "many of them that sleep in the dust of the earth shall awake," xii. 2, and how, after "he shall have accomplished to scatter the power of the holy people, all these things shall be finished," xii. 7. We thus collect that the scope of the prophecy of "the latter days," reaches far beyond the days of the Greeks in Asia, and that it comprehends a period of more than 2300 years, counted from the time of the vision, for it reaches even far beyond the present time; and that the events of "the latter days," according to present experience, must be looked for towards the latter half of this long period, beginning at least a thousand years or more after the

ADAPTATION OF CHAPTER VII,

CONCERNING THE TEN HORNS OF THE FOURTH EMPIRE, AND THE LITTLE HORN, TO THE TIMES OF THE GREEKS IN ASIA.

Text, xi. 4. " For his kingdom shall be plucked up, even for others beside those." *

Comment, Ch. xi. 5. *And the king of the south†* [PTOLEMY PHILADELPHUS] *shall be strong, and one of his princes* [AN- 1st horn. TIOCHUS THEOS] ; *and he* [PTOLEMY] *shall be strong above* 2nd horn. B.C. 285. *him, and have dominion : and his dominion shall be a great dominion.*

6 *And in the end of years they shall join themselves together; for the king's daughter of the south* [BERENICE ‡] *shall come to the king of the north to make an agreement : but she shall not retain the power of the arm ; neither shall he stand, nor his arm : but she shall be given up, and they that brought her,§ and he that begat her, and he that strengthened her in these times.*

7 *But out of a branch of her roots shall one* [PTOLEMY 3rd horn. B.C. 247 EUERGETES] *stand up in his estate, which shall come with an army, and shall enter into the fortress of the king of the north* [SELEUCUS CALLINICUS], *and shall deal against them, and* 4th horn. B.C. 246. *shall prevail.*

8 *And shall also carry captives into Egypt their gods, with their princes, and with their precious vessels of silver and of gold : and he shall continue more years than the king of the north.*

9 *So the king of the south shall come into his kingdom, and shall return into his own land.*

---

* That is, even for others beside the successors of Alexander, namely, in a future generation, for the followers of Mahomet who shall rule for 1300 years. Daniel therefore, giving no particulars concerning the four successors of Alexander, proceeds at once, v. 36, to the object of the vision, " the king " of the *latter days.* The interpreter, with a view to his own times, passing over Ptolemy Soter, Lysimachus, Cassander, and Seleucus Nicator, the four successors of Alexander, selects, out of more than twenty, *ten kings*, beginning with Philadelphus, and ending with Antiochus, and Philometer, who all lived nearly in his own days.

† King of Egypt, LXX.   ‡ Berenice, daughter of Ptolemy Philadelphus.
§ Callinicus.

date of the vision, B.C. 490.   It is in strict conformity,
therefore, with the abrupt transition in c. viii. 22, 23,
that in the same manner the angel should here suddenly transfer the vision from the times described in
c. xi. 4, to the times spoken of in c. xi. 36—" The
king shall do according to his will," that is to say,
"the king of fierce countenance," of the last end of
the indignation, representing, as we have said, the
great Mahomedan domination of these latter days in
the East, by the overspreading of which the " mighty
and the holy people " has been, since the year A.D.
627, trodden under foot, and by which "the daily
worship has been taken away, and the place of his
sanctuary cast down," viii. 11.   According to the
terms, however, of the marginal paraphrase, the chief
subject of the prophecy is made to refer, not to the
latter part of the period of 2300 years, but to the
three first centuries of that period, which is quite inconsistent with the preamble.   For we must bear in
mind that long after the troubles under Epiphanes,
or the destruction of Jerusalem by Titus, or the subjection of the people again by Hadrian, there yet remained a powerful Jewish population in Mesopotamia
presided over by the " Prince of the Captivity," and
also another large Jewish kingdom in Homeritis* in
Arabia Felix, which lasted for seven hundred years
even to the time of Mahomet.   And it is probable that
a memorial of, or substitute for the daily sacrifice†
was kept up in this kingdom, even to the final dispersion of the Jews, in A.D. 627, by the wilful king.

---

* See Milman's History of the Jews, vol. iii. book xxii.

† We know that an altar of sacrifice was kept up in the temple of Onias at
Heliopolis.   Josephus, Bell. Jud. vii. x. 3.

10 *But his sons* [SELEUCUS CERAUNUS and ANTIOCHUS THE GREAT] *shall be stirred up, and shall assemble a multitude of great forces: and one* [ANTIOCHUS] *shall certainly* 5th horn. B.C. 223. *come, and overflow, and pass through: then shall he return, and be stirred up, even to his fortress.*

11 *And the king of the south* [PTOLEMY PHILOPATOR] 6th horn. B.C. 222. *shall be moved with choler, and shall come forth and fight with him, even with the king of the north:* * *and he shall* B.C. 217. *set forth a great multitude; but the multitude shall be given into his hand.*

12 *And when he hath taken away the multitude, his heart shall be lifted up; and he shall cast down many ten thousands :*† *but he shall not be strengthened by it.*

13 *For the king of the north shall return, and shall set forth a multitude greater than the former, and shall certainly come after certain years with a great army and with much riches.*

14 *And in those times there shall many stand up against the king of the south* [PTOLEMY EPIPHANES]: *also the robbers* 7th horn. B.C. 205. *of thy people shall exalt themselves to establish the vision, but they shall fall.*

15 *So the king of the north shall come, and cast up a mount, and take the most fenced cities: and the arms of the south shall not withstand, neither his chosen people, neither shall there be any strength to withstand.*

[From verse 16 to verse 19 the interpreter proceeds to apply Ch. xi. 36–45, which really speaks of Mahomet as the wilful king, and the king of fierce countenance, to Antiochus the Great, the predecessor of Epiphanes.]

---

* Battle of Raphia, B.C. 217, between Antiochus the Great and Philopator.

† Forty thousand Jews slain at Alexandria.

The Prophecy continued from p. 116.

The king of
the latter
days, x. 14. Ch. xi. 36 And the king shall do according to his will; and he shall exalt himself, and magnify himself above every god (*col el*), and shall speak marvellous things against the God of gods (*El Elim*), and shall prosper till the indignation* be accomplished: for that that is determined shall be done.

37 Neither shall he regard the gods (*elohe*) of his fathers, nor the desire of women, nor regard any god (*eloah*): for he shall magnify himself above all.

38 But in his estate shall he honour the God (*Elah*)† of forces: and a god (*Eloah*), whom his fathers knew not, shall he honour with gold, and silver, and with precious stones, and pleasant things.

39 Thus shall he do in the most strong holds with a strange god (*Eloah*), whom he shall acknowledge and increase with glory: and he shall cause them to rule over many, and shall divide the land for gain.

40 And at the time of the end shall the king of the south ‡ push at him: and the king of the north shall come against him like a whirlwind, with chariots, and with horsemen, and with many ships; and he shall enter into the countries, and shall overflow and pass over.

41 He shall enter also into the glorious land, and many countries shall be overthrown: but these shall escape out of his hand, even Edom, and Moab, and the chief of the children of Ammon.

42 He shall stretch forth his hand also upon the countries: and the land of Egypt shall not escape.

43 But he shall have power over the treasures of gold and of silver, and over all the precious things of Egypt: and the Lybians and the Ethiopians shall be at his steps.

44 But tidings out of the east and out of the north shall trouble him: therefore he shall go forth with great fury to destroy, and utterly to make away many.

---

* See chap. viii. 19, " What shall be in the last end of the indignation."
† ALLAH, the god of forces, or of the sword.   ‡ King of Egypt, LXX.

ADAPTATION OF CHAPTER XI. 36–45,

CONCERNING THE WILFUL KING, TO ANTIOCHUS THE GREAT.

Text, Ch. xi. 36.   " And the king shall do according to his will."

Comment, Ch. xi. 16.   *But he that cometh against him* [AN- B.c. 200. TIOCHUS THE GREAT] *shall do according to his own will.*

Text, Ch. xi. 36.   " And shall prosper."

Comment, Ch. xi. 16.   *And none shall stand before him.*

[It is remarkable, that the interpreter ceases to comment after verse 36 of the text, and begins again to comment with verse 41. He thus declines to make any observation upon the several passages referring to the name of God; perhaps from reverential feeling for the sacred name of God, or, more pro-bably, from fear of the accusation of sacrilege, if he should apply these passages to the gods of Antiochus.]

Text, Ch. xi. 41.   " He shall enter also into the glorious land."

Comment, Ch. xi. 16.   *And he shall stand in the glorious land, which by his hand shall be consumed.*

17 *He shall also set his face to enter with the strength of his whole kingdom, and upright ones with him ; thus shall he do : and he shall give him the daughter of women* [CLEO-PATRA *], *corrupting her : but she shall not stand on his side, neither be for him.*

18 *After this shall he turn his face unto the isles, and shall take many : but a prince for his own behalf shall cause the reproach offered by him to cease; without his own re-proach he shall cause it to turn upon him.*

---

* Cleopatra, daughter of Antiochus the Great, wife of Epiphanes.

45 And he shall plant the tabernacles of his palaces between the seas in the glorious holy mountain;* yet he shall come to his end, and none shall help him.

CHAP. XII. 1. And at that time shall Michael stand up, the great prince which standeth for the children of thy people: and there shall be a time of trouble, such as never was since there was a nation even to that same time: and at that time thy people shall be delivered, every one that shall be found written in the book.†

2 And many of them that sleep in the dust of the earth shall awake, some to everlasting life, and some to shame and everlasting contempt.

3 And they that be wise shall shine as the brightness of the firmament; and they that turn many to righteousness as the stars for ever and ever.

4 But thou, O Daniel, shut up the words, and seal the book, even to the time of the end: many shall run to and fro, and knowledge shall be increased.

5 Then I Daniel looked, and, behold, there stood other two, the one on this side of the bank of the river, and the other on that side of the bank of the river.

6 And one said to the man clothed in linen, which was upon the waters of the river, How long shall it be to the end of these wonders?

* No explanation of this passage can be found in the history of Antiochus. When Jerusalem, however, was taken by the Mahomedans under the Caliph Omar, in A.D. 637, the patriarch Sophronius, alluding to Dan. viii. 13, is said to have exclaimed, "The abomination of desolation is in the holy place."— *Gibbon.* The Mosque of Omar, or "the tabernacle of his palace," has stood "on the glorious holy mountain" even to this very day.

† "The Book." That is the book of life. Rev. xvii. 8. According to the paraphrase, The Book, or Scripture of Truth.

Text, Ch. xi. 45. "Yet he shall come to his end and none shall help him."

Comment, Ch. xi. 19 *Then he shall turn his face toward the fort of his own land: but he shall stumble and fall, and not be found.*[*] B.C. 188.

ADAPTATION OF "THE TIME OF TROUBLE," (xii. 2.) TO THE DAYS OF ANTIOCHUS EPIPHANES AS THE LITTLE HORN.

20 *Then shall stand up in his estate* [SELEUCUS PHILO-PATOR) *a raiser of taxes in the glory of the kingdom: but within few days he shall be destroyed, neither in anger, nor in battle.* 8th horn. B.C. 187.

21 *And in his estate shall stand up a vile person* [ANTI-OCHUS EPIPHANES], *to whom they shall not give the honour of the kingdom: but he shall come in peaceably, and obtain the kingdom by flatteries.* 9th horn, or little horn. B.C. 175.

22 *And with the arms of a flood shall they be overflown from before him, and shall be broken; yea, also the prince of the covenant* [the High Priest ONIAS].

23 *And after the league made with him he shall work deceitfully: for he shall come up, and shall become strong with a small people.*

24 *He shall enter peaceably even upon the fattest places of the province; and he shall do that which his fathers have not done, nor his fathers' fathers; he shall scatter among them the prey, and spoil, and riches; yea, and he shall forecast his devices against the strong holds, even for a time.*

25 *And he shall stir up his power and his courage against the king of the south* [PTOLEMY PHILOMETER] *with a great army; and the king of the south shall be stirred up to battle with a very great and mighty army; but he shall not stand: for they shall forecast devices against him.* 10th horn. B.C. 181.

26 *Yea, they that feed of the portion of his meat shall destroy him, and his army shall overflow: and many shall fall down slain.*

27 *And both these kings' hearts shall be to do mischief, and they shall speak lies at one table; but it shall not prosper: for yet the end shall be at the time appointed.*

---

[*] Antiochus the Great, slain while robbing the temple of Jupiter Belus, in Elymais.

7 And I heard the man clothed in linen, which was upon the waters of the river, when he held up his right hand and his left hand unto heaven, and sware by him that liveth for ever that it shall be for a time, times, and a half; and when he shall have accomplished to scatter the power of the holy people, all these things shall be finished.

8 And I heard, but I understood not: then said I, O my Lord, what shall be the end of these things?

9 And he said, Go thy way, Daniel: for the words are closed up and sealed till the time of the end.

10 Many shall be purified, and made white, and tried; but the wicked shall do wickedly: and none of the wicked shall understand; but the wise shall understand.

11 And from the time that the daily sacrifice shall be taken away, and the abomination that maketh desolate set up, there shall be a thousand two hundred and ninety days.*

12 Blessed is he that waiteth, and cometh to the thousand three hundred and five and thirty days.*

13 But go thou thy way till the end be: for thou shalt rest and stand in thy lot at the end of the days.

END OF THE PROPHECY.

---

* When the wilful king is interpreted as representing the personification of the Mahometan domination, these periods of 1290 and 1335 days, or years, necessarily count from the time of Mahomet even to beyond the present day. The Marginal paraphrase fixes them to the times of Epiphanes, and thereby contracts these periods into literal days; though the interpreter does not attempt to explain them. They cannot, however, have reference to the times of Epiphanes because Daniel himself, we are told, shall stand in his lot at the end of the days.

28 *Then shall he return into his land with great riches ; and his heart shall be against the holy covenant : and he shall do exploits, and return to his own land.*

29 *At the time appointed he shall return, and come toward the south ; but it shall not be as the former or as the latter.*

ADAPTATION OF CHAPTER IX.
TO THE TIME OF TROUBLE UNDER EPIPHANES.

Text, Ch. ix. 27.   " And he shall confirm the covenant with many for one week."

Comment, Ch. xi. 30.   *For the ships of Chittim* shall come against him : therefore he shall be grieved, and return, and have indignation against the holy covenant: so shall he do ; he shall even return, and have intelligence with them that forsake the holy covenant.*

Text, Ch. ix. 27.   "And in the midst of the week he shall cause the sacrifice and the oblation to cease, and for the overspreading of abominations he shall make it desolate."

Comment, Ch. xi. 31.   *And arms shall stand on his part, and they shall pollute the sanctuary of strength, and shall take away the daily sacrifice, and they shall place the abomination that maketh desolate.*

ADAPTATION OF CHAPTER XII.
TO THE TIME OF TROUBLE UNDER EPIPHANES.

Text, Ch. xii. 10.   " The wicked shall do wickedly : and none of the wicked shall understand."

Comment, Ch. xi. 32.   *And such as do wickedly against the covenant shall be corrupt by flatteries : but the people that do know their God shall be strong, and do exploits.*

Text, Ch. xii. 10.   "But the wise shall understand."

Comment, Ch. xi. 33.   *And they that understand among the people shall instruct many : yet they shall fall by the sword and by flame, by captivity, and by spoil, many days.*

34 *Now when they shall fall, they shall be holpen with a little help : but many shall cleave to them with flatteries.*

Text, Ch. xii. 10. "Many shall be purified and made white, and tried."

Comment, Ch. xi. 35.   *And some of them of understanding shall fall, to try them, and to purge, and to make them white, even to the time of the end ; because it is yet for a time appointed.*

THE END OF THE PARAPHRASE.

* The Romans shall come, LXX.

To sum up the arguments upon which the supposed interpolations in the text of Daniel appear to
be established, it may be observed:

1st. That the questionable passages disturb the
continuity of the prophecy. For the text of the
latter half of chap. x. is full of repetition, and, as
every reader must have remarked, verses 20, 21, and
xi. 1. follow each other abruptly, unlike the clear
style of Daniel in other parts of the book; while by
separating the supposed comment from the text, the
flow and the continuity of the prophecy is restored.

2nd. That they destroy the consistency of the
prophecy. For the angel, who declares that he is
sent expressly to announce what shall befall the
Jews in "the latter days,"—which days, therefore,
must reach beyond more than 2300 years from the
date of the vision,— is, according to the present
arrangement, made to announce events which chiefly
occurred within little more than 300 years from the
beginning of the period; and, though minute indeed
in describing the persecutions of the comparatively
early days of Antiochus, his description there suddenly and abruptly stops, without any allusion to what
befell Jerusalem by Pompey, by Herod, or by Titus,
or to the persecutions which took place in the *latter*
days,—by the hand of the Romans, or of Mahomet,
of the Crusaders, or of the Inquisition. It is of yet
future events, however, even later than these, of which
the angel now comes to speak, viz. of those which
shall befall the Jews " in the last end of the indignation," in "the time of trouble," when their "redemption

draweth nigh ;" Luke, xxi. 28. Again, while Daniel
writes,—" I heard, but I understood not,"—" shut up
the words,"—" for the words are closed up and sealed
till the time of the end ;" ch. xii. 4, 8, 9 : the interpreter treats the prophecy as already unfolded to
Daniel, saying,—ch. x. 1, " Consider the thing, and
have understanding of it in vision."*

3rd. That they introduce Pharisaic conceits into
holy Scripture. For the doctrine of the administration of God's government by the authority of angels,
set over each kingdom of this world, who strive
with each other according to the conflicting interests
of their separate kingdoms, as gathered from chap.
x. 13-20;—a doctrine, as Dr. Pusey observes,†
"nowhere found out of Holy Scripture, and within
Holy Scripture only found in Daniel ;"—is, as observed by Bishop Horsley, "in truth nothing better
than pagan polytheism, somewhat disguised and
qualified."‡ When the passage, however, is viewed
as mere comment, this doctrine, which differs much
from the revealed doctrine of the ministration of holy
angels, under God, appears to be the offspring of
Rabbinism, not of the teaching of Daniel.§

* The vision was sealed, because the "end" was far distant.
St. John, on the other hand, writes, " Seal not the sayings of this
prophecy," " for the time is at hand ;" Rev. xxii. 10.

† Pusey on Daniel, p. 362. ‡ Horsley's Sermons, vol. ii. p. 21.

§ Concerning this strange doctrine, Dr. Pusey, p. 522, has
been compelled in consistency with the authorised text to write:
" Daniel taught, in the case of two great nations, Persia and Græcia, that they were under the care of eminent angels, princes with
God. For the angels of Persia and Græcia were manifestly good
angels, since they desired the welfare of their people, and they
contended with Gabriel and Michael before God." Auberlen,
equally carried away by the text, observes : " The glorious angel

K

4th. That the parts objected to in chap. xi. were not treated by Jews as prophecy before the birth of Christ. For, neither the authors of the two books of Maccabees, nor Josephus, have referred to this minute prophecy of the ten Syro-Grecian kings, while treating of that period of history, though both appear to refer to the words of chap. viii.

5th. That they destroy the perspicuity, and unity, of the book of Daniel, and contract the scope of the several prophecies contained in it. For thus, the 1290 days "from the time that the daily sacrifice shall be taken away, and the abomination of desolation set up," ch. xii. 11, together with the 1335 days, spoken of immediately after, 12, must, as fairly argued by Mr. Desprez, necessarily refer to the taking away of the daily sacrifice spoken of in chap. xi. 31, in the reign of Antiochus, and therefore can only be interpreted in literal days ; and thus also Daniel is made to hold out a special blessing to those who shall live patiently to the end of forty-five literal days more than their neighbours, after the restoration of the sanctuary. This day-day principle

who appears to Daniel, tells him that for twenty-one days he struggled with the angel at the head of the Persian monarchy, and that finally, by Michael's help, he subdued him." "That he had to enter upon a further struggle with that Persian angel, and that this would be succeeded by one with the Grecian." —*Prophecies of Daniel. Trans.* p. 57. Bishop Horsley, on the other hand, saw the danger and falsehood of the doctrine,—" by whatever name," he says, " these deputy gods be called, whether you call them gods, or demigods, or demons, or genii, or heroes, or angels, the difference is only in the name." " Confidently I deny that a single text is to be found in holy writ which, rightly understood, gives the least countenance to the abominable doctrine of such a participation of the holy angels in God's government of the world."

of interpretation, which must be applied throughout the book, leads to the conclusion, that all the prophecies of Daniel have already been long since fulfilled, though the mode of application of these several periods on this assumption cannot with any degree of accuracy be explained; for "the consummation," the resurrection, and the last coming of the son of man, clearly have not yet come to pass.

6th. That it is difficult to account for the following series of repetitions of the same phrases, almost exactly in the same order of continuity, except on the principle of text and paraphrase of the text.

Ch. x. TEXT.	Ch. x. COMMENT.
9. When I heard the voice of his words.	15. When he had spoken such words unto me.
9. My face to the ground.	15. My face towards the ground.
8. My comeliness was turned in me into corruption.	16. My sorrows are turned upon me.
8. I retained no strength.	16. I have retained no strength.
10. A hand touched me.	18. Then touched me one like, &c.
11. A man greatly beloved.	19. O man, greatly beloved.
12. Fear not, Daniel.	19. Fear not, peace be unto thee.
12. The prince of the kingdom of Persia.	20. The prince of Persia.
13. Michael one of the chief princes.	20. Michael your prince.
Ch. xi. 2. I will show you the truth.	21. I will show thee that which is written in the Scripture of truth.

1 ... 2

3

Ch. xi. COMMENT.	Chap. xi. TEXT.
16. Shall do according to his own will.	36. Shall do according to his will.
16. He shall stand in the glorious land.	41. He shall enter also into the glorious land.
19. He shall stumble and fall and not be found.	45. He shall come to his end and none shall help him.
	Ch. ix.
30. Forsake the holy covenant.	27. Shall confirm the covenant.
31. Shall take away the daily sacrifice.	27. Shall cause the sacrifice and the oblation to cease.
31. Shall place the abomination that maketh desolate.	27. For the overspreading of abominations he shall make it desolate.
	Ch. xii.
32. And such as do wickedly, &c.	10. The wicked shall do wickedly.
33. They that understand, &c.	10. The wise shall understand.
35. To try them and to purge, and to make them white.	10. Shall be purified, and made white, and tried.
35. Till the time of the end.	9. Till the time of the end.

4 ... 5 ... 6

7th. That they disturb the reckoning of the chronology of the Bible. For by the insertion of one single verse, chap. x. 1, which is not written in the first person, as is the style of Daniel in the following verse,* and which fixes the date of that chapter to the third year of Cyrus, the order of the chapters is inverted, by placing the date of chap. x. before that of chap. ix.: and a succession of eight kings of Persia is thus made to intervene between the time of the vision in the reign of Cyrus, and the reign of Darius Codomanus, the last king of Persia, conquered by Alexander. Whereas it is expressly declared by the prophet, that there shall stand up four kings only during that interval.† Again, by comparing this verse, chap. x. 1, with chap. xi. 1, which speaks of the " first year of Darius the Mede" as already past, a Median king, bearing the Persian title Darius, is introduced as reigning before Cyrus, who is not only not known in secular history, but by his intrusion here causes extreme confusion in this part of sacred history. For the Darius of the books of Haggai, Zechariah, and Ezra, who reigned at the close of seventy years of "indignation against Jerusalem," is thus made to be a different king from Darius who reigned at the close of seventy years of " desolation of Jerusalem,"‡ and the prayer of Daniel to God to restore and to build the sanctuary in the first year of Darius, is thus separated by at least seventeen, if

* See also, the same style, "I, Daniel," ix. 2, x. 7, xii. 5.

† Dan. xi. 2. Arces, who reigned but part of two years, is not referred to in the prophecy.

‡ See pp. 57, 58.

not forty-six years from the command from God to restore and to build the sanctuary in the second year of Darius. Again, by the introduction of this Median Darius, who we affirm never lived, as distinct from the Persian Darius, sometimes called the Mede, the historical book of Ezra is thrown into a state of extreme confusion. For Ezra tells us that the Temple of Jerusalem was completed in the sixth year of Darius, when Artach-Shashtha, that is Xerxes, was reigning with him, which we know was the case in B.C. 486; and this date well agrees with the age of Daniel's Darius, when that king is identified with the son of Hystaspes ; because he began to reign in, or transferred his seat of government to Chaldea, when about sixty-two years old. But when the Median Darius, whose age was sixty-two, is supposed to be an earlier king than the Darius of Ezra, in conformity with chap. x. 1, and xi. 1, then must the building of the Temple be thrown back to the beginning instead of the end of the reign of Darius son of Hystaspes, when Artach-Shashtha, or Xerxes, had probably not even been born. On the authority of these two doubtful verses all the commonly received interpretations of the book, both for and against its authenticity, have proceeded, when they assume that the unknown king, " Darius the Mede," was one who preceded Cyrus on the throne of Babylon, not one who came after him, though no such king can be found in secular history.

8th. The wilful king of xi. 36–45, after whose

removal, we are told, "the time of trouble" and the awaking of many from "sleep in the dust of the earth" shall immediately take place, xii. 1, 2, is evidently identified[*] by the interpreter with Antiochus the Great in xi. 16-19. Now this must necessarily be a false interpretation: because the time of the resurrection has not even yet arrived. The last of these passages, therefore, cannot be the writing of Daniel.

9th. If it is true that the fourth great empire predicted by Daniel, chap. ii., is the Roman empire, and that that empire was divided into ten parts, or horns, as described in chap. vii., then the interpretation which identifies these "ten horns" with ten Syrian and Egyptian kings who reigned before the Roman empire was divided, as set forth in chap. xi., must be a false interpretation, and not, therefore, that of Daniel.

We return now to Mr. Desprez's interpretation of Daniel, chap. ix. The desecration of the city and the sanctuary, and the ceasing of the daily sacrifice, as foretold in this chapter by the prophet, denote, he says, "that memorable epoch in the annals of the holy people, which witnessed a cessation of the daily sacrifice for three, or for three and a half years; an event without parallel in Jewish history, and which can only be explained with fairness of the profanation of the temple by Antiochus." "If the passage is not explained by the cessation of the daily sacrifice caused by the Syrian oppressor, it can never be explained at all."[†]

_____

* See pp. 121, 123, 125.   † Desprez on Daniel, p. 185.

To this observation we reply at once, that Mr.
Desprez has for the moment overlooked the fact,
that the event, though remarkable, has been paral-
leled in Jewish history, by a sudden cessation of
the daily sacrifice in the temple on a still more
memorable occasion, that is, in the days when a
Roman prince came against the city with his people,
and not only made the city desolate for a time, but
actually "destroyed the city and the sanctuary,"
in most strict conformity with the words of Daniel;
since which time till now it may be truly said, that
" by the overspreading of abominations" Jerusalem
has been made desolate, and trodden under foot,
and closed against the worship of the " holy people."
It must also be borne in mind that the ceasing of
the daily sacrifice as connected with this final destruction of Jerusalem by Titus (Dan. ix. 26, 27),
on the authority of Christ Himself, can only be
explained as occurring *after* the time of his ministry,
and *not* therefore in the time of the Maccabees.
For our Lord warned His disciples, saying, " When
ye shall see the abomination of desolation, spoken
of by Daniel the prophet, standing where it ought
not, (let him that readeth understand), then let them
that be in Judea flee to the mountains."* Now, the
only words of Daniel which can possibly be here referred to by our Lord, as words of future import, are
those contained in ch. ix. 26, 27, thus declared by Him
to have reference to the siege of Jerusalem by Titus.

Now, what does Josephus relate concerning the

* Mark, xiii. 14.

events of this siege? He writes, " Titus now commanded the soldiers who were with him to destroy
the foundation of Antonia (the castle which overlooked the temple); and having called Josephus to
him, — for he had been informed that on that very
day, being the 17th day of Panemus (Tamuz), that
which is called the perpetual sacrifice (ἰνδελεχισμὸν
καλούμενον) had been discontinued for want of men to
offer it, and that the people were thereby grievously
cast down in spirit," *—directed him to implore those
in possession of the temple no longer to pollute the
holy place by bloodshed, and to propose to them
that they might select whom they pleased to offer
for them the sacrifices thus discontinued. For Titus
was truly anxious to save the temple from destruction. Here, then, is a parallel event to that which
happened in the days of Antiochus, and one more
closely harmonizing with the words of Daniel than
that pointed out by Mr. Desprez. He, therefore, is
not only not justified in saying that the event foretold by Daniel can never be explained except in the
manner he proposes, but the full weight of our
Lord's evidence is thus absolutely set against his
mode of explanation.

There is one other preliminary remark which we
would make before examining Mr. Desprez's arithmetical exposition of the " Seventy Weeks." He
suggests that the Book of Daniel " may be partly
(that is, as regards the narrative) a compilation and
re-arrangement of more ancient annals, and partly

* Josephus, " Bell. Jud." vi. 2.

(that is, as regards the prophecies) the original composition of some learned and pious Jew who lived at a period subsequent to the *scenes* he describes; probably whilst his countrymen were still engaged in their patriotic struggle against Demetrius, and following up the advantages they had won from Antiochus Epiphanes;"* that is to say, between the death of Judas Maccabeus in B.C. 161, and the year B.C. 143, when all persecution ceased.†

"It will not require," he adds, "much argument to show that such a book, at such a time, may have afforded *material aid and encouragement* to the Jewish patriots;" "may have reminded them that the Lord knows how to deliver His servants, whether from a 'burning fiery furnace,' or from excruciating torture." This idea, that forged prophecies were now first fitted together with genuine legends, with the object of stimulating the valour of the patriots, is Mr. Desprez's modification of the view generally taken by writers of this class on the book of Daniel, that the book is forgery throughout; and contrasts with the apparently more reasonable proposition which we have advanced, that the genuine prophecies of Daniel now first began to attract unusual attention as apparently literally coming to pass, and that the fact of their fulfilment was considered sufficiently remarkable to justify their publication, with a comment, applying them to the events of the day. There is, indeed, good ground for believing, with Mr. Desprez, that the book of Daniel was thus made use

* P. 30.   † 1 Macc. xiii. 41.

of as an instrument in encouraging the Jewish patriots during their eventful struggle; and it is specially to the noble steadfastness and endurance of the
three young princes, Hananiah, Mishael, and Azariah,
when about to be cast into the flames, and to the
patient resignation of Daniel when about to be cast
into the den of lions, to which he must allude, when
speaking of the encouragement to be derived from
the *scenes* described by the writer. We agree with
him as to the value of these scenes for the assumed
purpose, and also of some of the prophecies, when
woven into the times of Antiochus by means of
chap. xi.; but it cannot be shown that the narratives
were then, for the first time, brought to light, nor
can we readily understand how such a prophecy as
that of chap. xi. could add to the effect of the narratives in the way of encouraging the patriots. Certainly the prophecy of the seventy weeks, chap. ix.,
would have afforded them anything but encouragement, supposing it merely to have informed the patriots that the anointed Judas had just been cut off,
and the daily sacrifice abolished, in literal accordance with this newly discovered prophecy, and that
desolations were determined " even until the consummation," then leaving off abruptly, without one
word of consolation.

We will not dwell upon the impiety and impru-
dence of this supposed "pious" Jew, thus putting
into the mouth of God prophecies of events only
just come to pass, and still fresh in the memory of
his readers, and thus producing them as new reve-

lations to the people, or upon the grossness of a
people, who could be imposed upon by such palpable
forgery. There is such glaring improbability in all
this as to destroy any such incongruous theory.
But the difficulty we would point out lies here:
That the noble Mattathias, father of Judas Maccabeus, who died in the year B.C. 168, and who was
the first to rouse his countrymen to resistance
against Antiochus, actually had on his death-bed
encouraged his sons "to be valiant and show themselves men," by reminding them of the steadfastness
of former Jewish worthies; pointing out how "Ananias, Azarias, and Misael, by believing were saved
out of the flame;" and how "Daniel, for his inno-
cency, was delivered from the mouth of lions."*
So that Mattathias, in B.C. 168, seven years before
the death of Judas, and before the time of the supposed forgeries, had referred to a history then extant, and, moreover, a history which we must
presume had been composed before his time, which
contained the very *scenes* which Mr. Desprez and
other critics suggest were brought forward in their
present shape some ten years later, for the first
time, and for the special encouragement of those
living under Demetrius. In the face of this evidence,
what ground, we are compelled to ask, have these
critics, beyond their own imagination, for teaching
that Daniel, chap. iii. or chap. vi., were first brought
forward after the year B.C. 161? And if there is no
ground for such teaching as regards chap. iii., then

* 1 Macc. ii. 59, 60.

also none as regards chap. i., in which is explained
how these four holy men came to be placed in the
position referred to by Mattathias; and again, if not
as regards chap. vi., then also not as regards chap. v.,
which leads to it.   Chap. ix. also, *primâ facie*, is
exempt from the supposition, as affording nothing
but discouragement to those who should then read
it, and so on.   So that, in fact, there appears to be
but small reason, if any, on the score of advantage
to the patriotic cause, for the composition of the
prophecies of Daniel after the year B.C. 161, and
sufficient reason, on the contrary, for believing that a
book containing at least the *scenes* referred to was, as
it professes to have been, written long before B.C. 168.
We take it for granted that the writer of the first
book of the Maccabees is not charged with any
piously-fraudulent intentions.   Here, then, are difficulties, *in limine*, which to an ordinary writer seem
to be insuperable in the way of the supposition that
the book in general was forged after the reign of
Antiochus.   Nevertheless, if philosophers are right
in teaching us that prophecy is out of place in the
ways of God towards man, and if they can really
show that the precise and plain wording of Daniel ix.
can be so fitted with exactness to the time and the
events of the reign of Antiochus, as not to be mistaken, then shall we be ready to recall and reconsider
the apparently inevitable conclusions at which we
have thus far arrived.

    We proceed, therefore, to set forth briefly the
three enigmatical expositions by which sceptical

commentators pride themselves upon having proved, beyond all fair question, that the seventy weeks were fulfilled in the times of Antiochus.

Enigma No. 1.

Seventy Weeks equal to 429 Years.

Mr. Desprez sets out with the intention "to keep imagination, which is apt to run wild on prophetic subjects, within due bounds, and to abide by the rules of sound and careful criticism."* We would ask him to consider how far imagination has been allowed to run wild, or been restrained, in the following summary of his own observations :—

"On the supposition," says Mr. Desprez, "that the 'seven weeks' represent fifty-four years, from the *assault* upon Jerusalem by Nebuchadnezzar, in B.C. 590, to the restoration by Zerubbabel in the first year of Cyrus, B.C. 536; that the 'threescore and two weeks,' starting *from the same terminus à quo*, represent 429 years, to the death of Judas Maccabeus in B.C. 161, to which must be *added* the 'one week,' significant of a period of seven years, during which Antiochus makes a covenant with the apostate Jews"—meaning by one week "added" to, one week *included within* the threescore and two — "we have arrived at a total of 54 + 429 + 7 = 490 years. Owing to the uncertain character of biblical chronology, it is possible that an approximation to

* Page 1.

complete numerical exactness is alone attainable; sufficient agreement, however, may be discernible between the prophetic records and their historical fulfilments to satisfy the general requirements of the arithmetical problem."*

The reader will no doubt be amused at this ingenious and complacent method of turning seventy weeks of years, or 490 years, into a period of 429 years, the exact interval between the two extreme dates. He will be curious also to know how the explicit words, "from the going forth of the commandment to restore and to build Jerusalem," become transmuted into the command of Nebuchadnezzar to assault Jerusalem; for which explanation, however, our limits compel us to refer to Mr. Desprez's ingenious work. We can only observe, that we are anything but convinced or satisfied with the soundness of this enigmatical mode of interpretation; nor do we think, with Mr. Desprez, that the exegesis of this mysterious volume is thus to be placed, "upon a basis that shall stand."† The enigma may thus be reduced :—

7 weeks, or 49 years are 54 years, counted from B.C. 590
62   „   434 „   are 429 „   do.   do.
1   „   7 „   = 7 „   ending   B.C. 161
———   ———   ———   ———
70 weeks, or 490 years=490 years, comprised within 429 yrs.

If this were the meaning of the supposed forger of this prophecy, we cannot comprehend why he

* Page 186.   † Page 187.

should not have written plainly, "from the going forth of the command to *assault* Jerusalem unto the cutting off of Messiah the Prince, shall be about *sixty-one* weeks." The prophet, however, has not so written.

Enigma No. 2.

Seventy Weeks equal to 441 Years.

Other writers, such as Harduin, Ekerman, Eichhorn, Maurer, Hitzig, Wieseler,—we take the names from Dr. Pusey's analytical list*—have seen in the anointing of "the holy of holies" by Judas Maccabeus in the year B.C. 165, that is, in the re-consecration of the temple of Jerusalem after its profanation, the prominent event which filled the mind of the writer of the seventy weeks' prophecy. They count, therefore, from the year B.C. 606, the supposed year of Daniel's captivity, down to the year B.C. 165, a period of exactly 441 years.

Now from B.C. 606 to B.C. 536, the supposed first year of the " anointed" Cyrus, is a period of just seventy years. This interval is assumed, therefore, (though erroneously if Darius the Mede is Darius son of Hystaspes), to represent the seventy years of "desolation" of Jerusalem of which Daniel speaks, in ch. ix. 2, and at the end of which time he prays for a restoration of the sanctuary. The angel, it is said, replies to him that, not seventy years, but seven times seventy years is the

* Pusey on " Daniel," p. 215.

time appointed, so that these 490 years must be considered merely as a prolongation of the original
"seventy," and to be counted, therefore, from the
same year B.C. 606. It matters not that Daniel
speaks emphatically of the command to build Jerusalem as the *terminus à quo* to be adhered to ; it is
determined by these critics, in spite of this insuperable obstacle, that the 490 years ought to begin in
B.C. 606, and end with anointing the "holy of holies"
in B.C. 165. The whole period, however, is, unfortunately, only 441, not 490 years. This matters
not. The want of precision is with the prophet, not in
the exposition. It would be tedious beyond measure
to go through the shifts and shuffles of the promoters of this arrangement, in their endeavours to
show how seven weeks, or forty-nine years, can
be supposed to be represented by seventy, thus
ending with Cyrus. It is quite clear that this
explanation cannot be made to tally with the prophecy. It does not even satisfy those who are
inclined to favour the same general view of the
subject.

7 weeks, or	49 years,	explained to be = 70 years.	
62 „	434 „	counted from B.C. 606	
1 „	7 „	from B.C. 172 to 165	
70 weeks, or 490 years, comprised within		. .	441 years.

There were those, no doubt, in the days of the
Maccabees who would have been inclined to have
entertained even such a perversion of the prophecy
as this. But we know that the day for such inter-

pretations had gone by at the commencement of
the Christian era. For it was from this prophecy
of Daniel (ix.), and from this prophecy only, that
pious Jews were led, as we read, at that very time
to collect about the temple waiting in daily expectation of the appearance of "the Christ."

Thus far, at least, we assume that the reader will
feel disinclined to agree with Dr. Williams, "that it
is clear beyond fair doubt that the period of weeks
ended in the reign of Antiochus Epiphanes." Let
us proceed, then, to examine another of these precious
enigmatical expositions, by which he would seem to
have arrived at this conviction.

ENIGMA No. 3.

SEVENTY WEEKS EQUAL TO 424 YEARS.

In the previous exposition the seventy years of
"desolations of Jerusalem" (ix. 2) are reckoned from
the fourth year of Jehoiakim, B.C. 606, that is, from
a point of time eighteen years before Jerusalem was
made desolate by Nebuchadnezzar. This manifest
contradiction has proved unsatisfactory to most candid inquirers. Some eminent expositors, therefore, such as Bertholt, Bleek, Rosenmüller, Ewald,
and others, have proposed to count correctly, with
Daniel, the seventy years of desolation of Jerusalem
from the year when the city was made desolate by
Nebuchadnezzar (2 Chron. xxxvi. 20, 21), an event
commonly though erroneously placed in the year B.C.

L

588. Now allowing, for the sake of argument, with these writers, that it had been announced to Daniel, in answer to his prayer, that Jeremiah's "seventy years" of desolation were to be lengthened out into 490 years, this lengthened period would thus seem to commence from the year B.C. 588. This arrangement seems at first sight to be an improvement on the last. For, if we count seven weeks, or forty-nine years, from B.C. 588 we come to the year B.C. 538, the commonly received date of the first year of Cyrus the Lord's "anointed," at Babylon, and this appearance of a Messiah at the expiration of "seven weeks" is considered not without reason to be highly remarkable and satisfactory, and something indeed which could hardly be looked upon as accidental. The cutting off of Messiah, however, at the end of 7 + 62 weeks, in this case, must of course have reference to some second Messiah in the days of the Maccabees, which is not quite so satisfactory.

The insuperable difficulty however still remains, that, counting from the year B.C. 588 to B.C. 164, the year of the death of Antiochus, an anointed prince, and soon after the anointing of the "holy of holies" by Judas, is exactly 424 years, not 490, that is, nearly sixty-one weeks, and not "seventy," nor "threescore and two," nor "seven and threescore and two," = 483, nor any period named by the prophet. To remedy this defect it is proposed, and even Ewald lends his name to the extraordinary suggestion, that the seventy sabbaths which are comprehended in seventy weeks are in this instance intended to be

thrown out of the calculation altogether, and that
the enigmatical writer of the book really intended
to express by the term "seventy weeks," not 490,
but 420 years, which number does not fall far short
of the actual interval of 424 years.

Some such explanation as this appears to be that
which comes home to the mind of Dr. Williams as
the most probable explanation of the words of the
prophecy, and as fixing the fulfilment of the weeks
beyond fair doubt in the reign of Antiochus. He
observes,*—"It can hardly be accidental that just
forty-nine or fifty years intervene between the *destruction* at the commencement of the captivity and
the advent of Cyrus in Babylon, or the restoration
under Zerubbabel, whether we follow the suggestion of Isaiah in calling Cyrus the Anointed, or that
of Zechariah in applying the term to Zerubbabel."
In reply to this remark we can only repeat the
question,—How is it possible that the words "to
bring back the captivity, and to restore Jerusalem"
—we make use of Dr. Williams' own translation†—
can, by any conceivable accident, barring the insan-
ity of the interpreter, be mistaken to represent "to
go into captivity and to destroy Jerusalem," which
were the assumed features of the year B.C. 588?

Again he observes, "It can hardly be accidental
that from certain epochs of the captivity to points
in the Maccabean struggle should be 434 years."
Now allowing for a moment that "to destroy," and

* Introduction to Desprez's "Daniel," p. xlii.
† P. xlii.

" to restore," may be taken as equivalent terms, we
agree with Dr. Williams that there may be something observable in the assumed fact that 434 years,
counted, not from B.C. 588, but from B.C. 608, should
be found to end in the death of the anointed priest
Onias, say in B.C. 174. Such, however, is not really
the fact. For though apparently so, according to
the common Biblical reckoning, we shall endeavour
to show in the course of the following pages that
the coincidence is merely the result of a mode of
computation introduced by the Rabbinical para-
phrast: that neither B.C. 588, nor B.C. 608, is the
true date of the event to which it is attached: and
that the interval between the supposed first captivity
in the reign of Jehoiakim and the death of Onias is
at most a period of 408 years, not of 434, nor of 441
years.

Again, Dr. Williams thinks that " the possibility
of the omission of Sabbatical years "— from the
period of seventy Sabbatical weeks — " opens room
for discrepancy," that is, for contradiction between
Daniel's words and facts. Now any supposition of
this sort may be possible on the assumption that the
words are forged. But if there is one thing in this
great prophecy which is definite and worthy of accurate explanation, it is its marked and inseparable
connexion with the sacred Sabbatical cycle. Daniel's
periods are expressed in " weeks," not in years. It
is the Sabbath which marks the division of days
or years into weeks, and to leave out Sabbaths
therefore, would be to destroy any computation by

weeks.   Considering also that it was, amongst other
neglects, for the neglect of the Sabbatical years, and,
as expressly stated, "that the land might enjoy her
Sabbaths," that the seventy years of desolation had
been inflicted, it would certainly be something
remarkable in the ways of God towards His people,
if after commanding them through Moses to keep a
perpetual observance of "Sabbaths of years" (Lev.
xxv. 2–10), that now, when "seventy weeks," or
seventy "Sabbaths of years," were announced as
determined on the people and the holy city, till the
fulfilment of their great expectation, the appearance
of Messiah the Prince, it should for the first time be
put forth by His prophet, or by any pretended prophet, that the computation of weeks should be made
exclusive of Sabbaths.   This is, perhaps, the most
astonishing and ill-conceived suggestion of all to
which this class of interpreters has been driven, in
the endeavour to fit the reckoning of the supposed
impostor to the historical facts before him.   The
scheme may be thus reduced:—

7 weeks, or	49 years =		49 years counted from		B.C.	588
			to first of Cyrus B.C. 538			
62 „	„ 434 „	are 364 „	ending in B.C. 175			
1 „	„ 7 „	is 11 „	ending in		B.C.	164

70 weeks, or 490 years are 424 + 70 Sabbaths = 494 = 424

Such, then, is the result of our examination of the
enigmatical mode of explanation of the prophecy.
It is sufficiently clear that the figures cannot be
made to correspond with the facts, when the

prophecy is interpreted as referring to Antiochus.
It is hardly worth while to take into consideration whether this may be accounted for on the
supposition that the supposed writer of the prophecy was ignorant of history, considering that
we believe the chronology of those by whom these
enigmatical figures have been put together to be
itself entirely corrupt. Be that, however, as it may,
no candid inquirer, we think, will admit that there
is any justification for Dr. Williams's assertion to be
derived from either of these enigmatical interpretations.

From the foregoing investigation then of the various modes of interpretation of the book of Daniel, it
would appear that the book has suffered in times
past, as much from the hands of zealous or care-
less friends, as it has from the enmity of open
foes ; that large interpolations, written with no
sinister purpose, but with the honest intention of
illustrating the prophet's words, had been introduced into the text, some time before the Christian
era, that is to say, before the publication of the
Greek translation called the LXX., and that those
interpolations had become so fixed and recognised
in all copies used in the early Christian Church, as
to have been adopted even into the later and re-
vised copies of Theodotion, of Jerome, and of other
translators. And thus the true text of Daniel has
been handed down to us obscured and mystified by
mere words of comment; while those who would
have expounded and made plain the text have lite-

rally, though unintentionally, fulfilled the words
addressed to the prophet : " Shut up the words, and
seal the book ;" " For the words are closed up and
sealed till the time of the end." xii. 4, 9. Again,
we have seen how a succession of rabbis, priests,
philosophers, and commentators, have, from time
to time, set their minds to expound the hidden
mystery of the prophecy of the " Seventy Weeks,"
that prophecy of prophecies, which nevertheless
still lies wrapped in obscurity amongst the treasures of this wondrous book ; how, by the application of a defective heathen scheme of chronology
to the interpretation of prophetic periods, which
would seem to run in measured cycles throughout
Holy Scripture, the true import of Daniel's periods
has become so distorted and obscured, as to leave
the impression upon many a reverent mind, that,
if indeed prophetic, they are incapable of any but
a vague interpretation ; and how at length the book
has fallen into the hands of merciless critics, who
have dragged it in triumph through the mire, as a
detected piece of fraud, and worthy only to be cast
amidst the heap of pious impositions by which mankind from time to time has been misled.

Yet if it is true, as we trust that we have succeeded in showing, that the text of the book has
been subjected to interpolation, then is it clear,
not only that it is not profane, as some would
persuade us, but, on the contrary, that it is the
bounden duty of all who think they can throw
light upon it, to question, to scrutinize, and to dissect

each chapter and sentence of the book, with the view, if possible, of restoring the integrity of the inspired text. Let us not be ashamed to submit the book for revision to the hands of those to whom it pleased the Almighty at the first to commit "the oracles of God." Let it undergo the scrutiny of God's own holy people, who, through times of deepest ignorance and darkness, have proved their fitness for the trust, by cherishing with scrupulous exactness each syllable and letter of the supposed sacred text; and who, in these days of enlightenment, with their knowledge of the language, and of Hebrew modes of comment, may yet be able to throw light upon the way in which, and the extent to which, corruption has crept in. Perchance, while lifting off the veil with which, in days gone by, they have thus but too carefully shrouded from their own eyes the Divine messages of the prophet, they may be led to perceive, how simply and how precisely his predictions of Messiah have been fulfilled, in the birth and cutting off of Him, who "came unto His own, and His own received Him not," and who, when in wilful blindness they rejected, reviled, and crucified Him, exclaimed in tender mercy on the cross, "Father, forgive them, for they know not what they do."

We now proceed to point out the manner in which the prophecy appears to us to have been literally fulfilled.

DANIEL'S PROPHECY OF MESSIAH
THE PRINCE.

WE have seen in the foregoing pages how about
the time of Antiochus Epiphanes, rather more than
a century and a half before the birth of Christ,
the prophecies of Daniel had become the subject
of intense interest amongst the Jews, owing to the
supposed literal fulfilment in that reign of certain
striking predictions of the prophet; and how even
that portion of ch. ix., which relates to the ceasing
of the "daily sacrifice" in the temple of Jerusalem,
which we know from our Lord Himself, was
written with reference to the time of the taking
of Jerusalem by Titus, had been prematurely interpreted in connexion with the reign of the Syro-
Grecian king. As time advanced, the interest in
these prophecies became more and more intense.
Prophetic interpretation in the days preceding the
coming of our Lord had become a subject of absorbing
occupation, much as it is in these our own days;
and the same great prediction concerning the
coming of "one like a son of man with the clouds
of heaven," to "set up a kingdom which should
never be destroyed," and to give "the kingdom
and dominion, and the greatness of the kingdom

under the whole heavens to the people of the saints
of the most high," which now, in the greater fulness of the times, is confidently looked forward to
by many devout interpreters as close at hand, was
then as confidently believed to be literally coming to pass, in the restoration of the "kingdom" to
Israel. It could hardly have been otherwise, if the
authoritative interpretations of the Scribes of that
day were allowed to pass as correct. For nothing
according to their interpretations seemed to intervene between the events then declared to have
come to pass, excepting only the appearance of the
prophet Elias, and the next great and glorious event
foreshadowed by all the prophets of Israel.

It was clear enough to all that the four successive empires of the heathen world, so distinctly
portrayed in ch. ii., had actually risen in succession
in accordance with the words of Daniel. It was,
as we have argued, so fully believed by Rabbinical
scribes, that the vision of the ten kingdoms, or
horns, of ch. vii., and of the little kingdom, or horn,
which should rise up amongst the ten, had been
fulfilled in the time of Antiochus, as to have
led to the incorporation of the historical comment
of ch. xi., with the text of the book of Daniel
itself. And it was then generally allowed, as we
may infer from the adoption of the same opinion
by Josephus, that the writers of the books of
Maccabees, however erroneous we may now consider their interpretation, had rightly interpreted
the events connected with that other "little horn,"

or kingdom, spoken of by Daniel in ch. viii. as having been already fulfilled in the days of the same Antiochus. The next great event, therefore, was the restoration of " the kingdom " to the saints of the Most High, that is, to the people of Israel; and a deep conviction had taken possession of the minds of the whole Jewish nation that that event was now close at hand. The book of Enoch, the 4th eclogue of Virgil, and the Sibylline Oracles, testify to the prophetic excitement then prevailing throughout all the world. Nor was the actual temporal position and influence of the Jewish nation at that time incommensurate with the great spiritual expectations which they entertained. The Jews in the days of Herod were already spread throughout every kingdom of the civilised world. In Mesopotamia, Media, Persia, Egypt, Arabia, Asia Minor, Greece, and Rome, their numbers and importance were great. Some of them had even allied themselves with noble families at Rome. Prodigious wealth was accumulated in Jerusalem, arising from the annual contribution of the half-shekel per head by every worthy Jew throughout the world towards the treasury of the temple. The splendour and magnificence of the kingdom of Herod the Great might be compared to that of Solomon himself; and in all his undertakings we are told that it was his ambition to surpass all that had been done before him. It is not improbable that Herod, or his flatterers, at times may have been disposed to think that he himself was that prince upon whom all expectation was fixed. Be

this as it may, the expectation was universal; and '
have the testimony of the Roman historians Tacit
and Suetonius to the fact, that "an ancient and t
varying tradition had prevailed, throughout the Ea
that at that time some one rising in Judæa shot
obtain dominion." So prepared, indeed, and waitii
were they in distant regions for the great event, tl
in the course of not many months after His birth
find wise men journeying from the East to Jud;
bearing kingly gifts, to present to him who v
"*born* King of the Jews," the star of whose i
tivity they had seen in the East.

Now it is to be remarked particularly, that it v
to the *birth* of a prince that the thoughts of pi(
men at that time were turned in Jerusalem. Isa
had written, "A virgin shall be with child and sl
bring forth a son." The inquiry made of the cl
priests and scribes by Herod was, "where Christ sho
be *born*," Matt. ii. 4. The words of Isaiah—"Unto
a child is *born*, unto us a son is given," had, as we le
from the Targum of Jonathan, been applied by J-
themselves to the expected Messiah. And it !
been announced to Mary, "that holy thing wh
which shall be *born* of thee shall be called the !
of God," Luke, i. 35. The appellation by wh
this expected child* was commonly referred
was "Messias," anointed, or "the Messias,"
anointed, or "Χριστὸς Κύριος," Christ the L-
words clearly adopted with reference to
Hebrew expression "Mashiach Nagid," Messiah

* Acts, iv. 27.

prince, of Daniel :* devout men and women were collected about the temple, waiting daily the appearance
of this Prince, who should save them from their enemies, and all who hated and oppressed them ; and so
nearly was the time of His arrival fixed and known
in Jerusalem, that to one aged priest in particular, it
had been revealed that he should not see death till he
had seen the Lord's Christ, Χριστὸς Κύριου.†

Such then being the state of ferment and expectation at Jerusalem, we learn from St. Luke, that,
while certain shepherds were keeping watch over
their flocks by night, a heavenly messenger suddenly
announced to them, " This day is *born* unto you, in
the city of David, a Saviour, which is Christ the
Lord," Χριστὸς Κύριος ; or, in other words, this day is
born unto you, the expected " Mashiach Nagid."
Thus, by every conceivable form of declaration, first
by obscure revelation to Isaiah of old, then to Mary
the mother of our Lord not long before the birth,
then to the shepherds on the very day of the birth,
and, lastly, to the wise men journeying from the East,
it was proclaimed that in the birth of the Messiah,
the glorious words of the prophets had been or
were to be fulfilled. Seeing then that the expecta-

* The word נָגִיד, *nagid*, is not commonly translated Κύριος,
though indeed the LXX translation paraphrases " ad Maschiach
nagid," as if written "ar nagid," πολιν Κυριου. Theodotion writes
Χριστου ηγουμένου. David, however, was *Nagid* over Israel, and so
also was Solomon, and " the son of David " was to sit upon the
throne of his father, therefore, as " Mashiach Nagid."

† Luke, ii. 26.

tion was thus literally fulfilled in the *birth* of a pri
of the house of David, we submit that it is neit
reasonable nor in conformity with Scripture, to p
over the birth of Christ in the reign of August
and to look onward to the reign of Tiberius, to
baptism of Christ, as Dr. Pusey and almost all ot
interpreters have proposed, for the fulfilment of 1
prophecy.* The words of the holy angel co
hardly have more distinctly proclaimed, "1
Seventy Weeks' prophecy of Daniel concerning
Messiah, is this day fulfilled by the *birth* of Christ
Lord in Bethlehem." We have no hesitation, the
fore, in affirming, that the consistency of Scriptu
can only be maintained by taking the birth of Chr
and not his baptism, nor his death, as the *termii*
ad quem of the prophecy concerning Messiah
Prince.

Taking then the birth of Christ as the fundamen
point of our interpretation, let it be observed, as
proceed, how plainly and naturally each separate
riod of weeks comprised within the seventy falls i
its own true position, and with what exactness ev
single date required for the verification of this prec
numerical prediction has been, either directly or
directly recorded, in sacred history.

For if " Jesus began to be about thirty years
age," as we are told, in the fifteenth year of Tiber

---

* Sir Isaac Newton, and some few other interpreters, h
seen that the fulfilment of the prophecy took place in the birtl
Christ, though unable to explain the several periods of wee
on that understanding, in connexion with the common reckonir

Cæsar,* at the time of his baptism, say after the month of August (for in August, B.C. 28, the reign of Tiberius began,) and either before the winter of A.D. 28 set in, or after the winter, in the early part of A.D. 29, then must the birth of Christ have taken place either about the autumn or winter of the year B.C. 3, or the spring of B.C. 2, that is to say, at the beginning or middle of the Sabbatical year B.C. 3–2, in the year 4711 or 4712 of the Julian period, which is in accordance with the opinion of Scaliger,† after much consideration of the subject: and if we count upwards from that date seventy Sabbatical weeks, or 490 years, we come to the Sabbatical year B.C. 493–2, which falls, as it ought to fall, in the reign of Darius the son of Hystaspes, king of Persia, in agreement, as we shall show, with Daniel's words.

The last year of the whole seventy weeks is thus precisely fixed, by St. Luke, to the Sabbatical year, B.C. 3–2: the first year of the period appears to be fixed, by Daniel, with equal precision: for Daniel, who was living at the beginning of the period, tells us that it was " in the first year of Darius, son of Ahasuerus, of the seed of the Medes, what time he was set over the realm of the Chaldeans," that the prophecy of the seventy weeks was delivered to him. And he elsewhere tells us that the first year of that king's reign over Babylon was when he was " about threescore and two years old."‡ We know of no reason which can be assigned why the age of the

* Luke, iii. 1.
† De Emend. Temp. p. 551.   ‡ Dan. v. 31.

king should be so precisely recorded, if not for the purpose of marking, though indirectly, the exact year of the delivery of this all-important prophecy; but if intended so to mark that event, then ought we to find, if our principle of interpretation is correct, that Darius son of Hystaspes, who we assume to be the same as Darius son of Ahasuerus, was about sixty-two years old in the Sabbatical year B.C. 493–2.

Now Ctesias, who lived at the court of Persia, and who is by far the best authority concerning the reigns of the kings of Persia which we possess, has left a record that Darius died at the age of seventy-two,* and Herodotus asserts that he died in the fifth year after the battle of Marathon, that is, in B.C. 485. If then we follow the reckoning of Herodotus, and Darius was seventy two in B.C. 485, he must have been sixty-two years old in the year B.C. 495, and therefore " *about* threescore and two years old," that is, in his sixty-third year, in B.C. 494. This computation may be thought sufficiently near to satisfy those who follow Herodotus, and who adopt the reckoning of Archbishop Ussher, who places the birth of Christ in B.C. 4. For thus, 490 years added to B.C. 4 would bring them to the sixty-third year of the age of Darius; making, however, the date of the prophecy and the birth of Christ thus to fall each one year too early, that is, in each case before the Sabbatical year had commenced. We are, however, satisfied that Herodotus is here slightly in error.

Both Herodotus and Ctesias are apparently agreed

* Ctes. Frag. Muller, p. 49.

that Xerxes, the son of Darius, came to the throne in
the year B.C. 486, by the direct appointment of his
father while yet alive, as related by the former of
these historians. For the difference between them is
that Herodotus assigns thirty-six years to the reign
of Darius ending in the accession of Xerxes, in B.C.
486, while Ctesias, more correctly we believe, allowing more years to Cambyses, reckons only thirty-one
years of Darius to the same date. Thus, according
to Ctesias, Darius came to the throne in the year B.C.
517, which is the very date inscribed in the Parian
Chronicle as that of his first year;* and this date
also agrees with a still extant tablet in the Serapéum
at Memphis, which records the birth of an Apis in the
fifth year of Cambyses (*i.e.* his fifth year over
Egypt†), which fell in B.C. 521, and its death at the
age of seven years and eight months, in the fourth
year of Darius, that is, in B.C. 514, thus making the
first year of his reign B.C. 517. Nevertheless, Herodotus is unquestionably right in assigning thirty-six
years to the reign of Darius, for this year of his reign
is found in Egyptian records,‡ so that he must, if
Ctesias is correct, have died in the year B.C. 483 or
482, having completed, or nearly completed, the

* Some have suggested an amendment of Selden's reading of
the marble. But Selden himself clearly had no doubt as to the
figures before him. For he charges the author of the chronicle
with a metachronism, and a manifest error. Marmor Oxoniensis,
p. 140.

† See a paper by the author on this subject, "Journ. Sac.
Lit." Oct. 1864.

‡ Vol. II. part 3, "Transactions of the Chronological Institute."

seventy-second year of his age. If so, his age would have been " about threescore and two," in the course of the Sabbatical year B.C. 493-2. This we believe to be the true reckoning of his reign, and the result is, that the vision in which the prophecy of the seventy weeks was revealed to Daniel, was probably seen in the early part of the year B.C. 492, just seventy Sabbatical weeks before the birth of Christ, and those weeks indeed, as we believe, the first seventy weeks of a great period of weeks comprehending the then future destinies of the Jews, commencing from the date of the dedication of the second temple.

Here let us pause for a moment to consider one or two interesting results to be derived from this precise determination of the date of the delivery of this prophecy. What are the words of the holy angel to Daniel ? " Seventy weeks are determined upon thy people and upon thy holy city." Now what is the meaning of the expression " holy city ?" When did Jerusalem first become the " holy city ?" Not when David conquered this stronghold from the Jebusites. Not when he fixed his palace on the Mount of Zion. But Jerusalem became the " holy city " when Solomon dedicated his temple to Jehovah, when the cloud descended and filled the house, and when the city together with its holy sanctuary constituted the " holy city." Now it is not of Jerusalem, but of the " holy city " that the prophet Daniel speaks, and we know that from the time of the dedication of the first temple, in the

twelfth year of Solomon, to the destruction of the
city and the sanctuary in the reign of Zedekiah,
was exactly 420 years, and that when these years
are added to the seventy years of desolation of
the city, or the seventy years during which the
land enjoyed her neglected sabbaths, ending about
the first year of Darius son of Ahasuerus, they
form a period of 490 years, or seventy weeks. So
that, reckoning in the Era of the "holy city,".
or in the Era of the first temple, the words of
the prophecy delivered to Daniel in B.C. 492 were
first fulfilled at the completion of the 490th year
of that Era ; while counting downwards from B.C. 492
to the birth of Christ they were a second time fulfilled in a period of exactly the same length of
time. This sixty-second year then of the age of
Darius, the son of Hystaspes, thus incidentally preserved in the Book of Daniel, is in fact for
chronological purposes the most important date in
all Scripture. It is the pivot upon which sacred
chronology turns. By means of it we are enabled
to compute with exactness upwards and downwards,
either to the building of the temple, or to the birth
of Christ, and to reckon also within strictly defined
limits the hitherto unknown years of the period of
the Jubilee ; and when taken in conjunction with the
period of 480 years recorded in 1 Kings, vi. 2, we
mount with exactness even to the year of the
exodus, to a point reaching nearly twice the distance of the Era of the Olympiads.

But if this date B.C. 492 be the true date of

Daniel's vision in the reign of Darius, then must the destruction and the "desolations of Jerusalem," in the reign of Nebuchadnezzar, have commenced just seventy years before this well-defined point of time ; because Daniel, at the very time of the vision, declared that he then "understood by books the number of the years, whereof the word of the Lord came to Jeremiah the prophet, that he would accomplish seventy years in the desolations of Jerusalem," chap. ix. 2, and therefore prayed for the immediate restoration of the sanctuary. Now seventy years added to the year B.C. 492–3 brings us to the year B.C. 563, in which year, therefore, unless our principle of interpretation is erroneous, we ought to find from history that Jerusalem was taken by Nebuchadnezzar and made desolate. On the contrary, however, as we have seen, both believers and unbelievers have, with one consent, agreed to fix the date of the fall of Jerusalem in the year B.C. 588. If tested, therefore, by the rule of "*quod semper, quod ab omnibus,*" we fear that a synod of chronologists would be inclined to pronounce decidedly against the interpretation we have now advanced. Nevertheless, we are satisfied that this is the true date of the destruction of Jerusalem by the Chaldeans. For it cannot be by chance that the Jewish historian Demetrius, who wrote a history of the kings of Judæa in the reign of Ptolemy Philopator, more than 200 years before the Christian era, should have recorded that "the last carrying away of captives" from Jerusalem by king Nebuchad-

nezzar mentioned in Scripture, which we learn
from the prophet Jeremiah was in the twenty-third
year of that king's reign,* took.. place in the year
B.C. 560, that is, as the author writes, 338 years
and three months before Ptolemy Philopator began
to reign 'in B.C. 222, from which we learn that the
latter part of the nineteenth year of the reign of
Nebuchadnezzar in which Jerusalem was destroyed,
may, by this computation, have fallen in B.C. 563 ;
and thus, on the authority of this Jewish historian,.
we are justified in placing the beginning of the
"desolations of Jerusalem" in B.C. 563, and the close
of the desolations in the sabbatical year B.C. 493–2,
and therefore also the vision of Daniel in that year,
as before determined.

But what historian, it may be asked, will support
Demetrius in this computation? We reply that to
all appearance it is remarkably confirmed by a passage in the gospel of St. Matthew, who seems to
found upon this particular date, so fortunately preserved,† a peculiar genealogical computation which
can in no other way be understood. For he reckons
that "from the carrying away into Babylon unto
Christ are fourteen generations." (Matt. i. 17.) But
how fourteen generations? We know from St.
Luke that there were no less than twenty-two generations from father to son between the times
mentioned. It is not, therefore, by such generations

---

* Jer. lii. 30. See Canon of Demetrius. Appendix A.

† Preserved amongst other fragments of chronology by Clem.
Alex. Strom. l. c. xxi.

that Matthew counts; on the other hand, we know that throughout the East a generation was counted as forty years. Numerous instances to this effect are to be found in the Old Testament, as also a remarkable instance in the "Zendavesta."* Now fourteen times forty years is a period of exactly 560 years, which added to the birth of Christ B.C. 3, brings us to the very year B.C. 563, for the carrying away into captivity at the destruction of Jerusalem, to which, therefore, St. Matthew must probably have referred.

Nevertheless, much difficulty will always be found in explaining how the three successive periods of fourteen generations spoken of by St. Matthew, in the above passage, were fulfilled; and as this rough mode of computation does not, and cannot be expected to bring out three precise periods of 560 years in exact succession, without which nothing decisive can be drawn from this peculiar record, we will not dwell upon this argument for more than it is worth, but turn to two other highly interesting modes of testing the accuracy of the reckoning of Demetrius, viz. to some of the most ancient manuscripts now extant in the world, and also to certain Egyptian monuments recently discovered bearing indirectly upon the times of the Jewish monarchy.

Amongst the *débris* of what may be called the library of one of the last kings of Assyria, lately brought from Nineveh to the British Museum, by

* 2nd Fargard, 134. "Every forty years two human beings are born of every two human beings, a pair, one male and one female child."

Mr. Layard, there have been found four, more or less perfect copies of a list of annual officers at Nineveh, reaching nearly from the beginning to nearly the end of the Assyrian monarchy. In this list are found the names of Tiglath-pileser, Sargon, and Sennacherib, kings of Assyria, who, we know from the Bible, were contemporary with Ahaz and Hezekiah, kings of Judah ; and the names are so grouped in the list, that the length of each successive reign can be ascertained by counting the intervening number of officers between the names of the several kings. Now three eminent Assyrian scholars, Sir H. Rawlinson, Dr. Hincks, and M. Oppert, having each separately examined the document, which is styled by Sir Henry the Assyrian Canon, and having compared it with astronomical records, had arrived at the conclusion that Sennacherib must have begun to reign somewhere about the year B.C. 704, according to Sir Henry, or about 702, as determined by M. Oppert and Dr. Hincks; and that Tiglath-pileser must have reigned somewhere about the year B.C. 743, or 744. While these pages, however, are passing through the press, Sir H. Rawlinson has announced the discovery of what he considers to be the record of a solar eclipse,* observed at Nineveh in the year B.C. 763, and registered in the eighteenth year before the accession of Tiglath-pileser, thus marking the first year of the

---

* See Index prefixed to the second Volume of the "Cuneiform Inscriptions," published by the British Museum in 1866, No. 52 ; and "Athenæum," 18 May, 1867.

reign of that king with mathematical precision, as
the year B.C. 745.   Again Sir H. Rawlinson on
examination of the historical tablets of Tiglath-pileser,
has pointed out that Tiglath-pileser, in the eighth
year of his reign, *i.e.* in the year B.C. 738, took
tribute of Menahem, king of Samaria, Rezin, king
of Damascus, Hiram, king of Tyre, and Yahu-
khazi, that is, Khuzzi-yahu, עֻזִּיָּהוּ, Uzziah, king of
Judah.*   Now, according to Demetrius, the last
year of Uzziah was B.C. 734, only four years later
than the year in which he paid tribute, according to
the Assyrian Canon.   But the last year of Menahem,
who reigned only ten years, was, according to Demetrius, B.C. 738 ; so that his reign cannot be raised
even one single year, if Rawlinson's statements are
correct, without producing discrepancy between the
Canon and Demetrius.   The reckoning, therefore,
of Demetrius appears to be exact.

The testimony of the Egyptian monuments to
the same effect, though not quite so precise, is equally
satisfactory.   M. Mariette, in the year 1856, discovered in the temple of Serapis at Memphis, a
series of the tombs of the sacred bull Apis, from
the epitaphs on which the length of the several
reigns, from Tirhakah, king of Egypt, to Amasis,
the king of Egypt conquered by Cambyses, may be
reckoned.   Sir Gardner Wilkinson, who examined
these monuments at Paris in 1856, writing to Mr.

---

* "Athenæum," 8 Mar., 15 Mar., 1862 ; August 22, 1863 ;
and 9 Feb. and 9 Mar. 1867.

Poole, observes, " The accession of Tirhakah cannot be placed earlier than B.C. 700, which would bring down the expedition of Sennacherib much later than in the Bible chronology."* Sir G. Wilkinson had not, however, then observed the overlapping of the reign of Apries, or Pharaoh Hophra, with that of Amasis, shown by the recorded death of Apis in the 12th year of Apries, and the birth of his successor in the 5th year of Amasis, by which the beginning of the reign of Apries must be lowered ten years, and the beginning also of the reign of Tirhakah must be placed even as low as B.C. 680, while the reign of Sevechus, or Sethos, will fall in B.C. 691. Now Herodotus informs us that Sethos was reigning in Egypt when Sennacherib came up against Egypt ; when Tirhakah, as we know from the Bible, was yet reigning in Ethiopia ; and when Hezekiah was in the 14th year of his reign ; all which fits in exactly with the precise statement of Demetrius, that Sennacherib carried away captives from Judæa 467 years and 9 months before the reign of Ptolemy Philopator ; that is, in Feb. B C. 688.

But now, again, our reckoning comes into direct collision with received ancient chronology, and has to undergo the test of an authority supposed by many to be of very great weight, we mean the well-known Canon of Ptolemy, the Alexandrian astronomer. For if the nineteenth year of Nebuchadnezzar fell, as we have said, in B.C. 563, then must his first year of course have fallen in the year

* " Monthly Review of Literature," Oct. 1856.

B.C. 582, which is directly opposed by the authority
of this Canon, which places his accession in B.C. 604,
a date accepted by Scaliger and other great chronologists up to this day. Fortunately, we are enabled
to appeal from this supposed decisive authority to
a still higher authority, viz. that of unerring astronomy, the most accurate test which can be brought
to bear upon chronological computations. The
test of a solar eclipse, the time of which may be
computed now almost as accurately as it could
have been registered when the event took place,
and still more that of a *total* solar eclipse, which
Mr. Airy declares to be at least ten times as valuable as any other eclipse of the sun for this purpose, when brought to bear upon the time of any
event in history, must necessarily outweigh any other
evidence of date which can be given on the subject.

We have so frequently had occasion in pursuit
of these inquiries* to refer to the *total* solar eclipse
of the year B.C. 585, as identified with that mentioned by Herodotus as having occurred during the
battle between Cyaxares, king of Media, and
Alyattes, king of Lydia, shortly before Nineveh was
destroyed by the Medes and Babylonians, and the
correctness of this date as attached to that event is
now so seldom called in question, that it is unne-
cessary to enter into any detail here upon this point.†

* "Trans. Chron. Inst." vol. ii. part 3.

† We regret to find that Professor Rawlinson, in his "Anc.
Monarchies," vol. iii. p. 210, seeks to accommodate this eclipse to
his chronology, not his chronology to the eclipse. He sets aside

It is sufficient to observe that Herodotus places the fall of Nineveh not long after that eclipse, and that Abydenus, treating of Babylonian history, places the accession of Nebuchadnezzar to the throne of Babylon immediately after the fall of Nineveh, all which well accords with the year B.C. 582, already pointed out as the date of the first year of his reign. So that the unquestionable accuracy of the date of the eclipse, the unusually precise record of Demetrius, the peculiar genealogical computation of St. Matthew, the evidence of the Assyrian Canon, the epitaphs of the sacred bulls in the Serapéum, and the exact record in Scripture of the age of Darius at the time when he began to reign over Babylon, all combine together in the most remarkable manner to lead to the date B.C. 582 as the first year of Nebuchadnezzar king of Babylon.

Now it is interesting to find that this is the very date to be derived from the reckoning of the ancient Chaldean historian, Berosus, who wrote four hundred years before the compilation of Ptolemy's Canon : while the system of Babylonian dates, in and after the reign of Nebuchadnezzar, introduced

the remarkable words, "day was *suddenly* turned into night," (ἐξάπινα) which is the peculiar feature of a total eclipse, and thus leaves himself at liberty to apply any partial eclipse of the sun to the event. And as one error leads to another, he feels himself compelled to expunge the name of king Deioces from the list of the Median kings, because his revolt from Assyria is thus pushed up into the reign of the powerful Sargon, instead of falling in the reign of Sennacherib, in which, as Josephus informs us, it took place.

by this latter document, which was wholly unknown
either to Africanus or to Eusebius, or to the very
learned Clement of Alexandria, has been the unfor-
tunate means of obscuring the true Babylonian
reckoning, even till the present day.   For Eusebius,
with all the most ancient authorities before him,
very plainly states that the king called Sardanapalus by the Greeks was the last of all the Assyrian
kings:* while Polyhistor, who copied from Berosus,
tells us that Sardanapalus was no other than Nabopalassar, the father of Nebuchadnezzar : from which
identification we are enabled to fix with exactness
the date of the reign of the last of the Assyrian
kings.   Abydenus, who also copied from Berosus,
fixes with accuracy the date of the termination
of the Assyrian empire under Sardanapalus just
167 years (erroneously written 67 in our copies
of Eusebius†) after the first Olympiad, that is, in

---

* Professor Rawlinson here throws off all respect for authority.
He makes Saracus, the last king of Nineveh, fall in the ninth
year of the reign of Cyaxares, when that king was about forty
years of age ; whereas Abydenus tells us that the marriage of the
grand-daughter of Cyaxares had already taken place before the
fall of Saracus. Herodotus gives twenty-eight years to the Scythian occupation of Asia, all comprised within the reign of
Cyaxares, Mr. Rawlinson finds not more than eight years for the
Scythian occupation according to his chronology. Abydenus tells
us that the Assyrian empire ceased in B.C. 610, Mr. Rawlinson
in B.C. 625. The Parian Chronicle (confirmed indirectly by an
Assyrian inscription, which lowers the common date of the reign
of Gyges,) places the first year of Alyattes, who fought with
Cyaxares, in B.C. 605, Mr. R. places his sixth year before B.C. 610.
† Eus. Auch. Part i. p. 39.

B.C. 610, and thus incidentally identifies that king with Nabopolassar : for Nabopolassar certainly began to reign in the year B.C. 625,—when the thrones of Babylon and Nineveh were still united,— as certified by a lunar eclipse in his fifth year, recorded by Ptolemy. This last king of Assyria is called, in the book of Judith, "Nabuchodonosor, who reigned at Nineveh." We read that in his twelfth year, that is, in B.C. 614, he slew Arphaxad, or Phraortes, the king of Media, an event also recorded by Herodotus.* Four years later, that is, in B.C. 610, Herodotus tells us that the Scythians (probably called in for the purpose) relieved the king of Nineveh from the vengeance of Cyaxares, son of Phraortes, and that, having conquered the Medes, the Scythians from henceforth became the arbiters of all Asia. Thus the empire of the Assyrians was virtually superseded by that of the Scythians, in B.C. 610, though Nineveh was not yet destroyed. Nabopolassar, however, or Nabuchodonosor, still lingered on the throne of Nineveh, by support of the Scythians, and in his eighteenth year, that is, B.C. 608, "there was talk in the house of the king of the Assyrians that he should, as he said, avenge himself on all the earth." A great army, therefore, of Scythians, Medes, and Persians, commanded by Holophernes, was poured into Syria, and marched even as far as Ashdod, with a view to the conquest of Egypt, at which place it was stopped by

* Herod. i. 102.

Psammetichus, the Egyptian king who purchased
peace, as related by Herodotus,* and also by the
book of Judith.†   Nothing can be more consistent
and accurate than all this history thus put together.
But now again Abydenus, still copying from Berosus, takes up the narrative, and informs us that
another king,‡ styled "Saracus," a king we must
assume set up by the Scythians, followed Sardanapalus on the throne of Nineveh, and ended his reign
by burning himself in his palace when that city was
finally besieged and destroyed by the Babylonians
and Medes.   Abydenus does not indeed state the
length of the reign of Saracus, but we have the very
best reason for believing that this siege took place
twenty-eight or twenty-six years after the coming of
the Scythians into Asia.   Herodotus, in three places,
marks the interval as twenty-eight years, which,
counted from the year B.C. 610, brings us to the
year B.C. 582 ; and Abydenus concludes his account
of the siege by stating that Nebuchadnezzar, on the
fall of Nineveh, took the throne of Babylon, and
surrounded the city with a strong wall. §   The
difference between the 1280 years counted by Castor
and Abydenus from Ninus to the termination of the
empire, and the 1306 years of Ctesias, counted from
the same point to the taking of Nineveh by the
Medes and Babylonians, is, however, only twenty-
six years.   These twenty-six years, therefore, end

---

* Herod. i. 105.   † Judith, ii. 28 ; iii. 1.
‡ Castor calls him Ninus.   § Euseb. Auch. Part i. p. 25.

in B.C. 584, when we may suppose that the final siege by Nebuchadnezzar and Cyaxares began.

All the earliest records, therefore, combine to fix the date of the first year of Nebuchadnezzar to the year B.C. 582: and those critics, we think, are in error, who in interpretation of the ninth chapter of Daniel, propose to count sixty-two weeks of years, or 434 years, from B.C. 608, as the beginning of the reign of Nebuchadnezzar to the death of Onias, the high-priest, in B.C. 174. Such a reckoning indeed suited the ideas of the Jewish interpreter who paraphrased the tenth and twelfth chapters of Daniel in the days of the Maccabees, and who, by two verses of comment, as we have seen, (ch. x. 1, and ch. xi. 1), succeeded in raising the first year of Darius the Mede in Babylon from the year B.C. 492 to B.C. 538, thereby raising also the reign of Nebuchadnezzar. But this arrangement, we submit, is the result of a chronology made to suit his own interpretation, and by it both sceptical and believing critics have ever since been led astray.

Again, we test the accuracy of our Biblical reckoning by counting upwards from the first year of Nebuchadnezzar, B.C. 582, that is, from the fourth year of Jehoiakim (Jerem. xxv. 1.), to the fourteenth year of Hezekiah, thus:—

			Years.
JEHOIAKIM	.	.	3
JOSIAH	.	.	31
AMON	.	.	2
MANASSEH	.	.	55
HEZEKIAH	.	.	15

106 + B.C. 582 = B.C. 688.

and we are thus led to the year B.C. 688 for the close
of the fourteenth year of Hezekiah. Now, this is the
exact reckoning which had been preserved amongst
the Jews. when Demetrius wrote ; for he places the
time of tne carrying away of captives from Judea
by Sennacherib, who threatened Jerusalem in Hezekiah's fourteenth year, with great precision, just
four hundred and sixty-six years and nine months
before the reign of the fourth Ptolemy,* that is, in
the month of February, B.C. 688. From which we
learn that the fourteenth of Hezekiah was concurrent with the two years B.C. 689 and 688, counting
from Nisan to Nisan. This direct historical testimony we look upon as of extreme value.

But Holy Scripture has, we believe, preserved
for our guidance a testimony even still more valuable ; one indeed which appears to bring the reckoning of the reign of Hezekiah into a position of
absolute precision, by a sign of a most remarkable character. This sign was foretold, in the first
place, for the confirmation of the drooping faith of
King Hezekiah, when heathen blasphemers threatened to raise their standard against the holy city ;
but it was recorded, we submit, with a fuller and
a deeper purpose for the instruction of after ages,
and specially, perhaps, with a view to cheer the
wavering faith of the Church in these days of
doubt and scepticism, when again blasphemers have
assailed the city of God. For shortly before the
invasion of Sennacherib,—say in the beginning of

* "Trans. Chron. Inst." vol. ii. part iv. p. 102.

B.C. 689, according to our reckoning,—we read that Hezekiah was sick unto death, and that in answer to his fervent prayer for recovery the Prophet Isaiah was sent to him to declare : " Thus saith the Lord the God of David thy Father, I have heard thy prayer—I have seen thy tears : behold, I will add unto thy days fifteen years, and I will defend this city," &c.*   "And this shall be a sign unto you, Behold, I will bring again the shadow of the steps, which it shall have gone down on the steps (Maaloth) of Ahaz with the sun, ten steps backwards," or "from the end." In these few words we appear to have brought before us a description of an instrument in the palace of Hezekiah, in use from the days of Ahaz, probably for marking the variation of the shadow cast by the sun from day to day.† The words "shadow of the steps" going " *down upon the steps*," are most expressive ; and we learn from them that—

1st. The "steps of Ahaz" were turned away from the sun.

For in that position only could they cast their shadow, or the number of illumined steps be varied, up or down the steps, according to the altitude of the sun. Now, the only conceivable use of a fixed instrument so placed would be to observe the rise and fall of the shadow from day

---

* Isa. xxxviii. 5, 6.

† " They say that Ahaz, by some contrivance, had erected in his palace certain steps (ἀναβαθμούς), which showed the hours of the day, and also measured the course of the sun." Glycas, Annal. Pars ii. p. 361.

to day, as the sun on the meridian gradually rose and fell between summer and winter, while passing from solstice to solstice. It is quite clear that no motion of the sun in its ordinary diurnal progress through the heavens would produce the effect described : and equally clear that the shadow cast by a gnomon placed at the head of such an erection of steps would, if the instrument were placed, as it ought to be, at an angle equal to the latitude of the place, say 31° 47′ for Jerusalem, travel upwards and downwards upon the steps, "with the sun," from winter to summer and summer to winter, marking meridian altitudes from day to day. We assume then that—

2nd. The "steps of Ahaz" were set at an angle of not more than 31° 47′, sloping away from the sun, in the plane of the meridian.

3rd. That a gnomon equal to about 2° 54′ 13″ was placed at the head of the steps, causing the shadow on the shortest day of the year to fall beyond the lowest step. The sun's altitude on that day being 34° 41′ 13″.

Such an instrument would indeed have been of the nature of what was called by Greek astronomers a Sciotheron, or shadow-taker, or more properly a Heliotropion, that is, an instrument formed to mark the turning of the sun at the tropics, then required for correct regulation of the seasons of the year, and of special service to the Jews, whose festivals were fixed in connexion with the seasons. Some such instruments must of necessity have been of early invention, and probably may have been known in the time of Homer. For we find a passage in the Odyssey, speaking of the "turnings of the sun," τϱοπαὶ ἠελίοιο, as to be found in what he describes as "an island called Syria."* While Diogenes Laertius, in his life of Pherecydes, clearly refers to this same instrument, whether natural or artificial, when he speaks of the Heliotropion preserved in the island of Syra. The Scholiast on this passage in Homer writes—"There, they say, was the cave of the sun, by means of which the turnings of the sun were exhibited;" that is, probably by means of a ray of light admitted through an aperture into the cave. Anaximander, according to Laertius, was the first Greek who adopted the use of Gnomons, and placed them on the Sciothera of Lacedæmon, for the purpose of indicating the tropics and equinoxes. These Sciothera were of a pyramidal form.†

The obelisk was the simplest, though most imperfect form of Heliotropion, marking indistinctly the length of the shadow in summer and winter. In Italy another simple form of Heliotropion may yet be seen in several churches. In Milan Cathedral a meridian line is marked on the pavement, upon which an image of the sun, cast through an

---

* Νῆσός τις Συϱίη κικλήσκεται (ἵπου ἀκούεις)
'Οϱτυγίης καθύπεϱθεν ὅθι τϱοπαὶ ἠελίοιο.

Odyss. l. xv. 402.

† See a valuable dissertation by Salmasius, on Sciothera and Heliotropia, Plin. Exerc. p. 447. "A Sciotheron is a pyramidal instrument, composed of four triangles surrounding the right angle of the triangles, for finding midday." Scholiast on Ptol. Geog.

aperture in the southern wall, travels backwards
and forwards from winter to summer, and summer
to winter. In Bologna a similar arrangement was
made in the church of St Petronia, in A.D. 1576,
and another by Dominico Cassini in A.D. 1645.
Again a similar sort of instrument was to be seen
in the observatory at Pekin, when visited by Du
Halde. "They had contrived (says P. Le Comte)
a gnomon in a low room." . . . "The slit which
the ray of the sun came through is about eight
feet above the floor, is horizontal, and formed by
two pieces of copper borne up in the air, which,
by turning, may be set nearer or farther from each
other, to enlarge or contract the aperture. Lower
is a table with a brass plate in the middle, on
which was drawn a meridian line fifteen feet long,
divided by transverse lines, which were neither
finished nor very exact. There are some small
channels round the table, for holding water so as
to level it."*

Now it is obvious in all these instances that if
a flight of steps were placed on the meridian line,
sloping upwards from the lowest step to within a
foot or so below the aperture, the ray or image of
the sun would travel up and down such steps from
solstice to solstice. Such then would appear to
have been the form of the Heliotropion of Ahaz.

Now on the day of the recovery of Hezekiah,
an extraordinary motion of the shadow was observed on these "steps of Ahaz," by the rising of the
shadow "ten steps" from the point to which it had

* Du Halde's "China," fol. 1741, vol. ii. p. 131.

"gone down with the sun." This effect, it will be observed, is spoken of as "a sign," not as a miracle. A sign, as we have suggested, not noted merely with reference to this king's doubting faith, but recorded also with a prescient view to the incredulity of later days. Let it be remembered that the cure of Hezekiah was effected not by miracle, but by the ordinary application of a lump of figs. The promise of his recovery was confirmed by the motion of the shadow on the dial of the palace. We are justified, therefore, in looking for some natural phenomenon by which to account for this peculiar motion upon the dial; and the obvious, if not only, way in nature in which a shadow caused by the sun could, with a regular and steady motion, be deflected downwards on such an instrument would be by the slow passing of the moon over the upper part of the sun's disk as it approached the meridian.* We inquire then of astronomers whether any such phenomenon occurred visible at Jerusalem at the beginning of the year B.C. 689. And we learn that a large partial eclipse upon the upper limb of the sun was visible at Jerusalem, on the 11th January, B.C. 689, somewhere about half-past eleven o'clock on that day.

---

* Dean Milman thinks the effect may have been produced "by a cloud refracting the light."—*History of the Jews*, vol. i. p. 385. A dark cloud no doubt might produce the effect of deflecting the shadow. But the cause in such case would have been so manifest to every one, and the effect so transient, that the phenomenon could hardly have been referred to afterwards as "a wonder that was done in the land." 2 Chron. xxxii. 31.

This eclipse, then, fulfils four of the main conditions required by the narrative to make it applicable to our chronological reckoning. 1st. It occurred about the year fixed by Demetrius as that of the king's illness. 2nd. It occurred while the sun was approaching towards, and passing over the meridian. 3rd. The obscuration was on the upper portion of the sun's disk, causing the point of light to be depressed downwards. 4th. It was visible at Jerusalem. But there is a fifth condition of the most stringent character, by the fulfilment or non-fulfilment of which, in combination with the other four, we may determine with moral certainty whether this eclipse was, or was not, the actual cause of the phenomenon observed by Hezekiah, viz. that the deflection of light during the eclipse should be capable of affecting the shadow on such an instrument as we have described to the extent implied by the words, "ten steps;" and also that the month of January, when this eclipse occurred, should be a month suitable for the development of such a phenomenon.

Now the passage of the moon over the face of the sun during this eclipse occupied about two hours and a half. But from the time of central conjunction when the obscuration was the greatest, and the point of light depressed to the lowest, to the time when the light from the upper portion of the sun's disk was released by the passing on of the moon eastward, was just about twenty minutes: and this, therefore, was the time during which the phenomenon of retrogression on the steps was exhibited under the eyes of the king. Assuming, then, that the time when the ascending shadow had travelled upwards to the tenth step coincided, or nearly so, with the time when the sun had reached its highest altitude for the day, at noon, we infer,—

4th. That the time of central conjunction during this eclipse was not later than from twenty to fifteen minutes before noon.*

It could not have been much earlier, because the phenomenon of the resting of the shadow for a time at its *apparently* highest point for the day, which preceded the promise that it should rise ten steps, has also to be accounted for : and this cessation of its motion upwards could not have taken place till about twenty-five minutes before noon, when the decreasing motion of the sun in declination, or slackening motion upwards as it approached mid-day, would have become counteracted by the coming on of the eclipse. Now, at twenty-five minutes before twelve, the sun's disk would have risen to the altitude of 35° 8' 13" ; and the highest visible point of light would, owing to the eclipse, then have been about 35° 4' 13" ; and at twenty minutes before twelve, or at the time of greatest obscuration, the extreme cusps of light pro-

* The exact time of conjunction cannot at present be determined with precision by astronomers. When this our reckoning, however, shall have been established, the retrogradation of the shadow in B.C. 689 may perhaps become the means of rectifying the lunar theory, both as regards time of conjunction, and also as to the number of digits eclipsed.

SUN'S ALTITUDE BEFORE AND AT NOON.

Phase at noon.

Moon's relative hourly motion in declination 5′ 44″ northward.
Right ascension, 29′ 33″ eastward.
Corrected for Jerusalem, 19′ 42″ eastward.
Altitude of the Gnomon, 34° 41′ 13″.

Sun's apparent semi-diameter . . 16′ 13″

Moon's „ „ . . 15 13

Phase at 20 minutes before noon.

SOLAR ECLIPSE AT JERUSALEM, 11TH JANUARY, B.C. 689.

duced by the intervention of the moon would still
have stood at about the same altitude, or at 35° 4',
just 23' of a degree below the highest point of light
at noon, as shown on the accompanying diagram.
The whole disk had now become raised above the
gnomon, yet no motion upwards of the shadow on
the steps had been observed for full five minutes.
The time shown by the dial apparently was mid-day.

Now the question is, to what extent would a
staircase rising at an angle of 31° 47' towards the
sun, with a gnomon so placed at the top as to cast
the shadow on the shortest day of the year to the
foot of the lowest step, be affected by a movement
perpendicularly of the point of light to the extent
of 23' of a degree. The effect, we know, would
be widely different at different periods of the year.

In the summer, when the sun is high in the
heavens, the shadow short, and falling from the gnomon upon the upper steps of the instrument, the
effect would be hardly perceptible; in the spring
or autumn the effect would be small, but somewhat
greater; but in the winter, when the sun is low,
the shadow long, and falling almost parallel with the
slope of the steps, the effect would be the greatest,
and on the 11th of January, B.C. 689, would have
been to the extent of neither more nor less than
one-twelfth of the whole range of steps.* This
extent of motion, then, is fully sufficient to satisfy

* Dean Stanley refers to an eclipse which occurred in Sept.
B.C. 713, as that which Thenius supposed to have been the one
which affected the dial. But the motion of the shadow would,
as he says, have been almost imperceptible at that time of the
year.—" *Lectures on the Jewish Church,*" 2nd *Series,* p. 486.

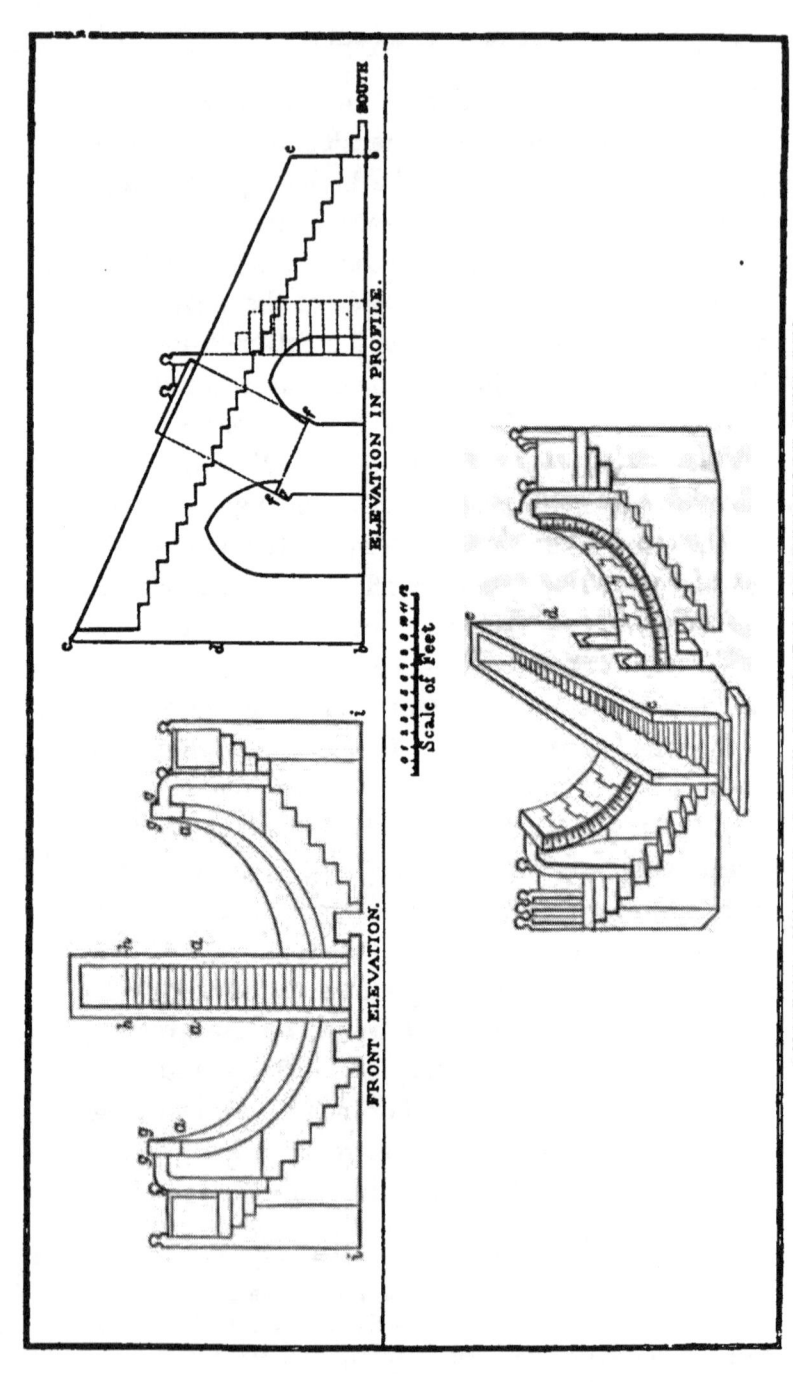

SOUTH

ELEVATION IN PROFILE.

Scale of Feet

FRONT ELEVATION.

ANCIENT SUN-DIAL AT THE BRAHMINS' OBSERVATORY, BENARES.

From Drawings by Lieut.-Col. Archibald Campbell, formerly Chief Engineer in the East India Company's Service.
"Philos. Trans." vol. lxxii.

the fifth condition required by the narrative. And whether the erection of steps was on a scale similar (though reversed in position) to the huge dials still visible in the ruined observatories at Delhi and Benares, the stair of one of which is one hundred and eighteen feet in length,* or whether it was, as we are satisfied, an instrument adapted to the interior of a chamber, if its length was divided into one hundred and twenty parts, the movement of the shadow to the extent of one-twelfth of the length would have affected it to the exact degree of "ten steps."† Neither a day or two earlier nor later, could the same degree of motion have been produced under the same conditions. In no year probably before or after B.C. 689 has the same com-

* See "Asiatic Researches of Calcutta," vol. v. p. 177.

† The Hebrew word which we have translated "from the end," may also be translated "hindwards," or "from the back part." Such a translation, if the phenomenon was witnessed in the open court, as some suppose, would suggest the idea that the "steps of Ahaz " may have been a double instrument sloping both *backwards* and forwards, north and south, to and from the sun, at the angle of the latitude of Jerusalem, 31° 47'. The slope on the south side would thus, as in every correctly formed dial, have been parallel with the axis, or *poles* of the earth, and the motion of the shadow from that slope would have marked the hours before and after noon. The slope on the north side, or hindwards, in the form of steps would, by means of a *gnomon*, as explained, have marked by the meridian shadow the day of the year, and the turning of the sun at the solstices. Such an instrument appears to be referred to by Herodotus, when he speaks of the *pole*, and *gnomon*, and the *twelve parts of the day* having been derived from the Babylonians. Herod. ii. 109. The Benares instrument is "the Pole." With an additional slope towards the north it would approach the form of a Sciotheron; with a gnomon also at the top it would form a Heliotropion.

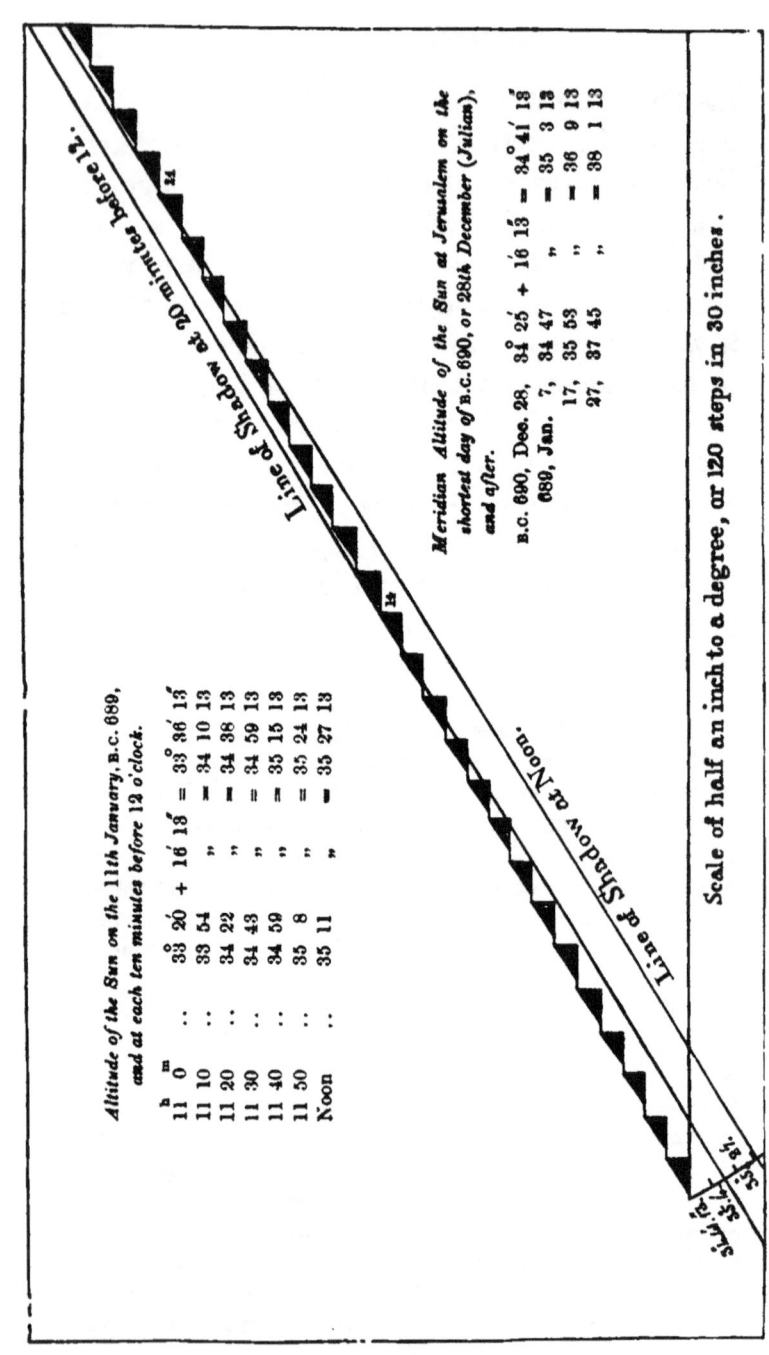

Altitude of the Sun on the 11th January, B.C. 689,
and at each ten minutes before 12 o'clock.

h	m					
11	0	::	33° 20′	+ 16′ 18″	=	33° 36′ 18″
11	10	::	33 54	,,	—	34 10 13
11	20	::	34 22	,,	—	34 38 13
11	30	::	34 43	,,	—	34 59 13
11	40	::	34 59	,,	—	35 15 13
11	50	::	35 8	,,	—	35 24 13
Noon		::	35 11	,,	—	35 27 13

Meridian Altitude of the Sun at Jerusalem on the
shortest day of B.C. 690, or 28th December (Julian),
and after.

B.C. 690, Dec. 28,	34° 25′	+ 16′ 13″	=	34° 41′ 18″
689, Jan. 7,	34 47	,,	—	35 3 13
17,	35 53	,,	—	36 9 13
27,	37 45	,,	—	38 1 13

Scale of half an inch to a degree, or 120 steps in 30 inches.

"SO THE SUN RETURNED TEN STEPS, BY WHICH STEPS IT WAS GONE DOWN."

bination of circumstances concurred. There is perhaps an additional reason for supposing that this fall
and rise of the shadow was in winter? For the time
of year appears to be pointed out by the word
" endwards," or " from the end," (אֲחֹרַנִּית) that is,
from the *lower* end of the steps towards which the
shadow had gone down. Now the lower end of the
steps could only have been the place of the shadow
in January or December, at the time of the winter
solstice. The use also of a cake of figs (דְּבֵלָה), that
is, of dried figs, on the occasion, seems to imply the
winter season. The eclipse, therefore, on the 11th
of January, near the time of noonday, and in the year
B.C. 689, so exactly falls in with all the conditions
required by the history, that we cannot doubt that
the 14th, or rather the end of the 13th year of
Hezekiah fell in the beginning of that year, and
that the day of the king's recovery from sickness
was the 11th day of January of that year.

How vividly is the scene in Hezekiah's palace
on that day presented before our eyes! We assume
with certainty that the sick and dying king was
incapable of movement and closely confined to his
chamber, and that all which is described as passing
between him and the prophet, and all that was
witnessed on the dial, could only have taken place
within the walls of that chamber. We see him
stretched upon his couch with his face turned de-
spondingly "towards the wall." The hangings of the
entrance are closed, for it is winter, and the darkness
of the chamber, which is in an inner court of the

winter-house,* is broken only by the flickeri⟨
upon the hearth.† An ornamental stru⟨
polished marble in the form of steps dimly
projecting in front of the wall to which h
reaching the length of some thirty feet from ⟨
at the north end towards the ceiling at th
end of the apartment. A broad beam ⟨
is seen shining down through an apertu
above, such as we have imagined in the
Syria, or which might be daily seen at Pek
Milan. It is the rays of the penumbra issui
the sun, whose disk is just beginning to ris
the gnomon, some five-and-thirty minutes bef⟨
day. It illumines the lower steps of the inst
while all the steps above are left in shade. T
falls near to where the couch of the king is
and around which in grief are standing his
his attendants, and his faithful minister, the ⟨
He watches the slow progress of the shadow u
on the steps, telling him that the day has
reached its middle course—the day, alas! wh
sibly may prove to be his last—and his t⟨
turn mournfully to days gone by in which
"walked before his God in truth, and serv⟨

* Jer. xxxvi. 20–22.

† The dial chamber of the palace was doubtless pla⟨
winter-house, for it was at the winter solstice chiefly
instrument would have been of use. The chamber n
been capable of being darkened, for the light on the lo
for twenty days about the solstice was only that of the ⟨
so to speak, and the motion of the shadow then could ⟨
been well observed in a dark place.

with a perfect heart." He seems to call in question the justice of the sentence pronounced against him, and complains aloud that his days are cut off, that he is going "to the gates of the grave," and is "deprived of the residue of his years." The progress of the shadow gradually slackens. It has already ceased to rise upon the steps. The hour of noonday apparently has arrived. That hour for marking which alone the instrument is formed. The prophet softly leaves the chamber, and is about to quit the palace, when, "before he had reached the middle court," he is commanded to return.* Quickly re-entering the chamber, he announces the promise of the king's recovery, and that on the third day he shall go up into the house of the Lord. "What shall be the sign," is the reply, "that the Lord will heal me and that I shall go up, &c.?" The prophet points to the shadow on the dial, which now for several minutes had been resting on a step full ten degrees below its proper altitude for the day. Like the days of Hezekiah, its progress upwards was cut off, and both had prematurely reached the zenith of their course. As compared with its position on the previous day at noon, the shadow had gone down. He predicts its movement upwards. And the words have scarcely left his lips when, to the amaze of the king and his attendants, it is seen gradually to ascend during the space of twenty minutes, till it has reached its highest altitude for the day. It is

* 2 Kings, xx. 4.

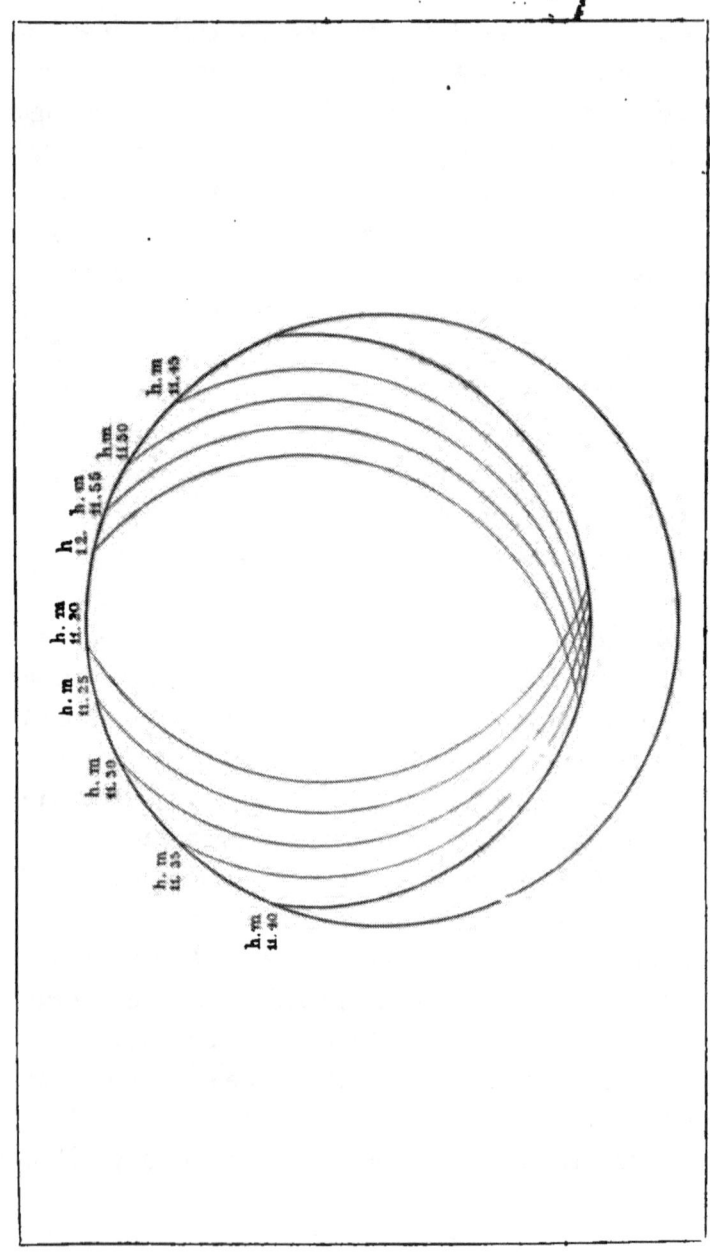

VARIATION OF THE POINT OF LIGHT FOR EVERY FIVE MINUTES BEFORE AND AFTER
CENTRAL CONJUNCTION;

enough. "He hath both spoken to me," he cries, "and He hath done it. I shall go softly all my days in the bitterness of my soul." How impressive, how appropriate is this sign that he shall "go up" into the House of the Lord. That he shall ascend the steps of the temple, chanting the solemn "songs of the steps," and praising and magnifying "the Lord of Lords, whose mercy endureth for ever."

The fame of this two-fold manifestation of the mid-day shadow and its predicted rise of ten degrees quickly spreads throughout the palace and the city. It is spoken of as a miracle. It reaches the invading army of the Babylonians. It is repeated on their return to the astrologers of Babylon. And the princes of Babylon send ambassadors to Hezekiah "to inquire of the wonder that was done in the land."*

But to return to the subject of the prophecy of the seventy weeks. Having thus defined with exactness the strict limits of the whole period of 490 years, as falling between the Sabbatical years, B.C. 3-2 and B.C. 493-2, and *that* in accordance with the first eleven propositions laid down for the interpretation of the prophecy in pages 56, 57, 58, and 59; it now remains to point out, in rectification of the common order of arrangement, how the several minor periods of "one week," "seven weeks," and "threescore and two weeks," comprised within, and making together, "seventy weeks," are to be accounted for in history, in conformity with pro-

---

* 2 Chron. xxxii. 31.

O

position 15, viz. that the "one week" must necessarily precede the "seven."

The first period then to be accounted for is
that of "one week," or seven years, counted from
the completion of the seventy years' desolation of
Jerusalem and commencement of the overthrow of
Babylon, say in the autumn of the Sabbatical year
B.C. 493, about twelve months[*] before the assumption by Darius of the government of that city and
province; and seven full years, reckoned from the
month Tishri of the Sabbatical year B.C. 493, would
end in the same month of the Sabbatical year beginning in Tishri B.C. 486. Now the end of this period
of seven years, or "one week," must also form the
beginning of the following period of forty-nine
years, or "seven weeks;" and this period of seven
weeks is declared to count "from the going forth
of the commandment to restore and to build Jerusalem." We have, therefore, to look for no other
event than the going forth of the commandment to
restore and to build "the holy city," as the point
of division between these two first periods of the
prophecy; and this "going forth," or going out,
or *fulfilment* of the commandment, ought to be
found to fall somewhere within the Sabbatical
year B.C. 486-5.

Now what do we read in Scripture concerning
the rebuilding of the city and temple of Jerusalem?
In Isaiah we read, "Thus saith the Lord" "of

---

[*] The final siege of Babylon lasted twenty months. Herod.
iii. 153.

Cyrus, He is my shepherd, and shall perform all my pleasure, even saying to Jerusalem, Thou shalt be built: and to the temple, Thy foundation shall be laid." Thus we learn that "the commandment" which should go forth to build Jerusalem ought to have proceeded from the mouth of Cyrus. And in Ezra, accordingly, we read that, " In the first year of Cyrus king of Babylon, the same king Cyrus made a decree to build the house of God," by which Jerusalem should a second time become the holy city. This decree, however, we know was not at that time carried into effect, but on the contrary was frustrated for many years by the Samaritans, so that even the existence of any such decree was quite unknown in the court of Darius when he was first "set over the realm of the Chaldeans." But on the petition of the Jews, in the third or fourth year of Darius son of Hystaspes, when that king was at Babylon, order was given to search for this decree, and it was found at last at Acmetha in the province of the Medes, and a second time promulgated by Darius.

And now if we turn to the book of Haggai[*] we find that on the 24th day of the month Sebat, that is in December, in the 2nd year of Darius, B.C. 490, the foundations of the Temple of Jerusalem were laid by Zerubbabel, and that in the month Adar, *in the sixth year of Darius*,[†] that is, in March B C. 485, some few months, we may pre-

---

[*] Haggai, ii. 18.   [†] Ezra, vi. 14

sume, after the re-issue of the decree, the building was completed, " according to *the commandment of the God of Israel, and the commandment of Cyrus*, and Darius, and Artach-Shashtha king of Persia." The dedication, by which event Jerusalem became once again the " *holy city*," also took ·place in the month Nisan of this year. This command from heaven, then, and this fulfilment of the original command of Cyrus, which had been so long laid aside, is without doubt the " commandment " spoken of by Daniel, from " the going forth," or completion of which to the time of Messiah should be " seven weeks and threescore and two weeks," that is, 483 years. The particularity with which this decree is marked as the " commandment of God," and " the commandment of Cyrus," which also had proceeded from the Lord God of heaven,* is sufficiently remarkable to satisfy those who dwell upon the word, *davar*,† as necessarily implying a command from God. But it is still more remarkable, that the time when this commandment was carried into effect is unmistakably fixed to some year in which Darius and Artach-Shashtha were reigning together on the Persian throne. We beg the reader's attention to the fifth and sixth chapters of the book of Ezra, in which the second contest concerning the rebuilding of the temple between the Samaritans and the Jews is narrated. It will be observed particularly that Darius, that is, the

* Ezra, i. 2.
† See " Dr Williams' Introduction to Mr. Desprez," p. lxi.

son of Hystaspes, was then appealed to to search in
"the treasure-house which is *there* at Babylon,"
v. 17, whether any decree had ever been issued by
Cyrus, for the rebuilding of the temple at Jerusalem, which seems to imply that the king was then
present in that city.   It also appears that now, for
the first time, Darius was styled "king of Assyria,",
vi. 22, as if he had but lately taken the government
over the realm of the Chaldeans: while Artach-
Shashtha, *at the same time*, is spoken of as reigning
king of Persia, vi. 14.   Now it was in the year
B.C. 486, in the fourth year after the battle of
Marathon, that Darius, we are told, felt himself
called upon to appoint his successor, who also from
that time was his coadjutor seated with him as king
on the throne of Persia. Herodotus relates that after
a contest between Xerxes and his brother, Xerxes
was declared to be the king's successor, and, as
Plutarch relates, was led by his brother to the
throne.   It is clear, then, beyond doubt that this
Artach-Shashtha of Ezra is the Xerxes of Herodotus: and those who think otherwise are bound to
explain in what other way this combination of two
Persian kings on the same throne in the reign of
Darius is to be accounted for.   Herodotus has correctly recorded that the name of the son of Atossa
and king Darius was Xerxes = Ahasuerus, and so
continues to retain that name throughout the reign
of this king.   Yet there is nothing in this to prevent
the supposition that he may have styled himself Artaxerxes on being raised to the throne. That he was

so styled, we know was the opinion of the LXX translator of Daniel, who, however faulty in his paraphrase in other respects, has, in translating ch. v. 31, preserved, we believe, the true interpretation of this passage. For he writes, " Artaxerxes, who was a Mede received the kingdom, and Darius full of days, and venerable with old age."* He here clearly refers to the elevation of Xerxes to the throne of Persia in the old age of Darius, and thus shows that the Jews of Alexandria had not at the time of this version adopted the false idea first introduced by Josephus, that " Darius the Mede " was Cyaxares, and that he reigned at Babylon before the first year of Cyrus. Like Ezra, he calls the associated king Artaxerxes, and thus we have good reason to believe that Xerxes, or Ahasuerus, who " in the *beginning* of his reign " (that is, of his local government) received an accusation against the Jews under the title Ahasuerus,† either at this time, which is most probable, or at some period before Ezra wrote, had assumed the loftier title " Arta-Xerxes." The words, " *in the beginning of his reign*," are alone significant, and may be assumed to point to a time when Ahasuerus, or Xerxes, though reigning as local king, was not yet in a position to style himself " king of kings," as in ch. vii. 12. We meet with the same expression in the

---

* Καὶ ᾽Αρταξέρξης ὁ τῶν Μήδων παρέλαβι τὴν βασιλίιαν, καὶ Δαρεῖος πλήρης τῶν ἡμερῶν καὶ ἴνδοξος ἐν γήρει.—LXX.

† Ezra, iv. 6.

annals of Shalmanezer, the king of the black-obelisk
in the British Museum, which runs thus :—

"*In the beginning of my reign*, when I had sat in state
upon the royal throne, I collected my chariots and my army,"
&c., &c.

"*In my first year*, I crossed the Euphrates in deep water,"
&c. &c.*

And again in the annals of Sennacherib, king of ,
Assyria, as translated by Mr. Fox Talbot:†—

"*In the beginning of my reign*, I destroyed the forces of
Merodach Baladan," &c. &c.

"*In my first year*, a certain man called Nebo, lord of names,
chief of Ararat, brought a gift of gold and silver."

So that we seem to gather from the book of
Ezra, that Xerxes = Ahasuerus had been appointed
subordinate king for some time before the death
of his father Darius, with the title Artach-Shashtha,
or Artaxerxes: that in the year B.C. 485 he was
styled "king of Persia," his father Darius being
styled "king of Assyria:" and that in his seventh
year, computed from his appointment as successor
of Darius, *i.e.* in B.C. 479, when he issued a decree authorizing the return of captives from Babylon, with Ezra,‡ after the death of Darius, he had
assumed the more lofty title of "Artaxerxes, king
of kings." This view of the early years of Xerxes·
on the throne of Persia is confirmed by an Egyp-

* "Dublin University Magazine," Oct. 1853. Dr. Hincks
styles the king Assur-yuchura-bal.

† Journ. R. Asiatic Soc. 1861.

‡ Ezra, vii. 12.

tian monument which, according to Dr. Birch, makes the 13th year of Xerxes (counted from his first appointment as local king) concurrent with the 36th, or last year of the reign of his father Darius.*

This change in the title of Xerxes, we think, affords the true solution of a difficulty in Thucydides, where he speaks of the flight of Themistocles to the court of Artaxerxes, though we know that the flight took place as early as B.C. 473, or 472, in the reign of Xerxes. Josephus also affirms that Ezra, who received his commission from Artaxerxes, came up to Jerusalem in the reign of Xerxes: † while the tradition of the Rabbis is, that Ezra came to Jerusalem in the seventh year of the new temple, that is, according to our reckoning, in the reign of Xerxes B.C. 479.

The chronology of the period may thus be re-capitulated : —

B.C.

495. The Babylonians under Belsharezar, or Belshazzar, son of Nabonadius, revolt from Persia, on the sailing of the Persian fleet for Samos. ‡

---

* "The principal inscriptions of Atauti are of the *thirty-sixth year of Darius*, whom he calls the beloved of the god Khem dwelling in Coptos. In one which bears the date of *this same year*, he gives also the *thirteenth* of Khishairsha, or Xerxes, whom he calls the son of Darius, mentioning both monarchs as if living." Loftus' "Chaldæa and Susiana," p. 412.

† Wars, ii. vi. 2 ; Ant. xi. v. 1.

‡ Herodotus, iii. 150, vi. 25. There were two expeditions to Samos, the first to reinstate Syloson, the second to reinstate the son of Syloson. We suggest that the revolt was on the second occasion, not the first.

B.C.

494. With a view to the approaching expedition against Babylon, Xerxes = Ahasuerus is appointed local king in
Persia, during the intended absence of Darius, and styled
Artach-Shashtha, Ezra, iv. 6, 7, all civil affairs being referred to him during the war.

493. The siege of Babylon, which lasts twenty months, is begun
in the early spring of this year, and the city is taken
by Zopyrus, in the reign of Darius according to Herodotus, in the reign of Xerxes according to Ctesias, towards
the end of B.C. 492.

492. Darius, according to the Parian Chronicle, having begun to
reign in Persia, in B.C. 517, and having reigned 36 full
years, must have died in the year B.C. 482-1. He was
72 years of age at his death, according to Ctesias. He
was " about threescore and two years old," therefore, in
B.C. 492-1, " when set over the realm of the Chaldeans."

491. " In the first year of his reign " over the Chaldeans, the
prophecy of the Seventy Weeks was delivered to Daniel.
It was delivered, we infer, in the first month, because " in
those days," ch. x. 2, 4,—that is, in the days mentioned in
ch. ix.,—Daniel was mourning " in the first month." And
this first month was the month Nisan. For the names of
the months in the reign of Darius referred to in the books
of Haggai, Zechariah, and Ezra, are not those of the
Persian months,—the names of which are found in the
Behistûn inscription,—but always those of the Jewish
months,* which were the same as the Babylonian, and
Assyrian. Having destroyed Babylon, he was now styled
king of Assyria, Ezra, vi. 22, and the years of his reign
were counted from Nisan, or April. The first month of
the first year of Darius was, therefore, Nisan, B.C. 491,
though he may have *begun* to reign in B.C. 492.

490. In October of this year the battle of Marathon was fought,
and lost. The Scythian expedition had also been disas-
trous, and injurious to the prestige of the Persian arms.
The power of Persia was shaken in the provinces, and
Egypt soon after revolted. The Jews, therefore, know-

---

* Zech. i. 7 ; vii. 1. Ezra, vi. 14.

B.C.

ing probably of the elevation of Daniel, and stimu-
lated by Haggai and Zechariah, without asking permission of the king, began to build the temple of Jerusalem,
though the building of it had been prohibited by Xerxes,
or Artach-Shashtha, in the absence of Darius (Ezra, iv.
21); and "in the 24th day of the 9th month, in the 2nd
year of Darius" (Haggai, ii. 10, 18), the foundations of
the temple were laid, that is, in Dec. B.O. 490.

489. The Samaritans endeavour to stop the building of the
temple without success, and appeal to Darius, still "there
at Babylon," Ezra, v. 5, 17.

488. In the fourth year of Darius, search is made for the decree
of Cyrus, which is found at last at Acmetha, in the
province of the Medes.—Ezra, vi. 2. But we may infer
from Zech. viii. 9, that the decree had not yet been found
in the ninth month of this year.

487. The building of the temple now proceeds by permission of
Darius, who confirms the decree of Cyrus (vi. 7), in this
or the following year.

486. In the fourth year after the battle of Marathon, Xerxes is
appointed by Darius successor to the throne of Persia,
and begins his imperial reign, Darius, according to Ctesias,
having reigned 31 years, counted from B.C. 517.

485. The temple of Jerusalem is finished by "the commandment of the God of Israel, and according to the commandment of Cyrus, and Darius, and Artach-Shashtha
king of Persia:" "on the third day of the month Adar,
which was in the sixth year of the reign of Darius
the king," that is, in March B.C. 585. And thus Jerusalem becomes again the "Holy City."—Ezra, vi. 14.

A more complete explanation of the fulfilment
of the first seven years, or "one week" of the
prophetic period, we submit, can hardly be desired.

And here, again, it is satisfactory to find upon
examination that this reckoning, and indeed this
whole interpretation, is the result of no newly-

invented theory, but that it is the same as that which was entertained in the East in the early periods of the Church. For Abulpharagius, surnamed Bar-Hebræus, who was born in the year A.D. 1226, tells us that he visited the province of Azerbijan, in Armenia, and searched the archives of the city Margan, where he extracted many things from Syriac, Saracenic, and Persian books, which he considered worthy to be preserved from oblivion; and after briefly narrating the history of the world from Adam to the birth of Christ he writes,* " In the days of Herod our Redeemer was born; and the ' seven' together with the ' sixty-and-two ' weeks of Daniel were completed, which together make 483 years, to be computed from the sixth year of Darius son of Hystaspes." Now, 483 years added to the year of the birth of Christ, bring us to the year B.C. 486. Again, he writes,† " There are collected from the time of the building of the first temple, that of Solomon, even to this year in which the second building was finished, 508 years ;" which leads us up to the year B.C. 993 for the building, and B.C. 996 for the first year of Solomon, which differs only three years from the date we had long ago determined from Deme-

---

* " Tempore hujus Herodis natus est Redemptor noster, finitæque sunt hebdomades septem una cum hebdomadibus 62 Danielis, quæ conficiunt annos 483, consolidandos ab anno sexto Darii IIystaspis."—P. 46.

† " Anno ejus (Darii fil. Hystaspis) sexto perfectum est templum, in mense Ijar, altum 60 cubitorum, latum viginti. Colliguntur anni a condito templo primo Salomonis usque ad hunc annum, quo structura altera finita est, 508."—Vol. i. p. 31.

trius and other sources to be that in which Solomon came to the throne.*

Let us here remark how strikingly applicable the whole of the last chapter of Haggai now becomes—written, as we assume it to be, in the second year of Darius, B.C. 490—when the building of the temple by Zerubbabel is placed in the latter years of that king's reign, instead of in the year B.C. 520.

The prophet in this chapter begins by pointing the attention of those few aged men in Jerusalem, who could still remember the splendour and glory of the first temple, to the poverty and nakedness of the building then standing before them, which had been gradually growing up since the days of Cyrus; and then encourages them with the words:—

"Thus saith the Lord of Hosts, yet once, *it is a little while,* and I will shake the heavens and the earth, and the sea, and the dry land; and I will shake all nations, and the desirable things (or precious) of all nations † shall come: and I will fill this house with glory, saith the Lord. The silver is mine and the gold is mine," "the glory of this house shall be greater than of the former," and in this place will I give peace:" (Haggai, ii. 6-9)

that is, while all the nations round about are stirred with commotion, the land of Judea shall be at peace.

Again to the same effect we read :—

* See Chronological Table, in Appendix.

† Καὶ ἥξει τὰ ἐκλεκτὰ πάντων τῶν ἐθνῶν.—LXX.

"Et commovebo omnes gentes, adferentque res desideratissimas."—ROSENMULLER. The verb is plural.

"Speak to Zerubbabel, governor of Judah, saying, I will shake the heavens and the earth; and I will overthrow the throne of kingdoms, and I will destroy the strength of the kingdoms of the heathen; and I will overthrow the chariots and those that ride in them; and the horses and the riders shall come down, every one by the sword of his brother. *In that day,* saith the Lord of hosts, I will take thee, O Zerubbabel, my servant, the son of Shealtiel, saith the Lord, and I will make thee as a signet: for I have chosen thee, saith the Lord of hosts." (Haggai, ii. 22.)

Here, then, we learn that within "a little while" after the year B.C. 490, when as yet the temple was unfinished, a time was coming when the political heaven and earth of the heathens should be shaken, and that while terrible war should be raging amongst the nations, the land of Judea alone should be at peace, and that "in that day" the government of Zerubbabel over Judea should be protected and established, as a signet on the finger of the Lord of hosts.*

Now we know from history that during the ten years between B.C. 490 and 480, between the battles of Marathon and Salamis, the kingdom of Persia was stirred to the foundations, while the whole power of the empire was gathering in preparation for a struggle with Greece, and for one of the mightiest convulsions which ever shook the heathen world;† which ended, as we know, with the overthrow of the vast armies of Xerxes, with the casting down of chariots and horsemen, and the humbling

* See Jerem. xxii. 24.

† Both Julian and Libanius speak of a ten years' preparation for this war: joining Xerxes and Darius together during the time. Ussher's Annals, p. 173.

in the dust of the pride of the great "king of kings." Precisely also within this interval we have seen that the sanctuary and city of Jerusalem were rebuilt, the authority of Zerubbabel exercised in peace, and, as Josephus records, the Jewish autonomy re-established throughout Judea.

Again we may observe how, the books of Haggai and Zechariah being thus brought down into their true chronological position, an answer is afforded to those who express surprise that no reference to the book of Daniel should be found in these books; for while, unknown to them, Daniel was praying at Babylon in B.C. 491 for the restoration of the city and the sanctuary, the prophets Haggai and Zechariah were in B.C. 490, bringing about at Jerusalem the practical answer to his prayer, by stirring up the people to perform the work. Now, also, we may perceive how the messengers of the Lord might walk to and fro through the land, and proclaim, "Behold, all the land sitteth still, and is at rest." *

Before we quit this part of the subject, let us observe with what peculiar fitness also the narrative in the sixth chapter of Daniel,—which describes how the kingdom, or satrapy of Babylon, or perhaps even the whole dominion of the Persian empire, was divided by Darius into one hundred and twenty lieutenancies, with three presidents over them,—falls in with the history of the reign of Darius, son of Hystaspes, when this subdivision of provinces is placed, not

---

* Zech. i. 11. See note p. 58.

in the year B.C. 538, as commonly arranged, but 46 years later, that is, in the year B.C. 492-1. Nothing can be more vague and incongruous than the narrative as now chronologically arranged. Rosenmuller observes upon this chapter, " That which Darius, son of Hystaspes, actually performed, the author of our book has attributed to Cyaxares II., the first king that reigned after Belshazzar, that is Nabonidus, the last of the Chaldean kings; which error leads him into another, that of calling Cyaxares Darius the Mede."

We have sufficiently shown that the author of the book of Daniel in this chapter is really speaking of Darius, son of Hystaspes, not of Cyaxares; yet at first sight there may appear to be some difficulty in our identification, arising out of this very chapter. For there is no better established fact, than that Darius in the early part of his reign divided his empire into *twenty* satrapies or tributary kingdoms, some of them exercising a considerable amount of independence. The policy of his government in the beginning of his reign was to leave undisturbed, as far as possible, the ethnical divisions of the kingdoms he had conquered : and at this early period we certainly read of no such minute division, as of one satrapy into one hundred and twenty parts : nor of the substitution of three presidents for one absolute governor. If then Daniel has truly recorded so great a change of policy with regard to the government of one of his provinces, towards the latter part of the reign of Darius, it seems

requisite for us to point out some evidence from
secular history of such a remarkable event having
actually taken place, and that about the year
B.C. 492–1.

Now we do find most striking evidence of such
a change of policy in the mind of Darius about the
very time upon which we have fixed, indicating that
the king in his later years had arrived at the wise
conviction, that popular local governments are far
more safely to be trusted in distant provinces than
powerful despots. For Herodotus relates that just
one or two years before the battle of Marathon, that
is, either in the B.C. 492 or 491, the king having
sent Mardonius, his general, at the head of the
Persian forces on an expedition towards Greece,
ordered him to pass through the great satrapy of
the Ionian provinces, and there to put down the
several despotic rulers throughout that turbulent
province, and to set up in their stead a series of
democratic local governments. Herodotus directs
the particular attention of his readers to this fact,
and speaks of it as likely to be looked upon by
them as incredible : yet, nevertheless, points to it
as justifying his own previous statement, that before
the empire of Persia had been consigned to the sole
dominion of Darius, such a popular form of government had actually been proposed for the whole
empire by Otanes, one of the seven conspirators
against the Magian.* Mr. Grote remarks upon

* Herod. vi. 43.

this passage of Herodotus,—" This was a complete reversal of the former policy of Persia, and must be ascribed to a new conviction, doubtless wise and well founded, which had recently grown up among the Persian leaders, that on the whole their unpopularity was aggravated more than their strength was increased by employing despots as instruments."*
Thus the satrapy of the Ionian provinces, which had revolted under Aristagoras, and which had proved itself equally difficult to govern with the province of Babylonia, became subdivided into numerous governments.

With regard to the satrapy of Babylonia, which comprehended also Syria,† and Judea, we know from the inscription at Behistun that it had revolted twice in the early part of the reign of Darius, and again that the city had been under siege for twenty months before its final destruction. Herodotus, however, has left us no particulars concerning its division into numerous lieutenancies. But here the testimony of the historical book of Ezra comes to our assistance as regards the Syrian section of that satrapy, and from Ezra we learn that subdivisions of government had also there taken place. For what are the popular governments of Judea under Zerubbabel, and of Samaria under Tatnai, set up about this same time, but counterparts of the local governments set up by Darius in the Ionian provinces? Josephus describes

---

* Grote's Hist. of Greece, chap. iii. p. 269.
† See Rawlinson's Herodotus, vol. iii. map.

the form of government in Judea under Darius as "an aristocracy mixed with an oligarchy,"*—a government differing widely from the despotic tyranny under which the Jews had suffered from the time of their return from captivity. The very words of Daniel seem to imply that an unruly independent spirit had now grown up even in the court of Persia, somewhat similar to what we find prevailing in Ionia. For he tells us how "the presidents and princes came tumultuously to the king," declaring that "all the presidents of the kingdom, the governors, and the princes, the counsellors, and the captains, have consulted together to establish a royal statute," to which they seem almost to have forced the king to consent. How different is this independent tone from that which had prevailed during the early despotism of the government of Darius! Yet it is quite in conformity with the democratic spirit described by Herodotus as prevailing in Ionia, just previous to the time of the battle of Marathon: and thus the sixth chapter of Daniel falls in well with the latter part of the reign of Darius, but by no means with the beginning of that reign. Again, this sixth chapter of Daniel also records an entire revolution in religious feeling at the court of Persia, soon after the capture of Babylon, which well agrees with the latter years of the reign of Darius. For soon after taking possession of the kingdom of Babylon in B. C. 492, we read that the King issued a proclama-

* Jos. Ant. xi. 4, 8.

tion, "that in every dominion of my kingdom men tremble and fear before the God of Daniel: for He is the living God."* And before the year B. C. 485, another decree, as we have seen, had gone forth authorizing the rebuilding of God's temple at Jerusalem, which hitherto had been strictly prohibited. Now it is remarkable, that about this very time, according to Persian historians, Darius began to encourage the propagation in his dominions of the religion of the Magi, which we know that he had persecuted to the death in the beginning of his reign. Zoroaster, or whoever the promoter of this religious reformation in Persia may have been, is said to have been the disciple of some Jewish prophet; and Dean Prideaux has argued, from his thorough knowledge of the Jewish religion and the sacred writings of the Old Testament, that probably he was of Jewish extraction.† Be this as it may, there was much affinity between the doctrines taught by this reformer and those of the Jews. He taught the existence of one Eternal Being, the immortality of the Soul, the resurrection of the body, the reward of the virtuous in a future state; and he is said to have spoken of the coming of that great Prince, whose appearance was looked forward to about the time of the birth of Christ; at whose birth the Magi came to pay Him adoration at Jerusalem. "Abu Mahommed Mustapha, in his life of Gushtasp (*i. e.* Darius son

---

* Dan. vi. 26.
† Prid. Con. Vol. i. p. 300.

of Hystaspes) relates, that after the king had reigned
thirty years (*i. e.* in B. C. 488) Zerdust appeared, a
wise man, who was author of the book of the Magi.
At first Gushtasp was disinclined to the new doctrine, but at length was persuaded, and adopted his
religion. He was among the disciples of Ozeir" (*i. e.*
Ezra.) * Thus the proclamation of Darius concerning the God of Daniel, and the issue of the decree
for the rebuilding of the temple of the living God,
do not inaptly fall in with the time of this religious
revolution in the latter years of Darius, between B.C.
492 and 485, where they are placed ; while, on the
other hand, we know that the building of the temple
had been obstructed throughout the reign of Cyrus,†
and that in the early part of his reign in Persia
Darius did all in his power to obstruct the influence
of the Magi, and to uphold the then prevailing worship, which was that of the heavenly host.

We now proceed to reckon the next period of
" seven weeks," or forty-nine years, which is to be
counted "from the going forth of the commandment to restore and to build Jerusalem." Here the
particular features of the period seem to be pointed
out by the words, " *the street shall be built, and
the wall, in troublous times.*" The limits of the
forty-nine years thus appear to be exactly defined.
The reissue of the command of the God of Israel and
of the command of Cyrus to restore the " holy city,"

---

* Hyde's Religio Veterum Persarum, p. 317.
† Ezra, iv. 5.

marks the beginning: the completion of "the wall" of the holy city marks the end. These forty-nine years, therefore, if counted from the autumn of the year B.C. 486, would end in autumn of the year B.C. 437. Now what does Josephus say concerning the building of the wall of Jerusalem by Nehemiah? After relating that the work was at length completed amidst great opposition from the surrounding people, and how the workmen were compelled to work with arms in their hands, as the prophet had foretold in "troublous times," he concludes thus: "This trouble he (Nehemiah) underwent for two years and four months, for in so long a time was the wall built, in the twenty-eighth year of the reign of Xerxes (Artaxerxes), in the ninth month,"* that is, in December 437. The dedication of the wall, we assume, took place in the following year, B.C. 436, at the time of the Jubilee.

The text of Josephus' copy of Nehemiah appears to have differed here from the text of our present copies of that book, or to have been somewhat fuller. He speaks of the coming of Nehemiah to Jerusalem in the 25th, not in the 20th year of Artaxerxes, as in our copies, possibly referring to a second visit to Jerusalem, after he had left it in charge of his brother Hanani, vii. 12. And the "two (three?) years and four months," during which he says that the wall was completed, seem to refer to the time spoken of by Nehemiah, v. 16: "Yea, also, I con-

---

* Jos. Ant. xi. 5. 8.

tinued in the work of this wall, neither bought we any land : and all my servants were gathered thither unto the work." The result is a fulfilment of the period of "seven weeks," with as much exactness as that of the two periods of "seventy weeks," and "one week."

But we have observed that this period of forty-nine years is the precise length of the period of a Jubilee, and we look therefore for some event marking the presence at this time of that peculiar year, and we find that it is appropriately marked by the consecration of the wall of Jerusalem in the beginning of the fiftieth year. For, as in our own days and country, it is the custom from time to time, for municipal purposes, to walk the boundaries of parishes, so in the days after the captivity, it was the custom in Judea to consecrate the boundaries of walled cities every fiftieth year, because the law affecting property within and without the walls was different as regarded re-entry in the year of Jubilee.* The registration of genealogies is also said to have been the work of the year of Jubilee,† and this we know was undertaken by Nehemiah in the year of the dedication of the wall.‡

There is something very remarkable in this division of 483 years, or sixty-nine weeks, into two periods of "seven" and "threescore and two weeks." The primary purpose was, as we have seen, to mark

---

* Lev. xxv. 29–30.   " Seder Olam Rabba," ch. xxx.

† Smith's "Dictionary of the Bible," vol. i. p. 1153.

‡ Neh. vii. 5; xii. 27.

the time of the rebuilding of the city and completion of the wall of Jerusalem. But this precise mention of "seven weeks," or 49 years, at the beginning of the combined period, seems also to imply that a new era or computation of Jubilees, which had necessarily been suspended during the captivity, was now intended to be commenced; and that, as in the days of Solomon, the computation was made from the consecration of the "holy city," so now again from the time of the restoration of the "holy city," a new computation was to commence, as every such era must, with a period of Jubilee. Ten Jubilee periods, of 49 years each, or 490 years, had, as we have seen, been accomplished in the year B.C. 492, and from thence a new period of seventy Sabbaths, or 490 years, was to be computed to Messiah. That the era of the Jubilees, however, in connexion with the Sabbatical years should now for the first time be broken, and that the new era should be computed, not from B.C. 492, but from a point seven years later, that is, from B.C. 485, may appear to some at first sight to be unsatisfactory, and to form a ground of objection to our chronological arrangement. Nevertheless, such is the precise command conveyed by the words of Daniel; seventy weeks are to be computed from the date of the vision, but "seven weeks" and sixty-two only, "from the going forth of the commandment;" and so the command seems to have been understood by Ezra. This break in the computation of the period of the Jubilee, forms in fact a striking confirmation of the correctness of our arrangement. For the Jewish tradition, as related by Maimonides,* is, that the old computation of the Jubilee was put an end to during the captivity, and that Ezra constituted, not the seventh, but the *thirteenth* year of the second temple the first sabbath, that is, the thirteenth year after the year B.C. 492, and the seventh year after the issue of the command to restore the holy city in B.C. 486. It is in the years of this new era, we think, that some of the numerical periods in Daniel connected with the future destinies of the holy people are specially to be reckoned.

The remaining period of "threescore and two weeks," or 434 years, "unto Messiah the Prince," requires no explanation. It was exactly completed between the autumn of B.C. 437, and the autumn of B.C. 3, about which time Christ was born, at the beginning of the Sabbatical year, about thirty years before the 15th year of Tiberius, and when Cyrenius was first made governor of Judea.† This date for the birth of Christ is again securely fixed by the record of a lunar eclipse at Jerusalem on the night of the 10th January, B.C. 1, not two months before the death of Herod the Great,‡ at whose death the

---

* Maimon. de Shemitta et Jubileo.

† Concerning the governorship of Cyrenius in Judea, see the researches of A. W. Zumpt, as set forth in Fairbairn's Hermeneutical Manual, p. 461.

‡ The thirty-four years' reign of Herod mentioned by Josephus, should not be counted from the autumn of B.C. 37, when he took Jerusalem, at which time the Jews refused to acknowledge him as king; but from the death of Antigonus, their law-

child Jesus, we may infer from Matt. ii. 16, may have been much under two years of age, which well agrees with our reckoning.

All that is predicted as about to happen " after threescore and two weeks," viz.— the cutting off of Messiah, the coming of a prince to destroy the city and the sanctuary, and the taking away of the daily sacrifice, which events took place in the reigns of Tiberius and Titus, we consider to have no reference whatever to the period of " Seventy weeks."

Such, then, we maintain, is the correct reckoning of the chronology of the Hebrew nation, from Solomon to the birth of Christ. Such is the plain and obvious reading of the words of the " Seventy Weeks'" prophecy. And such its precise and literal fulfilment in the birth of Jesus Christ. Divine providence and mercy predetermined the event. Divine wisdom and guidance fulfilled it. And, if the correctness of the reckoning be admitted, it is idle in the face of such exact fulfilment, to maintain that *Prophecy*, or the announcement of future events connected with the welfare of His creatures, is beneath the purpose and inconsistent with the ways of God towards men. It is idle to deny the *Inspiration* of the holy Daniel, thus

ful king, in B.C. 36. His thirty-fourth year ended in Adar B.C. 2. His thirty-fifth year, B.C. 2–1, being incomplete, was counted as the first year of Archelaus. For according to the Talmud, " a king who has reigned during the month Adar, has on the 1st of Nisan completed a year," and commences another,——" since one day of a year is considered to be a year."— *Treatise Rosh Hasshanah. Mishna Surenh.* Vol. ii. p. 300.

selected to convey this wondrous message to his people. It is still more idle, with Dr. Williams, to talk of "throwing overboard, as infected matter, all those directly Messianic interpretations in which Jesus of Nazareth is held to be distinctly, personally, foreseen as Christ."* And inasmuch as this foreknowledge and distinctness of announcement are above the reach or effort of human intellect, the whole circumstances connected with this great event partake of the *Miraculous.*†

We appeal then to our Jewish brethren, and ask what need is there, what room is there left for denying this the most wonderful event of their own most wonderful history ? What difficulty lies in the way of their confession, that this Offspring of the house of David, born at the appointed time, and in the appointed place; by whom, as they and all the world have seen, the destinies of mankind have been more deeply swayed than by any son of Adam till this day ; who sealed His mission by His death,

---

* Introduction to Desprez's Daniel.

† We are surprised and grieved to read in a recent able work, of Dr. Kalisch the following passages : "The gift of prophecy is nothing else but the gift of human reason and judgment, striving to penetrate through the veil of the future, and hence naturally liable to error." And again, "The belief in prophecy has the same origin as the doctrines of revelation, and inspiration, namely, the impossible supposition that the Deity enters into direct and personal intercourse with some men specially chosen." Kalisch's Leviticus, Part I. p. 454, and 457. Cannot the Almighty Creator of all things, the Father of Spirits, create an intermediate being through whom He may hold intercourse with man ?

and by the well-attested miracle of His resurrection from the dead ; can be any but their own expected Saviour, " Messiah, the Prince ?" We beseech them earnestly to consider the belief and teaching of Paul, the zealous Pharisee, the would-be persecutor of Christians, constrained to preach the love of Christ, " Messiah risen from the dead;" yet no way deviating from the strict and purest monotheism of his fathers. For Paul throughout his many epistles teaches, that as "there is but ONE GOD, the Father, of whom are all things, and we in Him," so also there is, distinct from the Father, " one Lord Jesus Christ, by whom are all things, and we by Him :" The Son of Man, or Man, by pre-eminence; the exalted, God-like pattern of humanity—of unfallen and immortal man ; for "this mortal must put on immortality," and "when Christ our life shall appear, then shall we also appear with Him in glory:" then will He " change our vile body, that it may be fashioned like unto His glorious body." He who made the world ; and the world knew Him not: He who was " slain from the foundation of the world ;" * "whom God hath raised from the dead :" † He who in the beginning conversed with Adam and with Abraham, in the form of man : He who in Daniel's vision, " like a Son of Man, came with the clouds of heaven, and came to the Ancient of days:" He who with Moses and Elias stood transfigured on the mount, in the form of man; "the image of the invisible God, the first-born of

* Rev. xiii. 8.   † Rom. x. 9.

every creature." For "God was in Christ (*i.e.* through the eternal Spirit) reconciling the world unto Himself," and Christ has taught us, that "no one hath ascended to Heaven, but He that came down from Heaven, even *the Son of Man who is in Heaven.*" He then who would profess the faith of Paul, and John, and Christ, must believe, not only that there is but ONE GOD, but also that there is "one mediator between God and men, the MAN Christ Jesus," "from above."

And yet most truly also is He "the only-begotten Son of God," inasmuch as He alone, before the foundation of the world, was begotten of the Father, through the Spirit, incapable of fall; perfect as God: and in Him alone "the fulness of the Godhead dwelleth bodily" from the beginning : God manifest in the flesh : "a mighty God," or heavenly potentate : "King of Kings, and Lord of Lords:" who when He shall come, "in the glory of His Father," to take His kingdom and to rule this world in righteousness, "this is the name whereby He shall be called, Jehovah our righteousness;" "for then shall the house of David be as Elohim, (*i.e.*) as the angel of Jehovah before them."* "Therefore let all the house of Israel know assuredly that God hath made that same Jesus, whom ye have crucified, both Lord and Christ."

Yet nevertheless, though Lord and Christ, though clothed with the glory of the Father, judge of this

---

* Zech. xii. 8.

world, as Son of man,* and also Son of God, though partaking to fulness of the Divine nature, and so inheriting the great name of God, though one with the Father, in the unity of the same eternal Spirit, a being, second to, distinct from, and incommensurate with "The King, eternal, immortal, invisible, the ONLY wise (or omniscient) GOD," "who only hath immortality, dwelling in the light which no man can approach unto; whom no man hath seen, or can see:" and distinct also from "the Ancient of Days," who, as the term implies, had been before Him. For He Himself impressed on His disciples, "My Father is greater than I," and spake to them of things known neither to the angels which are in Heaven, nor to the Son, but to the Father: He prayed to the Father; sits at the right hand of the Father; is our constant advocate with the Father; and when teaching the way of everlasting life with the Father, says, "This is life eternal, that they might know Thee the ONLY true GOD, and Jesus Christ whom Thou hast sent." And, therefore, the beloved disciple John, in his vision of the "New Jerusalem coming down from God," "saw no temple therein: for the Lord God Almighty, *and the Lamb*, are the temple of it." Yea, His apostles have taught us that we also may become "the sons of God," if, feeding on Him in our hearts, we will partake of the Holy Spirit of God, being "filled with the fulness of God,"† and so be one with Him, as He is one with the Father;‡ "partakers of the Divine nature,"§ through the

* John, v. 27. † Eph. iii. 19. ‡ John, xvii. 21. § 2 Pet. i. 4.

" divine power " of Jesus our Lord ; and yet not many Gods.

Let not our Jewish brethren, then, be deterred from the recognition of the " one Lord Jesus Messiah, their King and Saviour, either by those who would confound Him with the one Almighty and invisible God, thereby setting aside the mediator and advocate with the Father ; nor yet by those who would proclaim Him co-eternal and co-equal with the Father, thereby teaching, in contradiction of Moses and the prophets, two Almighty Gods. Such was not the teaching of the Apostle Paul. Paul is incessant in the repetition, of his distinction between "God the Father, and the Lord Jesus Christ." He tells us that, " at the name of Jesus every knee should bow, of things in heaven, and things in earth, and things under the earth ; and that every tongue should confess that Jesus Messiah is Lord, *to the glory of God the Father :*"* that when the Father " bringeth in the first-begotten into the world, he saith, Let all the angels of God worship Him," yea, that "unto the Son, he saith, Thy throne, *O God,* is for ever and ever." Yet, lest thereby the Son should be confounded with the Father, he adds, " God, *even Thy God,* hath anointed Thee with the oil of gladness above Thy fellows."† All power we know is given to Him in heaven and earth : " He hath put all things under His feet :" yet, nevertheless, " when all things shall be subdued unto Him,

* Philip. ii. 10, 11.   † Heb. i. 9.

then shall the Son also Himself be subject unto Him who put all things under Him."* Let us not shock our Jewish brethren by teaching that the manhood of Christ has been taken into God, for that is to detract from the pure divinity of God : but rather let us teach, that the divine Spirit of the invisible and unapproachable God has been poured " without measure" on that mighty celestial being, for whom, and by whom this world was made; "JESUS MESSIAH, the same yesterday, to-day, and for ever;" our Lord, and our God ; " the first and the last, which was dead, and is alive;"† the SON of MAN, who came down from heaven, "the SON of MAN, who hath ascended up where He was be-fore,"‡ " to His father and our father, to His God and our God,"§ and is "set on the right hand of the Majesty on high ; being made so much better than the angels, as He hath *by inheritance* ob-tained a more excellent name than they;"‖ even that great name which appertaineth to His Father from eternity.

But, to return to the subject of the prophecy, it has been remarked by a late eminent writer,¶ speaking contemptuously of the numerical periods of the book of Daniel, " What has the Holy Spirit to do with counting years, and months, and days ? In his kingdom, the only true and the only divine one, time and space are of a very subordinate im-

---

* 1 Cor. xv. 27, 28. † Rev. ii. 8. ‡ John, vi. 62. § John, xx. 17.
‖ Heb. i. 3, 4. ¶ Bunsen's " Hippolytus," vol. ii. p. 286.

portance, and wherever He has moved holy men in
the Church to say something respecting times, it
will be found that the subject of the prophecy is not
to be wholly external and idealess, but connected
with the great thoughts of God, and, finally, that
it offers to the mind a certain latitude, and to individual will and action all their energy."

We accept the concluding sentiments of this
passage as obviously true.   The coming of the
Saviour of the world, at the precise termination of a
predicted period of weeks of years, was indeed connected with the great thoughts of God.   But to say
that the Holy Spirit deigns not to take note of time
and space, and days and years, in connexion with
the affairs of this lower world, is as obviously untrue.   We cannot so gather from our reading of
Scripture, and especially of the Book of Daniel.
Hath not God set lights in the firmament for signs,
and for seasons, and for days, and for years?
Was it not commanded to the children of Israel to
keep holy each seventh day?   Was not the septennial division of years, and again the hallowing of
every fiftieth year, an express ordinance of God?
Not only have we before us, in the prophecy we
have been considering, a single instance of accurate
computation of years by the Holy Spirit, reckoned
in His own ordained calendar of sabbatic years and
jubilees—of an express announcement to Daniel the
beloved of the deep and gracious counsels of the
Almighty towards his people, through the medium
of a messenger from above, and again, of the fulfil-

ment of those counsels at the appointed time by the same heavenly messenger who appeared before the lowly Mary—but we also seem to arrive at an unlooked-for discovery from the examination of the numbers in this book, viz., that it has pleased the Almighty to forecast the destinies of His chosen people in fixed and measured cycles of this sacred calendar. For, as we have already seen, reckoning upwards from the birth of Christ to the release from captivity under Darius is a period of exactly 490 years; from thence to the dedication of Solomon's temple is a similar period of 490 years; and again from thence, according to the reckoning of the Second Book of Kings, to the mission of Moses to the children of Israel in Egypt, there is a third period of exactly 490 years; so that it may be said, with a considerable degree of precision, that the children of Israel have fulfilled their bygone destinies in three equal cycles of

70 weeks of years under the Tabernacle :

70 weeks of years, under the first temple, including 70 supplemental Sabbaths enjoyed by the land, during the captivity:

70 weeks of years under the second temple, even till the laying of the foundation-stone of the third temple, not made with hands, in the birth of Jesus Christ.

" Oh, house of Israel, cannot I do with you as the potter, saith the Lord ? Behold, as the clay is

Q

in the potter's, so are ye in mine hands, oh house of Israel."*

Now in the same degree that we are impressed with the conviction that these several periods have been literally fulfilled in the past history of God's holy people, and fulfilled according to His predetermined will and guidance, so shall we feel confident in the expectation that the several yet unfulfilled periods of the Book of Daniel, shall also be accomplished in the future history of this peculiar people; viz., the twice repeated period of "time, times, and a half," or 1260 years, during which the saints of the Most High shall be given into the hands of the little horn of ch. vii. 25—the 2400 years,† until the expiration of which the "sanctuary and the host shall be trodden under foot," ch. viii. 13, 14,—and the 1290, and 1335 years counted "from the time that the daily —— shall be taken away and the abomination that maketh desolate set up," xii. 11.

" Blessed be the name of God for ever and ever :" —" He changeth the times and the seasons: he removeth kings, and setteth up kings "—" he revealeth the deep and secret things: he knoweth what is in the darkness, and the light dwelleth with him." ‡

* Jer. xviii. 6.

† The reading of 2400, according to the Greek of Theodosion, instead of 2300, as in our ordinary Hebrew copies, is confirmed, as observed by Mr. Hatley Frere, by seven MSS. in Hebrew and Armenian, examined by the late Dr. Wolf, viz., two at Bokhara, one at Ispahan, one at Adrianople, one at Meschid, one at Ulshkelesia, one in Chaldæa. ‡ Dan. ii. 20–22.

THE PAPAL AND MAHOMEDAN LITTLE HORNS.

WE now dismiss the subject of the prophecy of the Seventy Weeks, trusting that we have succeeded in accomplishing one-half at least of the task we had undertaken, by proving from the unmistakable accomplishment of this the most remarkable prophecy in the book of Daniel, both the inspiration, and genuineness, of that holy book: and we turn once more to the consideration of the latter part of that other great prophecy of Daniel, which leads us down from the time of the Babylonian empire to the time of the second coming of the Son of man with the clouds of heaven. The first of these prophecies has relation to the coming of Messiah to be rejected of His people Israel, the second to the coming of Messiah " to be the glory of His people Israel." In the course of our observations, we have already disposed of the second, sixth, and ninth chapters of the book, and have also given reason for believing that a part of the tenth chapter, and the greater part of the eleventh, are not the words of the prophet, but the words of some zealous interpreter, endeavouring to apply the pro-

phecies of Daniel to his own times, and we have
nothing further to add concerning these two chapters.

The first, third, fourth, and fifth chapters of
Daniel relate chiefly to historical events, and do not
necessarily, therefore, come within the range of our
remarks, which are limited to the question of the
prophetic inspiration of the book.   There remain,
then, for consideration only three prophetic chapters, viz., the seventh, as connected with, and in
expansion of the prophecy of the great image, the
eighth, and the twelfth, upon each of which we propose to make a few observations.   And we think it
will appear, that the way to the interpretation of the
prophecies contained in them has already been
cleared and disencumbered of many difficulties.
We think also that the manifest fulfilment, even
under our own eyes, of the prophetic history of the
ten kingdoms of the fourth empire, and of the
"little horn," or kingdom which should arise up
amongst them, will afford almost as striking a proof
of the inspiration of the book of Daniel as is supplied by the prophecy of the Seventy Weeks.

To begin with ch. vii. We have seen how strongly
the Rabbinical interpreter in the days of the Maccabees was impressed with the idea, that " the fourth
kingdom upon earth," vii. 23, " dreadful and terrible," which we now so distinctly recognise in past
history as the Roman empire, was no other than the
empire of the Greeks in Asia, set up by the successors of Alexander the Great, the then last empire

which had appeared in the world ; that "the ten
horns of this kingdom," v. 24, were represented by
ten Greco-Egyptian and Greco-Syrian kings who had
already reigned, being a part of upwards of twenty
who succeeded Alexander in Egypt and Syria ; and
that the "little horn" which "came up among them,"
v. 8, which had "eyes like the eyes of a man, and a
mouth speaking great things," was no other than
Antiochus Epiphanes, one of the ten. Now the
obvious contradiction involved in this interpretation,
and that which proves that it cannot have been
dictated by the Holy Spirit, is, that if the ten horns
were to be represented by ten of the successors of
Alexander in Syria and Egypt, who have long since
passed away, which is undoubtedly the writer's meaning in chapter xi., the "little horn" from amongst
them must also have arisen *in those same days*, and
in that same country, and have also passed away ;
whereas, on the contrary, it is clearly foretold by the
Spirit that the power of this "little horn " shall last
till "the ancient of days did sit," v. 9, 11, 26, and
until "the greatness of the kingdom under the whole
heaven shall be given to the saints of the Most
High," which events have not yet come to pass. So
that it is impossible that Daniel's portrait of the
"little horn " of ch. vii. should be intended to represent the king Antiochus. Mr. Desprez and Mr.
Perowne,* therefore, consistently with the erroneous
indications of chap. xi., which place the time of

* See " Contemporary Review," vol. i. p. 104..

the ten kings, two thousand years ago, but inconsistently with the prediction of the prolonged power
of the " little horn " even to this time, both argue that
the " little horn" of the seventh chapter, and the
" little horn " of the eighth chapter, are one and
the same king, viz., Antiochus. While Dr. Pusey
and those who with him look upon the little horn
of chapter viii. as Antiochus, inconsistently with the
contents of ch. xi., which they suppose to be genuine,
and which speak of a power long since passed away,
argue that the little horn of chap. vii. must be
intended to represent some yet future Antichrist.
Both these views are made void by irreconcilable
contradictions, on the supposition of the genuineness
of chapter xi.   In the days of the Maccabees, the
first of these interpretations involved indeed no insuperable difficulty: for who could say that the
kingdom of the saints, or Jewish people, was not
then about to be established in the holy land, never
to be removed, or that the Son of man might not
then have soon appeared in glory?   We now, however, perceive from subsequent history that the idea
of making the successors of Alexander represent
the fourth kingdom, and the little kingdom to rise
out of its ten divisions, a king, or kingdom already
passed away, is manifestly impossible. Dismissing,
then, from our minds those portions of chapters x., xi.
which seem to contain a mere prosaic comment
of some Rabbinical interpreter, by whose unauthorised comment the above named writers, and many
others, have been led into such insuperable difficulties,

let us turn to the writings of a highly venerated
Jewish interpreter of this prophecy, of a later date; to
one whose spiritual and prophetic character is in
remarkable affinity with that of Daniel,—we mean
the inspired and beloved disciple St. John: who in
treating of these same periods of prophetic history
reaching yet into futurity, has guided our understanding of this chapter by the adoption of the same
symbols with those made use of by Daniel, and in
his interpretation of these symbols has clothed his
language with a prophetic style of diction in harmony with the style of the original vision.

St. John, in Rev. ch. xiii. sees in vision this
same "little horn" of Daniel, when he speaks of a
beast with "seven heads and ten horns," v. 1; and
we are sure of the identity of the horn and the
beast, because while the horn of Daniel has "a
mouth speaking great things," to the beast of St.
John is given "a mouth speaking great things,"
v. 5; while the horn of Daniel "wears out the
saints of the most High," to the beast of St. John
it is given "to make war with the saints and to
overcome them," v. 7; and while the saints are
given into the hands of the "little horn" until "a
time, times, and the dividing of time," or 1260 days,
to the beast that makes war with the saints it was
given "to continue forty and two months," or 1260
days. Now, St. John informs us, xvii. 7–12, that
the seven heads of this beast "are seven mountains;" that the ten horns "are ten kings which
have received no kingdom as yet;" and that these

ten kings shall give their power and strength unto
the beast.   So thát the beast, like the "little horn,"
rises from amongst the ten.   And then again upon
the self-same hills we see the beast arrayed in scarlet, v. 3, and a woman also clothed in the same
coloured garments, "drunk with the blood of the
saints," seated on the beast; and the plain interpretation is added, that this woman represents the city
then reigning over the kings of the earth, v. 18,
that is, Rome.   From this inspired interpreter, then,
we learn that the ten horns of the fourth kingdom
of Daniel were not in existence in the days of Antiochus, nor yet even in the days of St. John, and
that the seat of the "little horn" from amongst
them should be, not in Syria, but at Rome.

Again, we read in the seventh chapter of Daniel,
"I saw in the night visions, and behold, one like a
Son of man came with the clouds of heaven, and
came to the Ancient of days;" and in St. John,
chap. xiv. 14, "And I looked, and behold a white
cloud, and upon the cloud one sat like unto the
Son of man, having on his head a golden crown, and
in his hand a sharp sickle," wherewith to reap the
earth.   Thus, as in Daniel, so in St. John, still the
scene we find is laid in future time.   And in chap.
i. 7: "Behold, he cometh with clouds; and every
eye shall see him, and they also which pierced him:
and all the kindreds of the earth shall wail because
of him."*   So, that the latter portion of this chap-

---

* See the comment of J. Pye Smith, showing how this passage

ter of Daniel is appropriated and applied with extreme distinctness by St. John, to times which clearly have not yet come to pass. The Maccabean interpretation is at variance with St. John throughout. For a power rising in the east cannot be identified with one whose position is clearly fixed by St. John in the west. Nor can a power by whom the " daily sacrifice " was literally taken away, viz. Antiochus, be looked upon as even typical of a power in connexion with whom this peculiar act of impiety is nowhere spoken of. The little horn of ch. vii. is spoken of in that chapter, not so much as an impious king, as one puffed up with the arrogance of power. He persecutes even to blood the saints of the Most High, yet his distinguishing feature is not to destroy. His great words are spoken rather concerning than against the Most High.* The nature of his blasphemy hitherto is, not that he has rejected the daily worship of God, but that he has made his own word equal with that of God: and yet, perhaps, deeper and more heinous blasphemy may, in the nature of things, be expected from him and his people as the time of his destruction approaches; when his kingdom shall be full of darkness, and they shall blaspheme the God of heaven because of their pains.†

With regard to the period of " time, times, and a half "—the only period in this chapter requiring

has reference to the future establishment of the Jewish Church under the New Testament. Vol. i. p. 289.

* vii. 25.　　　　† Rev. xvi. 10, 11.

explanation—we are informed by Daniel that it will terminate at the time "when he shall have accomplished to scatter the power of the *holy people,*" xii. 7. In accordance with which St. John informs us that the oppressor of the saints, or *holy people,* " shall continue forty and two months," which is the same period: and again, that the two witnesses, one of whom we assume to be the Jews or *holy people,* the other persecuted Christians, shall prophesy in sackcloth during "one thousand two hundred and threescore days," or years. And this long period must necessarily be comprehended within "the times of the Gentiles:" for until those times are fulfilled, Jerusalem must be trodden under foot.*

Taking, then. the Apocalypse of St. John as the true interpreter of the Apocalypse of Daniel, how distinctly does the meaning of the seventh chapter of this prophet appear before our eyes! How prominently does the "little horn," "speaking very great things," stand out in history. Our eyes are directed to the seven hills of Rome. We are confined to the selection thence of one of the ten fragments into which the last, or Roman empire had at one time been divided. And we are compelled to look amongst them for a "little," but oppressive power, diverse from all which had preceded it, and "speaking very great things," which ought now to have existed, seated on those seven hills

* Luke, xxi. 24.

for the period of some 1260 years. Prejudice alone can prevent the recognition of the power here pointed out. It cannot be confounded with the kingdom of Antiochus. Truly has Pope Pius IX., as before referred to,* pointed out the kingdom sought for, when he writes, "By a peculiar disposition of Divine Providence it was ordered that when the Roman Empire was overthrown and divided into many kingdoms, the Roman Pontiff, in the midst of this diversity of kingdoms, and in the present state of human society, should possess a civil Princedom."

Now this "civil Princedom" is clearly no other than Daniel's "little horn." There is no other kingdom which rose out of the Roman empire which comes near to the description. The first thing that we are told, concerning this little horn is, that "there were three of the first horns plucked up by the roots" before it.† And accordingly within two centuries after the death of Gregory the Great, in A.D. 606, whose successor was invested with the title of "universal bishop," we find that Pepin, king of France, first, and afterwards the Emperor Charlemagne, had conferred upon the Pope, as the special patrimony of St. Peter, three principalities, viz. the Exarchate of Ravenna, seized from the dominions of the emperor of the East, Pentapolis, or a portion of the kingdom of the Lombards, and the city and

* P. 23.　　† Dan. vii. 8.

duchy of Rome; in virtue of which three temporalities the Popes have since assumed the triple crown. Again, we read, "Behold, in this horn were eyes like the eyes of a man." The prince of this little kingdom should be a seer, an ἐπίσκοπος, a Bishop. His eyes, however, should be worldly rather than spiritual; restless eyes, prying and searching into the affairs, not only of kings and kingdoms, but even into the affairs of private families and individuals. Again, " A mouth speaking great things." What can exceed the arrogance of this little temporal Princedom, claiming to itself the right to set up and depose earthly princes? What can exceed its spiritual presumption in claiming to absolve from oaths, to forgive sins, and the attribute of infallibility, which alone belongs to God? And "he shall wear out the saints of the Most High," " and they shall be given into his hand until a time, and times, and the dividing of time;" that is, God's holy people, the scattered seed of Abraham, shall be subject to his persecution during the whole period of his existence, 1260 days, or years. And accordingly the persecution of Judaism began with the rise of the Papal power in the seventh century, and has lasted till now. Till the seventh century, the scattered Jews had remained numerous and flourishing in Mesopotamia, in Spain, in Africa, and in Egypt; and, in Arabia, a Jewish kingdom of considerable power had existed for many ages, even from before the Christian era. Soon after the year A.D. 600, however,

"the laws of both Church and State," writes Da
Costa,* "concurred in the attempt to annihilate, if
possible, the Jewish faith, after Reccared, by abjur-
ing Arianism, had brought the whole of Spain under
the dominion of the Church of Rome and its Bishop.
Until that time, the Visigoths in Spain had, like
the Ostrogoths in Italy, shown favour to the Jews.
From henceforth the Romish clergy and the Gothic
kings seemed to vie with each other in multiplying
edicts and laws against the Jews, laws which have
been rightly designated as barbarous and absurd.
Like the edicts of Justinian in the East, they excluded 'the abominable sect' from all power or
jurisdiction over Christians; prohibited their marriage with Christians, and the celebration of their
weddings, sabbaths, and feasts, especially the Passover." Thus it is difficult to conceive anything
more complete than the correspondence between the
history of the Papacy and the prophetic history of
the "little horn."

It now only remains to be considered whether
anything may reasonably be said concerning the
time of the expiration of these 1260 years. And
here, as entering into the region of conjecture, we
shall be very brief. We are inclined to think that
this period has no connexion with the other four
periods above referred to, which relate to the east,
and not to the west. We see no room left for
doubt that these 1260 years mark the duration of

* Da Costa's "Israel and the Gentiles," p. 217.

the Papal power, whether spiritual, or temporal, or both combined. The history of this period now lies fulfilled before us. And we may either seek to gather the time of the end from the date of the beginning, or the date of the beginning from the end. Now the temporal power of the Papacy is evidently vanishing before our eyes. Though yet the vital spark of power is not extinct. Nay, we are led by Daniel to expect not so much its sudden destruction, as its gradual extinction by the consuming power of its adversaries. " The judgment shall sit, and they shall take away his dominion, *to consume and destroy it unto the end.*" * How long the spiritual power shall be allowed to survive the temporal, and to linger on in the ancient seat of its dominion, is a question also to be solved by time. Should we be disposed to fix the date of its commencement, at the time of the assumption by the Pontiff of the title of Universal Bishop in A.D. 607, then has the time of fulfilment already passed away in A.D. 1867. And this very date would seem to form a period not inapt from which to mark the beginning of the end. We have lived to see a crisis in the kingdoms of the West in the latter half of the year 1866, such as will form an epoch in the history of the nations of the world. The swallowing up and consolidation of petty kingdoms into mighty states in that year, has become the marked and normal feature of the day. It is now no longer possible that

* Dan. vii. 26.

the smaller fragments of the Roman empire should
continue to exist as separate kingdoms, while "multitudes are running to and fro,"* and the wheels
of locomotion are annihilating bounds and space.
The ten kingdoms of Daniel's fourth empire have
from henceforth ceased to exist.   And the once
stately bark of the civil princedom of the Pontiff
which rose amongst them, and so proudly sat triumphant on the sea of nations, now scarcely lives
amidst the upheaving waves and tempests of the
nations which surround it.   We cannot but believe
that we are living in days when the last end of the
prophecy of the four empires is being fulfilled before
our eyes with the same minute exactness, and perhaps with the same degree of absence of observation
by the outer world, as when, in fulfilment of that
other great prophecy we have been considering, our
blessed Lord Himself was born into the world,—
when "He was in the world," and yet "the world
knew it not."   Who can say that the fatal blow
which shall take away the temporal dominion of the
Pontiff has not already been delivered, and that
the process of gradual consumption is not even
now being carried on?   Of this, at least, we may
be certain, that this Papal princedom cannot, as
some would persuade us, be the kingdom of the
"stone cut out without hands," "which shall never
be destroyed."   For the destiny of the little horn is
to be consumed and destroyed unto the end.   The

* Dan. xii. 4.

body of the beast also connected with it must be
"given to the burning" flame.*   Again, the metropolis of Christ's spiritual yet visible kingdom upon
earth can never be identified with the city of Rome:
for we have the authority of the Great King himself
to declare, that Jerusalem is the city of the Great
King.†   Until this little "civil princedom" of the
Pontiff shall have been destroyed, and until the
scattering of the power of "the holy people" be accomplished, the spiritual reign of the saints of the
Most High upon earth cannot be revealed.

We now proceed to say a few words on chapter
viii., that is to say, on the prophecy of the ram and
the he-goat.   Here, again, we shall have to refer for
solution to the Revelation of St. John.   Meanwhile,
the removal of the greater part of chap. xi. as an unauthorised application of chapter viii. to the days of
the Maccabees, and the extinction thereby of Antiochus Epiphanes altogether from the field of view of
the prophet, will greatly facilitate the identification
of the "little horn," which is said to rise up towards
the *latter end* of the four kingdoms into which the
empire of the he-goat was to be divided.   As the
seat of the "little horn" of chap. vii. is fixed by St.
John to the seven hills of Rome, so is the seat of
the power of this second "little horn" of chap. viii.
fixed with equal precision to the countries neighbouring upon the Holy Land.   The two powers,
therefore, as we have said, can never properly be

* Dan. vii. 11.   † Matt. v. 35.

identified as one and the same, as is so earnestly
contended for by Mr. Desprez. The ram with the
two horns we are informed by the prophet himself
represents the kings, or kingdoms, of Media and
Persia: and the he-goat, as all admit, represents the
kingdom of Alexander the Great. The "little horn"
which shall rise up "in the last end of the indignation," we read, represents "a king of fierce countenance, and understanding dark sentences;" his distinguishing feature is, that "he shall *destroy wonder-
fully*," and "shall *destroy* the mighty and the holy
people," and "in peace shall *destroy* many," v. 24,
25. He is emphatically the *destroyer*. We look,
therefore, for a power whose characteristic feature
shall be trust in the sword. Now such a power
was Mahomet. For though it is true that almost
every chapter in the Koran is headed with the words,
—"In the name of the most merciful God," nevertheless the religion of Mahomet was chiefly propa-
gated by the sword. "The sword," says Mahomet,
"is the key of heaven and hell: a drop of blood shed
in the cause of God, a night spent in arms, is of
more avail than two months of fasting and prayer :
whosoever falls in battle, his sins are forgiven : at
the day of judgment his wounds shall be resplendent
as vermilion, and odoriferous as musk ; and the
loss of his limbs shall be supplied by the wings of
angels and cherubim." The time of his appearance
must fall during "the *last end of the indignation*,"
v. 19, that is, of the indignation against the Jewish
people. He waxes "great towards the south, towards

R

the east, and towards the pleasant land;" he casts
down *the place* of the sanctuary, that is, the city
of Jerusalem; and the sanctuary and the host are
to remain trodden under foot "unto two thousand
four hundred days," or years, "then shall the
sanctuary be cleansed." Again, this little horn
is identified with the king, or power, which
"shall do according to his will," xi. 36; who
"shall speak marvellous things concerning the God
of gods" (*El Elim*), and not regard the God of his
fathers, "nor regard any god" (*Eloah*), but shall
honour (מָעֻזִּים אֱלֹהַּ) Elah, or Allah of strongholds,
"the God of forces," as opposed to the God of
mercy and pity. He "*shall prosper till the indignation be accomplished,*" that is, until God's indignation
against the Jewish people shall have ceased. He
"shall plant the tabernacles of his palaces between the seas in the glorious holy mountain,"
xi. 45; and *immediately after his extinction the
people of Daniel shall be delivered,* "*every one
that shall be found written in the book,*" xii. 1.
In confirmation of this identification of the king of
fierce countenance with the wilful king, it will be
observed, that as in chap. viii. the king of fierce
countenance is spoken of immediately in connexion
with the latter end of the four kingdoms into which
the empire of Alexander was divided; so in chap.
xi., if we pass from v. 4 to v. 36, leaving out the
interpolated comment,* the king, who does according
to his will is spoken of immediately in connexion

* See pp. 112, 116.

with the same four kingdoms arising out of that of Alexander, "plucked up even for others besides those." Some of the distinguishing features of this fierce and wilful king mark the duration of his power as lasting even beyond the days in which we live, and others cannot be applied to the reign of Antiochus Epiphanes, even retrospectively. All the above characteristics are manifestly exhibited in connexion with the same remarkable power, viz. the warrior-prophet Mahomet, and Mahomedanism.*

Now St. John clearly portrays this same power in his description of the second woe trumpet, Rev. ix., where he speaks of the eruption of locusts from the abyss, as it were in breastplates of iron, with "the sound of chariots and many horses running to battle," and with a king set over them, whose name in the Hebrew tongue is Abaddon, but in the Greek tongue Apollyon, *the destroyer.* We know how "the holy people" were persecuted and destroyed by the Moslems under the fierce guidance of Mahomet, whose "dark sentences" and revelations are set forth in the pages of his own dark Koran, and how the fearful alternative of "the Koran or the sword" was offered by him to the Jewish communities in Arabia ; how tribes of peaceful Jews, who refused to accept the religion of the prophet, or the prophet himself as

---

* "Neither shall he regard the desire of women" (xi. 37). One of the distinguishing features of Mahomedanism is its utter disregard of sexual purity, so specially enforced by Christianity. Monkery, nunnism, celibacy, were evils which had been carried to excess in the days of Mahomet. The natural result of reaction was the license and laxity of polygamy.

their Messiah, were savagely destroyed "in peace;" how their religious worship, with the daily oblation, if not daily sacrifice, which was probably maintained in the Jewish kingdom of the Hamyarites even till the year A.D. 627, was then finally taken away, for "the transgressors had come to the full," and had now even set their minds to root out Christianity,* for they had "not the seal of God in their foreheads;"† how the sanctuary, or rather the "*place*" of the sanctuary, recently occupied by Christian Churches, was seized oy the Caliph Omar, and "the tabernacles of his palaces," that is, the mosque Al Aksa, and the Kubbat as Sakra, planted "in the glorious holy mountain," where they still remain; how the holy people have ever since been forbidden even to touch with the soles of their feet the holy ground; and how "the two witnesses" of the Most High, both Judaism and Christianity, are to this day prophesying in sackcloth and trodden under foot, till the power of the oppressor shall have been broken, though "without hand," and till the sanctuary of Jerusalem shall have been cleansed.

That the sanctuary of Jerusalem shall yet indeed be cleansed from Mahomedan pollution, we have not only the authority of Daniel, but that also of the Lord Himself, who has said, "Is it not written, My house shall be called the house of prayer *for all nations?*"‡ For this is a state of honour which

---

* Milman's "History of the Jews," vol. iii. p. 98; Sale's "Preliminary Discourse," pp. 29, 48.

† Rev. ix. 4.   ‡ Mark, xi. 17.

has yet to be realised by some future temple of Jerusalem.*

But some, perhaps, may be inclined to ask how could Mahomet, or his successors, have fulfilled the words of ch. viii. 11, as translated in our English version,—"by him the daily sacrifice was taken away,"—when we know that the temple of Jerusalem had been destroyed, and the sacrifices connected with it had already ceased to be offered, some five hundred years and upwards before the appearance of the false prophet. Nevertheless, reference is unquestionably made in this passage, either directly, or indirectly, to the perpetual morning and evening sacrifice of a lamb on the altar of the temple, as commanded by the law of Moses. It might indeed be argued, in reply to this question, that although the temple of Jerusalem was no longer standing in the days of the Saracens, yet, nevertheless, altars of sacrifice may have been retained by the dispersed nation, and the daily morning and evening sacrifice may have been offered thereon by the priests of that great community of Jews which flourished in Arabia even till the time of Mahomet. For we know from Josephus,† that in the temple of Onias, erected in Egypt some century and a half before the Christian era, an altar of sacrifice had been there set up, and that the daily sacrifices were continually offered up in that temple in the same manner as in the temple of Jerusalem. Such an

---

* See Ezek. xxxvii. 58.   † Ant. xiii. 3.

argument, however, is not necessary, and indeed
would not afford a satisfactory solution of the
difficulty. For the offering of sacrifices was forbidden by the law of Moses to the Jews excepting
only in the holy city: and the Sanhedrim at Jerusalem certainly never recognised the lawfulness
of the sacrifices in the temple of Onias at Heliopolis.
The probability is, therefore, that Jewish sacrifices ceased entirely after the destruction of Jerusalem. It will be observed, however, that in the
passage before us Daniel makes use neither of the
word "sacrifice," nor "oblation," when designating
the act of worship against which the hostility of
the Mahomedan little horn should be directed.
His words are simply, "by him the daily——was
taken away." When the prophet, in ch. ix. 27,
is intending to foretell the ceasing of the literal
daily sacrifice in the temple, at the time of the
destruction of Jerusalem by Titus, he makes use
of no such ambiguous expression; but speaks distinctly of the "sacrifice" (*zehbach*), and the "oblation" (*minchah*), as about to cease; both which have
accordingly, as far as we know, ceased to be offered
even till this day. In ch. viii. 11, 12, 13, both these
words are omitted, in three consecutive passages
relating to this impious act of the little horn.
Now the fact of the omission of these expressive
words, and the vagueness of expression applied to
this predicted interference with the daily worship,
seem to justify the construction, that the time referred to by the prophet was not a time when the

actual daily sacrifice could have been in operation, but when some daily offering in memory and in representation of the daily sacrifice may have been substituted by the dispersed Jews living within the dominions of the little horn. That some such daily offering was substituted by the Jewish priests, after the fall of Jerusalem, in place of the sacrifice of the lamb, may reasonably be assumed from the words of the Talmud, where it is said, "As the altar wrought atonement, during the time of the temple, so after its destruction, the table :"* that is, the table of the shewbread. Such, then, we consider to be the true construction of these words of Daniel.

The divine allegory of the sacrifice of "the Lamb of God that taketh away the sin of the world,"—"the Lamb slain from the foundation of the world,"—of the eating of the flesh, and drinking the blood of the Lamb—of the glorious exaltation of the Lamb to the throne of God—of the marriage of the Lamb,—of the preparation of His bride,— of the wrath and victory of the Lamb,—and of the salvation of all who are written in the Lamb's book of life,—the sacred legend of man's redemption and reconciliation with his God,—is the golden thread which shines throughout and unites the sacred texture of the Old and New Testament. It is the fundamental thought which has been gradually developed by prophets and apostles, and by Christ Himself, from beginning to end of holy

* See Kalisch's Leviticus, p. 62.

Scripture, from the time of the offering of the accepted lamb by righteous Abel, to the time referred
to in the last pages of the Apocalypse of St. John.
The leading of The Lamb to the slaughter, dumb,
and opening not his mouth, is the wondrous act
of loving mercy, prepared of old for man, which
was typified by the daily morning and evening sacrifice of the lamb without blemish in the temple of
Jerusalem: and so typified with the view of ac-
customing the minds of His creatures to a belief in
the all-powerful virtue and efficacy of perfectness
and innocence before the throne of God.* And it
is the offering up of the Lamb of God Himself,
which, we may infer from Ezekiel, shall hereafter
be commemorated, by the restored nation, in the
daily preparation of "a burnt-offering unto the
Lord, of a lamb of the first year without blemish,"

---

* We think that Dr. Kalisch has failed to explain the origin
of sacrifice, when he observes, that holocausts "express most
completely absolute submission to the power of the Deity," that
"they were designed by the law to keep alive the feeling of
humble dependence on Jehovah, and were used as a chief ac-
knowledgment of His theocratic rule:" and that "the command
to roast the Paschal lamb entire, so that no bone of it is broken,"
was "to symbolise the unity of the families and nation" of Israel.
These symbols are not expressive of the facts and feelings they
are said to represent. If there were any such feeling of submission
and dependence implanted in our nature in connexion with the
sacrifice of animals, how is it that this feeling has since died out,
and no longer seeks in pious minds to vent itself in such tokens
of submission? How is it, that this impulse to offer sacrifice,
which was universal, if inherent in our nature, ceased to exist
soon after the time of the great sacrifice of Christ?—KALISCH'S
Lev. pp. 156, 234.

to be sacrificed on the altar of the future temple, not, as under the old dispensation, every morning and evening, but "*morning by morning,*"—" by a perpetual ordinance unto the Lord." * The typical offering of the sacrificial lamb was the act of worship declared by Moses to be acceptable to the Most High, under the old covenant; the perpetual memorial of the death of the Lamb, by the eating (not sacrificing) of His flesh and blood—the blood of the new covenant—under the type of bread and wine, is the act of worship declared by the Lamb Himself to be acceptable to Him till His coming again : and the renewal in the cleansed sanctuary of Jerusalem of the " burnt-offering " morning by morning, in memory, we assume, of the lifting up of the Lamb between the third and sixth hours of the day, is the act of worship which shall hereafter be acceptable to the Most High, when, " as it is written, There shall (have) come out of Sion the Deliverer, and shall (have) turned away ungodliness from Jacob : for this is my covenant unto them, when I shall take away their sins." † To suspend, or take away the daily sacrifice in the temple, was looked upon by the Jews as one of the greatest calamities which could befall them.‡ To take away the perpetual memorial of the precious death of The Lamb, is on the face of it an act of the highest impiety. We cannot accuse the little horn of ch. vii. of any such impious act. On the contrary, the

* Ezek. xlvi. 13, 14, 15.   † Rom. xi. 26, 27.   ‡ See p. 136.

perpetual memory of the death of Christ has been ever faithfully preserved, in the daily mass, or sacrifice of Christ, upon the altars of the Papal horn. The charge against the Papacy is, that in place of the simple memorial of Christ's death, by the eating of bread, and drinking of wine, as commanded by Christ Himself, which is intelligible and acceptable to the humblest of mankind, a superstitious sacrifice, coupled with an inconceivable and revolting mystery, has been invented and substituted by its priests. But as regards the little horn of ch. viii., the charge against it is, of actually taking away and obliterating all trace in his dominions of the daily memorial of the sacrifice of the lamb, whether by Jew or Christian. In the creed of Mahomet Christ is looked upon as merely man. "Christ, the Son of Mary," he says, "is no more than an apostle : other apostles have preceded him : his mother was a woman, who did not pervert the truth : they both ate food." * He has not reached, but stumbled at the conception of a high celestial being begotten of God, perfect as Himself, "the image of the invisible, the first-born of creation." Though zealous indeed, and worthily so, for the indivisible unity of "the only true God," he has not recognised the divine person, and office of the Son of Man who came down from heaven, sent by God, and who, by inheritance, as Son of God, hath obtained a more excellent name than all the holy angels in heaven. The Koran denies that Christ was slain or cruci-

* Koran, ch. 5.

fied:* and despises and neglects His parting command, " Do this in remembrance of me." The religion of Mahomet thus proclaims itself the religion
of anti-Christ, —" He is anti-Christ who denieth the
Father and the Son."

Speaking of the eruption of the Saracens, like
locusts from the abyss, with their fierce destroying
leader at their head, St. John writes :—" The sun
and the air were darkened by reason of the smoke
of the pit." Now it is remarkable, that in the
Chronicle of Abulpharagius it is recorded, that " in
the sixth year of the Arabians," that is, in the year
A.D. 627, about which time, as we have seen, the
power of the holy people, and the daily memorial
of the sacrifice of the lamb, became extinct under the
destroying hand of Mahomet, " half the disc of the
sun was eclipsed, and darkness prevailed from the
preceding October even till June, so that it might
be said that the sun's disc was not completely restored during that time."† The Emperor Heraclius·
is said to have interpreted this phenomenon as intended to represent the partial darkness introduced
by the religion of Mahomet, which, having rejected
indeed idolatry for the worship of the one God, had
not however yet accepted the full truths of Christianity.

The consistency of this interpretation of the
little horn is complete, as long as the words of
chap. xi. do not stand in the way to complicate
it. On the other hand, if the whole of chap. xi.

---

* Koran, ch. 4.　　　　† Abulpharagius, vol. i. p. 101.

is to be accepted as an integral part of the original work of Daniel, Dr. Pusey, Mr. Desprez, Mr. Perowne, and many other interpreters, have shown how we are constrained to identify the little horn of chap. viii. not with Mahomet, but with Antiochus Epiphanes; who did, indeed, for three whole years, oppress and destroy the holy people, profane their sanctuary, and take away the literal daily sacrifice; but which interpretation entirely breaks down, inasmuch as he has not prospered " till the indignation be accomplished" upon the Jews, nor till the Almighty " shall have accomplished to scatter the power of the holy people." Again, these writers are quite at a loss to explain, with any appearance of probability, how the periods of 1290, and 1335 days, or years, have been fulfilled, which are to be reckoned "from the time the daily —— shall be taken away," even to the time when Daniel himself shall stand in his lot (xii. 13), and which must necessarily, according to their interpretation, be counted from the event spoken of in xi. 31, and also have ended literally in the reign of Antiochus. Gladly would we accept any reasonable explanation by which Antiochus Epiphanes could be made the type of the Mahomedan apostasy, and the genuineness of chap. xi. thereby made consistent with the genuineness of the remainder of the book. We confess, however, that we cannot fairly see our way to this result. A power rising up from amongst ten well-defined kings, successors of four notable kings, such as were the ten kings

who succeeded Ptolemy Soter, Lysimachus, Cassander, and Seleucus Nicator, may perhaps be said to
typify a power distinctly declared to be about to
rise during the latter times of these four kingdoms;
and Epiphanes so be made to typify the wilful king.
But how can this be reconciled with the passages of
apparent text and explanatory comment by which
it appears that the wilful king is represented or
typified by Antiochus the Great, not by Epiphanes?
For "the king" who "shall do according to his
will," who "shall stand in the glorious land," who
"shall come to his end, and none shall help him,"
and "shall prosper till the indignation be accomplished," cannot, according to the writer of chap. xi.,
16, 19, be identified with Antiochus Epiphanes, as
Mr. Perowne assumes, and as indeed he ought to be,
if typical of Mahomet or anti-Christ; nor is he by
that writer represented as the future anti-Christ
himself, as Dr. Pusey insists;* nor yet, again, can he
be supposed to represent the Roman or Papal power,
as inferred by Sir Isaac Newton, Bishop Newton, Mr.
Birks, and Mr. Elliot, arguing from the latter words
of the supposed interpolated passage (xi. 31–35).
For, as we have already shown,† he is there clearly
identified with no other than the father of Epiphanes, that is, Antiochus the Great, by the same
three characteristic expressions, "He shall do according to his own will;" "he shall stand in the
glorious land;" "he shall stumble and fall, and not

* Pusey's "Daniel," p. 95.   † See pp. 119, 131.

be found;" and, therefore, he is the king who immediately precedes the troubles under Epiphanes, not the king after whose fall the "time of trouble such as never was," begins.

As regards the long period of 2400 days, or years, during which the sanctuary and the host are to be trodden under foot, which, if even reduced to the lower reading of 2300, and interpreted in literal days, exceeds the term of six years, and is not therefore readily applicable to the profanation by Epiphanes, we think, with Mr. Hatley Frere, that it is intended to represent a period of Jubilee of Jubilees, or 49 times 49 years, = 2401 years; and we suggest that it should be computed from the commencement of the new era of Jubilee, beginning in B.C. 485, established by Ezra after the return from captivity.* In the year of Jubilee, according to the Levitical law, he who had alienated his inheritance was to return again into possession, and all slaves were to regain their liberty. The year of Jubilee of Jubilees, therefore, would seem to be a fitting period for re-entry of the holy people into their inheritance in the holy land, and for their release from their state of servility amongst the Gentiles. It is indeed a general expectation amongst the Jews that their restoration will take place at a time of Jubilee.

Now if we count 2400 years from the end, or autumn of the Sabbatical year B.C. 485, we come to

* P. 215, 216.

the autumn of the year A.D. 1916, which is the commencement of the Sabbatical year 1916–17, and A.D. 1917–18, or the year 2401, will therefore be the year in which a Jubilee of Jubilees, hereafter, will actually be completed. This, therefore, would seem to be a not improbable date for the cleansing of the sanctuary of Jerusalem. But the date of the cleansing of the sanctuary is accurately defined in chap. xii. 11, by these words, "From the time that the daily ———— shall be taken away, and the abomination that maketh desolate set up, shall be 1290 days," or years. If, then, we are right in the interpretation that Mahomet took away the daily ———— in A.D. 627, by counting 1290 years from thence, we are led with exactness to this same date, A.D. 1917, for the cleansing of the sanctuary of Jerusalem.

Now it must be observed, with reference to the reckoning of these 1290 years, that the omission of the words "sacrifice," or "oblation," in ch. xii. 11, teaches us that this period is not to be reckoned from the time when the literal daily sacrifice was caused to cease by the Romans, but from the time when "the daily ———— (i. e. the daily memorial of that sacrifice) was taken away, and the abomination which maketh desolate set up;" that is, from the time referred to in ch. viii. 11, which we have shown to have been the days of Mahomet and his successors. And in further confirmation of this interpretation, we may also point out, that about five or six years after the death of Mahomet, that is to say,

in the year A.D. 637, when Jerusalem was besieged
and taken by the Saracens, and when the Caliph
Omar, having entered the holy city, held conference
with the Patriarch Sophronius, on the site of the
temple of Solomon, and amongst other acts gave di-
rections concerning the erection and reconstruction
of the present mosques, the Patriarch, in reference
to these very words of Daniel, is said to have
secretly muttered to himself, while bowing before
the Caliph, " The abomination of desolation standeth
in the holy place."*

Again, "Blessed is he that waiteth and cometh
to the 1335 days," or years, that is, till the year
A.D. 1961–2. Now the blessing attached to the
termination of this last period marks it as an epoch
of extreme significance. It is the time of the end.
" But thou, O Daniel, shut up the words, and seal
the book, even to the time of the end."—"And
I heard the man clothed in linen, which was upon
the waters of the river, when he held up his right
hand and his left hand unto heaven, and sware by
him that liveth for ever," —"that when he shall
have accomplished to scatter the power of the holy
people, all these things shall be finished" (ch. xii. 11.)

With reference to this passage in Daniel, St.
John also writes (Rev. x. 5, 6, 7), "The angel which
I saw stand upon the sea and upon the earth lifted
up his hand to heaven, and sware by him that liveth
for ever and ever," — " that the time is not yet.

* Cedrenus, vol. ii. p. 746.   Temple of Jerusalem, by Jalal-
Addin, p. 183.

But in the days of the voice of the seventh angel, when he shall begin to sound, the mystery of God shall be finished, as he hath declared to his servants the prophets." It is then the "blessed" time of consummation, which is here alluded to, when that which is determined upon the desolate shall have been poured out (ix. 27); "when he shall have accomplished to scatter the power of the holy people;" and when at length the gracious promises spoken of by Isaiah shall be fulfilled, " Comfort ye, comfort ye my people, saith your God. Speak ye comfortably to Jerusalem, and cry unto her, that her warfare is accomplished, that her iniquity is pardoned; for she hath received of the Lord's hand double for all her sins." —" Prepare ye the way of the Lord, make straight in the desert a highway to our God."—" And the glory of the Lord shall be revealed, and all flesh shall see it together; for the mouth of the Lord hath spoken it." For, "as the lightning shineth from the east unto the west, so shall the coming of the Son of Man be." " At that time," says Daniel, that is, " at the time of the end," xi. 40, "shall Michael stand up, the great prince which standeth for *the children of thy people*, and there shall be a time of trouble, such as never was since there was a nation to that same time: and at that time *thy people* shall be delivered, every one that shall be found written in the book," that is, " in the book of life of the Lamb slain from the foundation of the world." And in allusion to the time here spoken of by Daniel, our Lord has said, " This gospel of the kingdom

s

shall be preached in all the world for a witness unto all nations; and then shall the end come." And again, "Immediately after the tribulation of those days shall the sun be darkened," &c., "and then shall appear the sign of the Son of Man in heaven: and then shall all the tribes of the land * mourn, and they shall see the Son of Man coming in the clouds of heaven with power and great glory."† "And when these things begin to come to pass, then look up, and lift up your heads" (*i.e.* ye children of Israel who shall be led captive into all nations), "for your redemption draweth nigh." ‡

But if at the end of the 1335 years, counted from the period of Mahomedan domination, the glorious epoch shall arrive which shall mark the termination of the warfare of Jerusalem, and the approaching period of the Son of Man, then should that epoch also mark the termination of " the times of the Gentiles." For our Lord Himself has said, that "Jerusalem shall be trodden down of the Gentiles till the time of the Gentiles be fulfilled."

Now the time of the Gentiles, or the time of the casting off of the Jews, is commonly reckoned as a period of " seven times" (Lev. xxvi. 17–28), or 2520 years.§ And as the casting off of the Jews had a twofold commencement, first partially in the breaking up of the kingdom of the ten tribes, never since restored, threescore and five years after the first year of Ahaz,‖ that is, in B.C. 654–3; and finally,

* Zech. xii. 10–14. † Matt. xxiv. 29, 20. ‡ Luke xxi. 28.
§ Faber's Sac. Cal. of Prophecy. ‖ Isa. vii. 8.

TIME OF INDIGNATION AGAINST ISRAEL,
Seven Times.

7 × 360 = 2520 years = 1260 × 2.

TIME OF THE GENTILES,
2520 years.

The ten tribes cut off,	The two tribes cut off,
B.C. 654-3.*	B.C. 560-559.*
2520 — 653 = A.D. 1867.	A.D. 1961 = 2520 — 559.

PERSECUTION OF THE LATTER DAYS.

PAPAL.	MAHOMEDAN.
Time, times and a half,	1335 days, or
1260 years + A.D. 607,	years + A.D. 627,
= A.D. 1867.	= A.D. 1961.

The sanctuary shall be cleansed after
1290 years + A.D. 627.
= A.D. 1917.

The sanctuary of Jerusalem shall be trodden
under foot, unto 2400 years, that is, unto
the year of Jubilee of Jubilees,
49 × 49 = 2401 years.
Era of Jubilee re-established by Ezra in B.C. 485.
2401 years — B.C. 485,
= A.D. 1916–17.

* See Chronological Table, Appendix A.

in the completion of the fall and captivity of **Judah,**
in the twenty-third year of Nebuchadnezzar, **that is,**
in B.C. 560–559, since which the house of David **has**
ceased to reign ; so in like manner may we **expect**
that it will have a twofold termination, at the **time**
of the restoration, when Christ shall set up **again**
the throne of his father David, and restore the **king-**
dom to Israel.   Accordingly we find that 2520 **years**
counted from B.C. 654–3 will lead us to the **eventful**
period of the world's religious history A.D. 1866–7 ;*
and counted from B.C. 559 will lead us to A.D. 1961–2.
We lay no stress on these numbers. They **may**
be as illusive as many which have been before **pro-**
posed.   Let them be taken or rejected **according**
to the inclination of the reader.   All we will **say is,**
that the period of the cleansing of the **sanctuary of**
Jerusalem is hardly capable of prolongation **beyond**
the year A.D. 1917, between which time and **now,**
however, great changes may be effected, both **re-**
ligiously and politically, in the position of the **holy**
people.

    We have now gone through the whole of **what**
we conceive to be the genuine prophetic **chapters of**
the book of Daniel: marking as we passed the **majes-**

---

    * The interest taken in the movements and opinions of the
Jews since the year 1866, cannot be more strongly marked **than**
by the fact, that an article on the Talmud in the " Quarterly **Re-**
view," in Oct. 1867, passed through six editions in the course of
a few months.   It is also remarkable that, since the year 1866,
both Jews and Christians have been thought worth to be taken **into**
the councils of the representative of Mahomedanism, at **Constan-**
tinople.

tic master-hand by which, with few but vivid lines, the world's history has been portrayed for more than two thousand four hundred years. We have seen the bright vision of the four successive heathen empires—the precise, yet complicated prophecy of the "Seventy Weeks," with the coming and cutting off of Prince Messiah—the rise, progress, and apparent fall in our days of the little "civil Princedom" of the Papacy, "diverse from the rest" —the spreading south, and north, and towards the pleasant land of the fierce, destroying kingdom of the Eastern little horn, or of Mahomet and his successors—both these latter kingdoms still clinging convulsively to their worn-out creeds, and dragging on a lingering existence—fulfilled with an exactness to strike with wonder every intelligent and unprejudiced observer. We have gathered with astonishment from this treasury of God's decrees how the destinies of the holy people, past and future, are cast in cycles in the sacred mould of Sabbath and Jubilaic years. With regard to slanders and objections raised against the book, we have seen how the Chaldee of Daniel is the same Chaldee, or nearly so, as that of his contemporary Ezra, not the Chaldee of the Targums, as alleged—how the first six prophetic chapters, which concern as much the heathen nations as the holy race, are naturally written in the dialect of the then dominant heathen kingdom in which Daniel lived; and how the remaining five, which especially relate to the last period of indignation against the holy people, in

the latter days, are appropriately written in the
Hebrew tongue—how the use of Greek and Aryan
terms falls in exactly with the position of the prophet in the central mart of commerce between
Greek and Aryan nations — how the prophets
Haggai and Zechariah, prophesying at Jerusalem
in the reign of Darius, son of Hystaspes, could
hardly be expected to make reference to the acts
and writings of Daniel at Babylon, living in the
reign of the same Darius — and how, least of all,
the Sadducean philosopher, Jesus son of Sirach,
could be expected to speak with distinction of a
book which treats of angelic beings, and of the doctrine of the resurrection from the dead. The hasty
and untenable objections, to which these observations are replies, recoil against the objectors in
favour of the genuineness of the book : and the result of our inquiry, and of the severe ordeal through
which the book has passed, is this :—

The book of Daniel, freed from unauthorised
additions, and from the reproach of forgery, is, as
it were, a hidden treasure brought to light,—a
heavenly pearl of wondrous worth long lost, now
found at last. "Shut up" and "sealed" for many
days, even "until the time of the end;" cast before
swine, and trampled under feet; it shines forth in
these latter days—days seen in distant vision by the
prophet, when multitudes are running to and fro and
knowledge is increased*—to shed its dazzling lustre

* Dan. xii. 4.

through the shrine of God, and guide the approaching footsteps of His saints.

Its clear, translucent oracles, obscured by scribes, and overlaid by comment—comment indeed confounded with the text; moreover, like the Ephesian image, authoritative comment, "not to be spoken against"—have long refused to yield response, except with a confused uncertain sound. A signal instance how the pure word of God by man's traditions may become of none effect.

Its sacred numbers, written in burning characters upon the shrine, telling of times and periods fixed in the decrees of the Most High, have been approached by wandering and bewildered Jews, rejoicing in their false and vicious reckoning —which errs to the extent of some century and a half between the destruction of the first and second temples*—and so, unable to discern the times, unskilled "to read the writing" like the wise men of old, they have returned to wander still in outer darkness, blind to the gracious promises which concern their peace. If Israel would resume her wonted place, her proud position of depository and teacher of the oracles of God, let her hasten quickly to remove the gross scholastic error of her sacred reckoning, which defaces the entrance of her yet gloomy halls.

Again, with less inaccuracy, but yet with error to the extent of more than twenty years in the short interval between the destruction of the first,

* See p. 68.

and building of the second temple, Christian **divines,**
expositors, and teachers, have sought to explain **the**
sacred numbers, and likewise have returned confounded and confused from the attempt.　The exceeding accuracy of the few words of Daniel **and of**
Ezra concerning the first kings of Persia, **under**
whom they lived, will yet put to shame the **critical**
acumen of professors in our seats of learning, **who**
unquestionably have missed their way amid **conflict-**
ing heathen records of those early kings.　Again **a**
signal instance how man's traditions make void **the**
word of God.

　　The history foreshadowed in the book of **Daniel**
is neither more nor less than the history of **that**
remote period foreseen by Moses, when his **people**
should lie scattered and persecuted over the **face**
of the earth; the period referred to also by our **Lord,**
under the expression "Time of the Gentiles:" **that**
is to say, the time of those successive Gentile **na-**
tions who should rule the world, from the day **when**
God's holy city and sanctuary were first **trodden**
under foot, to the day of the future **cleansing**
of the sanctuary; or, perhaps more correctly, **from**
the day of the casting down of the throne of **righteous**
David, to the re-establishment of that throne in **the**
kingdom of his most righteous Son, "who **shall**
reign over the house of Jacob for ever, and **of**
whose kingdom there shall be no end."　For " **in**
the days of those kings," writes Daniel, that is, **in**
the last days of the fragmentary kingdoms of **the**
Roman Empire, " shall the God of heaven set up **a**

kingdom never to be destroyed : and the kingdom
shall not be left to other people."

Now we have already observed that the date of
the overthrow of David's throne, and the last carrying
away of captives from Jerusalem, was the year B.C. 560,
as accurately laid down by the historian Demetrius;
and that from this date the domination of the Gentile
nations over the holy people, and the spread of Gentile learning and influence over the civilised world,
should be computed.   Nor is this year 560 a mere
fanciful and arbitrary date assumed for an immediate purpose.   On the contrary, we shall see that
it is the culminating point of a memorable epoch
in the history of God's government and education of
the human race—an epoch, when it pleased the Almighty, taking, as it were, His journey into a far
country, and saying to His servants, " Occupy till I
come," to withdraw His directing hand and guiding
influence from the affairs of men, and leave the full-
grown children of the world to work out their own
destinies by the bright light of reason and of intellect with which they were endowed.   In the world's
infancy God had walked with man.   Throughout
the period of its youth His tender fostering hand
was ever nigh, with signs and wonders, by angelic
messengers and prophets, to train the mind and fix
the principles of a chosen nation, selected from the
nations of the world to be His priests.   He gave
them a code of religious and moral law from Sinai,
—a code which could have proceeded only from the
hand of God,—suited to every age and nation of the

world. He trained them as examples of **purity and chastity** in the presence of the impure heathen. **He** stamped upon their hearts, in characters never **to be** effaced, amid the idolatry of the surrounding **na-** tions, the everlasting truth, " The Lord thy God **is** one Lord." He gave them the Holy Land **as a** possession, and set His sanctuary in the midst. **He** poured the abundance of His grace and Holy **Spirit** upon His servant David and the prophets, **with a** fulness of measure to which few have since **attained.** He committed the sacred oracles to their **charge;** and when thus fitted as lights to guide the **world,** partly in anger at their disobedience, but **more in** loving mercy to mankind at large, He **withdrew** from them His prophets and His fostering **hand,** and with a gracious promise of return, delivering **to** them a sacred roll, sealed up and closed, which **told** of what should befall their nation in the latter **days,** He cast them off, and scattered them as salt **upon** the surface of the earth.

Three periods may be marked in the history of the dispersion of God's people through the nations. The first when idolatrous Israel was carried off by Esarhaddon in B.C. 653; the second when Judah and Benjamin were carried to Babylon in B.C. 560; and the third when the house of Judah was scattered throughout the Roman world in A.D. 73. But it was at the second of these periods that the wisdom of the Gentile nations first came in contact and in competition with the wisdom of Israel. Gentile in- fluence and learning, the first dawn of which may be placed as early as the first Olympiad, B.C. 776, rose quickly into ascendancy after the date of the downfall of Judah. It was about the year B.C. 560, in which year we place the dream of Nebuchadnezzar, in the second year of his reign over the holy city, that Daniel, the representative of the captive people, surrendered, as it were, into the hands of the Gentiles the accumulated stores of heavenly wisdom, till then confined to the holy people, and took the chief position in the College of the Magi, or philosophers of Babylon ; from which time Grecian sages resorted to that city as the chief seat of learning. The barbaric empire of Nineveh, and the voluptuous, enterprising Tyre, had already fallen before the sword of the more enlightened kingdom of the Chaldees ; and, again, the glory of the Chaldees, and of the kingdoms of Lydia and Egypt, was soon to bow before the conquering hand of Cyrus, the Lord's anointed, "whose right hand I have upholden, to subdue nations before him," and whose first regnal year is fixed precisely in the year B.C. 560.

We refer the reader to an eloquent passage in Dean Stanley's History of the Jewish Church, written indeed from a somewhat different point of view from that which we have taken, but yet highly illustrative of the character of this great epoch in the world's history. The beauty of the extract will excuse its length.

Speaking of the last six-and-twenty chapters of Isaiah, he writes, " They take their stand on the times of the captivity, and from thence look forward

from the summit of the last ridge of Jewish history
into the remotest future, unbroken now by any intervening barrier." " The primeval period of mankind is drawing to its close; the ancient gigantic
monarchies and religions, known to us only through
their mighty conquerors, or their vast monuments,
are, as we have seen, passing away; the great ca-
tastrophe which is to wind up their long career, the
fall of Babylon, is already imminent. And in the
place of this great age is to begin that second period
of history which we term classical. Its commencement may be fixed almost to a year. It is with the
clearest right that the first date of the 'Fasti Hellenici,' the Grecian annals of our English Chro-
nologer, is fixed in the year B.C. 560." " From this
time forward that western world of Greece and
Rome rises more and more steadily above the
horizon, till it occupies the whole view." " In the
remoter horizon is the vision of a gradual ameliora-
tion of the whole human race, to be accomplished
not solely, or chiefly by the seed of Israel, but by
those outlying nations which were but just beginning to take their place in the world's history. In
the strains of triumph which welcome the influx of
these Gentile strangers we recognise the prelude of
the part which in the coming fortunes of the Jewish
Church is to be played, not only by Cyrus, and,
if so be Zoroaster, but by Socrates and Plato, by
Alexander and by Cæsar. It has been truly observed that the new elements which Christendom
received from the Greek, the Roman, and the

Teutonic world were almost as important as those which it received from the Jewish race. Its European, as distinguished from its Asiatic features, form one of the main characteristics which raise it above Judaism and Mahomedanism. To have recognised and anticipated this truth is the rare privilege of the Evangelic Prophet. This is the dawn of the new epoch of Jewish and universal history."*

It is, then, not the result of any forced interpretation of Scripture, but a literal fact, derived as well from history of the past as from this wonderful book of prophecy, that it has been, and is still decreed by the all-wise and all-merciful God, to scatter and diffuse His holy people — the literal seed of Abraham — throughout the Gentile nations ; and " to give the sanctuary and the host to be trodden under foot," for a period defined by Daniel as extending over 2400 years : a period manifestly not yet complete. And it is with equal certainty derived, both from the words of Daniel and of our Lord Himself, that this same sanctuary which is trodden down shall not long hence be cleansed, and that Jerusalem — even the literal Jerusalem — shall cease to be trodden under foot, when the time of the Gentiles shall have been fulfilled.

How is it, then, it may be asked, that the largest and most influential section of Christian interpreters

* Lectures on the History of the Jewish Church. Second Series, p. 577-581.

still approach the book of Daniel with the precon-
ceived opinion that the people of Israel are merely
a people of the past, the refuse and outcasts of a
bygone world?   And that to believe that such a
people as this can ever be resuscitated as a nation,
or that hereafter they shall have any office assigned
to them in the kingdom of the Son of Man, is looked
upon as appropriating the glories of the Gentile
church to a race for ever extinct and blotted out
from the sight of God?   Such a conviction has led,
and in our opinion must continue to lead, to gross
mis-interpretation of the words of Daniel.   And
here we find Drs. Williams, Pusey, Manning, and
Newman, united together in the same band, arguing
indeed from opposite extremes, yet, nevertheless,
enforcing different shades of the same opinion ; each
actively engaged in explaining away the direct
meaning of Holy Scripture, and in allegorising the
promises concerning Abraham and his seed, concerning David and the son of David, as if they had
reference only to the Gentile church.

Dr. Williams, who is the furthest in advance of
this party, and who laughs at the direct Messian-
isms of Dr. Pusey, tauntingly lays down " the general proposition, that personal Messianic prophecies
apply to the Lord Jesus, only in a manner corresponding to that in which was said of Israel may be
applied to the Church, the land of Canaan represents
heaven, the river Jordan stands for death, the sojourn in the wilderness for human life, the passage
of the Red Sea for baptism ;" and declares that

"only in proportion as the class of interpretations here glanced at is absolutely surrendered, will students or congregations have any key to the profound moral significance of the Old Testament, or to the method by which prophecy may become a persuasive, if not an argument in favour of Christianity."* While Dr. Pusey, who faithfully adheres to the literal application of the Messianic prophecies to our blessed Lord, is equally anxious to wipe out the traces of His holy people, and to exclaim against the holy city Jerusalem, spoken of by the Lord Himself as "the city of the Great King,"—"Down with it, down with it, even to the ground." Speaking of its past desolate condition, he writes,—"That desolation of 1800 years would not be less signal, if at any time the Jews should anew acquire property in Jerusalem, preparing the way probably for Antichrist."† Dr. Manning, in his recent work on "The Temporal Mission of the Holy Ghost," absorbed in the mysteries of his adopted church, scarcely recognises the operation of the Holy Spirit in the Jewish church of old, much less the future operation of the Holy Spirit on His people yet to come. While Dr. Newman, as before observed, takes refuge in horror in the Church of Rome, lest he should be contaminated even with the idea of a Protestant bishop seated in the literal Jerusalem. With this class of interpreters, if Israel is to be scattered, and their

---

* Preface to " Desprez," p. lxvi.

† Pusey's " Daniel," p. 189.

cities laid waste, it is literally upon Israel that the curse is to be poured out. But if, when speaking of the days when a righteous branch which shall be raised unto David, it is said, " In his days Judah shall be saved, and Israel shall dwell safely."* . . . " I will say, It is my people, and they [shall say, The Lord is my God,"† then is the promise to be interpreted as applicable, not to Israel, but to the Gentile church. They believe that the Son of David was born into the world, " a light to lighten the Gentiles," but they do not believe that He will hereafter sit on the throne of David, and " be the glory of His people Israel." They believe in the temporal mission of the Holy Spirit, but not in the future temporal mission of the Son of Man.‡ They understand the words, " A little while and ye shall not see me," but see no force in the words, " Again a little while and ye shall see me," "because I go to the Father." They realise the personal advent of the Son of Man in humility walking on this earth, and mixing with mankind, and rejected of His own ; but it is inconceivable to them that at His second advent He shall come unto His own again in glory, " that this same Jesus which is taken from you up into heaven shall so come in like manner as ye have seen Him go into heaven:" that He shall tread again upon this earth, mixing with mankind, and drinking again of the fruit of the vine : that " His

* Jer. xxiii. 6.   † Zech. xiii. 9.
‡ 1 Cor. xv. 24–28.

feet shall stand in that day upon the Mount of
Olives;" that all nations "shall go up from year to
year to worship the King, the Lord of hosts, and to
keep the feast of tabernacles :"* that they shall see
again His face, in that place which now is left desolate, and bowing in supplication before Him cry,
"Blessed is he that cometh in the name of the Lord."
They recognise the glory of the Son of God, but not
the full significance of His title Son of Man. They
are full of exalted expectations of the glories of the
Gentile "church triumphant," but unmindful that "if
the casting away of the Jews is the reconciling of
the world," the receiving of them shall be "as life
from the dead." For though "Blindness in part has
fallen upon Israel," it is not a greater blindness than
that which we are told may dim the eyes of the
Gentile church, and which may cause it, as assuredly it will cause it, to be cut off.

What is the history of the outward Church of
God from the beginning, from which, nevertheless,
a cloud of holy saints has been gathered, and is
gathering, even till the end? Is it not a history
of idolatry, rebellion, perversion of the word of
God, yet not of persecution, on the part of the
Jewish Church : of heresy, and schism, idolatry,
dark superstition, persecution, blood-guiltiness, and,
at length, of pride and arrogance reaching up to

* These perplexing passages in Zechariah are disposed of by
Bunsen and others, by placing Zechariah before instead of after
the end of the captivity; by orthodox interpreters the feast of
Tabernacles signifies figuratively the Christian religion.

T

heaven, on the part of its Gentile successor? In the Gentile church there sits arrayed in majesty a self-styled Vicar of Christ, claiming the attributes of God. Beside him, robed in scarlet, sit as lords the so-called successors of the lowly apostles. The kings of the earth are but as dust beneath their feet. The powers that be, with them, are not ordained of God. The very minor off-shoots of this towering Church rejoice in the appellation "High." All that is opposed to them is stigmatised as "Low." They treat with scorn the tables of God's commandments given from Mount Sinai, and set up in their stead their own strange devices. The "table of the Lord" entrusted to their care, has become their source of gain, the table of the money-changers.* The beautiful doctrine of the "bread which came down from heaven,"—the spiritual sustenance of faithful souls, —is degraded into worship of material bread. Professing the doctrine of the one only God, as taught by the Lord Himself in His own perfect form of prayer, "Our Father which art in heaven;" of the *only-begotten* Son of God, whose risen body hath ascended to His Father and our Father, to His God and our God; and of "the Spirit of truth which proceedeth from the Father," uniting Father and Son, and dwelling in the heart of every child of God, "that they may all be one, as thou, Father, art in me, and I in thee, that they also may be one in us;" their

---

* The offerings at the Lord's Table are cherished and promoted as "the churches' own richest treasure-mine."—"Clerical Journal," 31 Jan. 1867.

teaching is of three co-equal, co-eternal persons or existences, each with the perfect attributes of God, expressive only of three co-equal, co-eternal Gods. And last, as if to drive the world into revolt against the whole creed of Christendom, they teach the worship of the "mother* of God," and her immaculate conception; giving "pardon to the sinner, grace to the just, joy to the angels, glory to the holy Trinity,"† leading only by one further step to the dogmatic blasphemy, of the only-begotten mother of God.

If, as we believe it is, the doom of this corrupt and superstitious Church to succumb before the children of the despised and outcast race, it cannot be but in words of blasphemy that such arrogance shall be brought down from its lofty seat. The strong language of St. John concerning the Church of the seven hills, "Mystery, Babylon the Great, the mother of harlots and abominations of the earth, drunken with the blood of the saints and with the blood of the martyrs of Jesus," does but too justly represent the tyranny, the false doctrine, the corruption, the cruelty, the false miracles taught by this pernicious Church, and by its many base imitations.

---

* Mr. Newman calls upon us also for "religious affection and veneration" towards the "foster-father" of God. Why not also towards the brothers and sisters of God? The true answer to Mr. Newman is contained in Rev. xiii. 1 : "And upon his heads the name of blasphemy."—"Letter to Pusey," p. 33.

† Middleton's "Letter from Rome," Preface, p. 44.

Let us look around upon the three great sections of devout worshippers of the one Almighty God throughout the world, distinguished by their three separate seventh days of public worship,—Saturday, Friday, and Sunday. On the sons of Jacob scattered, though unmixed, in every quarter of the habitable earth: on the sons of Ishmael mighty in the East : on the sons of the Gentiles mighty in the West. All, here and there, is restlessness and commotion. The sons of Jacob, bending their eager eyes towards the holy city—to the place of their loved temple which is desolate—think upon her stones, and pray for repossession of the land of "everlasting covenant" with their fathers. There is "a noise" and "a shaking," as it were in the valley of dry bones, as if the bones were coming together, "bone to his bone," and that breath were being breathed again into the slain that they might live. The devout sons of Ishmael, with their eyes directed towards their temple at Mecca—preferring the cool waters of the well of Zem-zem to the soft flowing waters of Siloam, and the false prophet of Arabia to the great High-Priest of the order of Melchizedec—are conscious of their waning influence throughout the East. While the sons of the Gentiles, looking scornfully at Jerusalem, and straining their eyes into the far East, they know not where, in search of something, they know not what, are equally conscious of their utter incapacity to cope with the mighty work which lies before them, of bringing the heathen nations of the now opening East within the dominion of the Son of Man. Some with pious zeal are searching amongst the "fathers," hoping that some light out of darkness may from thence be cast upon their bewildered steps. Others are raking amongst the cast-off garments of mediæval ritualism, as if they thought to clothe themselves with righteousness, by putting on the outward garb of priests. While the great leaders of our own local Church, in the full sense of the weakness of division, are zealously seeking for union with Churches more corrupt than their own, in the hope that the combined weight of united Christendom may be enabled to withstand the shock with which the whole body now is threatened. The task, we believe, is hopeless. The superstitious teaching of Christendom, swayed by the directing influence of the Church of Rome, is driving thinking minds to infidelity. And except as regards its reformed and purer branches, sparsely scattered here and there, we fear that the Gentile Church is tending fast towards dissolution.

Another epoch in the world's history, and in the advancement of the human race, has come upon us. Gentile literature and science have done their beneficial work. Man's faculties and grasp of worldly things and things divine have become enlarged, and a deep longing for a nearer approach to, and knowledge of God pervades the Christian world—a longing not to be set at rest by that which satisfied the superstitious cravings of mediæval days. Things old are passing away. All

things around us are becoming new. The world
is rushing onwards along the stream of time, and
an alarmed and anxious cry is heard,—Whither
are we going? What is coming to pass? Who
will guide us through this uproar and confusion
which is overthrowing all established things? Yet,
nevertheless, the Providential hand which guides
the bark and rules the wave is nigh. We need
no other pilot for our guide. His chart is in our
hands, and we may know the way, if we will but
follow in the track as there laid down. If we will
cease to darken the plain word of God by mystical construction, if we will cease to doubt His
power to accomplish His designs, in the same literal
material sense in which they are foretold, however
mundane it may seem to our ideas — for what
more mundane than that which has already come
to pass, the eating, drinking, walking, dwelling of
our divine and heavenly Lord amongst the sons of
men,—then may we inquire, in the plain words of
Daniel, " How long shall be the vision concerning
the daily ———, and the transgression of desolation, to give both the sanctuary and the host to
be trodden under foot?" Or in the last words of
the apostles, with whom our Lord had spoken
for forty days before his ascension of the things
pertaining to the kingdom of God, "Lord, wilt
Thou at this time restore again the kingdom to
Israel?" And then shall we be prepared to listen
to the clear response, as uttered by the apostle
of the Gentiles, and interpreted long since by a

prelate of our Church. For, quoting the words
of St. Paul (Rom. xi. 11–15), Bishop Horsley
writes; " In these texts the apostle clearly lays
out the order of the business, in the conversion
of the whole world to Christ. First, the rejection
of the unbelieving Jews. Then the first call of
the Gentiles. Then the recovery of the Jews,
after a long season of obstinacy and blindness,
at last provoked to emulation, brought to a right
understanding of God's dispensations, by that very
call which hitherto has been one of their stumbling-
blocks: and, lastly, in consequence of the conversion of the Jews, a prodigious influx from the
Gentile nations yet unconverted, and immersed in
the darkness and corruptions of idolatry."* So
that, if this is a true interpretation of the teaching
of St. Paul, it is clear that the mighty religious
movement, which we all observe around us, is tending
ultimately towards the re-establishment of the " holy
people " as its final goal. The day of the rejection of
the unbelieving Jews is past. The day of the first
call of the Gentiles has lasted long enough to do
its work. And nothing intervenes between that
call and converted Israel's restoration, unless it may
be the fall of harlot-Babylon, by which the world
till now, both Jewish and Christian, has been held
in the thraldom of darkness and of bondage.

And when " Babylon is fallen, is fallen, that
great city, because she made all nations drink of

---

* Horsley's " Sermons," vol. i. p. 110.

the wine of the wrath of her fornication," God
shall not leave Himself without a witness upon
earth. We know, both from Daniel and St. Paul,
where then to look for the visible Church of Christ
which shall take up the work of God, "having the
everlasting Gospel to preach unto them that dwell
on the earth, and to every nation, and kindred, and
tongue, and people." While St. John joins in,
and informs us that he saw an "angel ascending
from the east, having the seal of the living God:"
that at the time of the fall of Babylon, he looked,
"and lo! a lamb stood on the Mount Sion, and
with him one hundred and forty-four thousand
having *his Father's name written in their foreheads,*"
and these one hundred and forty-four thousand are
said to be sealed "*of all the tribes of the children
of Israel,*" "and they sing the *song of Moses, the
servant of God,* and the song of the Lamb." It
is inconceivable that these words, though figurative,
can be intended to lead our minds to the idea of
a Church whose incense, altars, images, and crea-
ture-worship, proclaim its pagan origin,—on whose
forehead is written " Mystery, Babylon," and whose
seat is well defined as on the seven hills of pagan
Rome. But, on the contrary, they do distinctly
lead our thoughts to the lost and wandering sheep
of the house of Israel, and to their promised restoration to Mount Sion,—to that people, on whose
forehead is indelibly engraven the name of the
Father, and which, " as touching the election, is
beloved for the father's sake." We call to mind the

words of our blessed Lord, when announcing to the
woman of Samaria that the worship at Jerusalem
was soon about to cease, that nevertheless " Salvation is of the Jews." We believe, with St. Paul, that
" there shall come out of Sion the deliverer, and
shall turn away ungodliness from Jacob. For this
is my covenant with them when I shall take away
their sins." " For the gifts and calling of God are
without repentance."

We rejoice, then, in the fact that a Protestant
bishop is already seated at Jerusalem, representing
the purest form of Christ's religion in the world.
We shall rejoice with a more exceeding joy when
we shall see a master in Israel, placed at Jerusalem, representing the now gathering flock of He-
brew-Christians,* believers in Christ, yet glorying
in their nationality as of the seed of Abraham,
and so placed in communication with the heads of
our reformed Church.

For the name of Jesus is now no longer blas-
phemed by this devout and deeply-humbled people.
On the contrary, His name is honoured, and in
many instances His character and office far more
duly appreciated even by unbelieving Jews than
by many of the Church of Rome. Already that
one single prayer taught by the Lord Himself,
which sounds the key-note of the harmonious universal Church which shall prevail, when " the earth
shall be full of the knowledge of the Lord as the

* The Hebrew-Christian Alliance was first established in
1866.

waters cover the sea," would fall with more grace and dignity from the lips of the sons of Abraham, than from many who now mumble and mutter it over a rosary of Paternosters and Ave Marias.

We see already workmen on Mount Sion. The explorers of Palestine, like Zerubbabel and Jeshua released from bondage at Babylon, are excavating and mapping the ruins of the holy city. The minds of all the statesmen of the world are absorbed in the great coming question, who shall rise up and hold dominion in the East, or who shall " prepare the way of the kings of the East." We see already at the helm of State a Hebrew-Christian of consummate genius, raised up, as it were, like Joseph or like Daniel, to take a leading part in the destinies of this potent Gentile kingdom. May his mind be directed, and his remaining span of life prolonged, though not to finish, yet at least to set in motion, the great appointed work. Oh, may we soon behold throughout the East the valley rise, the hills made low, the crooked made straight, and the rough places plain, preparing the way of the Lord, making straight in the desert a highway to our God. We think we see the day, and that not far distant, when in the vast extended courts of the new temple on the Mount Sion, the song of Moses shall again be raised, from lips of thousands and of thousands of the re-stored seed of Abraham, made " unto our God, kings and priests," lifting their stout and manly voices to the skies, and crying,—

Give ear, O ye heavens, and I will speak; and hear, O earth, the words of my mouth.

My doctrine shall drop as the rain, my speech shall distil as the dew, as the small rain upon the tender herb, and as the showers upon the grass:

Because I will publish the name of the Lord: ascribe ye greatness unto our God.

He is the Rock, His work is perfect: for all His ways are judgment: a God of truth and without iniquity, just and right is He.

They have corrupted themselves, their spot is not the spot of His children: they are a crooked and perverse generation.

Do ye thus requite the Lord, O foolish people and unwise? is not He thy father that hath bought thee? hath He not made thee, and established thee?

Remember the days of old, consider the years of many generations: ask thy father, and he will show thee; thy elders, and they will tell thee.

When the Most High divided to the nations their inheritance, when He separated the sons of Adam, he set the bounds of the people according to the number of the children of Israel.

For the Lord's portion is His people; Jacob is the lot of his inheritance. . . . .

. . . .

While echoing back from hill and vale, far as the ear can reach, the distant voice of Christian pilgrims gathered from all the nations of the world, and winding in long procession towards the city, or camped in booths about the holy mount, "come up to worship the King, the Lord of Hosts, and keep the feast of tabernacles," is heard in softened sounds, chanting,—

We praise thee, O God; we acknowledge thee to be the Lord.

All the earth doth worship thee, the Father everlasting.

To thee all Angels cry aloud, the Heavens, and all the Powers therein.

To thee Cherubim, and Seraphim, continually do cry.

Holy, Holy, Holy, Lord God of Sabaoth;

Heaven and earth are full of the majesty of thy glory.

The glorious company of the Apostles praise thee.

The goodly fellowship of the Prophets praise thee.

The noble army of Martyrs praise thee.

The holy Church throughout all the world doth acknowledge thee;

The Father of an infinite Majesty;

Thine honourable, true, and only Son;

Also the Holy Ghost, the Comforter.

Thou art the King of Glory, O Christ.

Thou art the everlasting Son of the Father.

When thou tookest upon thee to deliver man, thou didst not abhor the Virgin's womb.

When thou hadst overcome the sharpness of death, thou didst open the Kingdom of Heaven to all believers.

Thou sittest at the right hand of God, in the glory of the Father.

We believe that thou shalt come to be our Judge.

We therefore pray thee, help thy servants, whom thou hast redeemed with thy precious blood.

Make them to be numbered with thy Saints, in glory everlasting.

O Lord, save thy people, and bless thine heritage.

Govern them, and lift them up for ever.

Day by day we magnify thee.

And we worship thy Name, ever world without end.

Vouchsafe, O Lord, to keep us this day without sin.

O Lord, have mercy upon us, have mercy upon us.

O Lord, let thy mercy lighten upon us, as our trust is in thee.

O Lord, in thee have I trusted, let me never be confounded.

And then, again, around, above, and from the skies, as if in dream, the voice of risen saints, whether in the body or out of the body we cannot tell, " as the voice of many waters, and as the voice of a great thunder, the voice of harpers harping with their harps," and singing a new song, which no man can learn excepting those alone who reach the holy mount, and crying,—

"Worthy is the Lamb that was slain to receive power, and riches, and wisdom, and strength, and honour, and glory, and blessing." "Blessing and honour, and glory and power, be unto Him that sitteth upon the throne, and unto the Lamb, for ever and ever."

REPLY TO OBJECTIONS.

1. As to the age of Daniel at his death.

It has been objected, that if Daniel lived, as we have argued, to the year B.C. 492, when Darius, son of Hystaspes, was about sixty-two years of age, and had been carried captive to Babylon in the third year of Jehoiakim, B.C. 583, at least ninety years before his death, and was (say) twelve years of age at the date of his captivity, he must have lived to the great age of 102, or upwards, which is assumed to be improbable.*

This objection we think is sufficiently answered by the explanation already given, that neither Josephus, nor any other ancient interpreter of Daniel, ever placed his captivity so early as the third of Jehoiakim's reign. But they are all agreed that the third year spoken of in Daniel, i. 1, is the third year of Jehoiakim's revolt from Nebuchadnezzar, B.C. 575, not 583, according to our reckoning, which makes all the difference required. For if, as we believe, he was carried to Babylon with

---

* The author can testify to an instance of longevity in a lady in Cornwall, who attained to the age of 104, retaining all her faculties.

Jechoniah in B.C. 575 or 574, and saw his last visions in the year B.C. 492, that is, eighty-two years after; his age when he died may not have been more than ninety-four, which is by no means incredible.

2. As to the title "Darius son of Ahasuerus of the seed of the Medes."

It is objected that Darius, son of Hystaspes, was a Persian, not a Mede. How then could Daniel, who was well acquainted with his lineage, speak of him "as Darius the Median?" And if he was son of Hystaspes, how could he be styled "son of Ahasuerus?" With regard to the first supposed difficulty, there is really none. Daniel, writing at Babylon, looked upon "Medes and Persians" as but one people. When the handwriting on the wall announced to Belshazzar that his kingdom was divided, and by the choice of the word U-pharsin, the Persians were specially pointed out as the conquering nation, the word is immediately interpreted by Daniel as signifying "the Medes and Persians." As late as the time of Thucydides, the war with Persia was called the Median war, and those who fell away to the Persians were said to Medize. Herodotus speaks of Cyrus as "king of the Medes," and of the fleet of Darius, son of Hystaspes, as "the Median fleet." The difficulty raised on the words "son of Ahasuerus," seems hardly reasonable from the mouth of those who look upon Darius son of Ahasuerus, as Cyaxares son of Astyages, or Astyages son of Cyaxares, and find no difficulty in identifying Ahasuerus of Ezra, iv. 6, with Cambyses. There should be no difficulty with such interpreters in allowing that Ahasuerus might also stand for Hystaspes. Nevertheless we cannot approve of such identifications. Daniel knew his own master's title, and has no doubt faithfully recorded it. Ahasuerus is unquestionably the equivalent in Hebrew for the Median title Cyaxares. It is also generally considered by modern linguists, that it is the equivalent of the Persian title Xerxes; and if so, there are two modes of accounting for this title being associated with Darius, one in connexion with Cyaxares the Mede, the other in connexion with Xerxes the Persian. The word "son" in Hebrew, all are aware, may also stand either for son-in-law, adopted heir, or successor on the throne. Now Cyaxares or Ahasuerus, the son of Astyages and uncle of Cyrus, left no male heir; he had married the Jewess Hadassah, which name is the same as 'Atossa, and he died, we may suppose, leaving her a widow. Darius the son of Hystaspes we know was an usurper, and every rebellious pretender to the throne of the Medes, in the days of Darius, as recorded in the still extant cuneiform inscriptions, claimed kinship with Cyaxares or Ahasuerus, like himself, as the last Median king; * as all Babylonian pretenders claimed to be descended from Nabonidus, the last Babylonian king.

If such, then, were the facts, what is more pro-

* See Behistun inscription. "Journal of R. Asiatic Society," vol. xiv. part I.

bable than that Darius, who sought to strengthen
his position with the Medes, should have married,
queen 'Atossa, or Esther, the widow of Cyaxares,
and so have claimed to be the rightful successor
to the throne of Media? Herodotus, who, at this
point is much astray in his chronological reckoning, attests, indeed, that Darius married 'Atossa,*
but he calls her the daughter of Cyrus instead of
aunt. For knowing nothing of Cyaxares son of
Astyages, the Mede, he could in no other way
account for the royalty of queen 'Atossa.

But there is another possible solution of the
difficulty, in connexion with Xerxes, if it is lawful
to suggest a very slight alteration of the present
text of Daniel. We have said that Darius took
the government of the Babylonian and Assyrian
provinces into his own hands, at the age of sixty-
two, that is, on the final conquest and destruction
of Babylon, under Belshazzar son of Nabonidus,
whom he had probably set up as tributary king
or viceroy, and that this took place in the year
B.C. 492. It was immediately after the fall of
Babylon also that he set out on his Scythian expedition,† from which he might never have returned. According, therefore, to the ordinary practice in Persia, he would, we may assume, have
appointed one of his sons to rule in his absence

---

* According to Persian tradition, the son of Gushtasp, or of
Darius Hystaspes, that is, Xerxes, was born of a Jewess, descended
from Saul. "Chronicle of Tabari," ch 119.

† Herod iv. 1

U

on setting off towards Babylon, and that son was probably Xerxes.

There is an Egyptian monument referred to by Dr. Birch,* which seems to confirm this suggestion. For, as Dr. Birch observes, the 13th year of Xerxes on this monument is made concurrent with the 36th of Darius. So that, if this 13th year commenced in B.C. 482, which, as deduced from the Parian chronicle, was the 36th year of Darius, the first year of Xerxes would have commenced in B.C. 494, that is, about the first year of the siege of Babylon. The Septuagint translator of Dan. ix. 1, reads, "In the first year of Darius son of Xerxes," οἱ ἐβασιλεύσαν, that is, "who (both) reigned over the realm of the Chaldeans." Now this use of the plural is very remarkable, and suggests the idea that the original words of the text were not "In the first year of Darius son of Xerxes," but "In the first year of Darius *and* Xerxes, who reigned," &c., *i.e.* in the first year after the fall of the city of Babylon B.C. 492, a reading which would bring the books of Daniel, Zechariah, and Ezra, into perfect harmony. Our own impression, however, is that Darius, son of Hystaspes, was the immediate successor of Cyaxares, either by adoption, marriage, or usurpation, and so called " son of Ahasuerus of the seed of the Medes."

3. It may be asked, How could Belshazzar, who drank out of the golden and silver vessels taken from

* See Loftus' " Chaldæa and Susiana," p. 412.

·· the temple of Jerusalem, Dan. v. 2, have been slain
on the occasion of that banquet in B.C. 492, when
we read in the book of Ezra that Cyrus, long before
that date, had delivered these same vessels to Mithridates the treasurer, and that they were brought by
Sheshbazzar to Jerusalem. Here apparently would
seem to be a difficulty. But if we refer to Josephus,
we find that these vessels were indeed delivered to
Mithridates, and were ordered also to be delivered
to Sheshbazzar, but not till the building of the
temple should be finished. As we know, therefore, that the decree of Cyrus for the building of
the temple was obstructed, and not put in execution
till the second year of Darius, B.C. 491, according
to our reckoning, it would appear that the vessels
of the temple may have been still retained at Babylon in B.C. 492.*

4. But, again, it may be asked, is it consistent
with history to place the final destruction of Babylon by Darius when he broke down the walls and
carried off the gates, so late as the year B.C. 493
or 492. Herodotus, we know, places the fall of Babylon after the siege of twenty months, early in the
reign of Darius. But there is every reason to
believe that he is here greatly in error. The extant inscriptions recording the events of the early
years of Darius, describe two captures of Babylon,
but neither of these would appear to have taken

* Josephus, Ant. xi. 1, 3.

place after so long a siege as twenty months, or in
a manner in any way corresponding to his description; while Ctesias, who is a far better authority
on Persian history, distinctly contradicts Herodotus
on this very point, telling us that all which is related by him concerning the taking of Babylon by
the stratagem of Zopyrus in the reign of Darius,
took place really in the time of Xerxes. Nevertheless both these accounts may be partially true.
For Xerxes, according to the Egyptian monument
referred to, became first associated with his father
in B.C. 494, and may either have accompanied
Darius in his expedition against Babylon in that
year, in which, if the siege was finished in B.C. 492,
the expedition must have set out, or he may
have remained as regent at Susa during the absence of Darius. On either of these suppositions
the accounts of Herodotus and Ctesias may, in
great measure, be reconciled. Of this, however,
we may be certain, that the walls and gates of
Babylon, as described by Herodotus, were not
taken away on the first taking of the city by Darius, because it revolted and had to be taken again
some few years after. Nor was this second capture
the one described by Herodotus, for Darius on
this occasion sent his general, and was not present in
person at the siege. It seems highly probable, therefore, that there was a third siege late in the reign
of Darius, and some time after the setting up of the
Behistun inscription. Again, Herodotus places the

last revolt of the Babylonians immediately after the sailing of the Persian fleet to Samos,* and this we take to be true. But the fleet of Darius sailed twice to that island, once to place Syloson on the throne, and a second time to restore Æaces son of Syloson;† and this second expedition took place, according to Clinton, in the year B.C. 494. Now during the Scythian expedition, which lasted only a few months, and which took place within three years after the revolt of Babylon, the Samian "prince" in command of the Samian fleet was not Syloson, as Herodotus would lead us to expect, but Æaces. This would be natural if the revolt had taken place in B.C. 494, the same year in which Æaces was set up, but not so probable soon after the elevation of Syloson. Herodotus, who had probably noted down correctly the connexion of the revolt with the sailing of the fleet, has, we submit, mistaken one occasion for the other when writing his history.

5. It has been remarked that, by placing the accession of Darius to the throne of Persia, with Ctesias and the author of the Parian Chronicle, in B.C. 517, we "ignore the really sound astronomical evidence (that, namely, which refers to lunar eclipses) on which the received chronology rests." For Ptolemy, by two eclipses recorded as occurring in the reign of Darius, "proves that he succeeded to the throne in B.C. 522–1."‡ The answer to this objection need be very brief. Ptolemy

* Herod. iii. 150.   † Ib. vi. 25.
‡ "Literary Churchman," 14 July, 1866.

has truly recorded two eclipses as occurring in certain years of the era of Nabonassar. These eclipses
have since been verified by modern astronomers,
and their dates are immoveably correct. Ptolemy,
however, adds, that one of these eclipses took place
"in the 20th year of that Darius, *who came after
Cambyses*," the other in the "31st year of the *first Darius*."* He also describes two other eclipses as having
happened during the archonships of Phanostratus and
Evander at Athens. Now it is not to be supposed that
eclipses were recorded at Babylon with the years
of Athenian archons attached; nor can it be believed that astronomical records at Babylon would
speak of a "*first* Darius" before a second had been on
the throne, or of that "Darius who came after Cambyses," except to distinguish him from some later
Darius. So that there is no proof that the connexion of these eclipses with Darius was not made at
a later date than the observation, and formed
no part of the original record. The only really
sound evidence to be derived from the canon of
Ptolemy as regards the reign of Darius is, that
Ptolemy adopted the reckoning of Herodotus in
preference to that of Ctesias and the writer of the
Parian Chronicle, in which we think he was wrong.
For the purposes of an astronomical manual it
mattered not to him which reckoning he adopted.
The relative distances of the eclipses one from the
other would in both cases have remained the same.

6. Lastly, there is a difficulty which attaches to

* Almagest. iv. 9.

the chronological arrangement which we have adopted, which requires much more serious consideration. The difficulty lies in connexion with the reign of Cyrus, king of Persia, concerning whom it was written, " He is my shepherd and shall perform all my pleasure; even saying to Jerusalem, Thou shalt be built, and to the temple, Thy foundation shall be laid;" the prince here referred to being undoubtedly the Cyrus, or Coresh, of the book of Ezra, who issued a decree for the rebuilding of the temple, in the first year of his reign over the kingdom of Babylon.* Now we have affirmed, with Demetrius, that the last carrying away of Jewish captives to Babylon, in the twenty-third year of Nebuchadnezzar, in the fifth year after the destruction of the city and temple of Jerusalem, took place in the year B.C. 560; which date there is sufficient ground for believing was also that of the first year of the reign of Cyrus, father of Cambyses as king of Persia. How, then, it may be asked, is this to be reconciled with the opening words of the book of Ezra, " Now in the first year of Cyrus, king of Persia, that the word of the Lord by the mouth of Jeremiah might be fulfilled," &c.? for the " word " referred to proclaims that Jerusalem should be restored after a period of seventy years of desolation. And how, again, if Nebuchadnezzar reigned twenty-two years after the year B.C. 560, as we affirm, Evil-Merodach two years, Nergal-sharezar four years, Laborosoarchod nine months, and Nabonadius seventeen years, in all more than forty-

* Ezra, v. 13.

five years, bringing us down to the year 514
for the last year of Nabonadius; and if, as the
Babylonian histories record, Cyrus at the end
of this time, or more probably some years earlier,
conquered Nabonadius giving him a government in
Carmania,—how, we ask, are these asserted facts
to be reconciled with the undisputed fact that
Cyrus, father of Cambyses, ceased to reign in the
year B.C. 530 (as generally supposed at the age of
seventy), and was succeeded by Cambyses in B.C.
529, who conquered Egypt in his fifth year, B.C.
525, as no one denies? Clearly they are irreconcilable. The old Christian chronographers, such
as Africanus and Eusebius, considered that the first
year of Cyrus spoken of by Ezra, was the year
B.C. 560, and that Jerusalem was destroyed about
thirty years before that date. Modern chronographers, such as Scaliger, Ussher, and Petavius, have
brought down the first year of Cyrus as king of
Babylon to the year B.C. 538 or 536. But there
is no ancient authority for this date, 538, as that of
the taking of Babylon. It has merely been adopted as
the date of the first year of Cyrus, as being the true
date of the year following the death of Astyages,
king of Media, whom Cyrus, his grandson, is supposed to have conquered. It is difficult also to
believe that the Cyrus of Ezra, in B.C. 538, issued his
decree for the rebuilding of the temple only twenty-
five years after the fall of Jerusalem, in B.C. 563, as
we place it.

A full and satisfactory explanation of this difficulty would require a somewhat lengthened treatise,

for which we have not space in this volume.* We can, therefore, only refer the reader to the few observations, which will be found appended, upon Persian chronology, in reconciliation of Herodotus, Ctesias, and Xenophon.† Both Ctesias and Xenophon, it is well known, vary considerably from Herodotus in their histories of the reigns of the kings of Persia and Media in the time of Cyrus. Practically, however, the testimony of both these historians has been set aside and neglected, owing to the winning style of the narrative of Herodotus, which has thrown them both into the shade. Almost the first lesson in ancient history imbibed in our youth from Herodotus is, that Cyrus, the grandson of Astyages, and son of Cambyses the Persian, and Mandane the Mede, and therefore called the Mule, dethroned his grandfather, Astyages, about seventy years before the battle of Marathon, that is, about B.C. 560, as generally supposed at the age of forty. But this idea is physically impossible, considering that his grandfather married in the year of the eclipse, in B.C. 585; that his great-grandfather, Cyaxares, continued to reign many years after the eclipse, and that Astyages reigned after him for thirty-five years, and was old when Cyrus was born.‡ So false a record must necessarily be at variance with

* The late Duke of Manchester, in a work of great research, was so perplexed with this period of history, that he arrived at the conclusion that Cyrus must have been Nebuchadnezzar I. and Cambyses Nebuchadnezzar II. "Times of Daniel," p. 128.

† See Appendix, A.

‡ Herod. i. 109.

the record of Scripture, if the record of Scripture is true. The solution of the problem, which we take to be the true one, may be thus shortly stated.

1st. Cyrus the Mule, the grandson of Astyages, was not the father, but the son of Cambyses, who conquered Egypt, as Xenophon relates.

2nd. He was not, and could not be, the king who dethroned Astyages, as just shown. Ctesias tells us distinctly that Herodotus was in error upon this point, and that Cyrus, who conquered Astyages, was in no way related to him. While Xenophon relates that grandfather and grandson lived together on the most amicable terms till the death of Astyages.

3rd. Cambyses, son of Cyrus,* and also father of Cyrus the Mule, was not merely a Persian noble, as Herodotus affirms, but that great king of Persia, Cambyses, who conquered Egypt in B.C. 525, and who had previously conquered Babylon by the hand of his son Cyrus, who acted as general of his army, in combination with his uncle, Cyaxares, but who had not yet been placed on the throne. Such is the history of Cambyses and Cyrus, grandson of Astyages, as related by Xenophon. So that Cyrus father of Cambyses, and Cyrus son of Cambyses, were two different kings of Persia. The latter, we affirm, was the king spoken of in the first chapter of Ezra; the former, he who conquered Astyages, and married his daughter, as related by Ctesias, some time between B.C. 560 and 538.

* Herod. i. 111.

APPENDIX A.

THE following treatise on the Sabbatical years and Jubilees
of the Jews, forms part of a chronological treatise comprehending Egyptian, Babylonian, Assyrian, Tyrian, Median,
and Lydian chronology, all based upon the fundamental date,
B.C. 583–2, as the date of the battle of Carchemish; fought
in the last year of Pharaoh-Necho, the first year of Nebuchadnezzar, and fourth year of Johoiakim, about the time
of the final destruction of Nineveh, and therefore soon after
the eclipse of Thales, now finally fixed by astronomers to the
year B C. 585, and twenty-five years lower than the commonly
received date. This treatise was published in the year 1863,
in the Transactions of the Chronological Institute of London.
The author was not at that time aware of a valuable treatise,
written by Dr. B. Zuchermann of Breslau, in the year 1857,
on the same subject. He has since procured that work, and
caused it to be translated, and it is published in the Transactions of the above Society. He is pleased to find that the
conclusion which he had arrived at, viz. :—that the period of the
Jubilee was not a cycle of fifty years, as generally supposed,
but a cycle of forty nine years, as maintained by Rabbi
Jehuda and the Geonim,—coincides with the opinion of Dr.
Zuchermann, and also that the series of computed Sabbatical
years after the captivity of the Jews at Babylon entirely
agrees with his computation. A perusal of Dr. Zuchermann's
treatise is strongly recommended to any one desirous of ac-
quainting himself with Jewish opinions and controversy on
the subject.

There are two difficult points, however, upon which Dr. Zuchermann has not sufficiently treated, and upon which the author trusts that he has thrown some light in the following observations.

The great difficulty which meets one at the threshold of the subject is, how to believe that any legislator, especially the supreme legislator over all, should have instituted the observance by his people of two successive years of fallow, during which neither seed should be sown nor fruit gathered out of the field, which, according to the law, as laid down in Leviticus xxv., would apparently have been the result in every fiftieth year, when after the completion of the forty-ninth year, which was Sabbatical, it was immediately followed by the year of Jubilee. This obvious difficulty has given rise to much difference of opinion; and many seeing the improbability of the correctness of such an interpretation of the law, have suggested that the Jubilee was not concurrent with the fiftieth, but with the forty-ninth, or Sabbatical year, which, on the other hand, is contrary to the words of Leviticus, xxv. 11.

The simple solution of the difficulty here suggested is, that the fiftieth year, or jubilee, was concurrent with the first year of the septennial cycle which followed the seventh Sabbatical year; and that it was not, as generally assumed, commanded to be observed as a fallow by the nation at large, but only by those who were the objects of the institution of the Jubilee, and who alone partook of its benefits, that is, those who, having dispossessed themselves of their inheritance within the previous forty-nine years, came again into possession in the fiftieth year. By means of this solution all difficulty in the nature of the original institution, or in the way of the early tradition of Rabbi Jehuda, is removed. For thus the fiftieth year or jubilee would have been a year of cultivation for the nation in general, as the first year of a septennial cycle, but a year of fallow for those few individuals only who came into re-possession of lands in that year.

Dr. Zuchermann again is at a loss how to fix upon any one year throughout the whole Jewish history as a year

actually observed, or computed, as a Jubilee, and this difficulty must ever remain, as long as erroneous chronological
reckonings such as are adopted both by Christians and Jews
continue to be applied towards the explanation of Holy Scripture. On the other hand, if there is sufficient ground for
adopting the reckoning proposed in the foregoing pages, it
will readily be seen how the whole series of Jubilees fall of
their own accord into place, and how when so arranged they
coincide with certain remarkable allusions in history pointing
to such years. The materials to be derived from Scripture
and Jewish tradition are amply sufficient, when properly
handled, for placing the whole question of the Sabbatical
years in connexion with the Jubilee on a secure foundation;
and to effect this, and to show the important bearing of these
sacred cycles upon sacred history, is the object of the following dissertation.

HEBREW CHRONOLOGY IN CONNECTION WITH THE SABBATICAL YEARS AND JUBILEES.

THE battle of Carchemish, in the year B.C. 583–2, or more accurately, in the spring of the year B C. 582, is the key to Hebrew chronology, because this battle was fought in the fourth year of the reign of Jehoiakim, king of Judah, as Jeremiah attests,* and from thence we compute with certainty, through the Hebrew Scriptures, the dates and reigns of the whole succession of kings of Judah, from the first year of Solomon, in whose reign Jerusalem was consecrated as the " holy city," to the last year of Zedekiah, when the " holy city " together with its temple, was destroyed by the Chaldeans.

We have already seen how the date of this battle, thus placed, being the date also of the first year of Nebuchadnezzar, and the last year of Pharaoh-Necho, king of Egypt, has led to the recovery of a very early mode of reckoning the chronology of the kingdoms of Assyria, Babylon, and Lydia —how the rise of the kingdom of Babylon under Nebuchadnezzar thus immediately follows the final destruction of Nineveh, soon after the eclipse of B.C. 585 — and how, in accordance with this fundamental date, Egyptian, Tyrian, and Median Chronology, in conjunction with the chronology of these other nations, form together one harmonious system.

The system of dates thus recovered is that which appears to have been entertained by learned men in the illustrious age of literature which followed upon the conquest of Asia by the Greeks, and is based accordingly, as we have seen, upon the authority of such writers as Berosus (quoted by Josephus, Abydenus, and Polyhistor), as Megasthenes, Manetho, Dino,

* Jer. xlvi. 2.

Demetrius, the author of the Parian Chronicle, and others of that early age of literature; while, on the other hand, with all due deference to Josephus, and the later Christian writers, such as Africanus, Eusebius, and especially Clemens Alexandrinus, as regards the valuable records of history and chronology which they have preserved to us, we have rejected their systematic chronographies as founded on an erroneous adaptation of heathen chronology to Scriptural events, and as, in fact, subversive of the plain Hebrew reckoning which it is our object now to re-establish.

If the battle of Carchemish, in the year B.C. 582, was fought in the fourth year of the reign of Jehoiakim, king of Judah, then must the succession of kings of Judah, as reckoned in the book of Kings, from Solomon to Zedekiah, have been as follows : —

Canon of the Reigns of the Kings of Judah, according to Demetrius.

Solomon	40 years from B.C.	993*
Rehoboam	17 ,, ,,	953
Abijah	3 ,, ,,	936
Asa	40 (41 current)	933
Jehoshaphat	25 ,, ,,	893
Jehoram	7 (8 current)	868
Ahaziah	1 ,, ,,	861
Athaliah	6 ,, ,,	860
Joash	40 ,, ,,	854
Amaziah	29 ,, ,,	814
Uzziah	52 ,, ,,	785
Jotham	16 ,, ,,	733
Ahaz	15 (16 current)	717
Hezekiah	29 ,, ,,	702
Manasseh	55 ,, ,,	673
Amon	2 ,, ,,	618

* Lepsius places the first year of Solomon in B.C. 992, and the first of Rehoboam in B.C. 953. But shortens the reign of Manasseh by 20 years.— Konigsbuch der Egypter. Tafeln, p. 8.

Josiah	.	.	.	31	(32 current)	616
Jehoahaz	.	.			3ms	586
Jehoiakim	.	.		11	„ „	585
Jechoniah	.	.			3ms	574
Zedekiah	.	.		11	„ „	573
						to
						563

Now, this arrangement of the chronology of the kings of Judah, derived from the date of the battle of Carchemish, is neither more nor less than that of Demetrius, the Jewish historian, who wrote in the third century B.C., and whose Canon of the reigns of the kings of Judah, as above set forth, has been reconstructed from three leading dates preserved by Clemens Alexandrinus in a passage which we shall presently quote.

Demetrius is spoken of by Eusebius,* in connexion with Philo, Aristobulus, Josephus, and Eupolemus, all Jewish writers; and he was, no doubt, one of those Hellenistic Jews who, under the domination of the Greeks in Asia, had adopted, as was then the custom, a Greek name. The works of Demetrius have not come down to us; and it is only through Josephus, Clemens Alexandrinus, Jerome, and Eusebius, that we have any knowledge of, or reference to, his writings. He is evidently referred to as a writer of considerable note.

The fundamental date from which Demetrius reckoned his chronology upwards, was the first year of the reign of Ptolemy Philopator, king of Egypt, from which it may be inferred that he lived in that king's reign, and wrote about the year B.C. 222. We have observed that this was a period of great learning and research. The successors of Alexander we know were promoters of literature in every branch. The historical records of the several Eastern nations under their dominion were then sought for and published in the Greek language; and the science of chronology, which was carefully studied at that time, boasts of the great name of Eratosthenes,

* Ecclesiastical History, ch. xiii.

the father of chronology, whose works are lost, and of the unknown writer of the Parian Chronicle,* both of whom must have been contemporary, or nearly so, with Demetrius. Demetrius wrote, therefore, rather more than 300 years after the death of Nebuchadnezzar, about the same length of time before Josephus, and 530 years before Eusebius. He is the first Jewish writer who has synchronised events in Jewish history with known periods in secular history; and writing, as we have observed, in an age of learning and cultivation, his testimony deserves to be looked upon with extreme reverence.

From Clemens Alexandrinus we learn that Demetrius wrote a history of the kings of Judah, and in a short passage from the *Stromata* † of that learned writer, we obtain an outline of his chronology from the time of Shalmanezer, king of Assyria, who overthrew the kingdom of Israel, to the reign of Ptolemy Philopator, the fourth king of Egypt, bearing that title. The passage runs thus :—

"Demetrius says, in his work concerning the kings of Judea, that the tribes of Benjamin and Levi were not carried into captivity by Sennacherib; but that from this captivity (*i.e.* in the reign of Sennacherib, by whom, according to Assyrian inscriptions, now extant, many captives were carried from Judea) to the last captivity from Jerusalem under Nebuchadnezzar (*i.e.* in the 23rd year of his reign), was a period of 128 years and 6 months. And that from the time when the ten tribes were carried away from Samaria (*i.e.* in the reign of Shalmanezer) to the reign of the fourth Ptolemy was a period of 473 ‡ years and 9 months, and from the carrying away from Jerusalem 338 years and 3 months."

Now, here is no loose reckoning in round numbers, which are, of course, always more or less inexact; but the passage quoted, as originally written, was clearly intended to convey a

---

* This Chronicle has been attributed by some to Demetrius Phalereus.

† Clem. Alex. Heinsii. Strom. i. p. 337.

‡ The figures are 573 in the present copies of Clemens. The context clearly requires 473.

statement of the exact dates, even to a single month, of three
captivities, which marked the transport of the children of
Israel from their own land into the cities of the Medes and
into the dominions of the king of Babylon.

Ptolemy Philopator began to reign in Nov. B.C. 222=221-2ᵐ

From thence to the 23rd year of Nebuchadnezzar　　338 3
　　　　　　　　　　　　　　　　　　　　　　　　————
　　　　　　　　　　　　　　　　　　　　　B.C. 559-5ᵐ
From thence to the invasion of Sennacherib, in
　　　　　　the 14th year of Hezekiah　　.　　.　　128-6
　　　　　　　　　　　　　　　　　　　　　　　　————
　　　　　　　　　　　　　　　　　　　　　B.C. 687-11ᵐ

Again, from the first year of Ptolemy Philopator=B.C. 221-2ᵐ

To the carrying away of the ten tribes　.　　.　　473-9
　　　　　　　　　　　　　　　　　　　　　　　　————
　　　　　　　　　　　　　　　　　　　　　B.C. 694-11ᵐ

So that, according to Demetrius, the deportation of captives
by Sennacherib took place in Feb. B.C. 688, that is, towards
the end of the 14th year of Hezekiah: the carrying away of
the ten tribes in Feb. B.C. 695, that is, towards the end of the
7th year of Hezekiah : * and the last captivity of Judah in Aug.
B.C. 560, or 23rd year of Nebuchadnezzar. From these three
leading dates it is easy to reconstruct, as we have done, the
whole list of reigns of the kings of Judah, which we have
denominated the Canon of Demetrius.

　　But again; the correctness of this Canon has been confirmed by the exact agreement of the date therein assigned
to the 4th year of Solomon, in which year the building of the
Temple of Jerusalem was commenced, viz. B.C. 990, with the
date of the commencement of the building as collected
through Josephus, from the Tyrian annals preserved by
Menander.†

　　　* The sixth year according to the Hebrew text, the seventh according to
Josephus.
　　　† See Tyrian Chronology. Trans. Chron. Inst. vol. ii. part iii.

From the flight of Dido in the 7th year of
    Pygmalion . . . . . B.C. = 846
To the 4th year of Solomon . . . . 144 yrs.
                               B.C. 990

Such is the well-defined outline of the Chronology of the times of the Hebrew monarchy, derived from three different sources of inquiry, and corroborated, as we have seen, by contemporaneous records recovered from the ruined palaces of the kings of Assyria.

We now propose to test the accuracy of this outline of Scripture chronology by the most rigid, and at the same time the most appropriate, test which can be applied to it, that is to say, its conformity or otherwise with a peculiar measure of time, which we know to have been in use amongst the Jews, and by which they are distinguished from all other nations in the world,—the sacred calendar of Sabbatical years and Jubilees. This calendar of consecrated years is the true test of the accuracy or inaccuracy of every scheme of Hebrew chronology which may be propounded : and as it is a striking proof of the utter worthlessness of the commonly received reckoning, that confessedly it draws no support from the Sabbatical years and Jubilees, and that the remarkable reference to such a mode of computation in the ninth chapter of the book of Daniel in no way can be made to fall in with that reckoning; so is the fact, of the simple manner in which each recorded Sabbath and Jubilee, and especially the prophetic words of Daniel, fall in with the proposed reckoning, one of the most interesting and conclusive arguments in favour of the arrangement of dates now before us. "Hallow my sabbaths, and they shall be a sign between me and you, that ye may know that I am the Lord your God."*

All Hebrew chronology ought necessarily to resolve itself into a series of septennial periods, marked by consecrated years of rest, during which it was ordained that the land

* Ezek. xx. 20.

should remain untilled, in conformity with the command,
" When ye come into the land which I give you, then shall
the land keep a sabbath unto the Lord.   Six years thou shalt
sow thy field, and six years thou shalt prune thy vineyard,
and gather in the fruit thereof; but in the seventh year shall
be a sabbath of rest unto the land, a sabbath for the Lord :
thou shalt neither sow thy field, nor prune thy vineyard.
That which groweth of its own accord of thy harvest thou
shalt not reap, neither gather the grapes of thy vine undressed; for it is a year of rest unto the land.   And the
sabbath of the land shall be meat for you; for thee, and for
thy servant, and for thy maid, and for thy hired servant,
and for thy stranger that sojourneth with thee, and for thy
cattle, and for the beast that are in thy land, shall all the
increase thereof be meat.   And thou shalt number seven
sabbaths of years unto thee, seven times seven years; and
the space of the seven sabbaths of years shall be unto thee
forty and nine years.   Then shalt thou cause the trumpet
of the Jubilee to sound on the tenth day of the seventh month."
. . . .   "And ye shall hallow the fiftieth year, and proclaim liberty throughout all the land unto all the inhabitants
thereof: it shall be a jubilee unto you; and ye shall return
every man unto his possession, and ye shall return every
man unto his family.   A jubilee shall that fiftieth year be
unto you : ye shall not sow neither reap that which groweth
of itself in it, nor gather the grapes in it of thy vine undressed."
. . . .   "And if thou sell ought unto thy neighbour, or
buyest ought of thy neighbour's hand, ye shall not oppress
one another: according to the number of years after the
Jubilee thou shalt buy of thy neighbour, and according unto
the number of years of the fruits he shall sell unto thee."*
   That the reckoning of these consecrated years was preserved by the Jews down to the time of the destruction of
Jerusalem by the Chaldeans, appears to be established beyond
dispute by one single incidental passage in the prophet Ezekiel.
While the armies of the Chaldeans were hovering over Judea,

* Lev. xxv. 2 15.

and threatening desolation to the land, he exclaims, "The time is come, the day draweth near: let not the buyer rejoice,. nor the seller mourn; for wrath is upon all the multitude thereof. For *the seller shall not return to that which is sold*, although they the (buyer and seller) were yet alive."* Here, then, is a clear reference to the law, that in the year of jubilee every man should return to his own possession. "That which is sold," says the law, "shall remain in the hand of him that hath bought it until the year of jubilee: and in the jubilee it shall go out, and he (the seller) shall return unto his possession."† Ezekiel also, with reference to yet future times, speaking of the portion of land hereafter to be appropriated to the prince, writes,—"If he give a gift of his inheritance to one of his servants, then it shall be his to the year of liberty;‡ after which it shall return to the prince."§

These incidental allusions by Ezekiel to the law of the jubilee clearly imply that he was addressing those who required no explanation of the nature of the law, and that the practice of buying and selling land by the years of the jubilee was then the common custom of the Jews, that is to say, before their captivity at Babylon. Whether, however, the remainder of the law, viz.—" ye shall return every man unto his family," that is, every slave shall become free in the year of jubilee, was carried into practice, is a more doubtful matter. But if the reckoning of the year of the jubilee was thus preserved, so also, of course, must the reckoning of the Sabbatical years have been preserved, as the one was computed from the other. That the practice of buying and selling land by the years of the jubilee was also in operation after the return from captivity, even till after the Christian era, appears from Josephus, who, speaking of the jubilee, writes, "This year also restores the land to its former possessors in the following manner:—When the jubilee is come, which name denotes liberty, he that sold the land, and he that bought it, meet together and make an

---

* Ezek. vii. 12.   † Lev. xxv. 13, 28.
‡ Called year of liberty because every slave became free in the year of Jubilee.
§ Ezek. xlvi. 17.

estimate, on one hand, of the fruits gathered, and, on the other hand, of the expenses laid out upon it. If the fruits gathered come to more than the expenses laid out, he that sold it takes the land again: but if the expense prove more than the fruits, the present possessor receives of the former owner the difference that was wanting, and leaves the land to him."[*] Josephus here describes what he knew to be the practical working of the law. Philo also tells us that the fiftieth year was practically a year of remission for slaves;[†] and also remarks that breeders of cattle in his days sent their herds to feed on the fallow lands in the year of Jubilee without fear of loss.[†] It is clear, therefore, that both before and after the captivity a register of the years of jubilee was kept; and this is the opinion even of Maimonides, who tells us that the fiftieth year *was computed*, though not kept as a jubilee, after the return from captivity: which, in our view, it was not intended that it should be, that is, as a year of fallow for the whole nation.

But though the *reckoning* of the sabbatical years and jubilees was thus correctly preserved for the daily secular purposes of the conveyance and reconveyance of land, there is every reason to believe that before the captivity, that is, during the whole period of the monarchy, the command to abstain from cultivating the land every seventh year was by no means observed, but on the contrary most wilfully neglected; so that this neglect came to be treated as a national sin. It is from the recorded period of non-observance of these Sabbaths, and from the precise period of punishment inflicted in consequence, that we are enabled with much certainty to fix the actual dates at which these consecrated years of fallow ought to have been observed. That these years were not observed by ten out of the twelve tribes of Israel, viz. — those ten tribes who revolted under "Jeroboam, who made Israel to sin," is made probable by the fact, that Jeroboam had instituted a feast in the eighth month[‡] at Samaria, with the implied object of

---

* Whiston's Josephus, Ant. iii, ch. xii. 3.

† Philo's Treatise on Festivals.

‡ 1 Kings, xii. 32.

preventing the observance of the feast of the seventh month at Jerusalem by those tribes; and we know that it was in the seventh month that the Sabbatical year began and ended, and that the ceremony which connected together the Sabbatical year and the jubilee, viz.—the sounding of the trumpet of the jubilee—was to be performed. The sin of Jeroboam, and the waywardness of the ten tribes, are constantly referred to in Jewish history, and at length the period of their contumacy was summed up by Ezekiel as a period of 390 years,* to be finished at the end of the yet forty years' contumacy of the house of Judah, in the final siege and destruction of Jerusalem, the " holy city," the chosen metropolis of the twelve tribes of Israel. Accordingly we find that this was the exact number of the years which elapsed from the first year of Jeroboam to the year of the destruction of the city by Nebuchadnezzar, as laid down in the accompanying table. There is the best reason also for believing that the national observance of the consecrated seventh year, by abstaining from the cultivation of the land, was neglected by the tribes of Judah and Benjamin, from the reign of Solomon to the same time, from the fact that the captivity at Babylon was to last for exactly seventy years, that the land might enjoy her seventy Sabbaths.† So that, taking the twelfth year of Solomon, or the year of the dedication of the temple of Jerusalem, as the true time of the establishment of the Jewish polity in the Holy Land, as contemplated by Moses,‡ and as the year in which Jerusalem " the holy city," was thus selected as " the city which the Lord had chosen out of all the tribes of Israel to put his name there,"§ and in which city from thenceforth all the feasts and ceremonies of the law were commanded to be observed,‖ and specially the ordinances connected with the three great feasts, including the feast of the seventh month,—

---

* Ezek. iv. 5.   † 2 Chron. xxxvi. 21.

‡ " Since the day that I brought forth my people Israel out of Egypt, I chose no city out of all the tribes of Israel to build an house, that my name might be therein." Solomon refers to these words at the time of the dedication. 1 Kings, viii. 16.

§ 2 Chron. xii. 13.   ‖ Deut. xvi. 2, 15, 16; xxxi. 11.

counting, we say, from the twelfth of Solomon, the first year of the holy city, to the year of the destruction of the holy city, there appear to have been exactly 420 years, during which this peculiar and remarkable ordinance, the Sabbatical year, had been nationally neglected by the Jewish people, being the complement of years of cultivation in a period of seventy weeks, or 490 years.

Nevertheless, as we have said, the register of these consecrated years, though not observed, must have been correctly preserved; and it is the register or calendar of Sabbatical years, which we desire to recover, as a test of the accuracy of our chronological reckoning.

The first question to be considered is, were the Sabbatical cycles reckoned in continuous and unbroken series? for if they were so, we may obtain the dates of the whole series by fixing the date of any one of them.

The learned Rabbi, Maimonides,[*] one of the most distinguished of Jewish writers, following the author of the Seder Olam Rabbah,[†] or Great Chronicle of the Jews, has maintained that the series of Sabbatical cycles, before the captivity, was not continuous, but broken by the intercalation of the year of Jubilee every fiftieth year; and this is the conclusion arrived at by many; and is indeed the opinion of the most recent writer on the subject, on a review of the whole question.[‡] But it will presently be seen,—and Maimonides himself does not dispute the fact,—that after the captivity, the Sabbatical years were observed in continuous septennial series, down to the time of the destruction of the second temple. And they are so observed in Palestine, even down to the present day.[§] So that, according to the opinion that the fiftieth year was originally intercalated, the law of Moses regarding the Sabbatical year would have been interpreted in one way by Joshua and the Jews who were instructed by

---

[*] Maimonides, ch. x. de Shemitha et Jubilæo.

[†] Seder Olam Rabbah, compare ch. xi. with ch. xv. Chron. Trans. vol. ii. Part ii.

[‡] See Smith's Dictionary of the Bible, voce Jubilee.

[§] Zuchermann, p. 4.

Moses down to the time of the captivity, and in another way
by Ezra and the great Synagogue after the captivity, a notion
which on the face of it is highly improbable. Nor, indeed, is
this idea acquiesced in by other Jewish writers. R. Jehuda,
and the Geonim (or the heads of the Jewish academies in Babylonia from the seventh to the eleventh centuries), maintained
that the year of Jubilee recurred every forty-ninth year, so
also do Scaliger, Petavius, Cunæus,* Pontanus,† Spanheim,‡
and our own Archbishop Ussher. Let us appeal then from
Rabbi Maimonides to that far more ancient and most eminent
master in Israel, whom we have just named, whose authority
on the subject of Levitical law, if we can ascertain it, is not to
be called in question.

Ezra, " the ready scribe in the law of Moses," " a scribe of
the words of the commandment of the Lord, and of his statutes
to Israel,"§ returned from captivity at Babylon, commissioned
by the king of Persia to re-establish in Jerusalem the forms
and ceremonies of the Jewish church, and to re-organise the
nation by setting magistrates and judges over the people, with
power to execute judgment, whether unto death, or to banish-
ment, or to confiscation of goods, upon those who disobeyed
the law of God and the king.‖ Now this Ezra, as Maimonides
observes,¶ reinstituted the observance of the Sabbatical year.
For the princes, Levites, and priests, entered into a covenant
at his command, amongst other things, that they " would
leave the seventh year (that is to say, cease from cultivating
the land in that year) and the exaction of every debt," that is
in the year of release,** and from this time forward to the
time of the destruction of the second temple, the religious
observance of the law was strictly fulfilled. Ezra, we assume,
had a distinct and accurate conception of what was commanded

---

* Critici Sacri, vol. vi.   † Pontanus de Sab. Ann.
‡ Spanheim, Chron. et Hist. Sac. p. 38.
§ Ezra, vii. 26.   ‖ Ezra, vii. 6–11.
¶ Maimonides, and the Jewish writers in general, state that this return of
Ezra was in the seventh year of the second temple, which we shall hereafter
show to be correct. He returned before Eliashib was styled high priest. Ezra,
x. 6–18.
** Neh. x. 31.

in the law — of how it had been neglected by the Jews in the times of the monarchy, and how, in obedience to the law, it ought to be observed for the future; and in the last chapter of the second book of Chronicles, which we may assume to have been written by him, he records his opinion. When speaking of the siege and capture of Jerusalem by the Chaldeans, he writes — "They burnt the house of God, and brake down the wall of Jerusalem, and burnt all the palaces thereof; and them which had escaped from the sword carried he away to Babylon, where they were servants to him (Nebuchadnezzar) and his sons until the reign of the kingdom of Persia."* He then concludes with this remarkable reference to the Sabbatical years, "to fulfil the Word of the Lord by the mouth of Jeremiah, until the *land had enjoyed her Sabbaths:* for, as long as she *lay desolate*, she kept Sabbath, to fulfil threescore and ten years."

These words were written by Ezra when the Jews were again settled in Judea, after their return from captivity, and when the seventy years' desolation of the land was looked back upon as an event past and fulfilled. There could be no doubt or misunderstanding, at that time, in the minds of Ezra and his contemporaries, after the event, as to the particular mode in which "the word of the Lord by the mouth of Jeremiah" had been accomplished: and Ezra accordingly has, in the above words, counted the period of desolation, and of sabbatical rest, without ambiguity from the date of the burning of the temple to the reign of the Persians at Babylon.

Jeremiah had declared, in the fourth year of Jehoiakim, "This whole land shall be a desolation and an astonishment: and these nations shall serve the king of Babylon seventy years."† He made no allusion, however, to the special reason referred to by Ezra, viz. — the long neglect of the septennial rests commanded by Moses, amongst other transgressions, why the period of punishment on the nation was measured

---

* That is, till the reign of the Persians at Babylon towards the end of the reign of Darius son of Hystaspes.

† Jer. xxv. 11.

out, as neither more nor less than threescore and ten years; nor did he define beforehand the particular event which should mark either the beginning or ending of the period. There had been much doubt and perplexity, we may assume, amongst the captives at Babylon as to the exact time when the term of their exile would cease. Some undoubtedly had counted the years from the fourth year of Jehoiakim, when the first invasion of the king of Babylon took place, and when Judæa first became a province of that kingdom, and had fondly hoped that the decree of Cyrus would have marked the completion of their servitude, and desolation of the land. Others, with the prophet Ezekiel, had begun to count their seventy years from the captivity of Jechoniah, eight years later. But, when it was seen that the decree of Cyrus was set at nought by the local governors of Judæa, and had become of no effect,—that the holy Temple of Jerusalem still remained cast down to the ground,— that the same desolation continued to reign throughout the land,—and also that the termination of the years counted from the captivity of Jechoniah had failed to bring relief, — there remained so much doubt and despondency in the minds of the people as to the predicted time of their restoration, that even in the very year when their term of punishment was accomplished, and the command went forth to carry into effect the decree of Cyrus, as if in despair, we read in the prophet Haggai concerning them, " This people say, The time is not come, the time when the Lord's house should be built." *

In the first year, however, of Darius the Mede, "what time he was set over the realm of the Chaldeans," the full term of seventy years' desolation of the city and Temple was on the point of completion: and both Daniel and Ezra, whose minds were intent upon the restoration of the "holy city" and sanctuary, perceived that the words of Jeremiah were now about to be acomplished. For the first time, also, the true import of the term of seventy years of "desolation" seems to have been apprehended. They have both fallen into the same

* Hag. i. 2.

manner of speaking concerning the mode and meaning of
that period, and have both expressed themselves almost in
the same words. Daniel, pondering over the words of Jeremiah, pronounces that the period of seventy years' desolation
spoken of by that prophet had reference to the " desolations
of Jerusalem."* Ezra, referring to the same words of Jeremiah, computes the period as threescore and ten years from
the burning of the city by the Chaldeans, which is precisely
the same mode of interpretation. The heavenly messenger
sent to Daniel, in the first year of Darius the Mede, proclaims,
" Seventy weeks " of years, or 490 years, " are determined †
or completed upon thy people, and upon thy holy city, to finish
the transgressions," &c.;‡ Ezra, dwelling upon the same idea,
relates historically, how on the expiration of threescore and
ten years counted from the burning of the city, which confessedly ended in the reign of Darius son of Hystaspes, the
land had enjoyed her full complement of threescore and ten
Sabbaths, or Sabbatical years, which is only another mode of
expressing that seventy weeks of years were then accomplished, according to the calendar of consecrated years,
counted from a more remote date. The idea intended to be
conveyed by both those sacred writers was primarily, though
Daniel also makes hidden reference to the future, that,
with the completion of the seventy years' desolation of the
city, a great period in the history of the Jewish Church had
been fulfilled, by the completion of seventy Sabbatical weeks
of years, upon the " holy city," and the holy land ; and Daniel
shows that these years were fulfilled about the first or second
year of Darius.

With regard to the king here referred to under the title
Darius, if decisive proof be required that both Daniel and
Ezra are speaking of one and the same king, viz.—Darius,
son of Hystaspes,—it is embodied in the fact, that the very

---

* Dan. ix. 2.

† The word "determined" (literally, cut out) may have reference either
to the past or future, that is, to years fulfilled or to be fulfilled.

‡ Dan. ix. 24.

same term of "seventy years," counted from the same point, viz. the destruction of the holy city and temple, is reckoned by Daniel as ending in the reign of Darius the Mede, by Ezra as ending in the reign of Darius son of Hystaspes.

Yet it is remarkable that many of the most able of commentators on this portion of sacred history, constrained and fettered by the conventional dates of heathen chronology, and following the hasty suggestion of Josephus, with a view to the adjustment of that chronology to Scripture, have been willing to believe that the king known to Daniel, only by the title Darius, was no other than Cyaxares son of Astyages, king of Media, who died before Darius son of Hystaspes had come to the throne: the result of which is, to set aside the concurrent testimony of four contemporaneous sacred writers, who have all placed the termination of the seventy years in the reign of the son of Hystaspes, and not earlier than that reign.

The testimony of Scripture to this effect is so clear and consistent, that it is difficult to understand how it could ever have been misapprehended. The Prophet Zechariah, who was living at Jerusalem at the expiration of the seventy years, writes, in the eleventh month of the second year of Darius son of Hystaspes, " O Lord of hosts, how long wilt thou not have mercy on Jerusalem, and on the cities of Judah, against which thou hast had indignation these threescore and ten years?"*

There can be no question that the years here referred to are the same "threescore and ten years" spoken of by Daniel and Ezra, as reckoned from the destruction of Jerusalem, and here declared to have ended in the second year of Darius. Again, two years later in the same reign, the same Prophet relates how messengers had been sent to Jerusalem by the Jews still dwelling at Babylon, to inquire of the priests, now that the Temple was being rebuilt, whether they should continue to fast in the fifth month, in commemoration of the

* Zech. i. 12.

burning of the Temple, as they had done from year to year, even " *those seventy years :*" * thus again marking the time of the fulfilment of those years in the reign of Darius son of Hystaspes.

Ezra, it is true, has related how, with a view to the fulfilment of the word of the Lord by the mouth of Jeremiah, Cyrus, in his first year as king of Babylon, had been induced to issue a decree for the rebuilding of the Temple of Jerusalem ; and many, no doubt, as before observed, trusted that the seventy years of servitude to the king of Babylon counted from the reign of Jehoiakim, were then about to cease. But Ezra must not be interpreted as contradicting himself. He does not say that the seventy years were fulfilled in the reign of Cyrus, but that with a view to their fulfilment a decree was issued; and having just before laid down that the seventy years of desolation and servitude spoken of by Jeremiah were to be computed from the burning of the city and Temple, he goes on to relate, how, with a view towards the fulfilment of the prophet's words, Cyrus issued his decree, and how the decree of Cyrus remained without operation, even "unto the second year of Darius."† That the servitude at Babylon did actually continue till that very year, we also learn from Zechariah, who, in the second year of Darius, writes, " Ho, ho, come forth, and flee from the land of the north, saith the Lord . . . *Deliver thyself, O Zion, that dwellest with the daughter of Babylon.*‡ So that Daniel, Zechariah, and Ezra, all concur in bringing the termination of the seventy years to the same date ; while Haggai, writing at Jerusalem, in the ninth month of the second year of Darius, fixes, as it were, the very day of reconciliation between the people and their offended God after their seventy years of punishment. He writes, " Consider now from this day and upwards, from the four-and-twentieth day of the ninth month, even from the day that the foundation of the Lord's temple was laid, consider it. Is the seed yet in the barn? yea, as yet the vine, and the fig-tree,

---

* Zech. vii. 5.   † Ezra, iv. 24.   ‡ Zech. ii. 6, 7.

and the pomegranate, and the olive-tree, hath not brought forth; *from this day will I bless you.*[*]   And this period of reconciliation is also very clearly referred to by Zechariah, who, in the second year of Darius, writes, " Thus said the Lord, I am returned to Jerusalem with mercies." . . . " Sing and rejoice, O daughter of Zion : for, lo, I come, and I will dwell in the midst of thee, said the Lord." . . . " The Lord shall inherit Judah his portion in the holy land, and shall choose Jerusalem again." . . . " As I thought to punish you when your fathers provoked me to wrath, saith the Lord of hosts, and I repented not : so again have I thought *in these days* to do well unto Jerusalem, and to the house of Judah."[†]   Unquestionably, therefore, the seventy years' desolation of Jerusalem, and the " threescore and ten " Sabbaths fulfilled during the desolation, had been completed before the second year of the reign of Darius son of Hystaspes.

But as, in common parlance, when we speak of seventy Sabbath days as past, we imply the fulfilment of seventy weeks of days, so when Ezra speaks of seventy Sabbatical years fulfilled, he implies the fulfilment of seventy weeks of years, or 490 years, of which 420 years should be accounted as ordinary years, and the remaining seventy years as Sabbaths.   Now we have already shown, that counting from the twelfth year of Solomon, when the dedication of the first Temple took place, and Jerusalem was thereby consecrated the " holy city," to the last year of Zedekiah, when the holy city and Temple were destroyed, was a period of exactly 420 years, as set down in detail in the accompanying table ; which, added to the " threescore and ten years " of penitential Sabbaths enjoyed by the land, during its period of desolation, make up the period of " seventy weeks " of years spoken of in the book of Daniel, as already determined or accomplished on the " holy city," in the first year of Darius.

So that literally in this first year, or just before, were accomplished the words, " Seventy weeks are determined upon thy people, and upon *thy holy city*, to finish the transgres-

sion, and to make an end of sins, and to make reconciliation
for iniquity, and to bring in everlasting righteousness, and to
seal up the vision and prophecy (that is, the prophecy of Jeremiah), and to anoint the holy of holies;" that is, to rebuild the
Temple or sanctuary of Jerusalem. But, again, if seventy
sevens of years, each with its appointed Sabbath, were exactly
fulfilled, neither more nor less, according to the calendar, in,
or before, the first year of Darius, then must that first year
of Darius have fallen during the close of or immediately after
a Sabbatical year, and so have been set down in that calendar.

Lastly, if Darius the Mede was the same as Darius son of
Hystaspes,—a fact which we consider to be established,—
then was this first year of the reign of Darius, that is, his
first year computed from the time when he was " set over
the realm of the Chaldeans," concurrent with the sixty-second
year of his age, that is, with the year B.C. 492; and the
autumn of this year, B.C. 492, must mark the termination of
the last of an uninterrupted series of Sabbatical cycles, which
is the point we have been aiming to arrive at.

Let us now recapitulate the several points which have been
established in the foregoing remarks. We have ascertained,—

1st. That a calendar of Sabbatical years and Jubilees was
preserved, and made use of in the ordinary transactions of
purchase and sale of land, before the time of the captivity.

2d. That seventy weeks of years, as computed in this calendar, were completed on the " holy city," in the last year of
the " desolations of Jerusalem."

3d. That these seventy weeks of years commenced with
the consecration of the holy city, in the twelfth year of Solomon.

4th. That the seventieth, or last year of desolation was
Sabbatical.

5th. That this seventieth, or Sabbatical year, ended in
the autumn of the first year of Darius son of Hystaspes,
reckoned from the time when he was " set over the realm of
the Chaldeans."

6th. That the autumn of this first year of Darius fell
in the year B.C. 492.

7th. That seventy weeks of years as computed before the captivity, comprised a period of exactly 490 years, not 500 years, and that the year of Jubilee, therefore, was not intercalated every fiftieth year, as suggested by Maimonides.

8th. That if the 490th or last year was B.C. 492, the first year or twelfth year of Solomon, was B.C. 982, which confirms the reckoning of Demetrius, which we have adopted.

Having thus confirmed the outline of our reckoning, and ascertained that the Sabbatical years, before the captivity, were reckoned in continuous and unbroken series, in the same manner as we shall find that they were reckoned after the return from captivity; and having also fixed the exact date of one year in the series, the restoration of the whole calendar of consecrated years and Sabbatical cycles, from the time of the division of the land of Canaan by Joshua, when the computation commenced, to the birth of Christ, is a matter of simple enumeration. The following is the remarkable result, showing that the whole period of existence of the Jewish church, from the mission of Moses to the birth of Christ, is divided into three exact and equal cycles of 490 years each, or seventy weeks, or ten complete Jubilaic periods of forty-nine years.

The first period is counted from the year B.C. 1471,—when Moses approached the Jews in bondage in Egypt, and when they were first selected as God's chosen people,—to the dedication of the temple of Solomon in B.C. 982, when the Jewish polity, as shadowed forth by Moses, was first established in the place which the Lord had chosen to put his name there.

The second period is counted from the dedication of Solomon's Temple to the release of the Jews from the seventy years' bondage at Babylon, in B.C. 492.

The third is counted from B.C. 492 to the birth of Christ, B.C. 3-2, and comprises the minor period of 483 years, or "seven weeks and threescore and two weeks," "from the going forth of the commandment to restore and to build Jerusalem unto Messiah the prince;" that is to say, of one period of jubilee, and sixty-two Sabbatical weeks of the sacred calendar, counted from the dedication of the second Temple

Y

in B.C. 486, or seventh year of Darius; when the Jewish laws and institutions were re-established, and from thenceforth observed, in a much more strict and perfect manner than had ever been effected in the days of the monarchy.

FIRST PERIOD OF THE JEWISH CHURCH,
COMPRISING 490 YEARS.

B.C.
1471   Mission of Moses, in the spring, say 12 months be-
        fore the exodus.
1470   Exodus, in the month, Abib, or Nisan.
1430   Entry into Canaan, in the month of Nisan.
1423   Divisions of the land, say in the month Tisri, 7½ years
        after the entry.
1417–6 The first Sabbatical year after the division of the land.

Calendar of Sabbatical Years and Jubilees.

B.C. 1417–6	1368–7	1319–8
1410–9	1361–0	1312–1
1403–2	1354–3	1305–4
1396–5	1347–6	1298–7
1389–8	1340–9	1291–0
1382–1	1333–2	1284–3
1375–4	1326–5	1277–6

1st Jubilee 1374–3. 2nd Jubilee 1325–4. 3rd Jubilee 1276–5.

1270–9	1221–0	1172–1
1263–2	1214–3	1165–4
1256–5	1207–6	1158–7
1249–8	1200–9	1151–0
1242–1	1193–2	1144–1
1235–4	1186–5	1137–6
1228–7	1179–8	1130–9

4th Jubilee 1227–6.   5th Jubilee 1178–7. 6th Jubilee 1129–8.

1123–2	1074–3	1025–4
1116–5	1067–6	1018–7
1109–8	1060–9	1011–0
1102–1	1053–2	1004–3
1095–4	1046–5	997–6
1088–7	1039–8	990–9
1081–0	1032–1	983–2

7th Jubilee 1080–9.   8th Jubilee 1031–0. 9th Jubilee 982–1.

SECOND PERIOD OF THE JEWISH CHURCH,

COMPRISING 490 YEARS.

SEVENTY WEEKS, OR TEN JUBILEES, FROM THE DEDICATION OF THE TEMPLE IN B.C. 982, TO THE RETURN FROM CAPTIVITY IN B.C. 492.

Calendar of Sabbatical Years and Jubilees.

B.C. 976–5	927–6	878–7
969–8	920–9	871–0
962–1	913–2	864–3
955–4	906–5	857–6
948–7	899–8	850–9
941–0	892–1	843–2
934–3	885–4	836–5

1st Jubilee 933–2. 2nd Jubilee 884–3. 3rd Jubilee 835–4.

829–8	780–9	731–0
822–1	773–2	724–3
815–4	766–5	717–6
808–7	759–8	710–9
801–0	752–1	703–2
794–3	745–4	696–5
787–6	738–7	689–8

4th Jubilee 786–5. 5th Jubilee 737-6. 6th Jubilee 688–7.

682–1	633–2	584–3	535–4
675–4	626–5	577–6	528–7
668–7	619–8	570–9	521–0
661–0	612–1	563–2	514–3
654–3	605–4	556–6	507–6
647–6	598–6	549–8	500–9
640–9	591–0	542–1	493–2

7th Ju. 639–8. 8th Ju. 590–9. 9th Ju. 541–2. 10th Ju. 492–1.

Return of the Jews from Babylon in B.C. 492–1, when Darius, in his first year, was about 62 years of age. Dan. v. 31; Zech. ii. 7.

THIRD PERIOD OF THE JEWISH CHURCH,
COMPRISING 490 YEARS.

B.C.

490   Building of the second Temple commenced.

485   Temple finished in the sixth year of Darius, in the month Adar.*

485   Temple dedicated in the autumn.

479–8 First Sabbatical year under the second Temple.

Calendar of Sabbatical years and Jubilees.

B.C. 479–8
472–1
465–4
458–7
451–0
444–3
437–6

First year of Jubilee 436–5 after "seven weeks" of years, ending with the dedication of the wall of Jerusalem.

Period of "threescore and two weeks"
"unto Messiah the Prince."

B.C.		
430–9	290–9	150–9
423–2	283–2	143–2
416–5	276–5	136–5
409–8	269–8	129–8
402–1	262–1	122–1
395–4	255–4	115–4
388–7	248–7	108–7
381–0	241–0	101–0
374–3	234–3	94–3
367–6	227–6	87–6
360–9	220–9	80–9
353–2	213–2	73–2
346–5	206–5	66–5
339–8	199–8	59–8
332–1	192–1	52–1
325–4	185–4	45–4
318–7	178–7	38–7
311–0	171–0	31–0
304–3	164–3	24–3
297–6	157–6	17–6
		10–9
		Birth of Christ 3–2

* The month Adar fell in the sixth year, the month Tisri in the seventh year, of Darius, and both in B.C. 485.

This threefold cyclical division of the times of the Jewish nation under the old covenant, is indeed a striking and remarkable result of our mode of reckoning Hebrew chronology, and leads to interesting reflections concerning the nature and degree of directing influence exercised by God in His providential government of the world. We shall return again to the consideration of this subject in our chronological sketch of Jewish history.

We now propose to verify, by direct historical testimony, the exactness of the dates of several years set down in the calendar as Sabbatical, both before and after the captivity, and so to confirm the soundness of the principle of continuous septennial division without intercalation. At the same time by verifying, by the same direct testimony, the exact date of one single year of jubilee, we shall show how the whole series of Sabbaths, from the time of Joshua to the building of the second temple, divides itself into Jubilaic periods of forty-nine years each, or seven weeks of years.

Nothing can be more certain than that the Jews religiously observed the consecrated years of rest after their return from captivity at Babylon. Long exile and affliction in the land of their enemies, in strict fulfilment of the words of their prophets, had left an impression on the mind of the nation never to be effaced, of the nearness and reality of the divine hand which directed their destinies, and a great and permanent change had thus been wrought in the character of the whole people. As the times of the first temple and of the monarchy had been marked by long periods of perverseness and neglect of the law of Moses, and by a weak and wavering belief, more frequently tending towards the idolatries of the surrounding nations than to the worship of the only true God ; so were the times of the duration of the second temple, from its restoration under Darius to its final destruction by Titus, characterised by extraordinary firmness and sincerity of faith, accompanied by a Pharisaical adherence to the strictest letter of the law. The observance of the Sabbath day was henceforth fenced in with restrictions of the minutest character, as regarded Sabbath journeys,

Sabbath burdens, and the performance of household duties, on that day of rest; while from the strict abstinence from cultivation of the land in the seventh year, the nation appears upon more than one occasion to have fallen into grievous straits for want of the necessaries of life, when suffering under the calamity of siege or invasion by their enemies.

The first well-established date of a Sabbatical year actually observed by the Jews, to which we shall refer, is the year of the siege and taking of Jerusalem by Herod the Great. Josephus tells us that this event happened in the year when Marcus Agrippa and Caninius Gallus were Consuls at Rome,[*] which year, by reference to a table of Consuls, we find to be the year B.C. 37. Josephus relates that the misery of the Jews was greatly increased towards the end of the siege, by the presence of the Sabbatical year, " which," to use his own words, " forced the country to lie still uncultivated, since we are forbidden," he says, " to sow the land in that year." [†] This extreme scarcity of provisions clearly indicates that the time spoken of was the second of the two Julian years covered by a Sabbatical year, for the Sabbatical year commenced in the seventh month, and extended from autumn in one year to autumn in the next. So that the year B.C. 38–7, that is, from seed-time in B.C. 38, to seed-time in B.C. 37, was Sabbatical, as set down in the calendar of consecrated years.

A second date of a Sabbatical year may be equally well established, viz., the year in which the high-priest Simon was slain, and his son John Hyrcanus took the high-priesthood. This event is placed by the writer of the first book of Maccabees in the month Sebat, or the eleventh month of the 177th year of the Seleucidæ,[‡] that is, in March B.C. 135. And we may assume that the siege of Jericho, which followed immediately upon the accession of Hyrcanus,— took place in the second of the two Julian years covered by a Sabbatical year,

---

* Jos. Ant. xiv. 16, 4.   † Jos. Ant. xv. 1. 1, 2.   ‡ 1 Macc. xvi. 14.

because Josephus writes, that while Hyrcanus in his first year, B.C. 135, is engaged in the siege of the fortress of Jericho, "that year on which the Jews are used to rest, occurs, ἐνίσταται; for the Jews," he says, "observe this rest every seventh year, as they do every seventh day."* Now, he tells us that, in consequence of the presence of the Sabbatical year, he was compelled to raise the siege, owing, we must assume, to scarcity of supplies for his army: and as this scarcity could not have occurred during the first three months of the year, just following the harvest, it must been felt during the nine months which fell in the second of the two Julian years. So that the year B.C. 136–5, or from seed-time in B.C. 136, to seed-time in B.C. 135, was Sabbatical, and so it is set down in the calendar.

A third well-established Sabbatical year is the year of the accession of Antiochus Eupator to the throne of Syria, or the year following the death of Antiochus Epiphanes, when the city of Jerusalem was besieged. This year Josephus informs us was the 150th year of the Seleucidæ, that is, the year beginning in April B.C. 163; and from the scarcity of food which prevailed, and the expression that the land " remained untilled," we may infer that the year named was the second of the two Julian years covered by the Sabbatical year. Josephus writes, Antiochus " placed a garrison of his own in the city; but as for the temple of Jerusalem, he lay a long time besieging it, while they within bravely defended it."— " But then their provisions failed them. What fruits of the ground they had laid up were spent, and the land remained untilled that year, because it was the seventh year, in which by our laws we are obliged to let it lie uncultivated."† The year, therefore, B.C. 164–3, that is, from seed-time in B.C. 164 to seed-time in B.C. 163, was Sabbatical, as set down in the calendar. The three years thus recorded in history as Sabbatical all occur at intervals from each other divisible into seven years, and are also all in septennial series counting

* Jos. Ant. xiii. 8, 1.　　　† Jos. Ant. ix. 3–5,

downwards from the Sabbatical year B.C. 492, already fixed; thus proving that the intercalation of the year of Jubilee after the 49th year was not in practice during the time of the second temple, as we have already shown that it was not under the first temple.

Let us now go back to the times before the captivity, during which a remarkable instance of two fallow years in succession, which could only take place when the Sabbatical year was followed by a Jubilee, is referred to by the prophet Isaiah, the dates of which have been fixed with precision by Demetrius. That historian, we have seen,* informs us that Sennacherib the Assyrian king had carried away captives from Judea in Feb. B.C. 688, having invaded and ravaged the country, we may assume, in the previous year, B.C. 689; and from the prophet Isaiah we learn that the year of this invasion was the fourteenth year of the reign of Hezekiah, which is B.C. 689, according to our table. Now, counting upwards without intercalation from the fixed Sabbatical year B.C. 493–2, or from either of the three years, we have just shown to have been actually observed as Sabbaths, we have set down the year B C. 689–8, that is, from seed-time in B.C. 689 to seed-time in B.C. 688, as Sabbatical in our calendar, and we have also set down the following year B.C. 688–7, as a year of Jubilee, counting downwards, without intercalation, in regular series of forty-nine years from the division of the land by Joshua. For, considering that there were counted exactly 490 years from the 12th of Solomon to the year B.C. 492, and that the 4th of Solomon was the 480th year from the Exodus, whether we take this year, B.C. 492, or the date of the battle of Carchemish, B.C. 582, as the fundamental date of Hebrew chronology, the year of the Exodus must necessarily have fallen in the year B.C. 1470. And, as the Israelites spent forty years in the wilderness, and seven years in subduing the land of Canaan, after which the land was divided amongst the tribes, the division of the land must have taken place in the

* P. 306.

year B.C. 1423, as set down in the accompanying table; * and
from this date the Sabbatical years and Jubilees are reckoned,
without intercalation, down to the year B.C. 689-8, which was
Sabbatical, and B.C. 688-7, which was the fifteenth year of Jubilee. If then there be truth in this reckoning, the fourteenth
and fifteenth years of the reign of Hezekiah must both have
been consecrated years of rest.

Now on reference to the history of these two years as
related by Isaiah, we find every reason to believe that the
fourteenth year of Hezekiah was Sabbatical, and also that
it was followed by a year of Jubilee. During the Sabbatical
year it was commanded, " Thou shalt neither sow thy field
nor prune thy vineyard; that which groweth of its own
accord of thy harvest thou shalt not reap "—" the Sabbath
of the land shall be meat for you." During the year of
Jubilee it was commanded, " Thou shalt not sow, neither
reap that which groweth of itself "—" *ye shall eat the increase
thereof out of the field.*" The meaning of the command is
this: the owner of the soil shall not be at liberty, during
the years of rest, to carry out of the field and appropriate
to himself the produce of the soil; but the spontaneous products of the soil shall be open to all, to gather *and eat in the
field.* The presence of Sennacherib's hostile army about
Jerusalem, of course, would have prevented the gathering
and eating of the fruits in the field; and with reference,
therefore, to his threatened attack on that city, Isaiah declares, " He shall not come into this city, nor shoot an
arrow there, nor come before it with shield," &c.—" and
this shall be a sign unto you," that is, a proof to you that
Sennacherib *shall not come near the city.* " Ye shall eat
this year,"—the fourteenth of Hezekiah,—" such things as
grow of themselves, and in the second year that which
springeth of the same; and in the third year sow ye, and

* Caleb, who had been sent in the second year after the Exodus to explore
the land, said to Joshua at the time of the division, — " Forty years old was I
when Moses sent me to spy out the land, and now, behold I am this day eighty
and five years old " (Josh. xiv. 7, 10), whence we learn that the Israelites had
employed seven years in subjugating the land.— Seder Olam Rabba, ch. xi.

reap, and plant vineyards, and eat the fruits thereof."[*] It
has been suggested by some, in explanation of this passage,
that the presence of Sennacherib's army near Jerusalem
would have prevented the cultivation of the land for two
successive years, thus compelling the people to subsist on
the spontaneous products of the land for that space of time;
and that no reference, therefore, is here made to the appointed
years of fallow. But this occupation of the land for two
years by the invading army does not well accord with the
sudden destruction of that army spoken of in the fourteenth
year;[†] nor can it be explained how the forced fallow of the
land for two years by Sennacherib's army could be construed
into a sign that Sennacherib's army should *not* approach
Jerusalem. On the other hand, it is obvious that the prophet
makes use of the very words which, in the book of Leviticus,
are applied to the Sabbatical year, and to the Jubilee, or
year of liberty—words needing no explanation to his hearers
in the presence of those two consecrated years; and it is
clear that the eating of the spontaneous products of the soil
could only be a sign in verification of the prediction of the
prophet, by their being gathered and eaten *in the field* by the
people, regardless of the threats of siege, and by their so
fulfilling the appointed duties of the consecrated years then
present, according to the law. The exact coincidence of
these two computed years of Sabbath and Jubilee with the
dates of two such years alluded to by Isaiah in the fourteenth
and fifteenth years of Hezekiah, leaves little room for doubt
that the first of these two years, B.C. 689–8, was Sabbatical,
and the second, B.C. 688–7, a year of Jubilee.

But if Demetrius has thus established that the fourteenth
year of Hezekiah, B.C. 689–8, was Sabbatical, he has also by
inference established that the fifteenth year of Asa, B.C. 920–19,
and the third year of Jehosaphat, B.C. 892–1, were Sabbatical
as set down in the calendar. Now, " Moses commanded
them, saying, At the end of every seven years, in the solemn-

---

* 2 Kings, xix. 29 ; Isa. xxxvii. 30.

† According to the annals of Sennacherib, found in his palace, he was no
more than one year in Judæa.

ity of the year of release, in the Feast of Tabernacles, when
all Israel is come to appear before the Lord thy God in the
place which He shall chose, thou shalt read this law before
all Israel in their hearing."*   And this reading and proclamation of the law is exactly what appears to have been performed in the two years just mentioned; for, although we
read nothing concerning the celebration of the Feast of
Tabernacles, which more probably was neglected than observed in those perverse and unworthy times, we do find that
in the fifteenth year of Asa, in the third month, before the
close of the computed Sabbatical year B.C. 920–19, when,
"after a long season, Israel had been without the true God,
and without a teaching priest, and without law "—" they entered into a covenant to seek the Lord God of their fathers
with all their heart and with all their soul."†   At this time,
therefore, the law must have been " read before all Israel in
their hearing."

Again, in the third year of Jehosaphat, that is in the
second half of the computed Sabbatical year, B.C. 892-1, thus
confirmed by Demetrius, that prince commanded the princes
and Levites to travel throughout the land, taking with them
the book of the law, and accordingly they " went throughout
all the cities of Judah, and taught the people."‡

Again, in the thirteenth year of Josiah, that is, in the
course of the second half of the Sabbatical year B.C. 605–4,
in the autumn probably of the latter of these two years, there
occurred a remarkable preaching of the law.   For in that
year the prophet Jeremiah commenced his forty years of
warning to the people of Jerusalem, which ended in the
destruction of the city :§ and that this preaching began about
the time of " the solemnity of the year of release," that is,
during the Feast of Tabernacles which immediately followed
the completion of the Sabbatical year, may reasonably be
inferred from the figurative allusion by the prophet to the
then actual state of fallow, or of ordained fallow, and to the

* Deut. xxxi. 10.   † 2 Chron. xv. 10.   ‡ 2 Chron. xvii.
Jer. xxv. 3 ; Ezek. iv. 6.

seed-time and cultivation which should then be about to commence. "Thus saith the Lord to the men of Judah and Jerusalem, Break up your fallow ground, and sow not amongst thorns. Circumcise yourselves to the Lord,"* &c. It can hardly be doubted that it was the seed-time and breaking-up of fallow, at the end of the seventh year then present to the minds of his hearers, which gave rise to this expression of the prophet; for although the observance of the Sabbatical year, we know, was neglected by the mass of the nation, in open defiance of the law, we are yet justified in assuming that some few devoted hearts at least were united with Jeremiah, and Hilkiah the high-priest, and the pious king Josiah, in their zealous endeavour at that time to revive the observance of the Mosaic ordinances and ceremonies.

Thus, in addition to the three Sabbatical years recorded by Josephus, and the Sabbatical year in the second year of the reign of Darius, already ascertained — making together four well-defined years of Sabbath after the Captivity — we have other four Sabbatical years before the Captivity, one of which is historically fixed, and the other three marked out by events appropriate specially to the close of the consecrated year, the dates of which are defined with equal precision; and as the intervals between these eight fixed periods are divisible by seven, the inference is unquestionable, that, from the reign of Solomon to the birth of Christ, the Sabbatical years were computed in unbroken series, without intercalation.

We have now cleared the way for a full understanding of the manner in which the year of Jubilee was computed, and are prepared to decide between five different modes of interpretation of this peculiar ordinance which have been suggested by different commentators.

1st. We may dismiss the idea that the year of Jubilee, or fiftieth year, was intercalated between the end of the seventh Sabbatical year and the beginning of the next period of seven weeks of years; for if, as we have shown, the Sabbatical years

* Jer. iv. 3, 4.

were reckoned in continuous septennial series, intercalation of course was impossible.

2nd. The idea of some that the Sabbatical years were reckoned in septennial series, but that the Jubilees were reckoned at intervals of fifty years in succession — thus disconnecting the Jubilee from the Sabbatical year — is untenable, because it is written, " The space of seven Sabbaths of years shall be unto thee forty-and-nine years. Then shalt thou cause the trumpet of the Jubilee to sound." So that the Jubilee must always have marked the close of the Sabbatical year, and so have been connected with it.

3rd. The idea of others, that the Sabbatical years were counted from Nisan to Nisan, and were concurrent with the ecclesiastical year, while the Jubilee was counted from Tisri to Tisri, with the civil year, is equally untenable, as disconnecting the sounding of the trumpet of the Jubilee in the seventh month with the closing of the seventh year.

There are but two modes of interpretation which are worthy of serious consideration, viz.: —

4th. That which identifies the year of Jubilee with the forty-ninth year — an opinion which has the support of many writers of great name;* and,

5th. That which identifies the Jubilee, or fallow year, with the first of the six years of cultivation which followed the Sabbatical year.

This latter interpretation, though at first sight paradoxical, we conceive to be the only true one. Against it, it is urged, with an appearance of great force of reason, that no wise legislator could have entertained the idea of compelling a whole nation to abstain from raising the means of subsistence for two successive years; and also that it is contrary to the terms of the law to suppose that a year of fallow could be concurrent with a year of cultivation: so that the only alternative left, as is assumed, is to identify the Jubilee with the

* Petavius, Calvisius, Strauch, Des Vignoles, Gatterer, and Franck. See Zuchermann, p. 10.

forty-ninth year. Both these objections, we submit, originate simply in a misunderstanding of the law.

At the close of the forty-ninth or Sabbatical year, on the tenth day of the seventh month, the trumpet of the Jubilee was to sound; and on that very day, with the sounding of the trumpet, every bondman became free to return to his family— every man to return to his own possession. Thus far, then, the Jubilee was identical with the year of release,* or Sabbatical year. The sole object of the institution was the recovery of freedom, and of alienated lands : and this object was completed on the day of Atonement which followed the completion of the forty-ninth year. But the fallow of the land which was to follow in the fiftieth year, we maintain was restricted to those few only who, during the past forty-nine years, had been compelled, by poverty, or otherwise, to alienate their property: for to these only were addressed the joyful words, — "It shall be a jubilee unto you, and ye shall return every man unto his possession:" "A Jubilee shall that fiftieth year be unto you, ye shall not sow, neither reap that which groweth of itself, &c. Where is the necessity for applying these words, as is assumed in the objection, to all occupiers of land throughout the nation? The proclamation of "liberty throughout the land unto all the inhabitants thereof," had reference only to those who had been in bondage: and in the same manner these words must be restricted to those only who regained possession of their land, and who, therefore, as a mark of gratitude, were called upon to offer up the firstfruits of their recovered property, by allowing the land to lie fallow, keeping a Sabbath unto the Lord, with its spontaneous produce free to all, to be gathered and eaten in the field. Under the law, thus interpreted, no fear of scarcity could arise from the non-cultivation of the few portions of regained land thus required to lie fallow in the second year; while, at the same time, the fiftieth year of fallow ordained for the few,

---

* The year of release was commanded to be observed by Ezra. (Neh. x. 1.) Maimonides tells us that slaves gave themselves up to revelry and rejoicing for several days before the day of atonement — as during the Roman saturnalia.

might, without contradiction, be commensurate with the first year of cultivation ordained for the many. Philo, as before observed, in his treatise on Festivals, does, indeed, say that the breeders of cattle took the liberty, in the year of Jubilee, of sending their cattle to feed on the most fertile plains, and that this license was not interfered with by the rich owners of the land. But this practice, if general, would seem to have been an act of benevolence somewhat beyond the law, unless, indeed, the permission here spoken of was given merely by owners of lands recovered in the year of Jubilee: for Maimonides, as we shall see, tells us distinctly that the observance of the year of Jubilee was not enforced under the second temple.

We are confirmed in the correctness of this view of the interpretation of the law, by the fact, that, with reference to apprehended scarcity arising from non-cultivation in the seventh year, the question is raised, and answered, "What shall we eat in the seventh year?"* But no such question is raised, or even hinted at, with reference to the two supposed successive years of general fallow, in the forty-ninth and fiftieth years, involving much more serious cause for alarm. The just inference is, that in the mind of the lawgiver no cause for apprehension was anticipated in the strict performance of the law of the Sabbatical year followed by the Jubilee, beyond what had already been disposed of and provided for in the words, "I will command my blessing upon you in the sixth year, and it shall bring forth fruit for three years, *and ye shall sow the eighth year;*"† which words can have no possible reference, except to the fallow of the seventh year; for the Jubilee, we are told, was the fiftieth year, and so, therefore, identical with the eighth, or first year of cultivation.

Our opinion, therefore, is distinct, that the fulfilment of the Jubilee was complete, as regarded the nation in general, at the termination of the forty-ninth year, and that it was computed accordingly at intervals of forty-nine years—that

* Lev. xxv.   † Lev. xxv. 21, 22.

the fiftieth, not the forty-ninth, was the year of Jubilee, to be observed as a year of fallow by those only who regained possession of land in that year—and that the year of Jubilee was commensurate with the first year of cultivation which followed immediately after the Sabbatical year.

And this, in fact, is the tradition preserved by Maimonides, as regards the mode of computation after the captivity, who writes, " After the destruction of the first temple the computation" (of Sabbatical years and Jubilees) "perished, because it was abolished" (that is, because it could no longer be observed): " the land then remained desolate for seventy years, after which the second temple was built, which lasted 420 years.* In the seventh year from the building" (which might be either the year B.C. 486, or 479, in our reckoning, counted either from the commencement or the finishing of the building) " Ezra returned and restored the computation a second time. From that year, therefore, they began to reckon another Sabbatical era, *and constituted the thirteenth year of the second temple* (B.C. 479) *Sabbatical.* They numbered from thence seven Sabbaths, and consecrated the fiftieth year. For, although the Jubilee was not celebrated under the second temple, yet the computation and consecration of the Sabbatical years was preserved:" and again, " The forty-ninth year was Sabbatical, the fiftieth the year of Jubilee: the fiftieth and last year, however, was the first of the six years of the Sabbatical week: and so on for each successive Jubilee." †

Thus we arrive at the same opinion as that entertained by Rabbi Jehuda, in the latter half of the second century, after Christ, which is expressed in these two sayings.

1st. " The year of Jubilee is included in the subsequent Sabbatical cycle."

2nd. " The fiftieth year counts in a twofold way." ‡

* No heed need be given to this false computation of 420 years. The traditional interpretation put upon the book of Ezra, however, is valuable.

† Maimonides de Schemittah et Jubilæo. Vorst's translation in Gantz' Chronology, p. 211.

‡ Zuchermann, p. 12.

And also at the same opinion as that entertained by a much earlier writer, viz.— the author of the "Book of Jubilees," who, according to Ewald, was a Jew of the first century before Christ, and living therefore when, as Philo informs us, the years of Jubilee were known and observed. This author, whose work has recently been discovered in an Ethiopic translation, "reckons by Jubilees of precisely seven weeks, i. e. of forty-nine years."*

Counting, then, according to this rule of computation, from the year B.C. 1423, when the land was divided amongst the tribes by Joshua,— Caleb, who was forty when he first searched the land, then being eighty-five years old,†— we find that the year B.C. 982-1, in which Solomon dedicated the temple of Jerusalem, was a year of Jubilee — that the year B.C. 688-7, or fifteenth year of Hezekiah, was a year of Jubilee, as already determined — and that the year B.C. 492-1, or the year when the building of the second temple was commenced, was also a year of Jubilee. And, as regards this latter date, it is confirmed by the tradition preserved by Rabbi Eliezer, one of the earliest of Jewish writers extant, some say contemporary with Gamaliel, the teacher of St. Paul,‡ in the first century A.D., others placing him as late as the fourth century. " Ezra, Jerubbabel the son of Schealtiel, and Jeshua the son of Jehotzedek," writes Eliezer, " went up from Babylon, and began to lament in the temple of the Lord." — " the Samaritans came against them in battle, 180,000 men. §   But how Samaritans? were they not Cutheans? called Samaritans, however, from the name of the city of Samaria. They also endeavoured to slay Nehemiah, as it is said, ' Come, and let us consult together in the villages,' &c. Moreover, before that they impeded the work of God (that is, the restoration of the temple) for two years, *even to the year of Jubilee.*"‖

* Ewald's History of Israel, vol. i. pp. 204, 205.
† Josh. xiv. 7-10.
‡ Vorst's Preface.
§ An instance of Oriental tendency to exaggerate numbers.
‖ Pirke, R. Eliezer. Vorst's translation, p. 101.

We now proceed to show how the calendar of Sabbatical years and Jubilees may be applied in illustration of the third period of the Jewish Church, or 490 years from Darius to the birth of Christ; and how the obvious reference in the ninth chapter of the book of Daniel to a series of Sabbatical years, hitherto an insuperable stumbling-block in the way of interpreters, is, on our principle of reckoning, made plain, so that he who runs may read.

We have observed that the words of Daniel in this chapter, " Seventy weeks are determined upon thy people and upon thy holy city," were accomplished on the termination of the last of the seventy penitential Sabbaths, which were fulfilled during the desolation of Jerusalem, ending in the first year of Darius, and that the words were so understood by Daniel himself, as containing a direct and special answer to his petition for the restoration of Jerusalem, concerning which he had so fervently prayed. Nevertheless, if there be truth in our reckoning, no one can fail to perceive that these same words were intended to cover a hidden and mystical meaning, referable to seventy weeks of years yet again to be accomplished on the people and the " holy city," terminating, as the event has proved, in the anointing of the " Most Holy," the heir to the throne of David, " Messiah the Prince," the Holy One of Israel.* So that, whether the words of the prophet be interpreted prospectively or retrospectively, they were literally fulfilled in the accomplishment of 490 years, or seventy Sabbatical weeks, as registered in the calendar.

Thus far the interpretation of the words of Daniel is plain and without difficulty. The difficulty which has ever existed, and which will continue to exist, in connexion with the common Biblical reckoning, is, how to interpret the following words, — " Know, therefore, and understand, that from the going forth of the commandment to restore and to build Jerusalem unto Messiah the Prince, *shall be seven weeks and three-score and two weeks:* the street shall be built again, and the

* Aben-Esra and Abarbenel both apply the words " holy of holies " to Messiah."

wall, even in troublous times. And after *threescore and two weeks* shall Messiah be cut off," &c. The repetition of the term, "threescore and two weeks," marks it as a defined period not to be passed over without separate interpretation. While the period of "seven weeks" is one of marked significance in connexion with the Sabbatical cycles. Nevertheless, in most modern explanations of the prophecy, these precise terms are left without any attempt at explanation, and the common notion is, that "seven weeks, and sixty-two weeks," is merely a mode of expressing a period of sixty-nine weeks: and in one mode or other, sixty-nine weeks are made to terminate either with the death or ministry of Jesus Christ. But this arrangement merely passes over the difficulty of the problem without solution. Others, such as Pontanus, Cuninghame,* and Sir I. Newton, clearly recognise the Jubilaic period in the words, "seven weeks;" and the first of these interpreters proposes to reckon the whole period as sixty-two weeks and seven weeks,† thus reversing the order of the weeks and Jubilee, as placed by the prophet, and placing the birth of Christ in a year of Jubilee: while Newton, to escape the difficulty, suggests that the "seven weeks," or period of Jubilee, form a separate and future period, terminating in the second coming of the Messiah. These two arrangements are both contradictory of the words which place the coming of "Messiah the Prince," at the expiration of sixty-two weeks, *not in the year of Jubilee.* All this is highly unsatisfactory, and merely illustrates the great difficulty, and, indeed, impossibility, of reconciling the weeks of Daniel with the calendar of weeks and Jubilees, in conformity with the common Biblical reckoning. This conclusion was so obvious to Prideaux, that, in a masterly treatise on the connexion of sacred and profane history, he boldly dismisses as erroneous the idea that Daniel

* "Synopsis of Chronology," p. 169. Ussher computes from his supposed 20th of Artaxerxes, B.C. 454, which is not even Sabbatical. Petavius from one year higher. Prideaux and Greswell from B.C. 458, Newton from 457; both Sabbatical, but not Jubilaic. Marshall from B.C. 445, counting in years of 360 days each.

† Pontanus. "Chron. de Sab.," p. 147.

has made any reference whatever in this prophecy to actual
Sabbatical weeks. Prideaux, in the preface to his great work,
writes, " I have in the series of this history taken no notice
either of the Jubilee or the Sabbatical years of the Jews, both
because of the uselessness, and also uncertainty, of them. They
are useless, because they help not to the explaining of anything either in the Holy Scriptures, or the histories of the
times which we treat of: and they are uncertain, because it
doth not appear when or how they were observed :" * and
again, " They act most out of the way in this matter, who
would confine Daniel's prophecy of the seventy weeks to so
many Shemittahs as if these seventy weeks fell in exactly
with seventy Shemittahs; that the first week began with
the first year of a Shemittah, or Sabbatical week, and
ended with a Sabbatical year, and so all the rest down
to the last of the whole number : and to this end some
have perplexed themselves in vain to find out Sabbatical years
to suit their hypothesis, and fix them to times to which they
did never belong: whereas the prophecy means no more
than by the seventy weeks to express seventy times seven
years, that is, 490 in the whole, without any relation to Shemittahs, or Sabbatical years."† It is needless to say that we
entirely dissent from these observations. Far more to the
purpose, in our opinion, are the words of the illustrious Newton, who remarks, " I content myself with observing, that, as
the seventy, and sixty-two weeks, were Jewish weeks, ending
with Sabbatical years : so the *seven weeks are the compass of
a Jubilee,* and begin and end with actions proper for a Jubilee."‡

It is interesting to observe the working of the mind of the
great philosopher under the difficulties of this question ; for it
is certain that he has laid down with truth and exactness some
novel points of chronology and interpretation, which, if he
had carried them to their just conclusions, would have led

* Prideaux's Connec.: Pref. p. xvi.
† Prideaux's Connec.: Pref. p. xix.
‡ Sir I. Newton, on Daniel, &c., p. 133.

him clearly to the solution of the problem. Yet, being unable to free himself from the fetters of the received chronology, it would seem that he has been driven to reject the legitimate results of his own sagacious reasoning, and to falsify historical facts worked out with much labour and ingenuity.

1st. As an astronomer, Newton adhered to the leading date, B.C. 585, as that of the eclipse of Thales: in which conclusion he has been confirmed, as we have seen, by the accurate calculations of modern astronomy.

2nd. He alone, of all interpreters, has identified " Darius, the son of Ahasuerus, of the seed of the Medes," with Darius son or successor of Ahasuerus, or Cyaxares II., whose father, Astyages, married in the year of the eclipse, B.C. 585; the necessary conclusion from which is, that as Darius " took the kingdom " (whatever that expression may signify) when about sixty-two years of age, that event could not have taken place less than about eighty or ninety years after his grandfather's marriage in 585, or, at any rate, till long after Darius the son of Hystaspes had been upon the throne. And since two mighty kings, bearing the same title, cannot be supposed to have been ruling at the same time over the same dominions, the identity of Darius the Mede with Darius son of Hystaspes is the only just result. And again, if this identification be correct, then must the son of Hystaspes have taken "the kingdom" in the sixty-second year of his age, that is, in B.C. 492.

3rd. Newton alone, of all interpreters, has pointed out that the completion of the wall of Jerusalem by Nehemiah the son of Hachaliah took place, as Josephus has related, in the twenty-eighth year of Artaxerxes Longimanus,* in the year B.C. 437, that is to say, just sixty-two Sabbatical weeks before the birth of Christ.

4th. He has also truly, as we believe, interpreted the " seven weeks " of Daniel, as signifying a period of Jubilee; and the " threescore and two weeks unto Messiah" as sixty-

* In our copies of Josephus it is written twenty-eighth year of Xerxes, bu this is clearly incorrect: Xerxes did not reign alone thirty-two years.—Nehem. v. 14.

two Sabbatical weeks, ending with the birth of Christ, B.C.
8–9 : the direct inference from which is, seeing that there is
no interval between the two periods, that these weeks must
have commenced in B.C. 485, and that a period of Jubilee was
completed in B.C. 436.

5th. By a searching and acute analysis of the books of
Ezra and Nehemiah, Newton alone, of all interpreters, has
pointed out that Nehemiah, the son of Hachaliah, was the contemporary and companion of Zerubbabel, and also of certain
priests who came up with Zerubbabel,* who sealed the covenant
with Ezra after his return to Jerusalem :† the result of which
discovery is, to place the sealing of that covenant, and the
contemporaneous events, not earlier than between fifty and
sixty years before the death of Nehemiah, or somewhere about
the years B.C. 480 or 490; for Nehemiah was alive in the
thirty-second year of Axtaxerxes, B.C. 433,‡ and lived probably
as late as the year B.C. 430.

6th.   Lastly, with Prideaux, he truly considered that " the
dispersed Jews became a people and city, when they first returned into a polity or body politic in the time of Ezra."§   And

---

* Zerubbabel was also contemporary with Mordecai who had been carried
captive eleven years before the destruction of the temple.

† Nehem. xii. 1-8 ; x. 1-9.

‡ Observations on Daniel, p. 131.   § The Peloponnesian war began in spring
(An. 1, Olymp. 87), as Diodorus, Eusebius, and all other authors agree.   It
began two months before Pythodorus ceased to be Archon (Thucyd. 1. ii.), that
is, in April, two months before the end of the Olympic year.   Now, the years
of this war are most certainly determined by the fifty years' distance of its first
year, from the transit of Xerxes inclusively (Thucyd. 1. ii.), or 48 years exclusively (Eratosth. apud Clem. Alex.), by the 69 years' distance of its end, or
the 27th year from the beginning of Alexander's reign in Greece, by the acting
of the Olympic games in its 4th and 12th years (Thucyd. 1. v.). and by three
eclipses of the sun and one of the moon, mentioned by Thucydides and Xenophon.   Now Thucydides, an unquestionable witness, tells us that the news of
the death of Artaxerxes Longimanus was brought to Ephesus. and from thence
by some Athenians to Athens in the 7th year of the Peloponnesian war, when
the winter half-year was running, and therefore he died (An. 4, Olymp. 88)
in the end of An. J. P. 4289 (B C. 425). suppose a month or two before mid-
winter. for so long the news would be in coming.   Now, Artaxerxes Longimanus
reigned 40 years by the consent of Diodorus, Eusebius, Jerome, Sulpicius, or 41,
according to Ptolemy's Canon, Clem. Alex. 1. 1, Strom., Chron. Alex., Abul-

if his inference be correct, that Ezra sealed the covenant with the priests who returned with Zerubbabel, then the just conclusion is, that the king in whose seventh year Ezra returned, who is called Artaxerxes, was in fact no other than Xerxes.

In these six propositions it would appear that Newton has, in fact, solved the difficulties of this perplexing, though plainly uttered prophecy, the sacred problem, which has baffled interpretation from the days of Clemens of Alexandria, and Africanus, to the present time; and it is difficult to believe that Newton could have been unconscious of the direct conclusions derivable from his own statement of facts. Being bound, however, in the chains of a conventional chronology, which rests, indeed upon the authority of the most charming and truthful of historians, but the most loose and untrustworthy of chronologists, he has been content to abandon the advanced and tenable position to which he had virtually attained, and to allow himself to be diverted into a series of untenable conclusions at variance with his premises, and into which no one has since found any inclination to follow him.

The eclipse which Herodotus distinctly places in the reign of Cyaxares I., the father of Astyages, he has in contradiction, of all authority, placed in the reign of Cyaxares II., the son of Astyages. The "seven weeks," so truly declared by him to represent "the compass of a Jubilee," he refers, as before said, to the time of the second coming of Christ. The sealing of the covenant by Nehemiah, together with Ezra and the priests, who came up with Zerubbabel, he places in the year B.C. 536, in the reign of Cyrus, instead of the year B.C. 479, or 7th year of Xerxes, thus leading to the most improbable inference that Nehemiah and Ezra must have both lived to

pharagius, Nicephorus, including therein the reigns of his successors, Xerxes and Sogdian, as Abulpharagius informs us. After Artaxerxes reigned his son Xerxes two months, and Sogdian seven months; but their reign is not reckoned apart in summing up the years of the kings, but is included in the 40 or 41 years' reign of Artaxerxes. Omit these nine months, and the precise reign of Artaxerxes will leave 39 years and 3 months. And, therefore, since his reign ended in the beginning of winter, An. J. P. 4289, it began between midsummer and autumn, An. J. P. 4950, B.C. 464.—(Newton, on Daniel, p. 139.)

the age of about 120 years. And he suggests that Darius the son of Ahasuerus, the mighty ruler over 120 provinces of the Persian empire, was a prince unknown in secular history, or monumental records, and nowhere alluded to, except in the Book of Daniel.

Now, when did the command—"to restore and to build Jerusalem"—go forth? Clearly at the time when, by the re-issue of the decree of Cyrus, the Jews were permitted to re-establish themselves as a body politic, and when the Jewish laws and institutions, both secular and ecclesiastical, were revived at Jerusalem. This, indeed, was not fully effected till the return of Ezra in the 7th year of Artaxerxes (Xerxes), B.C. 479; but the computation of the times of the "holy city" commenced seven years earlier, on the completion and dedication of the temple in B.C. 486-5; and from that date they began to reconstruct all that had been in abeyance during their captivity, and to compute the new reckoning of the year of Jubilee, as applicable to the restitution of alienated lands. The command to build Jerusalem was a command from God, and was merely confirmed by the decrees of the kings of Persia; and that command was given when the Lord God of heaven charged Cyrus to build him an house at Jerusalem, and fulfilled at the time of the completion of the new temple. The first words of the prophecy itself, as already interpreted, lead to this conclusion. For the seventy weeks determined upon the "holy city," as we have seen, were reckoned by the heavenly messenger, not from the capture of Jerusalem by David, but from the date of the dedication of the temple by Solomon. Jerusalem had long before become the seat of the throne of David, and the tabernacle and the ark of the covenant had long before the time of Solomon been brought up to the city; yet, not till the consecration of the temple did the times of the "holy city" begin to be reckoned. So, again, though many of the Jews had returned to Jerusalem in the reign of Cyrus, and though, no doubt, a tabernacle and altar had been set up for the celebration of the temple-worship immediately after their return, yet the holy city was not complete till the dedication of the temple in the sixth or seventh year of Darius, from which time the years of Jubilee were again to be reckoned. The completion of the temple is spoken of by Ezra in these emphatic words, as marking the importance of the epoch: " And they builded and finished it, according to the *commandment of the God of Israel,* and according to the commandment of Cyrus, and Darius, and Artaxerxes, king of Persia."* Josephus, also, very clearly marks this as the time of the re-establishment of the government in the hands of native rulers. Speaking of the great passover, which was celebrated at the time of the dedication, he writes: " They performed sacrifices of thanksgiving, because God had led them again to the land of their fathers, and to the laws thereto belonging, and had rendered the mind of the king of Persia favourable to them. So these men offered the largest sacrifices on these accounts, and used great magnificence in the worship of God, and dwelt in Jerusalem, *and made use of a form of government that was aristocratical, but mixed with an oligarchy, for the high-priests were at the head of their affairs,* until the posterity of the Asmoneans set up kingly government." †

The solution of the words of the prophecy, in conformity with the calendar of Sabbatical years and jubilees, stands, therefore, simply thus :—

1. The command to restore the temple, or sanctuary, went forth by the mouth of Haggai and Zechariah in the second year of Darius, in the year of Jubilee B.C. 491, seventy weeks before the birth of Christ.

2. The going forth of the command to restore and to build Jerusalem, that is, the " holy city," took place when the command formerly given by the Lord God of heaven to Cyrus, was

---

* Ezra, vi. 14. In the book of Esdras we read, " And they finished these things by the *commandment* of the Lord God of Israel, and with the *consent* of Cyrus, Darius, and Artaxerxes, kings of Persia." vii. 4, Διὰ προστάγματος τοῦ Κυρίου Θεοῦ Ἰσραὴλ, καὶ μετὰ τῆς γνώμης Κύρου, &c. Josephus writes, κατὰ τὰ προστάγματα τοῦ Θεοῦ Ἰσραὴλ καὶ μετὰ βουλήσεως Κύρου.

† Whiston's Josephus, Ant. xi. iv. 8.

re-promulgated and carried into effect in the **sixth year of
Darius**, that is, in the year B.C. **485, at the time of the**
dedication of the second temple, **sixty-nine weeks before the
birth of Christ.**

3. The wall of Jerusalem **was** dedicated by **Nehemiah,**
" in troublous times," after the expiration of " seven weeks,"
counting from the dedication of the temple, and in the **year of**
Jubilee B.C. 436, or 29th of Artaxerxes Longimanus; which
year of Jubilee is marked also by the examination of the genealogical registers in that year, and the consecration of **the**
city wall, which was one of the necessary ceremonies of the
year of Jubilee.*

4. The birth of Christ took place in the autumn or **winter**
of B.C. 3, in the beginning of the Sabbatical year, after " threescore and two weeks," counted from the dedication of the wall.

Thus far, then, as regards the Sabbatical years and Jubilees, and their use in illustration of the times of the **Jewish**
kingdom and commonwealth; and considering that the septennial division of time is one of the peculiar characteristics of
sacred history, even from the first six days or periods of creation and supplemental Sabbath, down to the sounding of the
seventh and final trumpet of the Apocalypse, and that the
peculiar reckoning by weeks of years was a special ordinance
of God to the Jewish nation, let no one hereafter, taking up
the subject of Daniel's weeks,—the one single occasion when
weeks of years are spoken of in the Bible after the time of
Joshua,—allow himself to be persuaded that the Sabbatical
years and Jubilees " are useless, because they help not to the
explaining anything in the Holy Scriptures," or that " they
act most out of the way who would confine Daniel's prophecy

---

* " As in the days of Joshua they were bound to pay tithes, to observe the
years of remission, and the jubilees, and also the walled cities were sanctified,
so at the entrance in the time of Ezra they were bound by the laws to pay tithes,
to observe the years of remission, and the jubilees, and they also sanctified their
walled cities." (Seder Olam, ch. xxx.) According to the opinion of Michaelis
and Ewald, the tables of genealogies were corrected and filled up in the **year of**
Jubilee. See Smith's Dictionary, *voce* Jubilee.

of the ' seventy weeks' to so many shemittahs, as if these seventy weeks fell in exactly with seventy shemittahs, each ending with a Sabbatical year."

Before we close these remarks, it is necessary to offer a few words in explanation of one of the principal features of this interpretation. How, it may be asked, are we to believe that Ezra returned to Jerusalem in the year B.C. 479, when he tells us himself that he received his commission in the seventh year of Artaxerxes, which year, according to our own reckoning, would appear to be B.C. 458?

With regard to this question, we read in the book of Ezra, " Now after these things," that is to say, after the repair and dedication of the Temple,—which is described by Haggai as lying "waste" in the second year of Darius,—" in the reign of Artaxerxes, king of Persia," "Ezra went up from Babylon," " and he came to Jerusalem in the fifth month, which was in the seventh year of the king." (Ezra, vii. 1–7.)

According to the common interpretation of the book of Ezra, which assumes that the dedication of the Temple took place in B.C. 516, and the return of Ezra in B.C. 458: Ezra is here supposed to declare that he came to Jerusalem fifty-eight years after the repair of the desolations of the Temple, and the history of the Jews is thus left blank during that long period. This, however, must be a false interpretation of the passage. For what does Ezra say in his prayer immediately after his return? " Our God hath not forsaken us in our bondage, but hath extended mercy unto us in the sight of the *kings* of Persia " (Darius and Artaxerxes, who had just commanded the Temple to be built), " to give us a reviving, *to set up the house of our God, and to repair the desolations thereof.*" It is not reasonable to assume, either that Ezra is here referring to a setting up of the house of God, and to desolations which had been repaired fifty-eight years before his time, or that so long an interval could have elapsed without producing some event in connexion with the Temple worthy of record in his history. He is evidently appealing to things present both to the eyes and hearts of his hearers, and when he tells us that " after

these things " he returned to Jerusalem, alluding to the repairs
of the Temple, he clearly points out the time of his return as
not long after the completion of those repairs.　The writer of
the Seder Olam, Maimonides, David Gantz, and all the Jewish
writers support this interpretation, affirming that he came
up in the seventh year of the second Temple, which, counted
from the completion of the building, was B.C. 479, or the
seventh year of Xerxes.　So that when Ezra styles this king
Artaxerxes, he is in fact speaking of the king commonly
known in secular history as Xerxes.* This is not only
the opinion and tradition of the Talmud and of modern Jews,
but was also the tradition and opinion in the days of Josephus,
who, in his history of the Wars,† speaks of the return of the
Jews from Babylon in the reign of Xerxes, and in the Antiquities writes, ' On the death of Darius, Xerxes, his son, took
the kingdom;' "Now about this time a son of Joshua, whose
name was Joachim, was the high-priest.　Moreover, there was
now in Babylon a righteous man, and one that enjoyed a great
reputation among the multitude.　He was the principal priest
of the people, and his name was Esdras."‡　Josephus then
goes on to say that Esdras returned to Jerusalem in the reign
of Xerxes, and during the high-priesthood of Joachim, not of
Eliashib, as commonly supposed.　This, again, appears to be
confirmed by Nehemiah, who, after giving a list of the priests
and Levites who came up with Zerubbabel, writes, "These
were in the days of Joiakim, the son of Jeshuah, the son of
Jozadak, and in the days of Nehemiah, the governor, and
of Ezra the priest, the scribe;"§ thus coupling the times of
Nehemiah and Ezra with those of Zerubbabel, who built the
temple.　This identification of Artaxerxes with Xerxes clears
up one of the greatest perplexities in the book of Ezra.　For
who has not stumbled when endeavouring to interpret the

---

* " Arta," is merely an affix common to many Persian names.　It signifies
great, according to Herodotus.
† Wars, ii. vi. 2.
‡ Whiston's Josephus, Ant., xi. v. 1.
§ Nehem. xii. 26.

fourth chapter of Ezra, where he speaks of king Artaxerxes,* who obstructed the building of Jerusalem : and who has not wondered at finding Artaxerxes coupled with Darius in the command to build the temple? Jewish commentators infer that Artaxerxes and Darius must therefore have been† one and the same king. Josephus, who was deeply tainted with the conventional heathen chronology of his day, supposes that Artaxerxes must have been Cambyses. While most modern interpreters would wish us to believe that Smerdis the Magian is the king here referred to. As if Ezra, who was about the court of Persia, was unacquainted with the true titles of the kings he speaks of. But if the Temple was finished in the year B.C. 486 or 485, as we have determined, then can there be no question as to who was the Persian king associated with Darius at that time. For Herodotus ‡ tells us that about that very time, that is to say, about four years after the battle of Marathon, which was fought in the year B.C. 490, Darius declared Xerxes, son of 'Atossa, to be his heir and successor, having at the same time raised him to the throne. (ἀποδέξας δὲ βασιλῆα Πέρσησι Δαρεῖος Ξερξεα.) Plutarch, also, copying from some other historian, relates how, on the decision of Darius, his elder brother made his obeisance, and taking him by the hand led him to the throne. It was, therefore, during that short interval only, between the appointment of Xerxes and death of Darius, when Darius and Xerxes were associated

---

* This Artaxerxes is called Ahasuerus, *i. e.* Xerxes, in the previous verse, in the Hebrew extract. By the Chaldee writer he is called Artaxerxes, his title at a later date. Ezra, iv. 6–8.

† " Ezras scriba adscendit è Babel Hierosolymam cumque ipso captivitas anno septimo Artaxerxis, uti conscriptum est in libro Ezræ, cap. vi. Atque ex narratione Seder Olam, cap. 30. Darius ædificavit templum ; omnes enim reges Persæ vocabantur Artaxerxes, uti omnes reges Ægypti vocitabantur Pharaones, prout explicabitur, &c. Itaque Ezras non tardavit in terram Israelis adscendere, anno enim sexto absoluta est ædificatio, et anno septimo ex Babel adscendit Hierosolymam. At vero si asseratur, Artaxerxem non fuisse Darium, tum mirum est cur Ezras non adscenderit toto tempore Darii, et integris sex annis Artaxerxis. Sed planum est hunc *Darium fuisse Artaxerxem.*"—" Chron. Sac. Prof." R. David Gantz, p. 56.

‡ Herod. vii. 2–4.

together on the throne, that the building of the **Temple could**
have been finished.*

But we have observed that Ezra, who was about the court
of Persia, must have been acquainted with the real title of the
king who gave him his commission; and if the real title of that
king was Xerxes, how does it come to pass that he gives him,
on three occasions, the title Artaxerxes? We have always
argued that Daniel, when speaking of Darius, his master, could
not be pointing to a king known by the title **Cyaxares**; and
Ezra, when speaking of Artaxerxes, could not, as we have just
said, have been referring to Cambyses or Smerdis.   How, then,
can he be supposed to be referring to Xerxes under **this title?**
The reply to this question we think is satisfactory.   There is
much reason for believing that Xerxes, or Ahasuerus, towards
the latter part of his reign, had assumed the title **Artaxerxes,**
and that it was during the time when he bore the latter title
that Ezra wrote his history.   We read, in the **Septuagint**
version of the book of Daniel, that " Artaxerxes, of the seed of
the Medes, took the kingdom, Darius being full of years, and
venerable with old age."   On the common supposition that the
Darius here spoken of was Cyaxares, these words have always
been, and ever will be, inexplicable; but, knowing as we now
do, that the son of Hystaspes is the king here referred to by
Daniel, it is unquestionable that the Artaxerxes who is here
declared to have taken the kingdom in the extreme old age of
Darius, was no other than Xerxes, and that Xerxes, therefore,
was known to the writer of this passage under the title Artaxerxes.   Again, Themistocles we know fled from Athens to
the court of Persia about the year B.C. 473, or 472, eight or
nine years before the accession of Artaxerxes Longimanus,
according to the canon of Ptolemy, Diodorus, Eusebius, Jerome,

---

* " Initium Xerxes cum patre incipientis imperare sumendum ab anno, qui
est quintus a clade Marathoniâ, Periodi autem Juliani 4227 = B.C. 487."—Scaliger de Emend. Temp. p. 406. Petavius writes, " Xerxes a patre Dario desig-
natus rex anno exacto tertio post cladem Marathoniam, quod anno circiter
Olympiadis 73 secundo contigit, Darii ineunte 35, J. P. 4227." Scaliger we
must presume intended to write quartus, not quintus. Both place the accession
of Xerxes one year too early. The date was B.C. 486.

and Sulpicius. Yet Charon of Lampsachus attests that he fled to the court of Artaxerxes; and Thucydides goes so far as to affirm that he fled to Artaxerxes, son of Xerxes. Much controversy has taken place upon this question; and while Ussher, Petavius, Kruger, Hengstenberg, and many others, are inclined to throw back the reign of Artaxerxes Longimanus eight or nine years earlier than the common date, Dodwell, Clinton, and others of equal authority, contend that Themistocles must have arrived in Persia so many years later than would appear from history. Plutarch informs us that Ephorus, Dinon, Clitarchus, and Heraclides, and the greatest number of authorities in his days, represented Themistocles as flying to the court of Xerxes. The only possible way of reconciling these conflicting opinions is by assuming that Xerxes had taken the title Artaxerxes when Themistocles arrived in Persia, and this we believe to be the solution of the difficulty.

We have already pointed out that the association of Xerxes with his father Darius, under the title of Ahasuerus,* may have taken place as early as the year B.C. 494; and in support of this opinion which we have rested much upon an Egyptian monument, on which Dr. Birch seems to think that the 13th year of Xerxes may be represented as concurrent with the 36th of Darius. Libanius countenances this view, when relating that Darius and Xerxes, united on the throne, made preparation for ten years after the battle of Marathon for the invasion of Greece;† while both Aristotle and Pliny ‡ speak of Darius as alive at the time of that invasion. This mode of computation certainly agrees well with the reckoning of Maimonides, who places Ezra's return in the seventh year of the new temple, which would thus be concurrent also with the seventh year of Xerxes, the 13th year of the new temple being B.C. 479. Pending, however, some further confirmation of this testimony of the monument, that Xerxes held some regal appointment under his father as early as B.C. 494, we may safely adhere to the direct testimony of Herodotus, that it was in the fourth year after the battle of

* Ezra, vi. 14.   † Ussher's Annals, p. 173.   ‡ Ibid. p. 175.

Marathon that Xerxes was appointed absolutely king, that is, in B.C. 486, and so reckon that Ezra returned to Jerusalem in the summer of the seventh year of that king's reign, B.C. 479, and that in the autumn of the same year he enforced the observance of the Sabbatical year (being the 13th from the commencement of the temple), as stated by Gantz, the Seder Olam, and Maimonides, and confirmed by the unvarying testimony of the Talmud.

This identification of Artaxerxes, who gave Ezra his commission, with Xerxes, son of Darius, which is so fully borne out by the internal evidence of the book of Ezra, forms a wonderful and exact confirmation of our whole scheme of reckoning. For thus the dedication of the second temple cannot be placed earlier than the year B.C. 486; and thus, therefore, the dates of the whole dynasty of kings of Judah must be lowered to the extent of about twenty-four years, which is required to place them in conformity with the dates of that invaluable record of those reigns, so often referred to— the Canon of Demetrius.

Continuation of Ezra's era of Sabbatical Years ending in the
Year of Jubilee of Jubilees, A.D. 1917.*

A.D. 5–6			
12–13	292–293	572–573	852–853
19–20	299–300	579–580	859–860
26–27	306–307	586–587	866–867
33–34	313–314	593–594	873–874
40–41	320–321	600–601	880–881
47–48	327–328	607-608	887–888
54–55	334–335	614–615	894–895
61–62	341–342	621–622	901–902
68–69†	348–349	628–629	908–909
75–76	355–356	635–636	915–916
82–83	362–363	642–643	922–923
89–90	369–370	649–650	929–930
96–97	376–377	656–657	936–937
103–104	383–384	663–664	943–944
110–111	390-391	670–671	950–951
117–118	397–398	677–678	957–958
124–125	404–405	684–685	964–965
131–132	411–412	691-692	971–972
138–139	418–419	698–699	978–979
145–146	425–426	705–706	985–986
152–153	432–433	712–713	992–993
159–160	439–440	719–720	999–1000
166–167	446–447	726–727	1006–1007
173–174	453–454	733–734	1013–1014
180–181	460–461	740–741	1020–1021
187–188	467–468	747–748	1027–1028
194–195	474–475	754–755	1034–1035
201–202	481–482	761–762	1041–1042
208–209	488–489	768–769	1048–1049
215–216	495–496	775–776	1055–1056
222–223	502–503	782–783	1062–1063
229–230	509–510	789–790	1069–1070
236–237	516–517	796–797	1076–1077
243–244	523–524	803–804	1083–1084
250–251	530–531	810–811	1090–1091
257–528	537–538	817–818	1097–1098
264–265	544–545	824–825	1104–1105
271–272	551–552	831–832	1111–1112
278–279	558–559	838–839	1118–1119
285–286	565–566	845–846	1125–1126

* Continued from p. 334.   † Siege of Jerusalem by Titus, a traditional
year of Sabbath.

Continuation of Ezra's era of Sabbatical Years ending in the Year of Jubilee of Jubilees, A.D. 1917.

A.D.			
1132–1133	1328–1329	1524–1525	1720–1721
1139–1140	1335–1336	1531–1532	1727–1728
1146–1147	1342–1343	1538–1539	1734–1735
1153–1154	1349–1350	1545–1546	1741–1742
1160–1161	1356–1357	1552–1553	1748–1749
1167–1168	1363–1364	1559–1560	1755–1756
1174–1175*	1370–1371	1566–1567	1762–1763
1181–1182	1377–1378	1573–1574	1769–1770
1188–1189	1384–1385	1580–1581	1776–1777
1195–1196	1391–1392	1587–1588	1783–1784
1202–1203	1398–1399	1594–1595	1790–1791
1209–1210	1405–1406	1601–1602	1797–1798
1216–1217	14`2–1413	1608–1609	1804–1805
1223–1224	1419–1420	1615–1616	1811–1812
1230–1231	1426–1427	1622–1623	1818–1819
1237–1238	1433–1434	1629–1630	1825–1826
1244–1245	1440–1441	1636–1637	1832–1833
1251–1252	1447–1448	1643–1644	1839–1840
1258–1259	1454–1455	1650–1651	1846–1847
1265–1266	1461–1462	1657–1658	1853–1854
1272–1273	1468–1469	1664–1665	1860–1861
1279–1280	1475–1476	1671–1672	1867–1868
1286–1287	1482–1483	1678–1679	1874–1875
1293–1294	1489–1490	1685–1686	1881–1882
1300–1301	1496–1497	1692–1693	1888–1889
1307–1308	1503–1504	1699–1700	1895–1896
1314–1315	1510–1511	1706–1707	1902–1903
1321–1322	1517–1518	1713–1714	1909–1910
Sabbatical year preceding the Jubilee of Jubilees.			1916–1917

JUBILEE OF JUBILEES, A.D. 1917–18.†

Blessed is he that waiteth and cometh to the thousand two hundred and five and thirty days. Dan. xii. 12; Rev. xiv. 13.

A.D. 1961.

* See Dr. Zuchermann's Treatise on the Sabbatical Cycle and Jubilee, p. 55. Trans. Chron. Inst. vol. iii. A recorded year of Sabbath.
† See p. 254.

APPENDIX B.

Compendium

OF

SACRED AND SECULAR CHRONOLOGY,

FROM THE YEAR B.C. 1000

TO THE DEATH OF CHRIST, A.D. 33.

KEY TO HEBREW CHRONOLOGY.

THE cardinal date in sacred history upon which the connexion between sacred and secular chronology turns is the year B.C. 582. In the spring of this year the battle of Carchemish was fought at the river Euphrates: in the year of the death of Pharaoh Necho (Jer. xlvi. 2, 26); in the first year of Nebuchadnezzar; in the fourth year of Jehoiakim, king of Judah (Jer. xxv. 1); soon after the fall of Nineveh according to Abydenus (Euseb. Auch. 27); which was after the date of the eclipse of Thales, B.C. 585 (Herod. i. 103, 106); and towards the latter part of the reign of Cyaxares, king of Media.

The outline of Hebrew chronology may also be computed with exactness, by tracing upwards from the beginning of Christ's ministry, in the 15th year of Tiberius (Luke, iii. 1–23); that is to say, from autumn A.D. 28, or spring 29, when he had completed his thirtieth year, as far as to the time of the Exodus under Moses.

I. The 15th of Tiberius began in Aug. A.D. 28, and ended in Aug. 29. Christ was born, therefore, thirty years earlier, either in the latter part of B.C. 3, or the beginning of B.C. 2, in the course of the Sabbatical year B.C. 3–2.

II. Seventy Sabbatical weeks of years, or 490 years, from the birth of Christ, counted upwards from autumn B.C. 2, bring us to autumn B.C. 492, or the year in which Darius, son of Hystaspes, was about 62 years of age (Dan. v. 31): for Darius came to the throne in B.C. 517 (Parian Chronicle), and certainly reigned 36 years, according to Egyptian monuments, that is to say, his last year was B.C. 482–1. He died at the age of 72 (Ctesias), and therefore was "about threescore and two years old" in B.C. 492–1, "when he was set over the realm of the Chaldeans" (Dan. ix.

2); that is, when having finally destroyed Babylon, he took the government of that city and Satrapy into his own hands.

III. Jerusalem lay desolate for 70 years (2 Chron. xxxvii. 21); that is, from the Sabbatical year ending autumn B.C. 562, till autumn 492, or 1st year of Darius, at Babylon.

IV. From the autumn of B.C. 562, the first year of captivity at Babylon, after the fall of Jerusalem in B.C. 563, to the dedication of the Temple of Jerusalem by Solomon in his twelfth year, in autumn B.C. 982, is 420 years according to the books of Kings and Chronicles. And since the twelfth year of Solomon was B.C. 982, his fourth year was B.C. 990.

V. The Exodus from Egypt was in the 480th year before the fourth year of Solomon, and therefore in the year B.C. 1470 (1 Kings, vi. 1).

The correctness of this outline of Hebrew chronology is proved beyond contradiction, by the conformity of the reckoning in detail with three eclipses of the sun, the paths of which have been accurately laid down according to the most recent astronomical tables.

I. With the eclipse of Thales, B.C. 585, which preceded the death of Necho II., and the first year of Nebuchadnezzar, as just explained.

II. With the eclipse at Jerusalem, on the 11th Jan., B.C. 689, which marks that year, from the month Nisan, as the 14th year of Hezekiah, in conformity with the record of Demetrius.*

III. With the eclipse recorded at Nineveh in the month Sivan, B.C. 763,† 18 years before the accession of Tiglath Pileser, in May 744, who took tribute of Menahem, king of Samaria, in 738, and as many before the death of Pul his predecessor, who received 1000 talents of silver from Menahem in 747 to confirm him on the throne.‡ All which is in exact agreement with the chronological position of Menahem, who reigned, according to Demetrius, from B.C. 747 to 737.

We shall henceforth argue from the annexed table of dates in Hebrew chronology, thus established, as from fixed data.

---

* See pp. 176. 181, 305.   † See p. 363.   ‡ 2 Kings, xv. 19.

KEY TO ASSYRIAN CHRONOLOGY.

THE general outline of Assyrian chronology may be collected with great exactness from the writings of Herodotus, Ctesias, Berosus, Abydenus, Castor, and Diodorus. Eusebius, who has quoted several of these authorities, though he himself has greatly misapplied them, tells us that Abydenus and Castor,— who were agreed in their Assyrian reckoning, excepting only that the one placed the termination of the Assyrian empire in the reign of Sardanapalus, the other in the reign of his successor, whom Castor calls Ninus,— had both preserved the names of the several Assyrian kings, from Ninus and Semiramis down to Sardanapalus, or his successor; and that, counting from Sardanapalus to the first Olympiad, was, according to Aby- denus, a period of 67 years. (Euseb. Auch. p. 39.) Eusebius, however, deviating from this authority to the extent of 24 years, places the fall of Sardanapalus in the 43rd year, *before* the first Olympiad, that is, in B.C. 819. That he has misin- terpreted the words of his author, and has here fallen into great error is obvious. For Abydenus elsewhere (Euseb. Auch. p. 27) states, that immediately after Sardanapalus reigned Saracus, and that it was in the reign of Saracus that Nineveh was destroyed, soon after which Nebuchadnezzar began to reign. So that it is quite clear that Abydenus is referring to times at least two centuries later than B.C. 819, and that he had counted, not 67 years before, but 167 after the first Olym- piad, to the end of the reign of Sardanapalus, that is, to the year B.C. 610. This record of Abydenus, thus corrected, is extremely valuable, inasmuch as it affords the means of recon- ciling several conflicting authorities; and on the faith of this early historian we propose therefore to make use of the year B.C. 610 as a fundamental date in Assyrian chronology.

Now Castor has recorded that 1280 years elapsed from the first year of Ninus to the breaking up of the Assyrian empire,

(Castoris Reliquiæ, Müller, p. 156). So that, according to this reckoning, Ninus the first king began to reign in the year B.C. 1889, and this we take to be correct. On the other hand, Ctesias counts from Ninus to Sardanapalus, in whose reign he supposes, wrongly, that the Assyrian empire had passed from the Assyrians to the Medes, 1306 years.*

Syncellus thinks that the reckoning of Castor, 1280 years, is to be preferred to the reckoning of Ctesias, 1300 years (so stated in round numbers).† But the precise record of Abydenus, that the Assyrian empire lasted till the year B.C. 610, enables us to show that both these reckonings have been correctly preserved. For neither Castor nor Abydenus has taken into account what Herodotus has faithfully related, viz., that the Assyrian empire was superseded by that of the Scythians, and that the Scythians held dominion over Asia for 28 years. At the end of that time, and after the date of the great solar eclipse in the reign of Cyaxares, in B.C. 585, which governs the chronology, Cyaxares, king of Media, destroyed Nineveh, and transferred the empire, not from the Assyrians, but from the Scythian intruders to the Medes.‡ The destruction of Nineveh by the Medes, then, is the event referred to by Ctesias, when counting the times of the empire as 1306 years: and this event, according to Abydenus, took place in the reign of Saracus, who followed Sardanapalus, not in the reign of Sardanapalus himself. Abydenus also tells us that the fall of Nineveh preceded the reign of Nebuchadnezzar, which began, as we have shown from Demetrius, in B.C. 582, after the eclipse of B.C. 585. Nineveh was therefore destroyed in B.C. 583. And if we add the 1306 years of Ctesias to that date, we arrive again at the same year, B.C. 1889, as that of the first year of Ninus, as already fixed by Castor. The Scythians, therefore, obtained the empire, having probably been called in by Sardanapalus to support it, in the year B.C. 610; and in the 28th year from that date Nineveh was finally destroyed.

---

* Concerning the exactness of this date see Clinton's "Fast. Hell." vol. i. p 263-1.

† Syncellus, Dind. vol. i. p. 318.   ‡ Herod. i. 106.

The only error of Ctesias is, that he supposed Sardanapalus to have been the last king of Nineveh instead of Saracus. The error of Castor is, that he mistakes the fall of Ninus, or Nineveh, for the fall of a king bearing that name.

Another important Assyrian date connected with Biblical history may be collected with exactness from Berosus, who tells us that after three successive dynasties at Nineveh, that is to say, of

49 Chaldean kings, who reigned	.	458 years.
9 Arabian kings	. . . .	145*
45 Assyrian kings	. . . .	526
		1129 years.

there rose up a Chaldæan king called Phul, who invaded the Assyrian empire, and subjugated it, we may assume, to the Chaldees. Now Phul, without question, is Pul, king of Assyria, who is mentioned in the Book of Kings as reigning in the time of Uzziah, king of Judah, and Menahem, king of Samaria, and who immediately preceded Tiglath Pileser (1 Chron. v. 26).

The reign of Tiglath Pileser is fixed with exactness in the Assyrian Canon, as beginning in the year B.C. 745–4, in the 19th year after the total solar eclipse of B.C. 763, recorded at Nineveh. The reign of Pul, the Chaldean invader, therefore, must have ended in the year B.C. 746–5, and have begun at some earlier date. If, then, we deduct 1129 years, the period embraced by the three above dynasties, from the date of the first year of Ninus, B.C. 1889, we come to the year B.C. 760, as the first year of Pul; who must have reigned, therefore, from the year B.C. 760 to 745. These figures taken together are so consistent, and place the reign of Pul so exactly where it must have taken place, according to fixed Hebrew chronology, that we cannot doubt that we have interpreted rightly the record of Berosus, and that Pul subjugated the empire of Assyria in that year.

* 245 is the figure in the original. We feel no hesitation in reducing the number by one century, in conformity with Castor and Ctesias.

The dates of the reigns of a series of **Assyrian kings**, that is, from the year B.C. 909 to B.C. 680, when **Esarhaddon** came to the throne, may be recovered with extreme exactness from the list of annual archons at Nineveh, deciphered by **Sir Henry Rawlinson** from clay tablets brought from the ancient city. And from Esarhaddon downwards it is easy to fill up from the Babylonian Canon and other sources the dates of the reigns in the following century to B.C. 583. The succession of kings of Assyria may be thus stated.

DATES DETERMINED BY THE ASSYRIAN CANON.[*]

	B.C
Commencement of the Canon. Accession of Bil-anir II.	90?
Asa, king of Judah, in his 26th year, sends presents to Benhadad, of Damascus, now about 20 years of age.[†]	90?
Accession of Tiglath-i-Bar	88?
Accession of Asshur-izir-pal, builder of the north-west palace at Nimrûd	88?
Jehu anointed king of Samaria, and Hazael king of Damascus, before the death of his father Benhadad [‡]	86?
Accession of Shalmanezer II., Black obelisk king . .	85?

In the 6th year of this king, Jehu being king of Samaria,[§] twenty-one years after the death of king Ahab, the Assyrians defeat the confederate forces of Benhadad and the kings of Hamath and of the sea-coast. Jehu pays tribute, as represented on the obelisk. But Ahab, who had set up his throne at Jezreel (probably one of the sons of Ahab, king of Samaria, who had escaped death when

---

[*] See "Athenæum," 18 May, 1867.

[†] The 2 Chron. xvi. 2. reads 36th of Asa. If written originally in numerals כ, 20, may have been mistaken for ל, 30; but Baasha, king of Israel, who died in the 27th year of Asa, was yet alive (xvi. 3). 26, therefore, is the true reading (1 Kings, xv. 21, 33).

[‡] 1 Kings, xix. 15.

[§] That Jehu was on the throne early in the reign of Shalmanezer appears from the fact, that the presentation of his tribute to that king forms the second bas-relief on the obelisk, as also the second tribute mentioned in his annals.

Jehu slew "seventy sons," the legitimate claimant
of the throne) is defeated, as confederate with
Benhadad, at the head of a small force of 10,000
men * 853

Death of Benhadad, now about eighty-six years of age*. 843

War with Hazael, now sole king of Syria * . . . 841

Accession of Shamsi-Bil 823

Accession of Bil-anir III. 810

Accession of Shalmanezer III. 781

Accession of Asshur-danan 771

In the year B.C. 765, which was the 21st of Uzziah,
and five years before the death of Jeroboam, king
of Israel, "*two years before the earthquake*"
(ch. i. 11), the prophet Amos foretells the death of
Jeroboam by the sword (vii. 1). With regard to
the earthquake he writes,—"Shall not the earth
tremble for this? . . . it shall rise up wholly as
a flood, and it shall be tossed up, and sink down,†
as the flood of Egypt" (viii. 8). "And it shall
come to pass in that day, saith the Lord God,
*that I will cause the sun to go down at noon, and
will darken the earth in the clear day.*" In fulfilment of which prophecy 765

An earthquake, (*si-hu.* Compare סַעַר, commotion ; or,
שֹׁאָה, ruin, Job, xxx. 14; σείω, to shake; σεισμός,
an earthquake), and also an eclipse of the sun
in the month Sivan (June), are recorded at
Nineveh in the archonship of Pur-el-salhe . 763

A total eclipse of the sun ‡ by calculation took place at
Nineveh, about midday, on the 15th June, B.C.

---

* See Dr. Hincks' translation of the Nimrûd obelisk, Dublin Magazine,
October 1853 ; and Rawlinson in "Athenæum," May 1867. Asa's presents to
Benhadad could not have been sent 89 years before Benhadad's death, as in
Oppert's reckoning, that is, in B.C. 932.

† The marginal reading, נשׁקעה, shall sink.

‡ The path of this eclipse, the only one capable of darkening the earth at
Samaria and at Nineveh, in the month Sivan, within fifty years, has been cal-
culated by Mr. Hind and Mr. Airy. This is the fundamental date of the Assyrian
Canon. The annular eclipse of June, B.C. 800, fixed upon by Oppert, is not
suitable, as incapable of darkening the earth in the clear day. Revue Archéol.
Nov. 1868.

B.C.

763, the dark shadow having previously passed
over Samaria,* where Amos had foretold it .   **763**

Pul invades Assyria. The empire becomes divided,
Rehoboam, king of Samaria, is slain, and there
is no king of Samaria for eleven years . . **760**

A succession of earthquakes at different places, are recorded at Nineveh down to the year . . **759**

Accession of Asshurlush as tributary to Pul . . . **753**

Menahem, king of Samaria, pays 1000 talents of
silver to Pul (2 Kings, xv. 19) to confirm him on
the throne **747**

Pul ceases to reign **745**

Accession of Tiglath-Pileser, nineteen years after the
eclipse, *i. e.* in the month of May (Jyar) . . **744**

Siege of the city of Arpad, in Syria, from B.C. 743 to . **740**

Menahem of Samaria, Rezin of Damascus, and Hiram
of Tyre, pay tribute to Tiglath-Pileser,† in 738, or **739**

Tiglath-Pileser takes tribute of Pekah in his 1st year . **734**

In this same year, the last of Uzziah, king of Judah,
whose name is also written Khazar-yahu, עזריהן,
Azariah, Tiglath-Pileser takes tribute of Yahu-
Khazi, that is, of Yahu-Khazar, or Azariah.‡

"The king," Tiglath-Pileser, "takes the hands of Bel,"
that is, removes his court to Harrân, in Mesopotamia, presided over by Bel§ .   .   . **728**

---

* Diodorus tells us that the Babylonians registered earthquakes as well as
eclipses. L. ii. Rhodom. p. 116.

† Annals of Tiglath-Pileser. The common Bible chronology, which place
the death of Menahem in B.C. 760, here absolutely breaks down. Opper
suggests a second Menahem, and a second reign for Pekah.

‡ See interchange of spelling in Hebrew names, 2 Chron. xxi. 17; xxii. 1, & 6,
The year B.C. 734, as the last of Uzziah, and first of Pekah, is so fixed in th
reckoning of Demetrius, who thus agrees exactly with the Assyrian Canon.

§ This expression has been taken to signify that Tiglath-Pileser now cease
to reign. But the same expression is made use of by Sargon when he too
Babylon, in B.C. 709. "I took the hands of the great Lord, the august go
Merodach," in other words, I reigned at Babylon. Sargon elsewhere says, "Th
great lord Bel-Dagon inhabits Mesopotamia." Tiglath-Pileser therefore, probabl
removed his seat of government to Harrân in Mesopotamia. We know from
the Jewish annals (2 Kings, xvi. 7) that he was still on the throne in the reig

B.C.

Shalmanezer (nominated king by Tiglath-Pileser ?) . 723
Sargon elected king by certain princes at Harrân . . 721
Begins to reign *de facto* 718
    Ahaz begins to reign in Judah in B.C. 717. Rezin
       of Damascus and Pekah of Samaria threaten to
       depose him (Isa. vii. 1–16). The prophet Isaiah
       declares, that before a certain child " shall have
       knowledge to cry My father, and My mother,"
       that is, before the expiration of two·years, " the
       riches of Damascus and the spoils of Samaria
       shall be taken away " (viii. 4). In fulfilment of
       which prophecy
Sargon besieges Samaria in the second year of his reign,
       and takes it towards the end of the third year,
       and carries into captivity 27,280 persons . 715
    (" Annals of Sargon," translated by Oppert, p. 4.)
    Pekah, king of Samaria, is dethroned in B.C. 715, and
       there is no king in Samaria for ten years. Sargon
       appoints his own rulers at Samaria. . .
    Ahaz meets Tiglath-Pileser at Damascus :* while
       Sargon goes down into Egypt. Boccoris king . 714
    Hoshea slays Pekah in 20th of Jotham = 4th of Ahaz 714†
Sargon takes Ashdod in person about the year . . 711
Sargon becomes king of Babylon (Archianus); conquers
       Merodach Baladan, son of Yakin (Mardocem-
       padus), who had reigned at Babylon for twelve
       years before him 709
       (" Annals of Sargon," p. 6.)
    Hoshea begins his reign in Samaria of nine years . 705
Sargon is assassinated on the 12th day of Ab (August) . 704
    Sennacherib his son claims the throne, and carries
       on two campaigns. Shalmanezer, probably father-
       in-law of Sennacherib (Tobit, i. 15), and nomi-
       nated king in B.C. 723, during the life of Tig-
       lath-Pileser, is the rightful heir, and now reigns.

---

of Ahaz, 22 years after the death of Menahem, that is, as late as B.C. 715, and
when the princes elected Sargon they were assembled at Harrân. See Oppert's
" Chronologie Biblique." " Revue Archéologique," Dec. 1868, p. 380.

    * 2 Kings, xvi. 10.   † 2 Kings, xv. 30.

Sennacherib's first campaign . . . . .

He places Belib-ni on the throne of Babylon.   **This**
king is called Belibus in the Babylonian Canon,
and his first year, which began in 603, is counted
from Thoth, or Feb. B.C. 702.

Sennacherib's second campaign.   After this time nothing
is related concerning him till the year B.C. 689 *

Meanwhile Shalmanezer, his father-in-law, besieges Samaria for three years (2 Kings, xvii. 5),
and takes the city in the year   6

Shalman-ezer is clearly the same as "Shalman," spoken of by the prophet Hosea at the time
of the destruction of Samaria, when the idol calf
of Beth-aven, or Bethel, was sent as a present to
King Jareb, *i.e.*, to his son-in-law San-ach-jarib
(Hosea, v. 13; x. 5, 6, 7). From which we know
with certainty that Shalmanezer and Sennacherib were contemporary princes, and reigned
on amicable terms, having divided the sovereignty of Assyria, as Tiglath-Pileser and Sargon
must have divided it in the early part of the reign
of Ahaz (2 Chron. xxviii. 16 ; 2 Kings, xvi. 7).
Shalmanezer besieges Tyre for five years in the
reign of Elulæus (Josephus, Ant. ix. xiv. 2).
Elulæus reigned 36 years in all, from B.C. 726
to 690.   He is the same as Il-ulæus of Babylon.‡

Sennacherib, in his third campaign, deposes Luliah, that
is, Elulæus, called king of Sidon, in his 37th year

In the beginning of the next year Hezekiah is sick.
As a sign of his recovery the shadow on the "steps

---

* Abydenus says of Sennacherib, " He was scarcely reckoned among
kings." Euseb. Auch. 26.   His campaigns are here inserted from Tay
Cylinder.   See Journal of R. Asiatic Society, vol. xix., Part 2.

† This is the recorded year of exile of the ten tribes, according to Dem
(see p. 306), and is also so reckoned on ancient grave-stones of Crimean
See Chowlson.   Mémoires de l'Académie Impériale de St. Petersburg, 1855

‡ See Tyrian chronology, and also Babylonian Canon, B.C. 726.   The
is compounded of El, and Ulæus, a river at Susa.   He probably first reign
Babylon and then at Tyre, and was dethroned by Sennacherib at Sidon.

B.C.

of Ahaz " returns ten degrees, which it had gone
down, caused by a large partial eclipse of the
sun, on the 11th Jan. 689 (Isa. xxviii. 7, 8),
visible at Jerusalem 689

In this same year Sennacherib invades Judea.
" The kings of Egypt," that is, Sevechus, and Zet,
or Sethos (Herod. ii. 141), and " the chariots and
horses of the king of Ethiopia," that is, of Tirhakah, come out to fight with him . . . 689

Sennacherib then takes 46 of the fenced cities
of Hezekiah, and tribute is laid upon him
of 30 talents of gold and 800 talents of silver
(" Annals of Sennacherib ").

Sennacherib, returning from Judea, after his fourth
campaign conquers Merodach Baladan . . 688

This is Merodach-baladan, the son of Baladan,* of
Isa. xxxix. 1, and the Messesi-Merodach of the
Babylonian Canon, whose last year at Babylon
is recorded in the Canon as B.C. 689 ; after which
anarchy and interregnum continue at Babylon
for eight years.

Sennacherib sets up his eldest son, Ashurnadin,
as king of Babylon, who rules but for a short
time.

Sennacherib's fifth campaign towards Balkh . . . 688

Sennacherib's sixth campaign towards the Persian Gulf . 687

The Babylonians set up Susubi as king of Babylon,
who is carried captive by Sennacherib.

In this year Sennacherib takes the title of Assur-
ach-erib, his father-in-law, Shalmanezer having
died (Tobit, i. 15–21).

Sennacherib's seventh campaign 686

Sennacherib's eighth campaign. Babylon revolts . . 685

Susubi escapes, and is placed again on the throne
of Babylon.† Sennacherib slain by his sons . 681

* That is, son of Merodach Baladan, son of Yakin, part of the name is
dropped, as in the instances of Shalman and Jareb.

† The position of these years of revolt within the period of interregnum at
Babylon affords strong evidence of the correctness of this arrangement of Sennacherib's reign.

Esarhaddon comes to the throne * .   .   .   .   .   (

    What follows is derived chiefly from the annals of
        Esarhaddon and Asshur-bani-pal.†

Esarhaddon overruns Egypt, drives away Tirhakah, and
        sets up Necho and nineteen other petty kings   .   (

This confederacy of petty kings lasts for fifteen years,‡
        till put down by Psammetichus in B.C. 653, whose
        reign is counted by Manetho from Feb. 654.

    Tirhakah recovers possession of Egypt   .   .   .   (

Accession of Asshur-bani-pal at Nineveh; Saosduchinus,
        Sammughes, or Saulmugina his brother, reigns
        at Babylon. Marlarmi is archon at Nineveh   .   (

Asshur-bani-pal seems to be the Acraganes of Castor,
        who reigned 42 years, from 667 to 625, and who
        immediately preceded Sardanapalus.

Asshur-bani-pal marches into Egypt, drives back Tir-
        hakah, and re-establishes Necho and the other
        confederate kings   .   .   .   .   .   .   (

Necho conspires with Tirhakah, and is sent captive to
        Nineveh .   .   .   .   (

Tirhakah takes Thebes, and afterwards recovers Upper
        Egypt   .   .   .   .   (

Asshur-bani-pal pardons Necho, and replaces him on the
        throne of Sais (say after two years' captivity) in
        662, the first year of his reign at Sais, according
        to Manetho. He reigns eight years at Sais   .

    Tirhakah dies after reigning 28 years   .   .   .

Urdumane, son of Tirhakah, slays Necho   .   .   .

Asshur-bani-pal takes tribute of Gyges, king of Lydia,
        who afterwards revolts and assists Psammetichus
        to throw off the yoke of the Assyrians, and dies .

Kiniladinus reigns at Babylon   .   .   .   .

Tobit dies at Nineveh in the 58th year of Israel's exile §
        (xiv. 11) .   .   .   .

---

* This date is fixed both by the Assyrian and Babylonian Canon.

† See Mr. George Smith's paper, "Zeitschrift f. Aegyptische Sprac." Sep.

‡ See Diodorus, l. 1, pp. 59, 60.

§ Tobit did not live 158 years. 58 must be the true figure. Which ca
represent his age, but the 58th year of the captivity of Israel.

B.C.

Nabopalassar, who is Sardanapalus (Polyhistor), called also
    Labynetus, and Nebuchodonosor, reigns at Nineveh   625
He slays Phraortes, or Arphaxad, in his 12th year*   .   614
He calls in the Scythians to defend the empire against
    Cyaxares, and they obtain possession of the govern-
    ment for 28 years   610
In his 18th year Holofernes leads the Assyrian army,
    together with the Medes and Scythians, as far as
    Azotus, or Ashdod (Judith, ii. 28; Herod. i. 105)   608
Judith dies in the 105th year of Israel's exile (Judith,
    xvi. 23) seventeen years after the death of Holo-
    fernes   591
Eclipse of Thales. Labynetus I. and Nitocris at Babylon †   585
Nineveh finally destroyed by the Medes and Babylonians,
    after the eclipse. Saracus perishes in the flames   588
Nebuchadnezzar, or Labynetus II., reigns at Babylon‡ .   582
Tobias dies in the 127th year of Israel's exile, and rejoices
    over Nineveh (Tobit, xiv. 14, 15)   .   .   .   569

N.B. Thus the book of Judith and the book of Tobit countenance the idea
that the era of Israel's exile was preserved by the descendants of the ten tribes,
and that it was the same as that which has been recorded on Crimean tombstones.

KEY TO EGYPTIAN CHRONOLOGY.

MANETHO, the Egyptian historian, in the reign of Ptolemy
Philadelphus, and at the request of that king, wrote the history of Egypt more than 250 years before Christ, for the information of the Greeks.

He has fixed two important epochs in Egyptian history,
in connexion with the Olympic era, telling us —

1. That the reign of Petubastes, the first king of the
    23rd Dynasty, was marked by the occurrence of the
    first Olympiad, " ἐφ' οὗ 'Ολυμπίας ἤχθη πρώτη."

* Judith, i. 15.   Herod. i. 211.
† Herod. i. 74, 185.   ‡ i. 77.

2. That Cambyses, the first king of the 27th Dynasty,
conquered Egypt in the fifth year of his reign over the
Persians, and reigned in Egypt six years. " Καμβύσης
ἔτη ἑ τῆς αὐτοῦ βασιλείας Περσῶν, ἐβασίλευσεν Αἰγύπτου
ἔτη, ϛ′." The fifth year of Cambyses, being the third
of the 63rd Olympiad, as known from other sources.

Within these two chronological points, aided by information
derived from a series of Apis tombs discovered by Mons. Mariette
at Memphis, and certain facts recorded on the monuments of
three of the kings of Assyria, we are enabled to fix the dates
of the Egyptian kings from Petubastes to Cambyses with great
accuracy.   All above the reign of Petubastes is, however,
involved more or less in conjecture.   Let us first count upwards
from Cambyses to Petubastes, making use in our progress of
the Apis tomb-inscriptions; and then let us count downwards
from Petubastes, making use of other sources of information.

1. The fifth year of Cambyses at Babylon, according to
the Canon of Ptolemy, was the year B.C. 525.   Diodorus also
records that Cambyses conquered Egypt in the third year
of the 63rd Olympiad,* that is, within the year beginning
in July 526, and ending in July 525 B.C.   We assume, then,
that Egypt was conquered in the course of B.C. 525, and that
Cambyses, being already a king, counted B.C. 525 as his first
year in Egypt.   Now there is a monument at Memphis, which
records the death of an Apis in the month Epiphi (the eleventh),
in the fourth year of the reign of Cambyses. †   This fourth
year of Cambyses recorded in Egypt cannot, of course, represent the year before his conquest of Egypt, but necessarily the
fourth of those six years in Egypt assigned to him by Ctesias
and Manetho; so that this Apis died in November, B.C. 522.
This may possibly have been the newly found Apis which was
wounded by Cambyses after his unsuccessful expedition against

---

* Diodorus Rhodom. p. 62.
† Brugsch, "Hist. d'Egypte," p. 266.

Ethiopia; but more probably it was that which was born in the 25th year of Amasis, rather more than 24 years before, since there is no intervening Apis tablet. They who from this monument infer that Egypt must have been conquered in B.C. 527, or 528, that is to say, in the second or third year of Cambyses, are not justified in thus setting aside Manetho, Diodorus, Ctesias, and the Canon, but are unquestionably in error.

Another Apis was born on the 28th day of the month Tybi, (the fifth month), in the fifth year of the reign of Cambyses, that is, in May, B.C. 521.

This Apis is recorded to have lived .	$7^y . 3^m . 5^d$
And to have died on the third day of the ninth month (Pachon), in the fourth year of Darius, that is, after he had reigned	3 . 8 . 3
Leaving from the birth of Apis to Darius .	3 . 7 . 2

So that from this monument we learn that Darius began to reign 3 years, 7 months, and 2 days after the birth of this Apis, that is to say, at the end of December B.C. 518, and his first year was, therefore, B.C. 517. This result is in such exact agreement with the Parian Chronicle, which places the first of Darius in B.C. 517, and also with the reckoning of Ctesias and Manetho, who give six years to the reign of Cambyses in Egypt, that no doubt can be entertained of the correctness of the reckoning here proposed of the reign of Cambyses over that kingdom.

II. Upon this secure foundation, then, we proceed to fix the reign of Amasis, who died, according to Herodotus, shortly before the arrival of Cambyses in Egypt. Manetho's record of the number of the years of his reign, that is, 44, is confirmed by monuments.[*] Assuming, then, that he died in the

* Brugsch, p. 261.

45th year of his reign, B.C. 525, which comprehends the six months of Psammecherites, his first year must have been concurrent with the year B.C 569, where it is commonly placed.

It is also to be remembered that an Apis had been installed on the 7th day of the month Thoth (January), in the 5th year of the reign of Amasis, that is, on the 17th January, B.C. 565.* It lived 18 years and 6 months, and died the 5th day of Pachon (September), in the 23rd year of Amasis, B.C. 547 :† that another Apis was born in the 25th year of Amasis (month unknown), that is, in B.C. 545,‡ and that this must be the same that died in the fourth year of Cambyses, in November B.C. 522, aged say 24 years and upwards, since no intervening monument marks the birth of an Apis between the 25th of Amasis and 5th of Cambyses.

III. Amasis conquered Apries, or Pharaoh Hophra of Scripture. Apries, however, was not put to death when Amasis came to the throne. On the contrary, he was so seated in the hearts of the people that he boasted that not even a god could dethrone him.§ And when Amasis conquered him, he did not venture to put him to death, but allowed him to dwell in his own palace at Sais for some years, till compelled by others to have him strangled. Now the number of years which Apries lived after his fall was probably not a few, considering that he was conquered in the year B.C. 569, and that Cambyses, who was placed on the throne of Persia when Darius was full 19 years old,|| that is, in B.C. 535, received his daughter in marriage in the place of a daughter of Amasis, whom he had demanded, not less than thirty-four years after his fall. So that we may assume that this daughter was born to Apries not earlier than about 560. We may indeed collect almost the

* The first day of Thoth fell on the 12th of January in this year.
† Brugsch, p. 262.
‡ The record of this Apis is in the Louvre.
§ Herod. ii. 169.
|| Ibid. ii. 209.

exact number of years of life thus accorded to him by Amasis
from the next Apis tablet, which records the birth of an
Apis in the 16th year of Necho II., on the 7th of Paophi
(February), which lived 17 years, 6 months, and 5 days,
and died on the 12th day of Parmuthi (August) in the
twelfth year of Apries. Now the question is, what was the
date of this twelfth year? We reply, that from the absence of
any intervening tablet between the twelfth of Apries and
fifth of Amasis, it may be inferred almost with certainty that
this twelfth year of Apries in which Apis died was the year
preceding the fifth of Amasis when the next Apis, as we have
seen, was installed: that is to say, that the twelfth of Apries was
the year B.C. 566, the following year, the fifth of Amasis,
being, as already determined, B.C. 565.

Thus we learn that Apries, who reigned 19 years, came
to the throne in B.C. 577, and was put to death in B.C. 559:
having reigned supreme for eight years, and for eleven years
after his defeat by Amasis. The exactness of this latter date
for the death of Apries is confirmed by Josephus. The prophet
Jeremiah, who went down into Egypt after the destruction of
Jerusalem, in B.C. 563, tells us that he had hidden certain stones
at the entry of Pharaoh Hophra's palace,* and predicted that
Nebuchadnezzar should "spread his royal pavilion over them;"
and then addressing the Jews, adds, "This shall be a sign
unto you."—"Thus saith the Lord, I will give Pharaoh
Hophra into the hands of his enemies, and into the hands of
them that seek his life."† Now Josephus tells us, with great
accuracy as to date, that in the fifth year after the destruction
of Jerusalem by Nebuchadnezzar, and in the 23rd year of his
reign, i. e. in the year B.C. 559, Nebuchadnezzar went down
into Egypt, conquered that country, slew the king then on the
throne (Apries, or Hophra), and set up another king (Amasis)
in his stead.‡ Apries was, therefore, strangled, either at the
instigation of Nebuchadnezzar, or, as Herodotus relates, of

* Jer. xliii. 10. † Jer. xliv. 30.
‡ Jos. "Ant." Hudson, p. 454.

certain of his enemies, in B.C. 559, and Amasis commenced his sole reign from this date. Apries, therefore, lived to the eleventh year after his defeat in his own palace at Sais.

Again, Clemens Alexandrinus synchronises the second year of Apries with the seventh year of Nebuchadnezzar, whose reign he places ten years lower than the Canon of Ptolemy, though still twelve years too high. If then Apries came to the throne in B.C. 577, his second year was 576. Now we have already fixed the seventh year of Nebuchadnezzar to B.C. 576–5.

IV. Psammuthis preceded Apries; and, according to the record on the Apis tablet last referred to, can have reigned not more than five full years, beginning therefore in B.C. 582.

In this year the battle of Carchemish, as we have said, was fought, and Necho II. conquered, falling "into the hands of those who sought his life."

V. Necho II. reigned sixteen full years and over, and his first year was counted from Jan. B.C. 598. This date is in agreement with a sepulchral monument at Florence,* which records that a certain Psammetichus, son of the lady Fekrot, who was born in September in the third year of Necho, and lived 71 years and four months, died in February in the 35th year of Amasis, that is, in the 35th year of his sole reign, B.C. 525. Now 71 years and four months counted upwards, from February, 525, bring us to September in the year B.C. 596, which year is the third of Necho.

VI. Psammetichus preceded Necho, and reigned, according to Manetho and the monuments, 54 years. His first year is counted from February, B.C. 652, though he came to the throne in 653.

The correctness of this reckoning is confirmed by a tablet which informs us that an Apis was born in the sixth month of

---

* Rosellini, vol. iv., p. 195.

the 53rd of this king's reign, that it was enthroned in his 54th year, lived 16 years, 7 months, and 17 days, and died in the second month of the 16th year of Necho, February, 583.* The 53rd year of Psammetichus was, therefore, B.C. 600, and his first year 652.

VII. We now follow Manetho alone as our guide, without the assistance of the Apis tablets, Memphis having fallen under the dominion of the Ethiopians for more than 50 years before the reign of Psammetichus; and, on his authority, we place the first year of Stephinates in B.C. 675, that is to say, 150 years and six months before the conquest of Egypt by Cambyses, and his two successors as follows, at Sais :—

XXVIth Dynasty, in Lower Egypt.

Stephinates reigns 7 years, counted from Feb., B.C.				675
Nechepsos	„	6	„	„	668
Necho I.	„	8	„	„	662
				to 655

Thus leaving an interval of three years between the last year of Necho, 655, and the first year of his son Psammetichus, 652, during which time Necho is slain by the Ethiopians, and Psammetichus takes flight into the marshes,† where we may suppose him to have remained for more than one year, and after which, having conquered his opponents, he began to reign supreme.

Thus far we conceive the dates of the several reigns to be in close accordance with authorities. We now venture with Eusebius to place the reign of Ammeres the Ethiopian as predecessor to Stephinates, and, as we believe, contemporary with Tirhakah.

VIII. Ammeres reigns 12 years, counted from B.C. 687-8.

---

* Mariette's Serapéum at Memphis, p. 28.

† Herod. ii. 152. Herodotus calls the Ethiopian king Sabbaco, but we know that it must have been Tirhakah, or his successor, from an Apis tablet which places the reign of Tirhakah almost immediately before that of Psammetichus.

And, if we now place the first year of **Petubastes**, in whose reign the first Olympiad began, as coeval with the year preceding the first Olympiad, or in B.C. 777, and trace downwards through the XXIIIrd dynasty, we fill up exactly the interval between Petubastes and Ammeres, thus—

XXIIIrd Dynasty, in Lower Egypt.

Petubastes reigns 40 years counted from B.C. 777
Osorcho   „   8   „   „   737
Psammus   „   10   „   „   729
Zet, or Sethos, or So 31   „   „   719
                                      to 689

IX. Again we trace upwards from Psammetichus, through the Ethiopians in Upper Egypt, and find that an Apis was born in the 26th year of Tirhakah the Ethiopian, and died in the 20th year of Psammetichus, proving that the last year of Tirhakah was not many years before the first of Psammetichus.

XXVth Dynasty of Ethiopians.

Allowing then three years after the death of Necho for the flight of Psammetichus into the Delta, and the putting down of his competitors, and 28 years more for the reign of Tirhakah, who died in 656, before Necho was slain, we bring the first year of Tirhakah to   .   .   683
Sevechus, his predecessor, reigned 12 years, counted from .   695
Sabbaco, who preceded Sevechus, 12   „   „   „   707
Boccoris, afterwards burnt alive by Sabbaco, reigns 6 years, having been placed on the throne of Egypt by Sargon in B.C. 714, and his years are counted from .   .   .   713

The only uncertain part of this arrangement lies in the position given to the XXIIIrd dynasty. Manetho does not say that Petubastes began to reign about the first Olympiad. This is merely our inference. For, unless such is his meaning, the mention of the Olympiad seems to tell us nothing. Manetho must have known the year of the reign of Petubastes in which the Olympiad began, and his object, we presume, was to give a chronological position to the reign. But if the accession of Petubastes is not intended to be made nearly concurrent with the first Olympiad, it is left in uncertainty to the extent of forty years. This adjustment of the XXIIIrd dynasty, however, is only of importance as regards the matter in hand, as showing how the reign of Zet, the last king of that dynasty, whom Lepsius and others identify with the Sethos of Herodotus, may thus fall in with the time of Sennacherib and Hezekiah, when Sethos is said to have reigned.

The true adjustment, on the other hand, of the XXIVth dynasty is of great importance, as showing how the accession of Boccoris to the throne of Egypt falls in with the 4th year of Sargon, king of Assyria, the date of which we have already ascertained.

The following appears to be the proper arrangement of the several dynasties counting downwards from Petubastes:—

MANETHO'S XXIIIRD DYNASTY.

						B.C.
Petubastes	40 years from	.	.	.	.	777
Osorcho	8 ,, ,,	.	.	.	.	737
Psammus	10 ,, ,,	.	.	.	.	729
Zet, or Sethos, or So, 31 ,, ,,		.	.	.		719–689

XXIVth Dynasty.

Boccoris, 6 years, counted from	.	.	.	.	713

Sargon, king of Assyria, marches an army into Upper Egypt, puts to flight the army of Sabbaco the Ethiopian king, and restores to the throne Pi-ir-u, or Pe-hor, or Boccoris, and lays tribute upon him. ("Annals of Sargon.")

XXVth Dynasty.

Sabbaco, 12 years .	.	.	.	.	.	707

Sabbaco captures Boccoris, and burns him alive. (Manetho.)

Hoshea, king of Samaria, sends messengers to So .	699
Sevechus, 12 years	. . . .	695

"The kings of Egypt (Zet and Sevechus) and the archers, and chariots, and horses of the king of

Ethiopia," that is, of Tirhakah, come out against
Sennacherib (" Annals of Sennacherib ").
XXVth Dynasty continued.

Ammeres, 12.	.	687–
Tirhakah, 28 years		683–65

XXVIth Dynasty.

Stephinates, 7.	.	67
Nechepsos, 6.	.	66

Esarhaddon, king of Assyria, overruns Egypt, drives
away Tirhakah, and sets up 20 petty kings as
rulers over Upper and Lower Egypt, amongst whom
are Necho and Nechepsos*   66

These kings rule Egypt, with interruptions, for
fifteen years, till 653. (Diodorus.)

Tirhakah recovers Egypt from the kings   . .   6

Asshur-bani-pal marches into Egypt and reinstates
the kings . . . . : . . .   6

Necho conspires with Tirhakah, and is sent captive
to Nineveh by the Assyrian generals . . .   6

Tirhakah recovers possession of Egypt for two years
till   6

Asshur-bani-pal pardons Necho, and after two years'
captivity replaces him on the throne of Sais.

Necho, 8.	.	6

Tirhakah dies after reigning 28 years   . . .   6

Urdumane, 2 years.   He slays Necho   6

Psammetichus puts down the confederate kings, after
they had ruled for fifteen years   6

Psammetichus	 54	6
Necho II.	 16	.
Psammuthis	 5	.
Aprics, or Hophra	 19	.
Amasis, 44 years from defeat of Apries . 34	alone	

XXVIIth Dynasty.

Cambyses	 6	.
Smerdis .	. . . . 7 months	.
Darius	 36	.

---

* "Campaigns of Esarhaddon and Asshur-bani-pal." by G. Smith.

KEY TO BABYLONIAN CHRONOLOGY.

			B.C.
Nabonassar . .	14	. . . . . .	747
Nadius . . .	2	. . . . . .	733
Chinzerus and Porus	5	. . . . . .	731
Ilulæus . . .	5	The Elulæus of Menander .	726
Mardocempadus .	12	Merodach Baladan, son of Yakin	721
Archianus . .	5	Sargon, king of Nineveh .	709
Interregnum . .	2		
Belibus . . .	3	Set on the throne by Senna-cherib	702
Apronadius . .	6	Asshurnadin, son of Senna-cherib	699
Regibelus . .	1	. . . . . .	693
Mesessimordac .	4	" Merodach Baladan, son of Baladan." Isa. xxxix. 1.	692
Interregnum . .	8	Susubi twice on the throne during this interval.	
Asaradinus . .	13	Esarhaddon, son of Senna-cherib	680
Saosduchinus . .	20	Sammughes, Saulmugina .	667
Kiniladinus . .	22	. . . . . .	647
Nabopalassar . .	20	Sar-Nabopal, or Sardana-palus (Polyhistor). .	625

The Scythian domination over Asia lasted for 28
years, from 610 to 583, till the destruction of Nineveh by Nebuchadnezzar and Cyaxares.

Herodotus proposed to himself (i. 106) to give the particulars of the fall of Nineveh at some future time, but has
omitted to do so. We may collect, however, from his narrative that the first act of the Scythians on coming into power
was to march an army towards Egypt. (i. 105.) They were
then bought off with presents by Psammetichus, and did not

proceed beyond Ashdod. This expedition is clearly the sa
as that described in the book of Judith (iii. 28), which end
in the same manner, and we learn from thence that Sardar
palus did not forsake the throne of Nineveh till after his 18
year. After his 20th year, however, he seems to have abs
doned that city to the Scythians, by whom, probably, Sarac
was there set up as king, and together with his queen Nitoc
he passed the remainder of his reign at Babylon. Syncell
properly counts 15 years only for his reign at Nineveh, that
till the entry of the Scythians; and from the year B.C. 610
582 is 29 years. Now this is the number of years given
Berosus, as cited by Josephus,* to Nabopalassar's reign befc
the accession of Nebuchadnezzar. Thus Nineveh was c
stroyed in the 28th year of the Scythian era, B.C. 583, N
buchadnezzar begins to reign in the 29th year, 582, which
the 4th of Jehoiakim, king of Judah, set up as a vassal of t
king of Egypt; and in the 30th year of the same era, which
called the 5th year of Jehoiakim's captivity (see LXX), tl
is of Jehoiakim's vassalage, as distinguished from his years
revolt (2 Kings, xxiv. 1), Ezekiel prophesies at the riv
Chebar. (Ezek. i. 1.)

Nabokolassar . . 43	Nebuchadnezzar, son of Na-	
	bopalassar†(Demetrius).	5

This year, B C. 582, is the date of the battle of Carche-
mish, and the fundamental date of our reckoning.‡
Nebuchadnezzar begins the siege of Tyre in his seventh
year, in the reign of Ithobal§   .   .   .   576–5
In his eighth year he carries away Jehoiakin captive to
Babylon (2 Kings, xxiv. 12)   .   .   .   5
In his nineteenth year he destroys Jerusalem .   .   5
He causes Apries, or Pharaoh Hophra, to be put to death   5

---

* Con. Apion. i. 19.

† The Chaldean kings from Nebuchadnezzar downwards are arbitra
placed in the Canon of Ptolemy. No eclipses are recorded as marking th
reigns. They are here regulated by the eclipse of Thales.

‡ P. 357.   § P. 383.

B.C.

Nebuchadnezzar having come to the 44th year of his reign
   dies, foretelling to the Babylonians that "a Persian
   mule shall come, and by the assistance of your
   gods shall impose upon you the yoke of slavery,
   the author of which shall be a Mede, the vain
   glory of Assyria" (Megasthenes) *   .   .   .   539

Evilmerodac begins to reign in the 37th year from Je-   538
   hoiakin's captivity.† He unites with Crœsus, and
   in his third year is slain in battle with Cyrus, son
   of Cambyses, and Cyaxares‡ early in 535.

Nergalsharezar reigns 4 years, from 535, and is slain on
   the taking of Babylon by Cyrus.§ The Rab-Mag.?‖

Laborosoarchod appointed king, reigns 9 months in   .   535

Nabonadius appointed regent during his minority .   .   535

   Babylon taken by Cyrus II., son of Cambyses, king
   of Persia, at the head of the armies of his father,
   and of Cyaxares, son of Astyages, though not yet
   himself a king (Xenophon)   532

Cambyses, on the death of his father, Cyrus I., becomes
   king of Babylon ¶ .   .   .   .   .   529 '

   Nabonadius remains governor of Babylon under
   Cambyses.

   Some few years after the fall of Babylon, according
   to Xenophon, and just 49 years and 3 months
   after Nebuchadnezzar began the siege of Tyre in
   576, according to the Tyrian annals,** Cyrus
   having married the daughter of Cyaxares becomes
   king of Media ††   527

---

* Euseb. Præp. Evan. i. 10.   Euseb. Chron. Auch. p. 30.
† 2 Kings, xxv. 27.   ‡ Xenophon, iv. ch. i. 8.
§ vii. ch. 5, 33.   ‖ Jerem. xxxix. 3.

   ¶ The regnal years of Cambyses were registered at Babylon. Ptolemy records an eclipse of the moon at Babylon in his seventh year, which took place in
B.C. 523. According to Diodorus, his fifth year fell in the 3rd year of the 63rd
Olympiad. And there is a document in cuneiform character, which has been
translated by Mons. Oppert, which bears date "20th Nisan, 6th year of Cambyses, king of Babylon, king of nations."—Revue Archéologique, Sept. 1866.

   ** See p. 383.

   †† Cyrus reigned probably seven or nine years during the lifetime of Cambyses.

Cambyses in his fifth year invades Egypt   .   .   .

During his absence in Egypt Cyaxares dies, and the whole empire revolts from Cambyses.

Nabonadius having revolted, Cyrus brings an army against Babylon, a second time, deposes him, and gives him the government of Carmania (Berosus) .   .   .   .

Nabonadius rules in Carmania till driven away by Darius, say in 516 (Megasthenes).

Cyrus now proclaims himself sovereign "over all the kingdoms of the earth," and as "king of Babylon " * issues his decree, on his return to Media, for the release of the Jews, and after a reign of nine years dies soon after the death of Cambyses, a mule without issue.

Before the death of Cambyses, Gomates usurps the throne, calling himself Bardes, or Smerdis, the son of Cyrus I., and brother of king Cambyses, by whom Bardes had been put to death.   He reigns seven months after the death of Cambyses .   .

Darius kills Gomates, and begins to reign   .   .   .

Naditabirus, who calls himself Nabuchodrosser, son of Nabonadius, revolts at Babylon.

Darius retakes Babylon, and slays Naditabirus   .   .

Aracus, calling himself Nabuchodrosser, son of Nabonadius, revolts at Babylon   .   .   .   .

Intaphres, sent by Darius, retakes Babylon and slays Aracus   .   .   .   .

Belsharezar, or Belshazzar,† son of Nabonadius, either placed there by Darius as governor, or usurping the throne of Babylon, revolts .   .   .   .

Darius, after a siege of 22 months, takes and finally destroys Babylon, being now about 62 years old (Dan. v. 31).   Darius now called king of Assyria.‡

* Ezra, v. 13.
† Journ. R. Asiatic Soc. vol. xix. part ii. p. 194.
‡ Ezra, vi. 22.

KEY TO TYRIAN CHRONOLOGY.

THE loss of the Tyrian annals, as translated by Menander from the public records, in which the length of the reign of each king was set down in order, and which were perfect in the days of Josephus, is a great privation to the chronologist. We are indebted to Josephus, however, for three very valuable extracts from these annals. By means of the first, we are enabled to fix with precision the first year of the reign of Cyrus, or Coresh, king of Persia; and by the third to fix with the same precision the first year of the reign of Solomon, both in accordance with the outline of our reckoning. The second extract, relating to Elulæus, confirms the date of the third campaign of Sennacherib. Tyre, we know, had flourished for several hundred years as a great emporium for commerce, with a navy which commanded the seas, till the time of Nebuchadnezzar, who besieged the city and put an end to its independent power. Concerning this siege Josephus writes, " In the records of the Phenicians we have this enumeration of the times of their several kings. Nebuchodonosor besieged Tyre for 13 years in the days of Ithobal their king. After him reigned Baal 10 years. After him were judges appointed, who judged the people,—Ecnibalus, the son of Baslacus, 2 months; Chelbes, the son of Abdeus, 10 months; Abbar, the high-priest, 3 months; Matgenus and Gerastratus, the sons of Abdelemus, were judges 6 years; after whom Belatorus reigned 1 year. After his death they sent and fetched Merabalus from Babylon, who reigned 4 years. After his death they sent for his brother Hirom, who reigned 20 years. Under his reign Cyrus became king of Persia. So that the whole interval (that is, from the first year of the siege to the 20th of Hirom), is 54 years besides 3 months. But in the 7th year of the reign of Nebuchadnezzar he began to besiege Tyre; and Cyrus the Persian took the kingdom in the 14th

year of Hirom."[*]   Thus the interval between the 7th of N
buchadnezzar, B.C. 576, and 19th of Hirom, is 49 years and
months; and the first year of the reign of Cyrus, therefor
was B.C. 527. This well accords with the idea that Cyru
son of Cambyses and Mandane, was born about B.C. 560, ?
years after his grandfather's marriage in the year of th
eclipse 585, and that he came to the throne in the reign of h
father Cambyses.[†]

The next extract has reference to the invasion of Phenic
in the days of Shalmanezer. Josephus writes, " And now th
king of Assyria invaded all Syria and Phenicia in a hosti
manner. The name of this king is also set down in th
archives of Tyre, for he made an expedition against Tyr
in the reign of Elulæus. And Menander attests to it, wh
when he wrote his Chronology, and translated the archives
Tyre in the Greek language, gives us the following history
' One whose name was Elulæus reigned 36 years. This king
upon the revolt of the Citteans,[‡] sailed to them and reduce
them again to submission. Against these did the king
Assyria send an army, and in a hostile manner overrun a
Phenicia, but soon made peace with them all and returne
back. But Sidon, and Acca, and Palætyrus revolted. An
many other cities there were which delivered themselves u
to the king of Assyria. Accordingly, when the Tyria
would not submit to him, the king returned, and fell up
them again, while the Phenicians had furnished him wi
threescore ships and eight hundred men to row them. An
when the Tyrians had come upon them in twelve ships, an
the enemy's ships were dispersed, they took five hundred me
prisoners, and the reputation of the citizens of Tyre w
thereby increased. But the king of Assyria returned, a
placed guards at their river and aqueducts, who should hind

---

[*] Joseph. cont. Apion. 1.

[†] It will be shown, when we come to treat of Persian chronology, how th
Cyrus, or Coresh, was son, not father of Cambyses, king of Persia, and th
he survived Cambyses probably not more than one or two years.

[‡] The people of Citium, in Cyprus, the Chittim of Scripture.

the Tyrians from drawing water. This continued for five years, yet still the Tyrians bore the siege and drank of the water out of the wells they dug.' This is what is written in the Tyrian archives concerning Shalmanezer, the king of Assyria." * Now we have observed that by means of this extract we are enabled to confirm with accuracy the date of the third campaign of Sennacherib. We have already found, by comparing the Assyrian Canon with the annals of Sennacherib on Taylor's Cylinder, that Luliah, or Elulæus, was dethroned by Sennacherib in his third campaign, in the year B.C. 690. From the same cylinder we have also learned that Hezekiah was attacked by Sennacherib in that same year. And from our fixed table of Hebrew chronology we are satisfied that the year 689 was the 14th year of Hezekiah, when according to Scripture he was again threatened. If, then, according to this extract, Elulæus reigned 36 full years, his first year must have been concurrent with the year B.C. 726.

Now, if we turn to Babylonian chronology, we find that Ilulæus, king of Babylon, came to the throne in the year B.C. 726. Assuming, then, the identity of Ilulæus of Babylon and Elulæus of Tyre and Sidon, the proposed adjustment of Hebrew, Assyrian, Babylonian, and Tyrian chronology, is at this point strikingly confirmed by this extract from Menander. But where, it may be asked, is the proof of this identity? We offer a few observations, which, though not affording absolute proof, show the high probability of this identification.

The Phœnicians, as Herodotus informs us,† came originally from the Erythræan Sea, or Persian Gulph; and we learn from Justin that they first established themselves upon the Assyrian lake,‡ that is, a lake in connexion with the river Euphrates, west of Babylon,—a position convenient for conducting the carrying trade from the Gulph through Babylonia,—and from thence, in course of time, they made their way to the coast of the Mediterranean Sea, first establishing themselves at Sidon, and after many years building the city

* Joseph. Ant. ix.; xiv. 2.

† Herod. i. 1.   ‡ Justin. xviii. 3.

C C

of Tyre. Aradus, Tripolis, Dora, and Joppa, we know were also numbered amongst the Phœnician cities. Strabo informs us that in his days there were islands in the Persian Gulph bearing the names of Tylus or Tyrus, Aradus, and Doracta,* which latter name Mr. Kenrick identifies with Dora;† and in the voyage of Nearchus up the Gulph we read of Sidodone, and Tarsia,‡ on the coast of Carmania; all which sufficiently indicates close commercial intercourse between Tyre and the Gulph. " From the Persian Gulf," observes Heeren, " they extended their commerce to the western peninsula of India, and the island of Ceylon." §

Tarsia we assume to be the Tarshish so frequently spoken of in Scripture, and Tyre is called by Isaiah " daughter of Tarshish;" ‖ as, in fact, born of the commerce between the Persian Gulph and the Western world. The coast of Carmania, or Tarshish, in the days of the opening of this commerce, when distant voyages by sea were unknown, was probably the point on the Gulph to which the trade by caravan from the far East — from " the ends of the earth " ¶ — was directed, and from thence distributed up the Tigris and Euphrates to the great cities of the world. We learn from Al-Edrissi, that in the ninth century of our era the town of Siraff, close to the site of Tarsia,** was a centre of Oriental commerce, which extended perhaps as far as China; †† and even as late as the sixteenth century, when the Eastern trade had fallen into the hands of the Portuguese, who were accustomed to voyages as far as the East Indies, the island of

---

* Strabo, xvi. 3.   † Kenrick's Phœnicia, p. 48.
‡ Vincent's Voyage of Nearchus, pp. 358–362.
§ Heeren's Manual of Ancient History. Eng. Trans. p. 27.
‖ Isaiah, xxiii. 10.   ¶ Psalm lxxii.
** When Jonah fled to Tarshish, it was probably to the Persian Gulph that he fled, not to Tartessus in Spain, as many suppose. He took ship probably at Opis, on the Tigris, a place so called by the Greeks, but which may have had the same derivation as Joppa, both being named by traders from the Gulph. It is a curious fact, as connected with Jonah, that some of the houses at Siraff are said to have been built with the bones of whales, showing the abundance of that fish in the Persian Gulph.
†† Vincent's Voyage of Nearchus, p. 365.

Ormuz on the same coast, somewhat nearer to the mouth of the Gulph, which superseded Siraff, was one of the principal stations of their trade. Thus the wealth of India and the distant East was transported in "ships of Tarshish" by way of the Euphrates through Babylonia towards Tyre; while much of the wealth of Arabia, which was also poured into Tyre, we learn from Aristobulus was carried by the merchants of Gherra, on the Arabian side of the Gulph, on rafts up the Euphrates to Thapsacus.* About two hundred and fifty miles below Thapsacus, according to Niebuhr, there was a canal of five hundred miles in length direct from the Euphrates to the Persian Gulph, a great and expensive work, and affording strong indication of the extent of the traffic to and from the Gulph.†

This traffic of the Tyrians with Tarshish, and the islands of the Persian Gulph, was in active operation nearly one thousand years before the Christian era, even in the days of Solomon, king of Israel and Judah, concerning whose wide dominion we read, that it should reach "from sea to sea, and from the river (Euphrates) unto the ends of the earth;" and to whom it is declared, "the kings of Tarshish and of the isles shall bring presents; the kings of Sheba and Saba shall offer gifts." ‡ Solomon we know had a fleet upon the Arabian Gulph, manned by the sailors of Hiram king of Tyre,§ by which immense produce of gold was annually imported from Ophir, on the coast of Africa. But in addition to this fleet we read that he had also another fleet,‖ expressly called "a navy of Tarshish," an expression understood by the writer of the book of Chronicles ¶ as a navy trading to Tarshish, which together with the "navy of Hiram," (who does not appear to have had a fleet on the Arabian Gulph), made once in three years a distant expedition, bringing back a freight of gold, silver, ivory, apes, and peacocks; a sufficient indication that this expedition was directed towards the East,

---

* Strabo, xvi. 3.   † Vincent's Voyage of Nearchus, p. 514.
‡ Psalm lxxii.   § 1 Kings, ix. 26, 27.   ‖ Ibid. x. 22.
¶ 2 Chron. ix. 24.

and not in the direction of the Mediterranean. Some have supposed that this " navy of Tarshish " sailed from the Arabian Gulph, and that, coasting the south of Arabia, it reached some distant point in the direction of India. But it is hard to believe that such skilful navigators as the Tyrians, who must have been well acquainted with the direct route towards the East by the Euphrates, and whose ally and associate, Solomon, was in possession of all the country lying between Tyre and the Euphrates,* and who moreover had built Tadmor, or Palmyra, within three days' journey of the Euphrates, with the express object of encouraging the commerce with Tipsah, or Thapsacus, a port on that river within his own dominions —it is hard, we say, to believe that two such skilful traders, in the days when navigation was chiefly conducted by the tedious operation of rowing, could have so far erred, as to have chosen a route towards the East more than a thousand miles greater in length than that by the river Euphrates. The very expression " navy of Tarshish," in conjunction " with the navy of Hiram," seems intended to distinguish this fleet from that which was built at Ezion-geber, which was merely manned with Tyrian sailors, but not accompanied by the fleet of Hiram.

About four hundred years later than the reign of Solomon, i.e. about the year B.C. 560, we have an account in the book of Ezekiel, written in the reign of Nebuchadnezzar, of the very same traffic of the Tyrians with the Persian Gulph. At this time Tartessus, or Tarshish, in Spain had been founded by the Tyrians, and silver, iron, tin, and lead, were imported from that colony. But after describing the traffic of the western world with Tyre, Ezekiel goes on to describe that with the East, naming in succession Damascus, Haran, Canneh, Sheba, Asshur, at that time comprehending all Mesopotamia, Chilmad, or Carmania, according to the Septuagint, Dedan, and Raamah, both placed by Bochart in the Gulph of Persia,† while the army of Tyre appears to have been composed partly

* 1 Kings, iv. 21–24.
† See Vincent's Dissertation on the xxvii. chapter of Ezekiel.

of recruits from Persia. Nebuchadnezzar, who had conquered Tyre after a siege of thirteen years, and who had built
Teredon,* near the mouth of the Euphrates, with the view of
keeping open the commerce of the Gulph with Babylon, had
possessed himself of the command of the whole traffic from
thence to Tyre, to the great enrichment of Babylon. After
the conquest of Tyre by Nebuchadnezzar, we find Baal reigning
over that city, who, we must presume, had been placed on the
throne of Tyre, by the king of Babylon; and about forty
years later we find from Menander that two kings in succession, viz., Merabal and Hiram, were called for from Babylon,
where probably they resided as hostages, to come and take
possession of the throne of Tyre. The connexion between
the two cities at that time was that of subordination on the
part of Tyre.

Again, about two hundred and thirty years after Nebuchadnezzar's invasion, that is, about B.C. 330, Alexander conceived the idea of diverting this great Eastern trade into new
channels. He subdued Tyre after an obstinate resistance,
and on his return to Babylon from the East sought to make
that city the capital of his empire. The Euphrates was still
navigable for ships of considerable size, and we find at this
period the same connexion of the fleets of Tyre with the
Euphrates as in former days. We learn from Arrian,† that
according to the ancient and common practice, which must
have been adopted by Hiram in the days of Solomon, and by
Ilulæus in the days of Sennacherib, Alexander transported no
less than forty-seven ships in pieces, on the backs of camels,
from Tyre to Thapsacus, where they were launched on the
Euphrates and carried down to Babylon, some being of the
size of five bank of oars. Alexander had constructed at
Babylon a harbour capable of holding one thousand ships, his
object being to conquer Arabia, colonise the islands in the
Persian Gulph, and monopolise the trade of the East; and in
the feverish contemplation of this expedition he was suddenly
overtaken by death.

* Euseb. Auch. p. 28. † Arrian, vii. 19.

Thus, then, we trace a close commercial connexion between Tyre and Babylon, extending over a period of six hundred and fifty years, during which the trade between the eastern and western parts of the world was carried on through those two cities; and during part of which time Tyre was in direct subjection to Babylon, receiving from thence her kings. We now return back to the particular reign of Elulæus of Tyre, in whose time the kingdom of Tyre was in a position of such power and importance, as to have imposed princes, even upon Babylon itself. In the reign of Elulæus, who was contemporary with Hezekiah, king of Judah, the prosperity of Tyre had reached the height of its grandeur. Isaiah, foretelling the destruction of the " joyous city," speaks of her merchants as " princes," " her traffickers," as " the honourable of the earth." These expressions imply great riches and magnificence on the part of her citizens. But, in addition to this, the prophet uses an expression concerning Tyre which implies extended dominion and imperial power, reaching over territories beyond the precincts of the little state. Tyre is designated the " crowning city," or, as otherwise translated, the dispenser of crowns— the setter-up of kings; * and the direction in which her dominion had extended is pretty clearly indicated to have been towards Chaldea. From the Assyrian inscriptions we learn that there was on the Euphrates a strongly fortified city bearing the name Tsur, or Tyre.† In the same chapter of Isaiah which proclaims the greatness and approaching downfall of Tyre, the prophet points out Chaldea as the stronghold of her greatness. For, suddenly breaking off from his denunciations against Tyre, he exclaims, " Behold the land of the Chaldeans. This people was not, till the Assyrian founded it for them which dwell in the wilderness. They set up the

---

* When Rezin and Pekah conspired to dethrone Ahaz, " and to set a king in the midst " of Judah, " even the son of Tabeal," Isa. vii. 6, it seems probable that Tabeal (qu. Tubaal) was a Tyrian Prince.

† See Rawlinson's map. Anc. Mon. vol. i. ; and Journal of Sac. Lit., new series, ix. p. 194.

towers thereof and the palaces thereof. He (the Assyrian) brought it to ruin. " Howl, ye ships of Tarshish (that is, ye ships which trade with the Persian Gulph) for your strength (that is, Chaldea) is laid waste."*

This passage alone is sufficient to indicate the occupation of the Euphrates in the time of Sennacherib by the fleets of Tyre. But the presence of the Tyrian fleet on that river is still more directly confirmed by the testimony of Assyrian inscriptions, the authority of which is decisive upon this point. In the annals of Sennacherib, recorded on Taylor's cylinder, we read, that this king, who had conquered Tyre in his third campaign, when in pursuit of his enemies, the Chaldeans, about three years later, who had taken refuge in the province of Elam, conducted his army over " the great sea of the rising sun,"—the Gulph of Persia—in " Syrian ships," that is to say, in those very ships of Tarshish spoken of by Isaiah, so well accustomed to the navigation of the Gulph, and so lately in the service of the king of Tyre : now, however, bewailing the loss of their stronghold in Chaldea, destroyed by Sennacherib. And much cause had the Tyrians for lamentation. For Sennacherib, we are told, had built Tarsus on the coast of Cilicia, and called it Tharsis or Tarshish,† borrowing the name from Tarshish in the Gulph, forming the city after the fashion of Babylon; and his views were now directed no doubt towards diverting the trade from its original route from the Gulph, through Babylon and Tyre, and directing it up the Tigris, through Nineveh, favouring the new port of his own construction on the river Cydnus.

Up to this time the commerce of the world, east and west, had centred in the markets of Tyre and Chaldea, and the ships in which this trade was carried on were denominated " ships of Tarshish." Notwithstanding, therefore, the position of the kingdom of Syria, with its capital Damascus, standing between Tyre and Euphrates —to which city no doubt large

---

* Isa. xxiii. 8-13.

† " Et Tarsum urbem, ipse ad similitudinem Babylonis condidit, quam appellavit Tharsin."—Euseb. Auch. p. 21.

tribute was paid for safe conduct—we cannot but conclud
that this vast trade by caravan to the Euphrates, and from
thence to Babylon and the Persian Gulph, was as much
under the control of the merchant princes of Tyre, as the
overland route through Egypt, in connexion with the same
Eastern trade, was lately under the direction of the merchan
princes of Great Britain. Considering then that we find a
fortified port established on the Euphrates, bearing the name
of Tyre—that in the reign of Elulæus a powerful Tyrian flee
occupied that river—that the pre-eminence of Tyre was such in
the days of Elulæus as to entitle that city to the designation
" crowning" or imperial city—and that during five year
of the reign of Elulæus at Tyre, or at Sidon, a king bearing
that title was seated on the throne of Babylon, on the line o
commerce which formed the source of Tyre's great riches—
it is not unreasonable to assume that the Tyrian dominion
had extended during that short period even to Babylon itself
or *vice versâ*, and that both these cities during some portion
of the 36 years' reign were subject to the same ruling hand.

The third extract is of great importance to chronology.
Josephus thus writes concerning Menander : " This Menande
wrote the acts that were done both by the Greeks and bar
barians, under every one of the Tyrian kings, and had taken
much pain to learn the history out of their own records
Now, when he was writing about those kings that had reigned
at Tyre, he came to Hirom, and says thus : ' Upon the death
of Abibalus, his son Hirom took the kingdom, lived 53 years
and reigned 34 . . . . Under this king there was a younge
son of Abdemon, who mastered the problems which Solomon
king of Jerusalem, had recommended to be solved. Now the
time from this king to the building of Carthage is thus calcu
lated,—upon the death of Hirom, Baleazarus his son took the
kingdom, lived 43 years, and reigned 7 years. After him
succeeded his son Abdastartus, who lived 29 years, an
reigned 9 years. Now four sons of his nurse plotted against
him and slew him, the eldest of whom reigned 12 years.
After them came Astartus, the son of Deleastartus, who live

54 years, and reigned 12 years. After him came his brother Astarymus, who lived 54, and reigned 9 years. He was slain by his brother Phelles, who took the kingdom, and reigned but eight months, though he lived 50 years. He was slain by Ithobalus, the priest of Astarte, who reigned 32 years and lived 68. He was succeeded by his son Baalzarus, who lived 45 years, and reigned 6. He was succeeded by Matgenus, his son, who lived 32 years, and reigned 9. Pygmalion succeeded him, who lived 56 years, and reigned 47. Now, in the seventh year of his reign, his sister fled away from him and built the city Carthage, in Lybia.' So that the whole time from the reign of Hirom till the building of Carthage amounts to the sum of 155 years and 8 months. Since, then, the Temple was built, at Jerusalem, in the 12th year of the reign of Hirom, there were from the building of the Temple until the building of Carthage 143 years and 8 months." [*] Some of the figures in this extract are corrupt, but all subsequent writers who have referred to this passage agree as to the sum total—143 years and 8 months; and, by comparing together the three variations of Josephus, Theophilus of Antioch, in the century after Josephus, and Syncellus, we obtain that same figure :—

	Josephus.	Theophilus.	Syncellus.	True Figures.
Hirom . . .	22	..	22	22
Baalzarus . .	7	17	17	17
Abdastartus .	9	..	9	9
Astartus . .	12	12	12	12
Astarimus . .	9	9	9	9
Phelles . . .	0 8^m	0 8^m	0 8^m	0 8^m
Ithobal . . .	32	12	32	32
Baalzarus . .	6	7	8	6
Matgenus . .	9	29	25	29
Pygmalion . .	7	7	7	7

143.8

Now, with regard to the building of Carthage, Niebuhr places the event 37 years before the first Olympiad, accord-

[*] Joseph. cont. Apion. i. 18.

ing to the Greek fashion of reckoning,—that is, in B.C. 813; and he considers this date "as historically certain as the date of the foundation of Boston or New York."*

Cicero[†] places the foundation of Carthage 39 years before the first Olympiad, in 815, Timæus writes 38 years. There must have been some authority for this reckoning; and we may agree with Niebuhr, that the actual foundation of the city was about the time referred to. But the founding of the city and the flight of the sister of Pygmalion are two very different things. Carthage was not built immediately upon the arrival of *Dido* in Africa. Strabo tells us that the island of Kothon, off the coast, was first occupied and fortified against the hostile Africans who opposed her landing on the main shore. Justin, from Trogus, tells us that a piece of land, as much as an ox-hide would cover, was first purchased on the coast,—a tradition which marks the difficulty in gaining her first footing in Africa. A citadel, called Byrsa, was then built. The people from the neighbouring country flocked there for the purpose of traffic, till at length the settlement assumed the appearance of a small state. Ambassadors were sent from Utica, another Tyrian colony; and the Africans, becoming desirous of retaining the strangers, with the consent of all, Carthage was at length built. For the foundation of the colony, therefore, we must look to other authorities. Now, Polybius was living at the time of the fall of Carthage, B.C. 146, and, as quoted by Appian,[‡] informs us that Carthage had flourished 700 years from the time of its foundation to the time when the city was destroyed. The epitomiser of Livy records the same number of years. Suidas, following, no doubt, these authorities, writes: "Scipio took the city after it had ruled over the surrounding nations 700 years." Solinus [§] is quoted by Scaliger to the same effect; and Orosius ‖ writes, "Diruta est Carthago septingentesimo post anno quam condita erat." The

---

* Anc. Hist. vol. iii. p. 159.   † Cicero de Republicâ, ii. 23.

‡ Appiani Punica, viii. 132.   § Scaliger, Fragmenta de Emend. Temp.

‖ Orosius, iv. xxiii.

colony of Carthage, therefore, was founded in the year B.C. 846, and Solomon began to build the Temple of Jerusalem 144 years before that time. The fourth year of Solomon therefore was B.C. 990, and his first year 993, as already determined.

Again, if we know the date of the fourth year of Solomon we know also the date of the fourteenth year of Hezekiah. For, according to Hebrew reckoning, there were exactly 301 years between the two dates. The date therefore of the fourteenth year of Hezekiah, which followed the third campaign of Sennacherib, was B.C. 689.

From these data, coupled with facts from the Assyrian inscriptions, we may form the following skeleton of Tyrian chronology, some of the intervals in which may yet further be supplied from time to time from the same sources :—

		B.C.
Building of Tyre, 240 years before the building of the Temple of Jerusalem *		1230
Abibalus	YEARS.	
Hirom	34	1001
Building of the temple of Jerusalem begun in the 12th year of Hirom .		990
Baalzarus	17	967
Abdastartus	9	950
Astartus	12	941
Astarimus	9	929
Phelles	0 8ᵐ	920
Ithobal	32	919
Baalzarus	6	887
Matgenus	29	881
Pygmalion	47	852
Dido founds a colony at Carthage in the 7th year of Pygmalion		846
Hiram pays tribute to Tiglath-Pileser		738
Metenna pays tribute to Tiglath-Pileser . . .		714

* Joseph. Ant. viii. 3, 1.

Ilulæus, who had reigned first at Babylon in **726, then at**
Tyre or Sidon, was besieged by Shalmanezer for
five years, and dethroned by Sennacherib after a
reign of 36 years in   .   .   .   .   .   .

Ithobal. The siege of Tyre, which was carried
on during the last 13 years of this reign,

begins in the 7th year of Nebuchadnezzar	13	
Baal	10	
Ecnibal	0	2⁰
Chelbes	0	10
Abbar	0	8
Mitgenus and Gerastratas . . .	6	
Belatorus	1	
Merabal	4	
Hirom	20	

     Cyrus set on the throne in the 14th year
     of Hirom   .   .   .   .   .   .

     Thus by means of one of these invaluable extracts fr
the Tyrian annals we ascertain that the year B.C. 990
the 4th year of Solomon, in which he began to build
temple of Jerusalem; and counting downwards from that da
according to the common reckoning of the reigns of the ki
of Judah, we arrive with precision at the year B.C. 582 (
fundamental date of our arrangement), as the date of the
year of Jehoiakim, king of Judah, and of the battle of C
chemish.

     Again, counting downwards from the battle of Carchem
to the year B.C. 575, or 7th year of Nebuchadnezzar, we
tain the precise year of the commencement of the siege
Tyre, and from thence, through the Tyrian records, ascert
the year of the accession of Cyrus, son of Cambyses, to
throne of Media, B.C. 527.

     Thirdly, in conformity with this outline of dates the
years' reign of Elulæus falls exactly within the year B.C. 7
or first of Ilulæus at Babylon, and the year 690, when Elul
was dethroned.

Lastly, we learn from this latter extract that the date of the first year of Ithobal, the priest of Astarte, who was the father of Jezebel, the wife of Ahab, king of Samaria, was B.C. 919; and that Ithobal was 36 years old when he came to the throne of Tyre. Now let us suppose that his daughter Jezebel was born in the year 932, when Ithobal was 23 years of age, which is not an unreasonable supposition, and that she was of about the same age as her husband Ahab. Jezebel, upon these assumptions, would have been 36 years old when Ahab came to the throne of Samaria in B.C. 896, according to Hebrew reckoning; she would have been left a widow in 875, when Ahab was slain at the battle of Ramoth Gilead, at the age of 57; and when she painted her face and was thrown out of window by command of Jehu fifteen years later, in the year 860, she would have attained to the age of 72. All this is so perfectly natural as to afford no slight testimony of the consistency of our dates as ascertained from Hebrew, Assyrian, and Tyrian chronology. And if we are justified in assuming that " Ahab of Jezreel," named in the Annals of Shalmanezer, the Black Obelisk king, as having been defeated by him in the year B.C. 858, at the head of his little contingent of 10,000 men and 2000 chariots, was not Ahab, king of Samaria, whose forces probably would have amounted to some six or eight times that number, but a son of king Ahab maintaining himself at Jezreel in opposition to the usurping dynasty; then will there be no need for the inference drawn by Sir Henry Rawlinson, on the one hand, that " the numbers in the Hebrew text of the Bible will have to be altered, between Hezekiah and Ahab, by about 40 years;" * or, on the other hand, for Dr. Oppert's most unreasonable proposition to thrust in 47 additional archons into the list of these annual officers at Nineveh contained in the Assyrian Canon, with the view of raising the date of the Black Obelisk king to a level with his assumed date for the reign of Ahab.

* Athenæum, May 18th, 1867

LYDIAN CHRONOLOGY.

LYDIAN chronology comes in contact with Scripture histo
through Crœsus the last king of Lydia, who, as we have se
was in alliance with Evilmerodac when that king was slain
battle by Cyrus in the year B.C. 535. Crœsus, in fear of t
rising power of the Persians, had consulted the oracle
Delphi, which warned him of the time when "a mule" shou
rule in Persia. And Nebuchadnezzar, his ally, with referen
no doubt to this same oracle, had warned the Babylonians, in B
539, of the coming of a "Persian mule" to enslave their countr
The fall of Crœsus could not, therefore, have taken pla
earlier than B.C. 534 ; and this year, or 533, we believe to
the date of the capture of Sardis, not B.C. 548, where it
commonly placed.

Mr. Clinton had collected together in his "Fasti Hellenici'
all the authorities bearing on this question, from which
would appear, that the only direct evidence in favour of tl
year B.C. 548 is derived from the comparatively late writer
Solinus and Eusebius. Solinus the grammarian, who live
in the second or third century of the Christian era, while r
ferring incidentally to the sudden recovery of speech t
the son of Crœsus, speaks of the event as having occurre
when "Cyrus victoriously entered Sardis in the 58th Olym
piad," B.C. 548 ;[†] which date, therefore, if Solinus is correc
would be the date of the fall of Crœsus. Solinus, howeve
who commonly follows Pliny as his authority, has probab
here inadvertently put the date of the accession of Crœs

* Vol. ii. p. 361.
† "Cum Olympiade octavâ et quinquagesimâ victor Cyrus intrasset Sar
Asiæ oppidum, ubi tunc Crœsus latebat, Atys filius mutus ad id, in voc
erupit vi timoris."—*Solin.* c. i. p. 8.

for the date of his fall, for his evidence is neither in harmony
with Pliny nor with other ancient writers. Let us refer to
more ancient authorities.

The five last kings of Lydia, according to Herodotus, and
according to the common mode of reckoning their reigns, are
usually placed thus,—

Gyges, who reigned 38 years from B.C. 718				
Ardys	„	49	„	„ 680
Sadyattes	„	12	„	„ 631
Alyattes	„	57	„	„ 619
Crœsus	„	14	„	„ 562
		———		to
		170		548

making a period of exactly 170 years, beginning in B.C. 718,
and ending in the year 548.

Dionysius of Halicarnassus, a historian of the same city
as Herodotus, who wrote some few years before the birth of
Christ, and therefore long before Solinus, and who, as a
native of a city not far from Sardis, had access no doubt to
the most authentic records concerning the kings of Lydia,
has a passage distinctly defining the limits of the history of
Herodotus, as comprised within a period of 240 years, beginning with the reign of Gyges, and ending with the invasion
of Greece by Xerxes, in . B.C. 479,—ἐν τοῖς τεσσαράκοντα καὶ
διακοσίοις ἔτεσι.* This computation would place the first year
of Gyges in the year B.C. 718, as above, and counting 170
years downwards from that date would bring us to the year
B.C. 548 for the last year of Crœsus. Thus it would appear
that Dionysius and Solinus are agreed, and this is the view
taken by Mr. Clinton and most other chronologists. But
Dionysius is here at variance with himself, and there has
been probably an error in transcribing the passage. For in
another passage Dionysius computes *about* 220 years from
Gyges to the flight of Xerxes,—ἔτεσιν ὁμοῦ διακοσίοις καὶ εἴκοσι.†

* Dionysius, tom. vi. p. 820.—Reiske.
† Ibid. tom. vi. p. 773.

Mr. Clinton suggests that the second passage should be corrected by the first, and that Dionysius "never could have meant to express the beginning of that kingdom (the Lydian) by 220 + 478, or B.C. 698, because that would bring the capture of Crœsus down to B.C. 528, when Cambyses was king of Persia." But the figure is not 220 exact, but *about* 220, that is to say, somewhat more or less than 220; and if we may suppose the exact number of years to have been 224 + 479, we should arrive at the year B.C. 703 for the first year of Gyges, and B.C. 534 for the fall of Crœsus. As regards the capture of Crœsus in the reign of Cambyses, which Mr. Clinton thinks so improbable, it is exactly what we are told by Xenophon was the fact. And he is not justified in thus arbitrarily setting aside the testimony of this historian. Xenophon tells us that "Cambyses king of Persia" was father of Cyrus, and that he was reigning in Persia when Crœsus was conquered by Cyrus; that Cyrus was not yet a king, and moreover that this Cambyses was the king in whose reign Egypt was conquered by the Persians. The emendation of τεσσαράκοντα for εἴκοσι is highly arbitrary, and without any appearance of probability about it, for no scribe could have copied in error εἴκοσι for τεσσαράκοντα if the latter word had been so written originally. The expressions also, "one hundred and forty years," and "*about* one hundred and forty years," do not sound compatible. Whereas the expressions one hundred and twenty-four years and *about* one hundred and twenty years are so. The first passage was therefore probably written originally with exactness thus,—ἐν τοῖς τεσσάρσι καὶ εἴκοσι καὶ διακόσιοις ἔτεσιν, and the copyist has hastily written τεσσαράκοντα for τεσσάρσι καὶ εἴκοσι, not so improbable an error. The result will show the probable correctness of this suggestion, for we shall hereby be enabled to reconcile Dionysius with himself, and also with all other authorities, excepting only Solinus and Eusebius.

If Gyges began to reign exactly 224 years before the beginning of the Persian war, in B.C. 479, which would place the beginning of that king's reign in B.C. 703; the several reigns of the kings of Lydia would stand thus :—

Gyges*	reigned 49 years, from B.C.				704–3
Ardys	,,	38	,,	,,	655–4
Sadyattes	,,	12	,,	,,	617–6
Alyattes	,,	57	,,	,,	605–4
Crœsus	,,	14	,,	,,	548–7
				to	534–3

Let us see what other ancient authorities say regarding these reigns. In the first place, Pliny,† writing in the first century, records that Caudaules, the predecessor of Gyges, died in the course of the 18th Olympiad, that is, between July B.C. 708 and July 704. Supposing him to have died in the latter half of the last year of the Olympiad B.C. 704, the following year, B.C. 704–3, would have been the first year of Gyges, as above. Again, Clemens Alexandrinus, in the second century, writes, Gyges began to reign *after* the 18th Olympiad, ἀπὸ τῆς ὀκτωκαιδεκάτης ὀλυμπιαδος.‡ If, therefore, Crœsus was deposed 170 years after the accession of Gyges, we have the authority of Dionysius, Pliny, and Clemens, for placing his deposition and the fall of Sardis in the year B.C. 534, or 533.

An interesting discovery made by Sir Henry Rawlinson confirms the lower date thus assigned to the reign of Gyges. In the *Athenæum* of the 8th March, 1862, Sir Henry writes : " In examining the many fragments of the historical tablets of Asshur-bani-pal, the son of Esarhaddon, which crowd the shelves of the British Museum, with a view of arranging, if possible, one complete copy of the annals for publication, I have within this few days lighted upon a passage which had

---

* We venture to interchange the figures connected with the reigns of Gyges and Ardys, giving 49 years to the former and 38 to the latter, on the authority of the annals of Asshur-bani-pal, which make the last year of Gyges concurrent with the revolt of Psammetichus in B.C. 654. Both Eusebius and Syncellus also give 38 years to Ardys.

† Nat. Hist. xxxv. 8.

‡ Clemens Alex. Strom. i. p. 327.

previously escaped my observation, but which I have now found repeated in a more or less perfect state on several of these mutilated terra-cotta records. The passage is of great interest, as it furnishes the first point of undoubted contact between Greek and Assyrian history. Asshur-bani-pal states as follows: ' Gyges was king of Lydia, a country on the sea-shore, and so far off that the kings, my fathers who reigned before me, had never even heard the name of it. In obedience to my royal proclamation (the proclamation is given at length, and invites all people to do homage and offer tribute to Asshur-bani-pal, king of Assyria, on pain of incurring the vengeance of Asshur, king of the gods) the said Gyges sent his officers to my presence to propitiate me, &c. &c.' " Now nothing can be more probable than that this proclamation was issued by the Assyrian king on his accession to the throne, and we collect from the Canon of Ptolemy that the reign of Esar-haddon, his father, ended in B.C. 668.* So that it is not un-reasonable to assume that the proclamation was made in the year 667. Gyges was therefore still on the throne 14 years after the date of his death as placed by Mr. Clinton. And if con-temporary with Psammetichus, he must have lived till the year B.C. 654.

Again the Parian Chronicle, composed in the reign of Ptolemy Philadelphus, 264 years before the birth of Christ, and far more ancient therefore than Dionysius, Pliny, or Clemens, places the accession of King Alyattes in the year B.C. 605, as above. This authority is extremely valuable from its antiquity, and coincides again with the evidence of the three before-named writers. For if Alyattes reigned 57 years from the year B.C. 605, his son, Crœsus, must have begun to reign in B.C. 548, and have ceased to reign in B.C. 534. Mr. Clinton has indeed observed that " we can only guess the number 341 (in the Chronicle) equivalent to B.C. 605." But this is not a true statement of the case. There are only two numbers, viz., 331 and 341, which can possibly be applied to

* Page 379.

what the marble records concerning Alyattes, consistently
with what remains upon the marble. The numbers run
thus:—

From the time when Terpander, &c.   CCCLXXXI
From the time when Alyattes, &c. XXXI
From the time when Sappho .   .   CCCXX . .

The second number, which is imperfect, must, we know,
have been less than CCCLXXXI. What remains of the
number is inconsistent with either CCCLXXI or CCCLXI.
It was, therefore, originally written either CCCXXXXI. or
CCCXXXI. Now 331 + B.C. 264 (the radix of the Chronicle), is equivalent to B.C. 595, and no one, I presume, would
venture to place the first year of Alyattes so late as that year.
Undoubtedly, 341 + 264 = B.C. 605, is correct, and so Selden,
Prideaux, and Marsham, have proposed to fill up the date.

This ancient chronicle once contained another very important date for which we are seeking; viz., the date of the capture of Sardis by Cyrus. When Selden examined the marble, in
1628, the date, unfortunately, was wholly obliterated. These
words, however, still remained legible, concerning the time
when Crœsus consulted the oracle, at Delphi: . . . . . .
. . . Αφ' ου Κροισος . . . Ασιας . . . .
Δελφος α . . . . ΔΔΔΔΙΙ . . . . . .
It has been proposed to fill up the spaces thus: Αφ' ου Κροισος
εξ Ασιας εις Δελφους απεστειλεν . . . .;
and if the remains of the number were correctly read by
Selden, there can be little doubt that (converting the Greek
into Roman figures) . . . . XXXXIL. should be
read CCLXXXXII., that is, 292 + B.C. 264, equivalent to the
year B.C. 556. But if the writer of the Chronicle really considered that Crœsus consulted the oracle in that year, he must
have differed much from Herodotus, as regards the length of
the reign of Alyattes; and we know not how much also he
may have differed with regard to the years of Crœsus. The
Chronicle would thus be at variance with the principal autho-

rity. We may, however, suspect some incorrectness in copying the remains on the marble. If, with Prideaux, we read:
Αφ' ου Κροισος της Ασιας εβασιλευσι, και εις Δελφους απεστειλεν, thus
making the date refer to the time of the *accession* of Crœsus to
the throne; and may also conjecture that the numbers, which
we know were not very distinct in the time of Selden, were
originally ΔΔΔIIII., instead of ΔΔΔΔII., equivalent in Roman
figures to CCLXXXIIII., that is, to 284 + 264 = B.C. 548, the
Chronicle and Herodotus might thus be brought into perfect
unison with each other, as regards the length of the reigns,
and the date, B.C. 548, for the accession of Crœsus would be
thus firmly established.

Diogenes Laertius, about the third century, in his life of
Periander, king of Corinth, informs us that Periander died
during the reign of Alyattes, king of Lydia, and confirms his
statement thus: "Sosicrates (who wrote about 200 years, B.C.)
asserts that he died 41 years before Crœsus, before the 49th
Olympiad." "Before Crœsus," certainly cannot mean before
the death of Crœsus, but almost necessarily before his accession to the throne. "Before the 49th Olympiad" signifies in
the course of the 48th = B.C. 588–585; and Laertius elsewhere
tells us that Periander's reign ended 40 years after the 38th
Olympiad,—that is, in the 48th. If so, we count 41 years
downwards from the year B.C. 588, and arrive at the year B.C.
548 for the accession of Crœsus, as derived from Dionysius
and other authorities, and his last year therefore would be the
year B.C. 534. Thus, the preponderance of ancient authority
seems to determine the date of the fall of Sardis to the year
B.C. 534; and Solinus, followed by Eusebius, are the only
direct authorities for placing the event in B.C. 548, just the
whole length of the reign of Crœsus earlier than other authors.
The only way in which we can account for this discrepancy
is by supposing, as already suggested, that Solinus, writing
from memory, has inadvertently affixed the date of the accession of Crœsus to the time when he was dethroned by
Cyrus. He is not an author much to be relied upon for
exactness; and we must remember that the date quoted by

him is only incidental, and not part of the subject-matter of the passage. Syncellus differs from Eusebius, and places the accession of Crœsus in the year B.C. 550,* and his fall in 536, two years earlier than we have placed it.

When Crœsus, after his fall, reproached the oracle of Delphi with having deceived him, it replied: " Let Crœsus know that he was made prisoner three years later than the Fates had ordained." † The fall of Sardis, therefore, in B.C. 534 well agrees with other history, being the fourth year after the death of Nebuchadnezzar, who, when dying, uttered the words of the oracle. On the other hand, the chronology which places the death of Nebuchadnezzar and the dethronement of Astyages by Cyrus about the year B.C. 560, and the fall of Crœsus in B.C. 548, in no way fits in with this rejoinder of the oracle.

There are two other circumstantial pieces of history related by Herodotus, which confirm the conclusion arrived at, that Crœsus ceased to reign after the year B.C. 537. With the view of strengthening himself against the rising confederacy of Medes and Persians, Crœsus had not only entered into alliance with the Babylonians and Egyptians, who sent auxiliaries, but also sent ambassadors to Athens and Sparta, seeking assistance from the Greeks. Now, Herodotus relates that when the embassy arrived at Athens they found that city in a state of internal commotion, and unable to enter into foreign undertakings; for Pisistratus, the tyrant, having been already twice driven from the throne into exile, and on the second occasion having remained absent for ten years,‡ had now for the *third time* just obtained forcible possession of the government. Now, the date of the first usurpation of Pisistratus,—viz. B.C. 560,— is a point not to be disputed. This is one of the few perfect dates which remained in the Parian Chronicle at the time it was discovered. Clinton, who carefully examined the history of the Pisistratidæ down to the

---

* Syncellus, Chron. Dindorf, vol. ii. p. 237.
† Herod. i. 62. ‡ Herod. i. 91.

time of the battle of Marathon, has arranged the several periods of tyranny and exile thus: * —

YEARS.		YEARS.	B.C.
1. Pisistratus usurps the tyranny		6	560
Birth of Hippias . . .			
7. First exile		6	554
13. Second tyranny . . .		1	548
14. Second exile		10	547
24. Third tyranny . . .		10	537
34. Death of Pisistratus . .			527

If these dates are correct,—and they cannot be far from the truth,—Crœsus must have sent to Athens in or after the year B.C. 537, and must have been deposed after that time.

The embassy to Sparta was more successful. The Spartans promised to enter into alliance with Crœsus; but, as usual, were slow in moving. As an earnest, however, of their friendship, they sent him, as a present, a magnificent brazen bowl, chased with figures, and capable of containing 300 amphoræ. This bowl did not reach its destination. The Spartans affirmed that it had been captured by the piratical fleet of Samians while on its way to Lydia; while the people of Samos affirmed that it reached Lydia just after Crœsus had been taken prisoner by Cyrus, and that those to whom it was entrusted sold it in the island. The assertion of the Samians, whether true or false, marks the time of the sending of the bowl as the last year of the reign of Crœsus. The question is,—Does this account suit best with the year B.C. 548, or B.C. 534?

To revenge this insult, we are told that the Spartans sent an expedition against Samos, and against Polycrates, the ruler of that little naval state, in the days when Cambyses invaded Egypt.† This invasion of Egypt, we know, took place in the year B.C. 525.‡ If Crœsus had fallen in the year B.C. 548,

---

* Fast. Hell. vol. ii. 44.

† Herod. iii. 44.　　　　　　　　　　‡ Page 370.

and the seizure of the bowl had taken place in that year, then must the Spartans have suppressed their anger for a period of twenty-three years, which seems somewhat inconsistent. Retaliation sought after the year B.C. 525 seems to be more consistent with the fall of Crœsus and the capture of the bowl in B.C. 534.

The chronology of Herodotus, according to the present text, is in an inconceivable state of confusion at this point. For he adds, that the Corinthians also joined with the Spartans against Polycrates to revenge an insult of the Samians, inflicted about the same time that the bowl was taken from the Spartans, and in the days of Periander and Alyattes. Now we have already seen that Periander died in the year B.C. 588, forty-one years before Crœsus began to reign, and sixty-three years before the expedition of the Spartans against Polycrates. So that an insult in the days of Periander must have taken place fifty-five years before the taking of the bowl. Herodotus here is greatly at fault, if the text is correct. The confusion arises out of his one leading error, in confounding the days of Cyrus, father of Cambyses, who married the daughter of Astyages, and who was contemporary with Periander, with the days of Cyrus, son of Cambyses, and grandson of Astyages, who was contemporary with Crœsus and Cambyses, who married Mandane.

KEY TO MEDIAN CHRONOLOGY.

THE chronology of the Medes, from the time of their revolt from Assyria to the time of their falling under the sway of Persia, is chiefly to be derived from Herodotus, who thus records the length of the first four reigns:—

Deioces, the first king of Media reigned 53 years
Phraortes, his son   „   22 „
Cyaxares, his son   „   40 „
Astyages, his son   „   35 „

Making together a period of 150 years.

Now, assuming the correctness of the length of each of these separate reigns, it will be sufficient, if we can determine with exactness the chronological limits of any one of them, to establish the correct position of all four reigns throughout the 150 years. Let us, then, select, for the purpose of examination, the reign of Cyaxares, the third Median king.

In his reign a remarkable solar eclipse is spoken of as having led to important events in Median history, and this eclipse affords the means of fixing the time of the events with extreme accuracy. Cyaxares had been at war for six years with Alyattes, king of Lydia, during which no great advantage had been gained on either side. While they were engaged in fighting their last battle, suddenly both armies were involved in total darkness, or, as Herodotus describes it, day was *suddenly* * turned into *night.*† Such sudden and total darkness,

---

* ἰξαπίνης, " suddenly." The sudden failure of light on this occasion forms an important element in considering the nature of the eclipse. An eye-witness of the total eclipse in Norway in 1853 observes: " As long as the least bit of the solar disk was visible, there was a diminution of light, though not absolute darkness; but, the moment the disk was completely covered by the moon, darkness was as suddenly produced as when in a room the last candle out of several is put out."

† Herodotus, lib. i. 74.

ECLIPSE OF THALES B.C. 585.

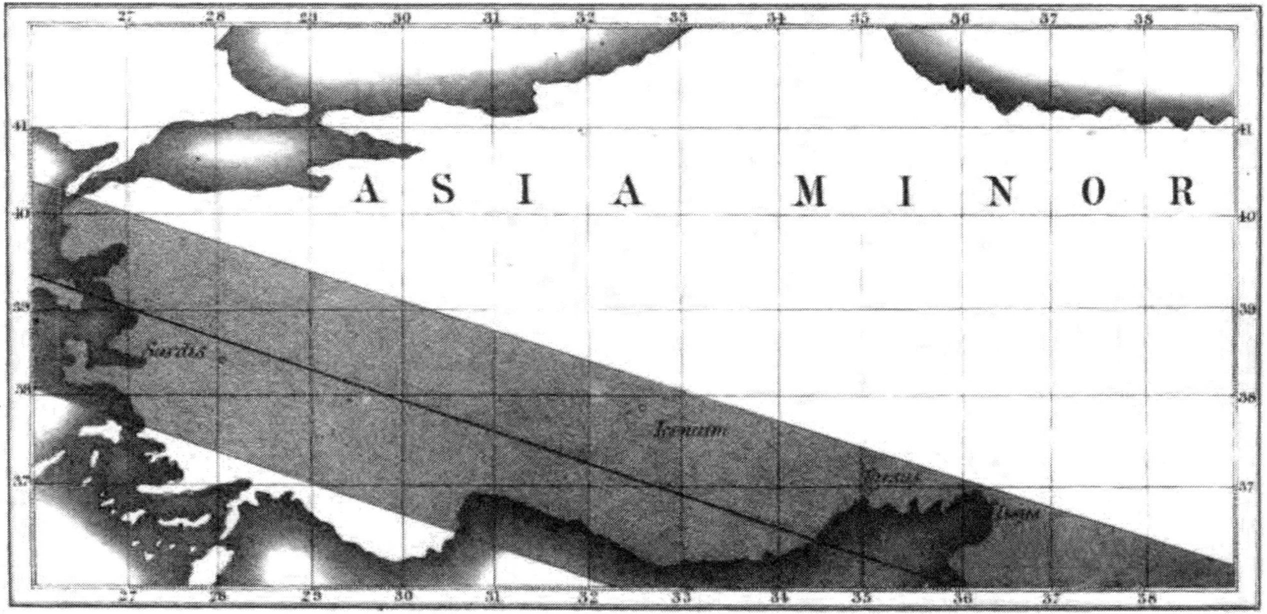

ASIA MINOR

Copied from M.r Airy's Map and calculated according to Hansen's tables.

it is well known, can only be produced by a total eclipse of the sun—a very rare occurrence at any particular spot in the world. No partial eclipse, however large, as instanced by the almost total eclipse which occurred in this country on the 15th of March, 1858, in any degree approaches the awfulness of a total solar eclipse, as described by those who have witnessed the phenomenon.* There was nothing in the effect of the eclipse of March 1858 (though the apparent diameters of sun and moon were so nearly equal, that it was doubtful beforehand whether the eclipse would be total or annular) which would have attracted the attention of two contending armies. On the occasion, however, of the battle between the Lydians and Medes, the armies were so stricken with awe that they desisted from the fight. Peace was forthwith made between the two kings, and sealed by a matrimonial alliance between Astyages, the son of Cyaxares, and Aryenis, the daughter of Alyattes. Both the *sudden* darkness and the effect created mark a total eclipse. Herodotus adds, that this eclipse had been predicted to the Ionians by Thales, as about to happen in their country in the very year in which it occurred.

If, then, we can fix the date of this eclipse, we shall of course know the date of this important battle, which, we are told, preceded the fall of Nineveh,† and obtain one fixed point in the reign of Cyaxares. We shall also know the very year of the marriage of Astyages, grandfather of Cyrus, a date of extreme value, from which to estimate the probable time of the events which occurred in his grandson's reign. Now, there are only three eclipses which were total in that part of the world during the fifty years which elapsed between B.C. 630 and 580, within which interval the battle must have been fought, which can possibly be supposed to have occasioned the sudden darkness which led to such results—viz., the eclipses

---

* "The phenomenon, in fact, is one of the most terrible that man can witness; and no degree of partial eclipses gives any idea of its horror." Airy's Lecture at Roy. Inst., Feb. 4, 1853.

† Herod. lib. i. 103–136.

of B.C. September 610, May 603, and May 585. The astronomers Mayer, Costard, and Stukely, in the last century, calculated, according to their imperfect knowledge of the moon's secular acceleration, that the eclipse of B.C. 603 was that which put an end to the battle between the Medes and Lydians;[*] and Dr. Hincks till his death endeavoured to contend for that date.[†]   The eminent German chronologist Ideler,[‡] on the authority of the astronomer Oltmanns, his countryman, fixed upon the year B C. 610, which for a long time was generally received: and this is the date adopted by Mr. Grote.[§]   Both these years well agree with the reckoning of the common chronology.   They are both, however, at variance with the ancient traditional date, which, by Pliny,[‖] is fixed to the 4th year of the 48th Olympiad, B.C. 585; and Clemens Alexandrinus[¶] and Solinus,[**] who speak of the 50th and 49th Olympiads, can only point to the same eclipse.

The attention of astronomers was recalled by the author to this subject [††] in the year 1852, and till within not many years of this time the determination of the true date of this eclipse has been a matter of investigation with several eminent European astronomers, as being a question of great importance in connexion with the lunar theory, independently of its historical interest.   In the course of their investigation, the supposed position of the moon's shadow during each of the three eclipses referred to came under consideration, and was subjected to the test of its conformity with the actual known position of the moon's shadow during several eclipses of a later date.

In the year B.C. 310, just 300 years later than the eclipse of B.C. 610, we read, in Diodorus [‡‡] and Justin,[§§] that Agathocles, tyrant of Syracuse, while conducting his fleet from

---

[*] Philosophical Transactions, A.D. 1754.   [†] Athenæum, Aug. 16, 1856.
[‡] Handbuch der Chron. vol. i. p. 209.
[§] Grote's History of Greece, vol. iii. p. 314, note 2.
[‖] Hist. Nat. ii. 12.   [¶] Clem. Alex. Strom. i. p. 302.
[**] Solinus, cap. xv. p. 25.   [††] Athenæum, Aug. 1852.
[‡‡] Diodorus, lib. xx. p. 735.   [§§] Justin, Hist. lib. xxii. c. v.

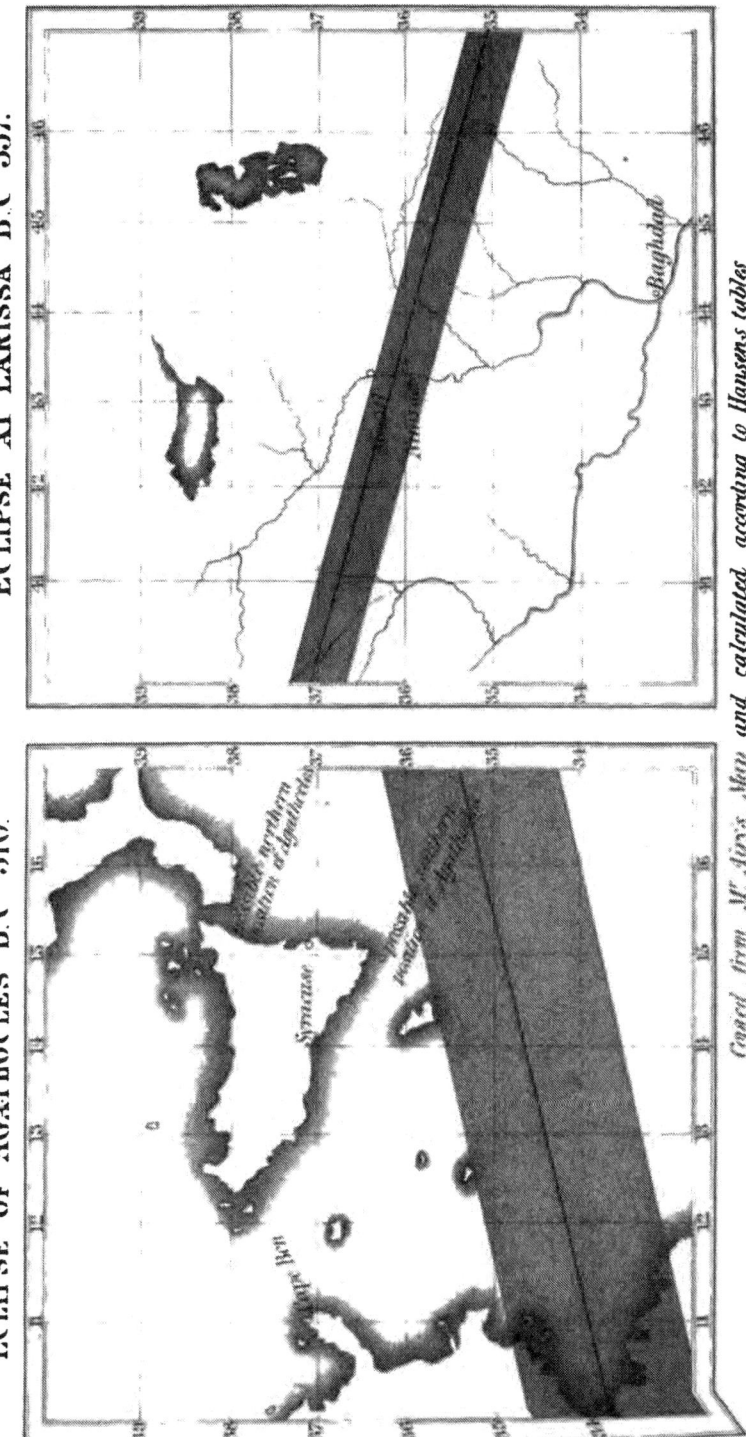

ECLIPSE OF AGATHOCLES B.C 310.

ECLIPSE AT LARISSA B.C 557.

Copied from M. Airy's Map and calculated according to Hansens tables

Syracuse to a spot near Cape Bon, on the coast of Africa,* fell under the shadow of an eclipse. His fleet had been chased by the Carthaginians on leaving Syracuse the preceding day, and is said to have escaped in the darkness of night. On the following morning, about eight or nine o'clock, a sudden darkness came on, which greatly alarmed his crew, and the stars appeared. On the morning of this eclipse, we are certain that Agathocles must have been somewhere within eighty or a hundred miles north or south of Syracuse, and the shadow of the total eclipse which enveloped his fleet must therefore have fallen within those limits. Now it is found, by calculation, that the same theory which would bring the moon's shadow, in the year B.C. 610, so as to throw the zone of total darkness anywhere over Asia Minor, would necessarily so lower the position of the shadow of the eclipse in the year B.C. 310, as to throw it upon the continent of Africa far too much to the south for any possible position of the fleet of Agathocles to have been touched by it: and the same theory which would raise the position of the shadow in B.C. 603 from the line of the Red Sea and Persian Gulph, so as to cause the zone of total darkness to pass anywhere near Asia Minor, would so raise the position of the shadow in the year, B.C. 310, as to throw it far too much to the north for any possible position of Agathocles to have been reached by it: while the theory which brings the shadow of the eclipse of B.C. 585, where ancient history leads us to infer that it passed,—viz., through Ionia, and therefore through the centre of Asia Minor, and on the direct road leading from Lydia to Media, also throws the shadow of the moon in the time of Agathocles within a hundred miles of Syracuse, where we are certain from history that it must have passed. Such is the nature of the proof, the details of which may be seen in Mr. Airy's valuable paper in the *Philosophical Transactions* of 1853, that the historical date, B.C. 585, or 4th year of the 48th Olympiad,

* Mr. Airy's paper, Phil. Trans. 1853.

is the true date of this eclipse;* and with the registered
motions of the moon for upwards of one hundred years before
him, at Greenwich Observatory, and with a practical knowledge therefore of the laws which regulate her motions, he has
expressed his opinion, " that the date B.C. 585 is now established
for the eclipse of Thales beyond the possibility of doubt."† The
new Lunar and Solar Tables of the German astronomer
Hansen, published in 1857 by our Board of Admiralty, lead
to the same result, as set forth in the accompanying maps:
since which Mr. Airy has published another paper in the
Memoirs of the Royal Astronomical Society of 1857, testing
his former conclusions with regard to the eclipse of Thales, by
the eclipse of Larissa in B.C. 557, and the eclipse of Stiklastad
in A.D. 1030, and substantially confirming those conclusions. Thus the date of the eclipse, now scientifically fixed
by the highest astronomical authority, ·coincides with the
date handed down by tradition; and it would seem to be
a mark of extreme hardihood to deny the result of this
concurrent testimony. Nevertheless, some have been found
warmly contending against it, feeling that the current chronology of the period is shaken to the foundation by this decision.

Thales is said to have predicted a good olive-crop, and
Anaxagoras to have foretold the fall of an aerolite. In a note
with the initials H. C. R., to Rawlinson's Herodotus, it is observed : " The prediction of this eclipse by Thales may fairly
be classed with the prediction of a good olive-crop, or of the
fall of an aerolite. Thales, indeed, could only have obtained
the requisite knowledge for predicting eclipses from the Chaldeans; and that the science of these astronomers, although
sufficient for the investigation of lunar eclipses, did not enable
them to calculate solar eclipses,—dependent as such a calculation is, not only on the determination of the period of recur-
rence, but on the true projection also of the track of the sun's
shadow along a particular line over the surface of the earth,—

* See also Mr. Hind's Letter to the Athenæum, 28th August, 1852.
† Lecture at the Royal Institution, Feb. 1853.

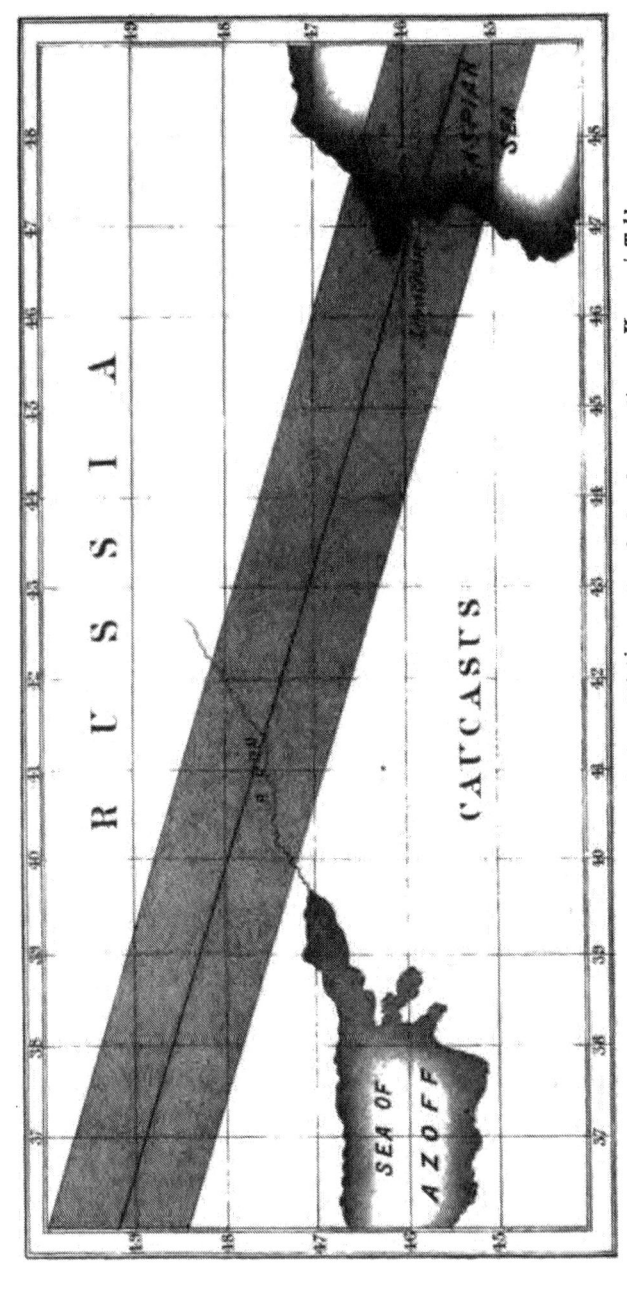

ECLIPSE · OF · B. C. 610.

Drawn according to data furnished by Mr Airy; and calculated according to Hansen's Tables

Vincent Brooks Day & Son Lith

may be inferred, from our finding that in the astronomical canon of Ptolemy, which was compiled from the Chaldean registers, the observations of the moon's eclipse are alone entered." * In reply to these observations, I quote the words of Mr. Airy: † "I think it not at all improbable that the eclipse was so predicted : and there is one easy way, and only one, of predicting it,—namely, by the *saros*, or period of 18 years, 10 days, 8 hours nearly. By use of this period, an evening eclipse may be predicted from a morning eclipse ; but a morning eclipse can rarely be predicted from an evening eclipse (as the interval of eight hours after an evening eclipse will generally throw the eclipse at the end of the *saros* into the hours of night). The evening eclipse, therefore," of B.C. 585, May 28, "which I adopt as being *most certainly the eclipse of Thales*, might be predicted from the morning eclipse" of B.C. 603, May 17. . . . . "No other of the eclipses discussed by Baily and Oltmanns present the same facility for prediction." Sir Henry Rawlinson has correctly stated the difficulty in those days of projecting on a map the true line of any coming eclipse; but the peculiar facility, without need of any such scientific projection, of anticipating that an eclipse would be visible in Ionia, on the 28th May, B.C. 585, from the fact of a large partial eclipse having occurred there on the 17th May, B.C. 603, again confirms the decision, that it was that, and no other eclipse, which Thales could have led the Ionians to expect.‡

Considering, then, that, according to our ablest astronomers, the eclipse of B.C. 585 is the only one which could have

---

* Rawlinson's Herodotus, vol. i. p. 212.

† "Proceedings of the Royal Astronomical Society," vol. xviii. p. 148.

‡ Sir G. C. Lewis, "Astronomy of the Ancients," p. 88, observes, "Thales is reported to have predicted the eclipse to the *Ionians*. If he had predicted it to the Lydians, in whose country the eclipse was total, his conduct would be intelligible ; but it seems strange that he should have predicted it to the Ionians, who had no direct interest in the event." Sir C. Lewis forgets that Miletus in Ionia was the birth-place of Thales, and that a shadow, covering two degrees of latitude, passing through Ionia would also necessarily cover Lydia.

been total on the line between Media and Lydia during fifty years, from B.C. 630 to 580,—that all ancient tradition affixes the date B.C. 585 to the battle between the Medes and Lydians, and that the solar eclipse in that year is the only one which could have been foretold by any astronomer of that early time, I assume it to be a fact established for ever, that the battle between the Lydians and Medes was fought in the year B.C. 585, and that Cyaxares, king of Media, was in that year in the full vigour of his power.* This one fact, however, is subversive of the whole scheme of Median and Persian Chronology as generally adopted, which places the death of Cyaxares in or about the year B.C. 595, ten years before the battle could have been fought; whereas it is clear, from Herodotus, that he must have lived several years after that event.

Another remarkable event connected with the reign of Cyaxares, from which we are enabled to define still more closely the time of his reign, is the final destruction of Nineveh and the Assyrian empire by the Medes under his command. The destruction of Nineveh is the last event in the reign of Cyaxares mentioned by Herodotus, and appears, therefore, to have happened, as already observed, after the conclusion of the Lydian war in B.C. 585. The Lydian war, he tells us, had been carried on by the king of Media, in the time of Labynetus, or Nabopalassar, ruler of Babylon, and somewhere within those 28 years when the Scythians held supreme power throughout all Asia. From which we have inferred that Labynetus was then local or tributary ruler of Babylon under the Scythians.† In the meanwhile, Cyaxares, having grown powerful in Media, prepared to shake off the yoke of the Scythians. He had strengthened himself already by the marriage of his son, Astyages, to the daughter of the king of Lydia in B.C. 585.

---

* In treating of Lydian chronology it has been already shown that Alyattes, king of Lydia, came to the throne in B.C. 605. A six years' war in his reign, therefore, could not have ended either in B.C. 603 or B.C. 610.

† Herodotus does not speak of him as king of Babylon, but as Λαβύνητος ὁ Βαβυλώνιος, lib. i. 74.

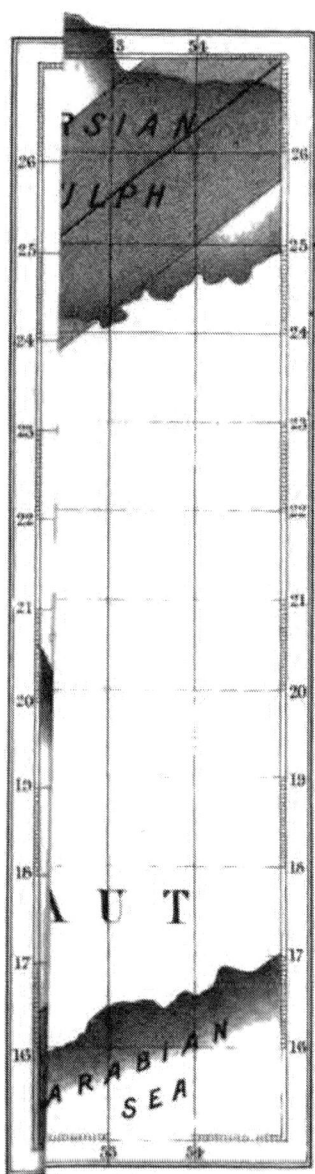

nsens tables

Turn'd Brooke . . . l . la . nd

He now, as we learn from Abydenus,* formed another
alliance by marrying his daughter, Amuhea, to Nebuchadnezzar, son of Nabopalassar, or Labynetus, ruler of Babylon,
who was acting as general of the armies of the king of
Nineveh.†

The Babylonians headed by Nebuchadnezzar (for Nabopalassar was now too infirm for war), and the Medes under
Cyaxares (the Nebuchodonosor and Ahasuerus of the book of
Tobit), now besieged Nineveh, which fell after a long siege,
Saracus, king of Nineveh, who had probably been set upon
that throne by the Scythians, on the expulsion of Nabopalassar the usurper, perishing in the flames. If we allow two
years for preparations and for the siege of that great city, after
the termination of the Lydian war, we shall arrive at the year
B.C. 583, as the date of the final destruction of Nineveh, in
which year we have already fixed the event. But if Cyaxares
was living in the year B.C. 583, and reigned only 40 years, he
could not have come to the throne earlier than the year B.C.
622; and his father, Phraortes, who, we are told, was slain in
battle by a king of Nineveh, could not have died earlier than
about the same year.

Who, then, was the king of Nineveh in the year B.C. 622,
of whom Herodotus speaks, who slew Phraortes? Undoubt-

* Euseb. Chron. Arm. Aucher., part 1, p. 27. Abydenus here speaks of the
daughter of Astyages, not of Cyaxares, having married Nebuchadnezzar. But
he or his copyist has probably written Astyages for Astibares, who was Cyaxares,
as we may infer from a fragment of Eupolemus (Müller's Frag. vol. iii. p. 229),
who records an expedition of Nebuchadnezzar and Astibares against Syria and
Judæa. The same error may have led Cicero and Solinus to have placed the
eclipse of Thales in the reign of Astyages, which is clearly incorrect.

† Nabopalassar, or Sardanapalus, must at this time have been of a great age,
and died, as we have reckoned, in B.C. 582; so that his office of general was
more nominal than real, and it was probably rather as ruler of Babylon, than as
general, that he was about this time commanded by Saracus to oppose the invasion of Necho. He had usurped the throne in the year B.C. 525, when we may
presume that he was not less than from 30 to 35 years of age, so that he was
probably nearer 80 years old than 70 at his death. Accordingly we learn,
through Athenæus, that Cleitarchus affirmed, "in his fourth book of the life of
Alexander, that Sardanapalus died of old age after having lost the empire of
Syria" (i e. Assyria). Athenæus, lib. xii. p. 529.

edly Nabopalassar was then king of Babylon, as fixed by the
eclipse registered at Babylon in his 5th year, in the 127th
year of the era of Nabonassar, or B.C. 621; and we know
from Polyhistor's Chaldæan history, that Nabupalsar, or Nabopalassar, was king of Nineveh, as well as king of Babylon.
Phraortes, therefore, was slain by Nabopalassar. This fact,
thus ascertained, enables us to fix the precise year of the
death of Phraortes, and of the accession of Cyaxares, with a
great degree of certainty. For Phraortes, king of Media, was
the same as Arphaxad, king of Media, of the book of Judith,
who, according to the Vulgate edition of that book, was slain
in the 12th year of the king of Nineveh: and the 12th year
of the reign of Nabopalassar over Nineveh and Babylon was
B.C. 614. Phraortes therefore was slain in that year, and
Cyaxares came to the throne of the Medes in the year B.C.
613.

We thus obtain the dates of the accession of each of the
four kings of Media, as follows:—

Deioces	.	. 53 years from B.C.	688	
Phraortes	.	. 22	„	635
Cyaxares	.	. 40	„	613
Astyages	.	. 35	„	573 to 539

Thus the first year of the kingdom of the Medes under Deioces
fell in the year B.C. 688, that is, where Josephus places it, in
the time of Sennacherib; and the death of Astyages in the year
B.C. 539, as confirmed by two copies of the Babylonian Canon,
which identify Nabonadius with Astyages, and place the last
year of his reign in that year. The identification we know is
wrong, but the true date of the death of Astyages has been preserved. This arrangement of Median Chronology apparently
clears up one of the greatest perplexities in the account which
Herodotus gives of these times. Herodotus, as we have seen,
counts 150 years from the first of Deioces to the last of Astyages. But when he comes to speak of the conquest of Astyages by Cyrus, he writes: "The Medes thus became subject

to the Persians, after ruling over Asia beyond the river Halys, for 128 years, excluding the time of the Scythian dominion." Now 128 years plus 28, is equal to 156 years; and 156 years and 150 years, calculated from the same point, cannot both end in the last year of Astyages. The explanation of the difficulty is perfectly simple. For we have already observed that, though the Scythians entered Asia in B.C. 610, and remained there 28 years, their sovereignty was counted only from the time when Nabopalassar, or Sardanapalus, abandoned Nineveh for Babylon, in B.C. 605, reducing the period to 22 years, which, added to 128, make up the 150 years.

Such is the well-defined outline of Median Chronology, from Deioces to Astyages, as deduced from Herodotus, and, as we believe it, to have been understood in ancient times; which alone also is consistent with the ruling date, B.C. 585, which no ancient authority ever doubted was the date of the eclipse of Thales.

With the death of Astyages, who is said by Herodotus to have left no male heir, the empire of the Medes is abruptly terminated by that historian, who from thenceforth considers that Cyrus, father of Cambyses king of Persia, became supreme and sole monarch of the whole Perso-Median empire. In this conclusion there can be little doubt that Herodotus was mistaken. This accomplished historian has selected from the various traditions current amongst the Persians in his day, what he conceived to be the true history of the rise of the Persian empire under Cyrus. But he warns us at the same time that other histories of Cyrus were then extant. Another equally accomplished Greek of a later date has thought it necessary to correct his statements. Xenophon, who had mixed with Persians of the highest rank of his day, and had made careful inquiries of them with a view to his History of Cyrus, has handed down to us a widely different account; and has given a lively history of the political state of Media and Persia after the death of Astyages. He shows us that, while Media and Persia were bound together in close confederacy, and by family alliance, after the death of Astyages, each of those

E E

kingdoms still retained its own independent prince. He tells
us, that Astyages had a son named Cyaxares, who was heir to
his dominions; that simultaneously with the reign of that son
over such portion of his dominions as remained unsubdued by
the Assyrians, Cambyses was reigning in Persia; and that
Cyrus, son of Cambyses, had not yet come to the throne. Now,
one or other of these two histories is certainly untrue. If
Cyrus, father of Cambyses king of Persia, conquered Babylon
when sole monarch over all Asia, Cambyses, son of Cyrus, and
Cyaxares, could not have been reigning independently in
Persia and Media when Babylon was taken by Cyrus, son of
Cambyses king of Persia.

We are enabled to adjudicate between the two historians,
on the evidence of a contemporary witness of the highest
character. The Jewish captive, Daniel, himself of royal extraction, had raised himself to the highest positions both in
the Babylonian and Persian states. He must have been perfectly acquainted with the persons and politics of the reigning
princes of his day. And no one was more competent to give
a correct description of the political state of Media and Persia
about the time of the taking of Babylon. Now Daniel has
left us incidentally, in a few words, so perfect a picture of the
political relations of those kingdoms in his days, as to enable
us to decide between the conflicting accounts of Herodotus
and Xenophon without fear of error. He pictures the Medo-
Persian empire, just before the taking of Babylon, in B.C. 492,
under the symbol of a ram with two horns;[*] and these two
horns, he tells us, represent the two kings, or kingdoms, of
Media and Persia. Nothing can be more distinct and decisive
than this image as regards the duplex character of the empire.
While placing Media, not Persia, nominally as the foremost
kingdom, he tells us, that the horn, or kingdom, which rose
last, viz. Persia, had then become the prevailing power; and this
twofold, yet united empire, he describes as extending itself
westward, and northward, and southward, from *Susa*, on the

* Dan. viii. 20.

river Ulai, in the province of Elam. Thus the provinces of Media and Persia, in the days of Daniel, formed together one kingdom. Neither of the two was subject to the other, but both combined to form one federal State, and so remained for a while, after Susa had become the principal seat of government. In conformity with this symbol of federal union and equality, we read, therefore, in the Book of Esther,* written after the fall of Babylon, of the " *power of Persia and Media,*" as distinguished from " the nobles and princes of the provinces," and also of the " Book of the Chronicles of the *Kings of Media and Persia.*" The Behistun inscription,† almost in the same words as Esther, speaks throughout of " *Persia and Media,* and the dependent provinces ;" and Daniel refers to the " laws of the *Medes and Persians,*" and declares that the kingdom of Babylon shall be " *divided and given to the Medes and Persians.*"‡ The contemporary evidence of Daniel, there- fore, establishes the accuracy of Xenophon, as regards the confederate character and equality of Media and Persia even as late as B.C. 492, the time of the taking of Babylon, and also as regards the titular precedence of Media up to that time ; and as decidedly sets aside the opinion of Herodotus, that Media had then become a subject province. The kingdom of Media did not cease to exist with Astyages; but some Median prince must have inherited the throne of that kingdom. When Xenophon, therefore, affirms that Cyaxares, son of Astyages, was that prince, there is every reason for believing that he has stated the truth, and that a fifth Median king really reigned. I assume it then to be a fact that Cyaxares II. succeeded his father Astyages in Media.

Xenophon has been very particular in his account of the war with Babylon, in B.C. 535, and of the first capture of that city by the Medes and Persians in the reign of Cyaxares II. ; but, having affixed no dates to his history, we are unable to

---

* Esther, i. 2 ; x. 2.
† Journal of the Royal Asiatic Society, vol. xv. p. 137.
‡ Dan. v. 29.

collect from the narrative how long Cyaxares II. remained on
the throne. All we know is, that if his father Astyages ceased
to reign in B.C. 539, Cyaxares must have begun to reign in B.C.
538. There is yet, however, another historian of these times
to be consulted, who relieves us from this difficulty.

While Xenophon has preserved the history of this second
Median king, bearing the title Cyaxares; a Hebrew writer—
some say Jehoiakim, son of Jeshua, the high-priest—has preserved the record of a second king, bearing, in the Hebrew
language, the title Ahasuerus, the first of that title having
also been king of Media. Now, there can be little doubt that
Ahasuerus and Cyaxares are one and the same title, for two
reasons :—

I. Because Nineveh was conquered, according to Herodotus, by Cyaxares I.; and the Median king who conquered
Nineveh, according to the book of Tobit, is called Ahasuerus.

II. Because the Hebrew title שׁורֹשׁ, without the vowel-
points, is "Achshurush," or "Achsurus," which, allowing for
the difference of languages, is the same as the Greek title
Αξαρις, or "Axares," and the Median title "U-akstarra,"* as
given in the Median transcript of the Behistun inscription,
which represents the title Cyaxares. The first syllable "Cy,"
in Cyaxares, we know, is merely an affix signifying "king," as
in the instances Ké-Cobab, Ké-Caus, Ké-Khosru, Ké-Lhorasp,
Ké-Gushtasp, in the Zendavesta.†

Cyaxares II. of Xenophon, therefore, is Ahasuerus II. of
the book of Esther; and it follows from this identification,
that Cyaxares, fifth king of Media, reigned not less than fourteen years; so that, if he came to the throne in B.C. 538, he
must still have been reigning in the year B.C. 525, when Cambyses, husband of Mandane, was on the throne of Persia, and
when Egypt was conquered, as Xenophon relates. We learn
from the Behistun inscription that several pretenders to the
Median throne made claim to it, as "of the race of U-akstarra,"

---

* Journal of the Royal Asiatic Society, vol. xv. part 1, p. 125.
† Zend. vol. ii. p. 422.

the last king; and that finally the province fell under the sole dominion of Darius, son of Hystaspes, who is himself described by Daniel as "son (or successor) of Ahasuerus of the seed of the Medes," which is the same expression as "of the race of U-akstarra."

There were, then, in all five kings of Media who reigned as follows:—

Deioces	53 years .	.	. B.C.	688
Phraortes	22 „	.	. „	635
Cyaxares I.	40 „ = Ahasuerus I.	„	613
Astyages	35 „	.	. „	573
Cyaxares II.	14 „ = Ahasuerus II.	„	538
			to 525

RECAPITULATION.

FROM the foregoing investigation of the times of the Hebrew monarchy, in connexion with the chronology of the neighbouring nations of the East, we have collected: —

I. That a colony from Tyre was founded at Carthage in the 7th year of the reign of Pygmalion, in the year B.C. 846 (pp. 392-4); and that the building of the Temple of Jerusalem was commenced, in the 4th year of Solomon, in the 144th year before that date, that is, in B.C. 990, just 25 years below the common date.

II. That according to the annals of Shalmanezer II., recorded on the Black Obelisk in the British Museum, Benhadad, king of Damascus, died about the year B.C. 843; from which we have inferred, that Asa, king of Judah, who in his 26th year sent presents to Benhadad, could not have presented his offering to that king earlier than about B.C. 908, that is, 65 years before Benhadad's death, or 25 years later than the common date (p. 363).

III. That from the solar eclipse registered at Nineveh, which occurred in the year B.C. 763, it is reckoned that Tiglath-Pileser, king of Assyria, who came to the throne in the 19th year following, began to reign in May B.C. 744; and since Pul, the predecessor of Tiglath-Pileser, received 1000 talents of silver from Menahem, king of Samaria, to set him on the throne, on which he reigned but 10 years, and Tiglath-Pileser, according to his own annals, about his 8th year, also took tribute of Menahem, we have inferred that that tribute was taken in the 9th or 10th year of Menahem in the year 738 or 739, about 25 years below the common date (p. 364).

IV. That from the Assyrian Canon, it appears that Sennacherib came to the throne in August B.C. 704; and since Shalmanezer, who destroyed Samaria, is the same as Shalman spoken of by Hosea (x. 14) when Samaria was about to be destroyed, and when the calf of Bethaven was about to be sent to king Jareb, or San-ach-jareb (x. 5, 6), Samaria was destroyed in the time of Sennacherib, not less than 17 years later than the common date (p. 366).

V. That the exact date of the destruction of Samaria by Shalmanezer is recorded by Demetrius as the 474th year before the reign of the 4th Ptolemy, or B.C. 696; and that this date is confirmed by the reckoning on tomb-stones now extant in the Crimea, which count from this year, being just 25 years lower than the common reckoning (p. 366).

VI. That the partial eclipse of the sun visible at Jerusalem on the 11th January, B.C. 689, which alone of all eclipses about that time, as being near the winter solstice, could have caused the shadow to have gone down and to return on the dial, or steps of Ahaz, "ten steps," falls in with the 14th year of Hezekiah, king of Judah, according to the same reckoning, just 25 years lower than the common date (p. 177).

VII. That the eclipse of Thales, which preceded the fall of Nineveh, and the accession of Nebuchadnezzar, and which marks the year of the marriage of Astyages, took place in the year B.C. 585, just 25 years lower than the commonly received date of that event, B.C. 610.

VIII. That according to the annals of Esarhaddon, that king towards the close of his reign set up in Lower Egypt, about the year B.C. 669, 20 petty kings, or nomarchs, whose government, according to Diodorus, who speaks only of 12 kings, lasted for 15 years, that is, till the year B.C. 653, when Psammetichus took the throne; and since Psammetichus reigned 54 years, and Necho II. 16 years, the fall of Necho and the battle of Carchemish took place in B.C. 582, just 25 full years lower than the common date.

IX. That according to Demetrius the last carrying away of captives from Jerusalem by Nebuchadnezzar, in his 23rd year, took place in the year B.C. 560, just 25 years below the common date (p. 306).

X. That the decree of Cyrus commanding that the temple of Jerusalem should be built could not, therefore, have been issued in B.C. 560, as supposed by Africanus and Eusebius; nor even so early as B.C. 538, or 536, as determined by Scaliger and his contemporaries, and now generally received; since the decree for the restoration would thus have fallen 25 or 27 years only after the destruction of the temple (p. 296).

XI. That the years of the reign of Darius spoken of by Daniel, Haggai, and Zechariah, are counted from the year B.C. 492, when Darius was 62 years of age; 46 years lower than the commonly received date for Darius the Mede, B.C. 538.

XII. That from the first year of Darius B.C. 492 to the birth of Christ is 70 weeks of years, or 490 years.

KEY TO PERSIAN CHRONOLOGY.

FROM the data thus collected it is clear beyond dispute, that the reckoning of the times of the Hebrew monarchy, as commonly received, has been set throughout exactly 25 years above the true dates: that the destruction of the city and temple of Jerusalem, in B.C. 563, took place about the time of the rise of the Persian monarchy under Cyrus, father of Cambyses king of Persia: that the seventy years' desolation of the temple and city was nearly concurrent with the first seventy years of the Persian monarchy: and that Cyrus, the first king of Persia, could not, therefore, have been the "Cyrus" spoken of by Ezra, as having released the Jews from captivity, and as having commanded that the temple should be rebuilt.

Who, then, we have to inquire, was Cyrus spoken of by Isaiah in the words, " He is my shepherd, and shall perform all my pleasure?" Who was that Cyrus, king of Persia, who, according to Ezra, declared, " The Lord God of heaven hath given me all the kingdoms of the earth: and He hath charged me to build Him an house at Jerusalem?"

Now, we have but three original authorities on the subject of the rise of the Persian empire, viz., Herodotus, Ctesias, and Xenophon. Let us first inquire what Herodotus says concerning Cyrus and his successors.

Herodotus, speaking of the pedigree of Cyrus, father of Cambyses king of Persia, names —

B.C.

1st. Cyrus, concerning whom nothing is related.*
2nd. Cambyses, son of Cyrus, who married Mandane, daughter of Astyages ; and who, he says, was not a king.†

* Herod. i. cxi.   † Herod. i. cvii.

B.C.

3rd. Cyrus, son of Cambyses and Mandane, called the Mule,
  who is said to have conquered Astyages his grandfather, to have overthrown the kingdoms of Lydia
  and Babylon, and to have died in battle with
  Tomyris, after reigning 29 years, say from . . 559

4th. Cambyses, son of Cyrus, great-grandson of Astyages,
  who conquered Egypt, and is said to have reigned
  8 years from 529

5th. Smerdis, the Magian, who reigned 7 months . . 522

6th Darius, son of Hystaspes, 36 years from . . . 521

7th. Xerxes, son of Darius, 21 years from   . . . 486

This is the reckoning of Persian Chronology which has
been hitherto universally accepted, on the assumption that
the eclipse of Thales took place either in B.C. 610, or 603. It
is, however, palpably incorrect. For Astyages married in the
year of the eclipse in B.C. 585, and could not, therefore, have
had a grandson of sufficient age to take the throne in 559, or
a great-grandson of an age to take the throne in 529. We
have no hesitation, therefore, in setting aside the arrangement
of Herodotus as absolutely mistaken.

Nevertheless, Herodotus has faithfully recorded that there
was a king of Persia who overthrew Crœsus, and who captured
Babylon, called Cyrus ; and that he was the son of Cambyses
son of Cyrus, and of Mandane daughter of Astyages, and
therefore, called " the Mule." The evidence of the Delphic
oracle, warning Crœsus against a mule who should reign in
Persia, and the last words of Nebuchadnezzar concerning the
Persian Mule,* go far to establish these facts. He has also
truly recorded that Cambyses was set on the throne of Persia
when Darius was between nineteen and twenty years of age.
Herodotus, however, has mistaken Cambyses who married
Mandane, and conquered Egypt, for the son, instead of the
father of Cyrus the Mule : and he is also incorrect in supposing that Cyrus had issue. For Cyrus " the Mule " twice conquered Babylon, and when Babylon was taken and destroyed

* See p. 381.

for the last time by Darius, that king was derided by the Babylonians, who exclaimed, "When mules bring forth then may Babylon be taken;" which seems to imply that Cyrus the Mule, now dead, had left no issue, and that one only of his race, that is, of a race of mules, was capable of taking that city. Cambyses, son of Cyrus, who reigned in Persia, could hardly, therefore, be the son of Cyrus the Mule.

Ctesias, who resided for many years in Persia in the reign of Artaxerxes Mnemon (whereas Herodotus was only a visitant there for a time), has deliberately contradicted Herodotus on this point, and has left the following record of the succession of Persian kings:—

B.C.

1. Cyrus, the founder of the Persian empire, who conquered Astyages, and afterwards married his daughter; and having reigned 30 years in Persia, died of a wound received in battle with Amoræus, say in 530 . . 560

2. Cambyses, son of Cyrus, who conquered Egypt, and reigned 18 years over the Persians, (having come to the throne when Darius was 19 or 20 years old)[*] 535-6

3. The Magus, who reigned 7 months after the death of Cambyses 518

4. Darius, son of Hystaspes, who reigned 31 years . . 517

5. Xerxes, son of Darius 486

Ctesias informs us that Cyrus who conquered Astyages was in no way related to him at the time of the conquest, and not therefore his grandson; and is altogether silent concerning the capture of Babylon by this prince. This Cyrus, wounded in battle with Amoræus, is evidently the same king as he who was slain in battle with Tomyris,[†] and whose son Cambyses, according to Herodotus, married Mandane; yet a king quite distinct from Cyrus the Mule, the grandson of Astyages.

Xenophon, who wrote about the same time as Ctesias, and probably adopted his reckoning in his life of Cyrus, sets at rest all difficulty on this point. For he says, "Cyrus is said to have had for his father Cambyses king of the Persians. It is agreed that he was born of a mother named Mandane: and Mandane

* Herod. i. 208, 209.　　† The one name is a corruption of the other.

was the daughter of Astyages, king of the Medes." * Cyrus, he tells us, acted as leader of the joint forces of the Medes and Persians, and first conquered Crœsus, then Babylon, during the reign of his father Cambyses in Persia, and of Cyaxares king of Media. His conquests, therefore, were accomplished between the years B.C. 536 and 518. Crœsus, we have seen, was conquered in the year B.C. 534, and Babylon was taken say in the year B.C. 532. The years of Cambyses are counted as king of Babylon, after the death of his father, from 529; for Cyrus, his son, was not yet a king when he took Babylon. It was not till he had taken that city a second time, after he had married the daughter of Cyaxares, with whom he received the kingdom of Media, nor till after the death of Cyaxares, and the revolt of the whole empire from Cambyses, nor also till the death of that king, that he could proclaim himself sovereign of all the kingdoms of the earth, in B.C. 518. It was then that he issued his decree for the rebuilding of the temple of Jerusalem, to which no heed was given by his successor, Darius, till twenty-six years after, when it had been forgotten by all except by the Jews themselves, and he died soon after the death of his father Cambyses, after a reign of nine years.

From this analysis of the records of the three Persian historians it would appear,—I. That not one only, as Herodotus supposes, but two kings bearing the name Cyrus reigned in Persia: one the father of Cambyses and the conqueror of Astyages, the other the son of Cambyses, who conquered Babylon in the reign of his father, and afterwards released the Jews. II. That there was but one Cambyses son of Cyrus, not two, viz., he who was king of Persia, and conquered Egypt. III. That the whole Persian empire revolted from Cambyses while he was in Egypt; and that after his return from Egypt Cyrus proclaimed himself universal king, on the second capture of Babylon.

That such is the true history, is confirmed by extant cuneiform inscriptions. For Darius on the rock of Behistûn writes, "Cambyses son of Cyrus, of our race (that is, son of Cyrus I.), he was king before me"—"when Cambyses proceeded to Egypt,

---

* Cyropædia, ch. ii.

then the state became wicked,"—"the whole state becar
bellious. From Cambyses it went over to him (Gon
both Persia and Media, and the other provinces."

And upon a brick found at Senkereh, the legend
which is translated by Sir H. Rawlinson, we read—

"I am Cyrus, son of Cambyses, the powerful king."

The true succession of Persian kings, therefore, d
from Persian inscriptions, is, that which has been preser
Ctesias and Xenophon, thus—

1. " Cyrus, of our race," father of king Cambyses.
2. " Cambyses the powerful king."
3. " Cyrus, son of Cambyses the powerful king."
4. Darius.

And since Darius declares himself on the rock t
been the immediate successor of Cambyses, this " Cyr
of Cambyses " must have reigned during the life of his
as Xenophon relates.   This, therefore, is Cyrus II.

That Herodotus has constructed his history of Cyru
the exploits of these two different Persian princes bearir
name, appears from the writings of native Persians, whc
of two great kings; the first Kai-Khosru, the hero of the
Shah-Nameh, the second Coresh, who released the Jews
cerning the first of these kings, Sir William Jones wri
shall only doubt that the Khosrau of Firdausi was the
of the first Greek historian, and the hero of the oldest p
and moral romance, when I doubt that Louis Quator
Lewis the Fourteenth were one and the same French
And again: " Whatever our chronologers may say, i
easy to conceive that the Jews were delivered by this
the name Coresh has no affinity with the Persian
Khosru, and we cannot suppose any corruption in the
text; whereas all the Persian writers agree that a
named Coresh, who was sent by Bahaman, son of As
to govern Babylon, in the room of Baltasar, actually pr
the captive Jews, and permitted them to rebuil
temple."*

* Sixth Discourse on the Persians, p. 106.   Short History of
411.

The chronicle of Tabari records that, after the death of Kai-Khosru, Lohrasp (Cambyses) took the throne ; that Gushtasp (Darius Hystaspes) succeeded him; and that in the reign of Gushtasp, a general named Coresh, governor of 'Irâq, was sent against Nabuchodonosor (Nabonadius), who ruled at Babylon, and that having captured this prince he sent him to Balk. After this, Coresh took the throne of Babylon, and immediately released the children of Israel from captivity.*

With regard to the time of the death of Cyrus the Mule, whether immediately after the death of Cambyses, or early in the reign of Darius, it is difficult to determine with exactness. A passage from Megasthenes, however, throws much light upon the question. He tells us, that, after Nebuchadnezzar, " his son Evil-merodach reigned, who was forthwith slain by his son-in-law Neriglissar (Nergal-sharezar).† To him (Evil-Merodach) there remained one surviving son, Labosoracus, whose fate also was to have fallen by a violent death. He then commanded that Nabonedochus (Nabonadius) should be placed on the throne, to whom it by no means belonged of right. When Babylon was taken (that is, the second time) Cyrus gave to this king the principality of Carmania. *Darius the king drove him away from that province.*"‡

This account of Megasthenes, though not much at variance with the chronicle of Tabari, differs somewhat from that of Berosus as copied by Josephus, inasmuch as Nergalsharezar is said to have appointed Nabonadius king or regent before his own death. Berosus gives two years to Evil-merodach, four to Nergalsharezar, nine months to Laborosoarchod, and seventeen years to Nabonadius, in all twenty-three years and nine months from the death of Nebuchadnezzar in B.C. 539. This reckoning leads us down to the year 516 for the fall of Nabonadius, and the accession of Cyrus. It is highly probable, however, as Megasthenes relates, that Nergalsharezar, who, on

* Zotenberg's Translation of Tabari, p. 495.

+ Possibly Nergal-sharezar, the Rab mag, (Jerem. xxxiv. 3) without whose sanction probably no king could be enthroned.

‡ Euseb. Auch. p. 30.

the death of Evil-merodach, in 536 or 535, may have taken command of the Chaldee army and carried on the war with Cyrus, may have appointed Nabonadius, a man of ability in Babylon, and who had married a daughter of Nebuchadnezzar (Dan. v. 10), to act as regent during his absence, while Labo-rosoarchod, son of Evilmerodach, was nominated king. And thus the reign of Nabonadius of seventeen years would be counted, not from the death of Nergalsharezar, but from B.C. 535. If, then, with Megasthenes we place Nabonadius on the throne about the year 535, his seventeenth year, when he was conquered by Cyrus must have been the year 519. Megasthenes tells us that Nabonadius was still reigning in Carmania when Darius came to the throne in 517, and by him was driven away. Now, the fact, that Nabonadius reigned in Carmania till the beginning of the reign of Darius, is most important, as fixing the reign of that king, and, therefore, also the death of Cyrus, many years later than where it is commonly placed.

The cardinal date of our arrangement (see p. 357) is the year B.C. 582, when the battle of Carchemish was fought, in the first year of Nebuchadnezzar; and his last year therefore was 539. The first year of the reign of Darius, son of Hystaspes, 517, is also a fundamental date (see p. 374). Between these two dates Nabonadius must have reigned.

Megasthenes and Berosus, who both lived in the time of Alexander, had, we conceive, equally correctly preserved the succession of Babylonian kings. Abydenus also, we think, has correctly abstracted that history. Josephus has slightly varied from Berosus, as regards Nergalsharezar, in order to lengthen out the time. While Polyhistor, followed by the writer of the Canon of Ptolemy, has entirely vitiated the record, by placing the reign of Cyrus for nine years, and Cambyses for eight years, between the reigns of Nabonadius and Darius.

Lucian writes, " Cyrus, the ancient king of Persia, as Persian and Assyrian annals attest, with which also Onesicritus, the historian of Alexander, seems to agree, when about one hundred years old inquired after each of his friends individually, and hearing that most of them had been put to death by his son Cambyses, who had given out that this was done by his command, being deeply afflicted with shame and grief at the atrocities of his son thus reflected upon himself, put an end to his life." Lucian has evidently put the lives of grandfather and grandson together to make the life of one Cyrus. His testimony is, however, valuable, to the effect that Cyrus died either in or after the reign of Cambyses.*

John of Malala has preserved some particulars connected with the death of Cyrus otherwise unknown. His death took place, he says, after a naval combat with the Samians, who after the overthrow of Crœsus had obtained the empire of the seas. It appears that he conducted a naval expedition against the Samians, which must have taken place in or after the time of Polycrates, the contemporary of Cambyses, and that having been worsted, he returned home and was slain. Pythagoras the Samian is quoted as authority for the fact that he died in war, which is said also to have been recorded in the Chronography of Africanus.†

The Cyrus who died after a naval battle with the Samians, can hardly be identified with Cyrus I. who was slain in war with Amoræus, or Tomyris, far in the east. Cyrus I., if we trust Herodotus, left his body unburied in the hands of Tomyris. It is then the tomb of Cyrus II. which is spoken of by Arrian as seen in the days of Alexander, and which is still extant at Murghâb, or Pasargadæ.

The conclusion arrived at is—

I. That Cyrus, son of Cambyses king of Persia, conquered Evil-merodach in B.C. 536 or 535; that he deposed Crœsus in 534; that he took Babylon for the first time in 532; that he became king of Media in 527, from which date the nine years of his reign are counted; that he took Babylon a second time in 519; and that Cyaxares being now dead, and Cambyses, his father, having died in 518, on his return from Egypt, he became universal monarch in that year.

II. That in the year B.C. 518, "he made a proclamation

* Lucian. Macrobii.
† Joan Mal. p. 158. Dindorf.

Hebrew Chronology adjusted to the Sabbatical Years and Jubilees.

B.C.	Kings of Judah.	Kings of Israel.		Kings of Assyria.	Remarks from Holy Scripture.
880	14 Jehosaphat	17 Ahab		7 Asshur-izir	Benhadad attacks Samaria, 1 Kings, xx. 1.
9	15	18		8 pal?	
8	16	19		9	
7	17	20	Era of the Temple.	10	
6	18	21		11	
5	19	22		12	Ahab slain in battle at Ramoth-gilead. 1 Kings, xxii. 34.
4	20	1 Ahaziah		13	
3	21	2		14	
2	22	1 Joram		15	
1	23	2		112 16	
870	24	3		17	
9	25	4		18	
8	1 Jehoram	5		19	
7	2	6		20	
6	3	7		21	Benhadad comes against Samaria. 2 Kings, vi. 24.
5	4	8		22	
4	5	9		23	
3	6	10		24	
2	7	11		25	
1	1 Ahaziah	12		122 26	Death of Jezebel, say at the age of 72.
860	1 Athaliah	1 Jehu		27	Hazael anointed king before the death of Benhadad.*
9	2	2		28	Wounds Jehoram, 2 Chron.
8	3	3		1 Shalmane-	Jehu slays 70 sons of Ahab.
7	4	4		2 zer II.	
6	5	5		3	Hazael now leads the army of Benhadad, owing probably to the infirmity of his father.
5	6	6		4	
4	1 Jehoash	7		5	
3	2	8		6	The Assyrians defeat the confederate forces of South Syria, Egypt, Arabia, and Palestine, at Aroer,† in B.C. 853.‡
2	3	9		7	
1	4	10		132 8	
850	5	11		9	Ahab of Jezreel (probably one of the sons of Ahab not slain by Jehu) associated with Benhadad's army.
9	6	12		10	
8	7	13		11	Annals of Shalmaneser.
7	8	14		12	
6	9	15		13	
5	10	16		14	
4	11	17		15	Death of Benhadad in B.C. 843.§ Ibid.
3	12	18		16	
2	13	19		17	
1	14	20		142 18	Shalmaneser takes tribute of Jehu. Ibid.

* 1 Kings, xix. 15; 2 Kings, viii. 15.
† "From Aroer, even Gilead and Bashan," 2 Kings, x. 33.
‡ Rawlinson: Athenæum, 18 May, 1867.
§ Benhadad, probably now 86 years of age. See B.C. 908.

present Cambyses, son of Cyrus, who is recorded on the rock
.at Behistûn as the immediate predecessor of Darius. So
strongly is this inference impressed upon the mind of Mons.
de Saulcy, that in a recent work upon the books of Ezra
and Nehemiah, he has not hesitated to pronounce that
" C'est l'écrivain sacré qui se trompe, ou bien plutôt c'est un
copiste maladroit qui a écrit le nom Artakhchacta au lieu de
Kambouziah." *

Accepting, however, the book of Ezra as it is written, it is
clear :—I. That the name of King Cambyses does not occur
in that book, where it ought to occur, if the common reckoning
were the true one. II. That, as has already been observed,
the names Ahasuerus and Artaxerxes probably represent one
and the same king. III. That Artaxerxes, or Artachshastha,
who in conjunction with Darius, in his sixth year as King of
Babylon, B.C. 485, sanctioned the completion of the Temple,
could be no other than Xerxes, or Ahasuerus, who in the
year 486, four years after the battle of Marathon, was raised
to the throne of Persia by his father Darius, and then, or soon
after, probably assumed the title Artaxerxes.†

The omission, then, of the name of Cambyses in the book
of Ezra between the reigns of Cyrus and Darius, confirms the
conclusion that Cyrus who issued the decree was not Cyrus
I., whose successor was Cambyses, but Cyrus II., the son of
Cambyses, who reigned during the life of his father, and who
immediately preceded Darius.

Now we have seen from the Tyrian annals, which were
perfect in the days of Josephus, that Cyrus began to reign in
the fiftieth year counted from the 7th of Nebuchadnezzar, B.C.
576, that is to say, in the year 527, which was in the time of
Cambyses.‡ And if, as commonly reckoned, he reigned nine
full years, his death may be placed either at the end of the
year B.C. 518, or the beginning of 517, as already surmised.

* F. de Saulcy. Etude Chronologique des livres d'Esdras et de Nehemie,
p. 73. 1868.
† See pp. 349, 350.   ‡ P. 384.

F F

Hebrew Chronology adjusted to the Sabbatical Years and Jubilees.

B.C.	Kings of Judah.	Kings of Israel.		Remarks from Holy Scripture.
1000	27 David			
9	28			
8	29			
7	30			Hiram sends cedar trees
6	31			and fir trees to David
5	32			for the Temple. 2
4	33			Chron. ii. 8.
3	1 Solomon			Solomon makes a treaty
2	2			with Hiram, king of
1	3			Tyre.
990	4			Solomon begins to build
9	5			the Temple in the
8	6			480th year from the
7	7			Exodus, the 481st
6	8			from the mission of
5	9			Moses,‡ B.C. 990.
4	10	[8th month*		
3	11 Temple fini	shed 11th year		
2	12 Temple ded	icated †	1	Zion becomes the "Holy
1	13		2	City" in the year of
980	14			Jubilee, the 490th
9	15			year from the mis-
8	16			sion of Moses, B.C.
7	17			982.
6	18			
5	19			
4	20			
3	21			
2	22			
1	23		12	Solomon finishes his
970	24			Palace in the 20th
9	25			year from the founda-
8	26			tion of the Temple.
7	27			2 Chron. viii. 1.
6	28			
5	29			
4	30			
3	31			
2	32			
1	33		22	

The vertical label in the fourth column reads: **Era of the Temple.**

* 1 Kings, vi. 38.   † viii. 2.   ‡ vi. 1.

Secular Chronology adjusted to Hebrew Chronology.

B.C.	Kings of Tyre.	Kings of Egypt.	Remarks from Secular Writers.
1000	2 Hiram		
9	3		
8	4		
7	5		
6	6		
5	7		
4	8		
3	9		
2	10		
1	11		
990	12		Temple of Jerusalem built,
9	13		according to Josephus
8	14		copying from Menander,
7	15		in the 144th year before
6	16		the flight of Dido to Car-
5	17		thage,* which took place
4	18		in B.C. 846. (See p. 395.)
3	19		
2	20		
1	21		
980	22		
9	23		
8	24		
7	25		
6	26		
5	27		
4	28		
3	29		
2	30		
1	31		
970	32		
9	33		
8	34		
7	1 Baalzarus		
6	2		
5	3		
4	4		
3	5		
2	6		
1	7		

* Josephus, Ant. ix. xiv. 2.

Hebrew Chronology adjusted to the Sabbatical Years and Jubilees.

B.C.	Kings of Judah.	Kings of Israel.		Remarks from Holy Scripture.
960	34 Solomon			
9	35			Jeroboam takes refuge
8	36			with Shishak, king of
7	37			Egypt, till the death
6	38			of Solomon.*
5	39			
4	40			
3	1 Rehoboam	1 Jeroboam		Secession of the 10 tribes
2	2	2		of Israel from the Holy
1	3	3	32	City 390 years before
950	4	4		the destruction.†
9	5	5		In the fifth year of
8	6	6		Rehoboam Shishak
7	7	7		comes against Jeru-
6	8	8		salem.‡
5	9	9		
4	10	10		
3	11	11		
2	12	12		
1	13	13	42	
940	14	14		
9	15	15		
8	16	16		
7	17	17		
6	1 Abijah	18		
5	2	19		
4	3	20		
3	1 Asa	21 Nadab		" The land had rest."
2	2	22		2 Chron. xiv. 6.
1	3	1 Baasha	52	
930	4	2		
9	5	3		
8	6	4		
7	7	5		
6	8	6		
5	9	7		
4	10	8		
3	11	9		Zerah the Ethiopian makes war
2	12	10		on Asa.
1	13	10 11	62	2 Chron. xvi. 9.

Era of the Temple.

* 1 Kings, xi. 40.   † Ezek. iv. 1-5.   ‡ 1 Kings, xiv. 25.

Secular Chronology adjusted to Hebrew Chronology.

B.C.	Kings of Tyre.	Kings of Egypt.	Remarks from Secular Writers.
960	8 Baalzarus		
9	9		
8	10	1 Sesonchosis	
7	11	2 or	
6	12	3 Shishak	
5	13	4	
4	14	5	
3	15	6	
2	16	7	
1	17	8	
950	1 Abdastartus	9	
9	2	10	
8	3	11	
7	4	12	
6	5	13	
5	6	14	
4	7	15	
3	8	16	
2	9	17	
1	1 Astartus	18	
940	2	19	
9	3	20	
8	4	21	
7	5	22	
6	6	23	
5	7	24	
4	8	25	
3	9	26	
2	10	1 Osorchon	Jezebel, the daughter of Ithobal, born about this time. P. 397.
1	11	2	
930	12	3	
9	1 Astarimus	4	
8	2	5	
7	3	6	
6	4	7	
5	5	8	
4	6	9	
3	7	10	
2	8	11	
1	9	12	

The dates of the reigns of the Kings of Egypt down to the year B.C. 777 are in some degree conjectural.

Hebrew Chronology adjusted to the Sabbatical Years and Jubilees.

B.C.	Kings of Judah.	Kings of Israel.	Era of the Temple.	Kings of Assyria.	Remarks from Holy Scripture.
920	14 Asa II.	12 Baasha			Covenant renewed in the Sabbatical year, 2 Chron. xv. 10. Deut. xxxi. 10-11.
9	15	13			
8	16	14			
7	17	15			
6	18	16			
5	19	17			
4	20	18			
3	21	19			
2	22	20			
1	23	21	72		
910	24	22			
9	25	23		1 Bil-anir?*	
8	26	24		2	Asa sends presents to Benhadad, 2 Chron. xvi. 2, 3, in the days of Baasha. See note, p. 362.
7	27	1 Elah		3	
6	28	2		4	
5	29	3		5	
4	30	1 Zimri		6	
3	31	1 Omri		7	
2	32	2		8	
1	33	3	82	9	
900	34	4		10	
9	35	5		11	
8	36	6		12	
7	37	7		13	
6	38	1 Ahab		14	Ahab marries Jezebel, daughter of Ithobal, king of Tyre. Jos. Ant. viii. 13, 1.
5	39	2		15	
4	40-41	3		16	
3	1 Jehosaphat	4		17	
2	2	5		18	The book of the law read in the Sabbatical year, 2 Chron. xvii. 9.
1	3	6	92	19	
890	4	7		20	No rain for three years in the reign of Ahab. 1 Kings, xviii. 2.
9	5	8		1 Tiglath-i-	
8	6	9		2 bar?	450 priests of Baal slain by Elijah. xviii. 40.
7	7	10		3	
6	8	11		1 Asshur-izir-	
5	9	12		2 pal?	
4	10	13		3	
3	11	14		4	
2	12	15		5	
1	13	16	102	6	

* The names of the kings of Assyria, as deciphered by Rawlinson, are not certain. Their dates are fixed, being calculated from the eclipse of B.C. 763, eighteen years before the accession of Tiglath-pileser.

Secular Chronology adjusted to the reckoning of the Hebrews.

B.C.	Kings of Tyre.	Kings of Egypt.	Remarks from Secular Writers.
880	2 Mytgenus	13 Osorchon II.	
9	3	14	
8	4	15	
7	5	16	
6	6	17	
5	7	18	
4	8	19	
3	9	20	
2	10	21	
1	11	22	
870	12	23	
9	13	24	
8	14	25	
7	15	1 Sesonchosis	
6	16	2 II.	
5	17	3	
4	18	4	
3	19	5	
2	20	6	
1	21	7	
860	22	8	
9	23	9	
8	24	10	
7	25	11	
6	26	12	
5	27	13	
4	28	14	
3	29	15	
2	1 Pygmalion	16	
1	2	17	
850	3	18	
9	4	19	
8	5	20	
7	6	21	
6	7	22	The colony of Carthage founded in the 7th year of Pygmalion, 700 years before the destruction of Carthage, in B.C. 146, and 144 years after Solomon began to build the Temple of Jerusalem. See p. 394.
5	8	23	
4	9	24	
3	10	25	
2	11	1 Tachelothis	
1	12	2 II.	

Hebrew Chronology adjusted to the Sabbatical Years and Jubilees.

B.C.	Kings of Judah.	Kings of Israel.	Era of the Temple.	Kings of Assyria.	Remarks from Holy Scripture.
880	14 Jehosaphat	17 Ahab		7 Asshur-izir pal?	Benhadad attacks Samaria, 1 Kings, xx. 1.
9	15	18		8	
8	16	19		9	
7	17	20		10	
6	18	21		11	
5	19	22		12	Ahab slain in battle at Ramoth-gilead. 1 Kings, xxii. 34.
4	20	1 Ahaziah		13	
3	21	2		14	
2	22	1 Joram		15	
1	23	2	112	16	
870	24	3		17	
9	25	4		18	
8	1 Jehoram	5		19	
7	2	6		20	
6	3	7		21	Benhadad comes against Samaria. 2 Kings, vi. 24.
5	4	8		22	
4	5	9		23	
3	6	10		24	
2	7	11		25	
1	1 Ahaziah	12	122	26	Death of Jezebel, say at the age of 72.
860	1 Athaliah	1 Jehu		27	Hazael anointed king before the death of Benhadad.*
9	2	2		28	
8	3	3		1 Shalmanezer II.	Wounds Jehoram, 2 Chron.
7	4	4		2	Jehu slays 70 sons of Ahab.
6	5	5		3	
5	6	6		4	Hazael now leads the army of Benhadad, owing probably to the infirmity of his father.
4	1 Jehoash	7		5	
3	2	8		6	The Assyrians defeat the confederate forces of South Syria, Egypt, Arabia, and Palestine, at Aroer,† in B.C. 853.‡
2	3	9		7	
1	4	10	132	8	
850	5	11		9	Ahab of Jezreel (probably one of the sons of Ahab not slain by Jehu) associated with Benhadad's army.
9	6	12		10	
8	7	13		11	Annals of Shalmaneser.
7	8	14		12	
6	9	15		13	
5	10	16		14	
4	11	17		15	
3	12	18		16	Death of Benhadad in B.C. 843.§ Ibid.
2	13	19		17	
1	14	20	142	18	Shalmaneser takes tribute of Jehu. Ibid.

* 1 Kings, xix. 15 ; 2 Kings, viii. 15.
† "From Aroer, even Gilead and Bashan," 2 Kings, x. 33.
‡ Rawlinson : Athenæum, 18 May, 1867.
§ Benhadad, probably now 86 years of age. See B.C. 908.

Secular Chronology adjusted to the reckoning of the Hebrews.

B.C.	Kings of Tyre and Sidon	Kings of Egypt		Kings of Babylon	Kings of Lydia / Media	Remarks from Secular Writers.
720	15 Iluæus 7	10 Psammus.		2 Mardoc-		A plurality of kings of Assyria is spoken of at this time. The court of Tiglath-pileser having been probably first removed to Harrân, afterwards to Damascus. Sargon second on the throne.
9	16 and 8		Zet, or 1	3 empa-		
8	17 Meten- 9		Sethos, 2	4 dus		
7	18 na 10		or So 3	5		
6	19 11		4	6		Metenna still reigning at Tyre.*
5	20 12		5	7		Tiglath-pileser, lord paramount, in his third Syrian campaign, by the hand of Sargon takes Samaria, deposes Pekah, and sets up Hoshea. Annals of Tig. Pil.; Annals of Sargon.
4	21 13		6	8		
3	14 (Tyre)	1 Bocco-	7	9		
2	15	2 ris	8	10		Sargon lays tribute on Bocooris in 714.
1	16	3	9	11		Sargon succeeds Tiglath-pileser 711, three years before he takes Babylon. Annals of Sargon.
710	17	4	10	12	Kings of Lydia.	
9	18	5	11	1 Archi-		Sargon, or Sarru-yakina-arku, king over Babylon.
8	19	6	12	2 anus,		Sabaco, the Ethiopian, kills Boccoris, and the Ethiopians possess Upper Egypt for 52 years till B.C. 655. Herod.
7	20	1 Sab-	13	3 or Sar-		
6	21	2 baco	14	4 gon		
5	22	3	15	5	Gyges	
4	23	4	16		1	Sargon dies in the month Ab, in the year of the archonship of Pakharbil, B.C. 705-4. Assyrian Canon.
3	24	5	17		2	
2	25	6	18	1 Belibus	3	
1	26	7	19	2	4	
700	27	8	20	3	5	Sennacherib counts his first year from B.C. 704. Sets up Belibus in 703, whose years are recounted from 702.
9	28	9	21	1 Aprona-	6	
8	29	10	22	2 dius	7	
7	30	11	23	3	8	
6	31	12	24	4	9	
5	32	1 Seve-	25	5	10	Shalmanezer besieges Tyre for five years, in the reign of Iluæus, who reigns 36 years. Josephus Ant. ix. xiv. 2.
4	33	2 chus	26	6 [lus	11	
3	34	3	27	1 Regibe-	12	
2	35	4	28	1 Mesessi-	13	
1	36	5	29	2 mordac,	14	
690	(Sidon)	6	30	3 or Me-	Kings of Media. 15	Sennacherib in his third campaign, in 690, drives Iluæus from Sidon, and then captures many of the cities of Judah from Hezekiah. Annals of Sennacherib.
9		7	31	4 rodach	16	
8	Tubaal	8 Amme-	1	Baladan,	1 Deio- 17	
7		9 res	2	son of	2 ces. 18	
6		10	3	Baladan.	3 19	
5		11	4	Is. xxxix. 1.	4 20	Eclipse of the Sun at Jerusalem, 11th Jan. 689.
4		12	5		5 21	
3		1 Tirha-	6		6 22	Sennacherib attacks Egypt, in the reign of Sethos, or Zet, in 689.† Herod. ii. 141.
2		2 kah	7		7 23	
1		3	8		8 24	

* Annals of Tiglath-Pileser II. by G. Smith. Zeitschrift. Jan. 1869. p.15.

† Tirhakah, king of Ethiopia, not yet king of Egypt, comes to the assistance of Sethos, king of Egypt, and Hezekiah. 2 Kings, xix. 9.

Hebrew Chronology adjusted to the Sabbatical Years and Jubilees.

B.C.	Kings of Judah.	Kings of Israel.	Era of the Temple.	Kings of Assyria.	Remarks from Holy Scripture.
880	14 Jehosaphat	17 Ahab		7 Asshur-izir pal ?	Benhadad attacks Samaria, 1 Kings, xx. 1.
9	15	18		8	
8	16	19		9	
7	17	20		10	
6	18	21		11	
5	19	22		12	Ahab slain in battle at Ramoth-gilead. 1 Kings, xxii. 34.
4	20	1 Ahaziah		13	
3	21	2		14	
2	22	1 Joram		15	
1	23	2	112	16	
870	24	3		17	
9	25	4		18	
8	1 Jehoram	5		19	
7	2	6		20	
6	3	7		21	Benhadad comes against Samaria. 2 Kings, vi. 24.
5	4	8		22	
4	5	9		23	
3	6	10		24	
2	7	11		25	
1	1 Ahaziah	12	122	26	Death of Jezebel, say at the age of 72.
860	1 Athaliah	1 Jehu		27	Hazael anointed king before the death of Benhadad.*
9	2	2		28	
8	3	3		1 Shalmanezer II.	Wounds Jehoram, 2 Chron.
7	4	4		2	Jehu slays 70 sons of Ahab.
6	5	5		3	
5	6	6		4	Hazael now leads the army of Benhadad, owing probably to the infirmity of his father.
4	1 Jehoash	7		5	
3	2	8		6	The Assyrians defeat the confederate forces of South Syria, Egypt, Arabia, and Palestine, at Aroer,† in B.C. 853.‡
2	3	9		7	
1	4	10	132	8	
850	5	11		9	Ahab of Jezreel (probably one of the sons of Ahab not slain by Jehu) associated with Benhadad's army.
9	6	12		10	
8	7	13		11	Annals of Shalmanezer.
7	8	14		12	
6	9	15		13	
5	10	16		14	
4	11	17		15	Death of Benhadad in B.C. 843.§ Ibid.
3	12	18		16	
2	13	19		17	Shalmanezer takes tribute of Jehu. Ibid.
1	14	20	142	18	

* 1 Kings, xix. 15; 2 Kings, viii. 15.
† "From Aroer, even Gilead and Bashan," 2 Kings, x. 33.
‡ Rawlinson: Athenæum, 18 May, 1867.
§ Benhadad, probably now 86 years of age. See B.C. 908.

Secular Chronology adjusted to the reckoning of the Hebrews.

B.C.	Kings of Tyre.	Kings of Egypt.	Remarks from Secular Writers.
880	2 Mytgenus	13 Osorchon II.	
9	3	14	
8	4	15	
7	5	16	
6	6	17	
5	7	18	
4	8	19	
3	9	20	
2	10	21	
1	11	22	
870	12	23	
9	13	24	
8	14	25	
7	15	1 Sesonchosis	
6	16	2 II.	
5	17	3	
4	18	4	
3	19	5	
2	20	6	
1	21	7	
860	22	8	
9	23	9	
8	24	10	
7	25	11	
6	26	12	
5	27	13	
4	28	14	
3	29	15	
2	1 Pygmalion	16	
1	2	17	
850	3	18	
9	4	19	
8	5	20	
7	6	21	
6	7	22	The colony of Carthage founded in the 7th year of Pygmalion, 700 years before the destruction of Carthage, in B.C. 146, and 144 years after Solomon began to build the Temple of Jerusalem. See p. 394.
5	8	23	
4	9	24	
3	10	25	
2	11	1 Tachelothis	
1	12	2 II.	

Hebrew Chronology adjusted to the Sabbatical Years and Jubilees.

B.C.	Captivity of Judah.		Age of Daniel.	Kings of Egypt.	Kings of Babylon.	Remarks from Holy Scripture.
520	43			5 Camby-	16 Nabonadius	"Now in the first year of Cyrus, king of Persia" (and of Babylon, Ezra, v. 13). "the Lord stirred up the spirit of Cyrus, king of Persia, and he made a proclamation." Ezra, i. 1.
9	44	"For as long as she		6 ses 1	17 Cyrus II. 1	
8	45			Cyrus 2	2	
7	46	2 Chron. xxxvi. 21.		1 Darius 3	Darius 3	
6	47			2		
5	48			3	Naditabirus	
4	49			4		
3	50			5		
2	51			6		
1	52		75	7		
510	53			8		
9	54			9		
8	55	During the captivity the land enjoyed her Sabbaths.		10		
7	56	lay desolate she kept Sabbath, to fulfil threescore and ten years,		11		
6	57			12		
5	58			13		
4	59			14		
3	60			15		
2	61			16		
1	62		85	17	Aracus	
500	63			18		
9	64			19	1 Belshazzar	
8	65			20	2	
7	66			21	3	"In the third year of the reign of King Belshazzar" Daniel was "at Shushan, the palace," that is, at the seat of government. Dan. viii. 1, 2. "And in the reign of Ahasuerus," in the beginning of his reign." Ezra, iv. 6. "And in the days of Artaxerxes." iv. 7. "In that night was Belshazzar slain." Dan. v. 30. "Darius took the kingdom, being about 62 years of age." Dan. v. 31. Now styled King of Assyria. Ezra, vi. 22.
6	67			22	4	
5	68			23	5	
4	69			24 Xerxes 1	6	
3	70			25 2	7	
2				26 3	8	
1	1 Darius		95	27 4	1 Darius, king	
490	2 king of			28 5	2 of Assyria	
9	3 Assy-			29 6	3	
8	4 ria			30 7	4	
7	5			31 8	5	"And they builded, and finished it (the Temple), according to the commandment of this God of Israel, and according to the commandment of Cyrus, and Darius, and Artaxerxes King of Persia." Ezra, vi. 14. Temple finished in Adar in 6th year of Darius. v. 15.
6	6			32 9	6	
5	7			33 10	7	
4	8			34 11	8	
3	9			35 12	9	
2	10			36 13	10	Temple dedicated in Nisan 7th year of Darius. v. 16
1				14		

* The 6th verse of Ezra. iv., is written in Hebrew, the 7th verse is in Chaldee. Xerxes is called Ahasuerus by the first writer, and by his later title, Artaxerxes, by the second writer.

Secular Chronology adjusted to the reckoning of the Hebrews.

B.C.	Kings of Media.	Age of Darius.	Kings of Persia.	Remarks from Secular Writers.
520	7 Cyrus II.		10 Cambyses 17	Cambyses reigns 11 years (Manetho), 18 years (Ctesias).
9	8		11 ... 18	Cyrus appoints Nabonadius to a principality in Carmania. Berosus.
8	9		Smerdis	
7	1 Darius		1 Darius	Darius begins to reign in 517. Parian Chronicle.
6	2		2	Darius expels Nabonadius from Carmania.
5	3		3	Naditabirus revolts at Babylon. Abydenus.
4	4		4	Behistûn inscription.
3	5		5	
2	6		6	Darius divides his empire into 20 or 22 satrapies,
1	7	44	7	according to national divisions. Ibid.
510	8		8	Darius marries 'Atossa, that is, Hadassah, or Esther, widow of Cyaxares, or Ahasuerus, and is so called "son," that is, heir or successor to Ahasuerus. Dan. ix. 1. Xerxes, son of 'Atossa, is named after his foster-father.
9	9		9	
8	10		10	
7	11		11	
6	12		12	
5	13		13	
4	14		14	
3	15		15	
2	16		16	
1	17	54	17	Aracus revolts at Babylon. Behistûn inscription.
500	18		18	
9	19		19	Belsharezar,† son of Nabonadius, set up as local king of Babylon by Darius.
8	20		20	
7	21		21	
6	22		22	
5	23		23	
4	24		Ahasuerus* 1	Xerxes, or Ahasuerus, is appointed ruler in Persia and Egypt, while Darius besieges Babylon for 22 months, on the revolt of Belshazzar.
3	25	62	25 ... 2	
2	26	63	26 ... 3	Babylon taken by Darius, and its gates and walls destroyed.
1	27	64	27 ... 4	
490	28		28 ... 5	Darius divides his empire into 120 small provinces. Dan. vi. 1. His policy now being to promote municipal and popular governments. Herod. vi. 43.
9	29		29 ... 6	
8	30		30 ... 7	
7	31		31 ... 8	Jerusalem becomes again the Holy City.
6	32 Xerxes or		Artaxer- 9	Darius reigns 31 years, according to Ctesias. Xerxes is now seated on the throne during the last years of Darius, and takes the title Artaxerxes. See p. 348.
5	33		1 ... xes 10	
4	34		2 ... 11	
3	35	72	3 ... 12	Darius died at the age of 72 (Ctesias), i.e. in his 73rd year.
2	36		4 ... 13	
1			5 ... 14	

* Loftus' Chaldæa and Susiana, p. 412.

† Journ. R. Asiatic Soc. vol. x. Part ii. p. 184.

Sabbatical Years and Jubilees.

	B.C.				
	480		6	Xerxes, called Artaxerxes by Ezra.	Ezra comes to Jerusalem and enforces the observance of the Sabbatical year,* which completes the first week of the new era of the second Temple, that is to say, the first of the "seven weeks and three score and two weeks," unto Messiah.
	9	■	7		
1st week	8		8		
	7		9		
	6		10		
	5		11		
	4		12		
	3		13		
	2	■	14		
2nd week	1	■	15		
	470		16		
	9		17		
	8		18		
	7		19		
	6		20		
	5	■	21		
3rd week	4	■	1	Artaxerxes	
	3		2	Longim*.	
	2		3		
	1		4		
	460		5		
	9		6		
	8		7		
4th week	7	■	8		
	6		9		
	5		10		
	4		11		
	3		12		
	2		13		
	1	■	14		
5th week	450	■	15		
	9		16		
	8		17		
	7		18		
	6		19		
	5		20		
	4		21		
6th week	3	■	22		
	2		23		
	1		24		

* "Upon the death of Darius, Xerxes, his son, took the kingdom. There was now in Babylon a righteous man " . . . " he was principal priest of the people, and his name was Esdras."—Josephus, Ant. xi. 5, 1.

APPENDIX. 461

Sabbatical Years and Jubilees.

B.C.				
7th week and Jubilee	440 9 8 7 6 5 4 3 2 1	25 26 27 28 29 30 31 32 33 34	Artaxerxes Longim².	Wall of Jerusalem completed in December.* Dedication with trumpets in the year of Jubilee, at the end of seven weeks. Unto Messiah the Prince 62 weeks. Nehemiah returns to Susa. Nehem. xiii. 6.
1st week after the Jubilee 2nd week	430 9 8 7 6 5 4 3 2 1	35 36 37 38 39 40 41 1 2 3	Darius Nothus	
3rd week	420 9 8 7 6 5 4 3 2 1	4 5 6 7 8 9 10 11 12 13		
4th week 5th week	410 9 8 7 6 5 4 3 2 1	14 15 16 17 18 19 1 2 3 4	Artaxerxes Mnemon.	

* "And this trouble he (Nehemiah) underwent for two years and four months, for in so long a time was the wall built, in the twenty-eighth year of the reign of Xerxes (Artaxerxes) in the ninth month."—Josephus, Ant. xi. 5, 6.

Sabbatical Years and Jubilees.

B.C.			
	400	5	Artaxerxes
	399	6	Mnemon
	8	7	
	7	8	
	6	9	
	5	10	
6th week	4	11	
	3	12	
	2	13	
	1	14	
	390	15	
	9	16	
	8	17	
7th week	7	18	
	6	19	
	5	20	
	4	21	
	3	22	
	2	23	
	1	24	
8th week	380	25	
	9	26	
	8	27	
	7	28	
	6	29	
	5	30	
9th week	4	31	
	3	32	
	2	33	
	1	34	
	370	35	
	9	36	
	8	37	
	7	38	
10th week	6	39	
	5	40	
	4	41	
	3	42	
	2	43	
	1	44	

Sabbatical Years and Jubilees.

B.C.				
360		45	Artaxerxes Mnemon	
11th week	9	1	Ochus	
	8	2		
	7	3		
	6	4		
	5	5		
	4	6		
	3	7		
12th week	2	8		
	1	9		
350		10		
	9	11		
	8	12		
	7	13		
	6	14		
13th week	5	15		
	4	16		
	3	17		
	2	18		
	1	19		
340		20		
	9	21		
14th week	8	1	Arces	
	7	2		
	6	1	Darius Codo-	
	5	2	manus	
	4	3		
	3	4		
	2	5		
15th week	1	1	Alexander the	Kingdom of the he-goat.
330		2	Great	
	9	3		
	8	4		
	7	5		
	6	6		
	5	7		
16th week	4	8		
	3	1	Ptolemy Soter	
	2	2		
	1	3		

Sabbatical Years and Jubilees.

B.C.		
320	4	Ptolemy Soter
9	5	
8	6	
17th week 7	7	
6	8	
5	9	
4	10	
3	11	
2	12	
1	13	
18th week 310	14	
9	15	
8	16	
7	17	
6	18	
5	19	
4	20	
19th week 3	21	
2	22	
1	23	
300	24	
9	25	
8	26	
7	27	
20th week 6	28	
5	29	
4	30	
3	31	
2	32	
1	33	
290	34	
21st week 9	35	
8	36	
7	37	
6	38	
5	1	Ptolemy Phi-
4	2	ladelphus
3	3	
22nd week 2	4	
1	5	

Sabbatical Years and Jubilees.

B.C.			
280		6	Ptolemy Phi-
9		7	ladelphus
8		8	
7		9	
6		10	
23rd week 5	▮	11	
4		12	
3		13	
2		14	
1		15	
270		16	
9		17	
24th week 8	▮	18	
7		19	
6		20	
5		21	
4		22	
3		23	
25th week 2	▮	24	
1	▮	25	
260		26	
9		27	
8		28	
7		29	
6		30	
5		31	
26th week 4	▮	32	
3		33	
2		34	
1		35	
250		36	
9		37	
8		38	Ptolemy Euer-
27th week 7	▮	1	getes
6		2	
5		3	
4		4	
3		5	
2		6	
28th week 1	▮	7	

H H

Sabbatical Years and Jubilees.

B.C.				
240	■	8	Ptolemy Euer-	
9		9	getes.	
8		10		
7		11		
6		12		
5		13		
4		14		
29th week 3	■	15		
2		16		
1		17		
230		18		
9		19		
8		20		
30th week 7	■	21		
6	■	22		
5		23		
4		24		
3		25		
2		1	Ptolemy Phi-	The capture of Samaria, Senna-
1		2	lopator	cherib's invasion, and the fall of
220	■	3		Jerusalem, calculated by Deme-
31st week 9		4		trius from the first year of Phi-
8		5		lopator. See pp. 305, 306.
7		6		
6		7		
5		8		
4		9		
3	■	10		
32nd week 2		11		
1		12		
210		13		
9		14		
8		15		
7		16		
6	■	17		
33rd week 5		1	Ptolemy Epi-	
4		2	phanes	
3		3		
2		4		
1		5		

Sabbatical Years and Jubilees.

	B.C.			
	200	6	Ptolemy Epi-	
	9	7	phanes	
34th week	8	8		
	7	9		
	6	10		
	5	11		
	4	12		
	3	13		
	2	14		
35th week	1	15		
	190	16		
	9	17		
	8	18		
	7	19		
	6	20		
	5	21		
36th week	4	22		
	3	23		
	2	24		
	1	1	Ptolemy Phi-	
	180		lometer	
	9			
	8			
37th week	7			
	6			
	5	1	Antiochus Epi-	
	4	2	phanes	
	3	3		
	2	4		
38th week	1	5		
	170	6		
	9	7		
	8	8		
	7	9		
	6	10		
	5	11		
	4	1	Antiochus Eu-	
39th week	3	2	pator	Siege of Jerusalem in the Sabbatical year.*
	2	1	Judas Macca-	
	1	2	beus	

* Jos. Ant. xii. 9, 3–5.

Sabbatical Years and Jubilees.

B.C.			
160	3	Judas Macca-	
9	4	beus`	
8	5		
7	6		
40th week 6	7		
5	8		
4	9		
3	10		
2	1	Jonathan	
1	2		
150	3		
41st week 9	4		
8	5		
7	6		
6	7		
5	8		
4	9		
3	1	Simon	
42nd week 2	2		
1	3		
140	4		
9	5		
8	6		
7	7		
6	8		
43rd week 5	1	John Hyrca-	Siege of Jericho in the Sabbatical
4	2	nus	year.*
3	3		
2	4		
1	5		
130	6		
9	7		
44th week 8	8		
7	9		
6	10		
5	11		
4	12		
3	13		
2	14		
45th week 1	15		

* Jos. Ant. xiii. 8, 1.

Sabbatical Years and Jubilees.

B.C.		
120	16 John Hyrcanus	
9	17	
8	18	
7	19	
6	20	
5	21	
46th week 4	22	
3	23	
2	24	
1	25	
110	26	
9	27	
8	28	
47th week 7	29	
6	30	
5	1 Aristobulus*	
4	1 Alexander	
3	2 Jannæus	
2	3	
48th week 1	4	
100	5	
99	6	
8	7	
7	8	
6	9	
5	10	
49th week 4	11	
3	12	
2	13	
1	14	
90	15	
9	16	
8	17	
50th week 7	18	
6	19	
5	20	
4	21	
3	22	
2	23	
1	24	

* Josephus fixes the reign of Aristobulus 481 Years (read 381 years) and 3 months after the return of the Jews from Babylon. 381 + 105 = B.C. 486, the era of the second Temple. Ant. xiii. xi. 1. See p. 303.

Sabbatical Years and Jubilees.

B.C.		
80	25 John Hyrcanus	
51st week 9	26	
8	1 Hyrcanus II.	
7	2	
6	3	
5	4	
4	5	
3	6	
52nd week 2	7	
1	8	
70	9	
9	10	
8	11	
7	12	
6	1 Aristobulus II.	
53rd week 5	2	
4	3	
3	4	Jerusalem taken by Pompey.
2	5	
1	6	
60	7	
9	8	
54th week 8	9	
7	10	
6	11	
5	12	
4	13	
3	14	
2	15	
55th week 1	16	
50	17	
9	18	
8	19	
7	20	
6	21	
5	22	
56th week 4	23	
3	24	
2	25	
1	1 Antigonus	

Sabbatical Years and Jubilees.

	B.C.			
	280		6	Ptolemy Phi-ladelphus
	9		7	
	8		8	
	7		9	
	6		10	
23rd week	5		11	
	4		12	
	3		13	
	2		14	
	1		15	
	270		16	
	9		17	
24th week	8		18	
	7		19	
	6		20	
	5		21	
	4		22	
	3		23	
25th week	2		24	
	1		25	
	260		26	
	9		27	
	8		28	
	7		29	
	6		30	
	5		31	
26th week	4		32	
	3		33	
	2		34	
	1		35	
	250		36	
	9		37	
	8		38	Ptolemy Euer-getes
27th week	7		1	
	6		2	
	5		3	
	4		4	
	3		5	
	2		6	
28th week	1		7	

H H

Sabbatical Years and Jubilees.

A.D.

A.D.				
1	3 Archelaus	32		
2	4 Augustus	33		
3	5	34		
4	6	35		
5	7	36		
6	8	37		
7	9	38	Archelaus' banished in his 9th year, and his
8		39	goods disposed of in the 37th year from the
9		40	battle of Actium. Jos. Ant. xviii. ii. 1.
10		41	Wars, ii., vii. 2.
11		42	
12		43	
13		44	
14	1 Tiberius	45	Tiberius begins to reign in Aug. A.D. 14.
15	2		
16	3		
17	4		
18	5		
19	6		
20	7		
21	8		
22	9		
23	10		
24	11		
25	12		
26	13		
27	14		
28	15		
29	16		Jesus Messiah baptized, being about 30 years
30	17		old, in A.D. 29. in the 46th year of Herod's
31	18		temple, in the 15th year of Tiberius.
32	19		Luke, iii. 1.
33	20		Death of Messiah the Prince, in the year 33, in
34	21		the 19th of Tiberius, on Friday, 15th of the
35	22		month of Nisan, on the day of the full
36	23		moon, 1st April.
37			
38	1 Caligula		
39	2		
40	3		

London :—STRANGEWAYS & WALDEN, Printers, Castle St., Leicester Square.

CPSIA information can be obtained
at www.ICGtesting.com
Printed in the USA
BVHW042311190219
540553BV00020B/104/P